Absolutely
Dylan

VIKING STUDIO BOOKS
Published by the Penguin Group
Viking Penguin, a division of Penguin Books USA Inc.,
375 Hudson Street, New York, New York 10014, U.S.A.
Penguin Books Ltd, 27 Wrights Lane,
London W8 5TZ, England
Penguin Books Australia Ltd, Ringwood,
Victoria, Australia
Penguin Books Canada Ltd, 10 Alcorn Avenue, Suite 300,
Toronto, Ontario, Canada M4V 3B2
Penguin Books (N.Z.) Ltd, 182–190 Wairau Road,
Auckland 10, New Zealand

Penguin Books Ltd, Registered Offices:
Harmondsworth, Middlesex, England

First published in Great Britain as *Oh No! Not Another Bob Dylan Book*
by Square One Books Ltd. 1991
Published by Viking Studio Books 1991

1 3 5 7 9 10 8 6 4 2

For Square One Books:
Publisher: Colin Larkin
Editorial and Production team: Susan Pipe, Aileen Tyler,
Thomas Collier, Johnny Rogan, Victoria Webb, Pat Perry,
and Mustafa Sidki. Special thanks to Paul Hunter and Chris Seaber
(who always wanted to get his name in a Bob Dylan book)
Design: Chestnut Mare Studios
Art Editors: Arthur Grangelin and John Bauldie
Marketing: John Eley
Photography: Norman Feakins
Cover photograph: David Michael Kennedy

Photographic credits
Colour:
2, 25, 33, Mauro De Marco. 5, Letty Kop. 7, 8, 15, 28, 34, Peter J Carni.
9, 14, Susan Wallach Fino. 11, John Patterson. 12, Heike Gossling.
16, Christian Levaux. 19, Courtesy Heike Gossling. 21, John Hume.
26, Nancy Cleveland. 29, Peter Howard. 31, Grazia Cioffi.
36, Gesine Zweig. 37, Jurg Bollinger. 32, CBS.
Black and White:
10, Brian Shuel. 13, 180, Columbia Records.
14, 210 bottom, 211, 214 left, Nancy Cleveland. 140, 214 right, Susan Wallach Fino.
148, 152, 219, Willem Meuleman. 149, 218 bottom, Leo Perez.
159, Bob Bedoian. 214 bottom, Helge Ottesen. 188 left, Chris David.
191, Dennis Grice Collection.

CIP data available

Printed in MEXICO

Absolutely Dylan

Patrick Humphries *Text*

and

John Bauldie *Notes*

VIKING
STUDIO
BOOKS

DEDICATION

To the memory of Stephen Grater

To the future of Thomas Dylan Brooke

THANKS TO: Dave Davies in the basement; Ian Woodward who keeps on keepin' on; Peter Hogan for reminding me just what it is I'm doing here; Pete Flanagan, Roger Bateson; Mark Smith, Paul Taylor, Dick Wallis, Mark Seaman, all those years ago; Jonathan Morrish; Mike Sharp; John Hersov; Bill Brooke, destroyer of clichés and slayer of ironies, Kathleen Beegan; Martin Carthy; Clinton Heylin; John Bauldie; Elizabeth M.Thomson; Bob Shelton, for finally nailing 'Rosebud' down; Roy Carr, the real McCoy; Larry the Lamb, Steve and Phil ("the shoeless hunter") Jump, for Madchester memories; Annie Bristow, for allowing me four hours to tell the world it's not only rock 'n' roll; Colin Larkin; Johnny Rogan and finally, Susan Gwendoline Parr, my glad-eyed lady of the Midlands. (PH).
Michael Krogsgaard and Clinton Heylin, whose Master Of The Tracks and Stolen Moments have proved invaluable reference guides, and to all Telegraph subscribers, now and then. Thanks also to Andy Bell and Mick Lawson for help with memorabilia. (JB).

CONTENTS

MINNESOTA STATE DEPARTMENT OF HEALTH
Division of Birth and Death Records and Vital Statistics
CERTIFICATE OF BIRTH

54389 858
Registered No._____

1. PLACE OF BIRTH: STATE OF MINNESOTA
County St Louis
Township
Village
City Duluth
No. St mary's Hospital St.
(If a hospital or institution give its NAME instead of street and number)
Length of mother's stay before delivery:
In hospital or institution_____yrs._____mos. 1 days
In this township, village or city 7 yrs._____mos._____days

2. USUAL RESIDENCE OF MOTHER
State Minnesota
County St Louis
Township
Village
City Duluth
No. 519 3rd Ave East St.
Is residence within limits of city or incorporated village? yes

3. Full Name of Child Robert Allen Zimmerman

4. Sex m 5. Twin, triplet, or other 6. Number in order of birth 7. Length 20½ in and Weight 7# 13oz 10gms 8. Legitimate? yes 9. Date of birth 5 - 24 19 41 (Month, day, year)

15. Full name FATHER Abram H. Zimmerman

16. Full maiden name MOTHER Beatrice Stone

11. Color or race Jewish 12. Age at last birthday 29 (Years)

17. Color or race Jewish 18. Age at last birthday 35 (Years)

13. Birthplace (Municipality or county) Duluth minn.

19. Birthplace (Municipality or county) Hibbing minn

14. Usual occupation manager Stock Dept

20. Usual occupation Housewife

15. Industry or business Standard Oil Co.

21. Industry or business

22. Children born to this mother
These totals MUST include THIS child
(a) Total No. of children born to this mother 1
(b) No. born alive and now living 1
(c) No. born alive but now dead
(d) No. born dead

23. Premature? Weeks of gestation 24. Cause of this stillbirth Before labor During labor

25. Was 1% silver nitrate used to prevent infant blindness? Yes No

CERTIFICATE OF ATTENDING PHYSICIAN, MIDWIFE, PARENT OR OTHER INFORMANT
I hereby certify that I attended the birth of this child, who was Alive at 9:05 P M. on the date above stated, and that the above facts as given are true to the best of my knowledge, information and belief.
James R. Manley M.D.
SIGNATURE OF PHYSICIAN, MIDWIFE, PARENT OR OTHER INFORMANT

I have checked the above facts and find they are correct.
Mrs. A. H. Zimmerman
(Actual Signature of Father or Mother)
519 3rd Ave East
(Mailing Address)

Date Signed 5-27-41 Address Duluth
(Signature)

Given name added from a supplemental report received_____19_____
Date Received by Local Registrar MAY 28 1941 19_____ Address_____
JUN 12 1941 REC'D
REGISTRAR
Filed pursuant to authority received and filed in the Minnesota State Department of Health on_____

Evidence indicates that the above certificate was filed May 28, 1941

STATE OF MINNESOTA)
COUNTY OF HENNEPIN) SS

I hereby certify that the above is a true and correct copy of the official record on file with the Section of Vital Statistics Registration of the Minnesota Department of Health.

Dated at Minneapolis

June 26, 1978

Deputy State Registrar
Minnesota Department of Health

Any alterations shown were made under the authority of Minnesota Statutes 1971, Section 144.172 and the regulations of the Minnesota Department of Health.

This is a facsimile copy of the official entry in the records of the State of Minnesota. Copyright Reserved©

At the Freewheelin' sessions October 1962

FOREWORD

BLUFF YOUR WAY INTO BOB DYLAN: A GUIDE FOR BEGINNERS

*Tongue-tied?
*Nervous in the company of those who plainly
know more about everything than you?
*Like to be fluent in something, anything?

This handy course will make you an expert on one of pop music's most influential figures in only six handy lessons. Who is it? Robert Zimmerman, that's who! Who's he?

Bob Dylan was christened Robert Zimmerman, so there you are, that's something you've learnt already!

Bob Dylan has made over 30 long playing records (albums) and many of them have featured highly in the charts, so a working knowledge of his career would be a Personality Plus for even the most tongue-tied person.

Bob Dylan fans are easy to recognise, they are elderly, male and frequently bearded. Their conversation tends to be staccato and monotonous, which is why you'll slip into their company like fingers into a glove! By lesson 6 if the conversation's becalmed, you'll be able to pose the question "Why wasn't the 'nightingale's code' version of 'Visions Of Johanna' included on Biograph?" And just watch the response!

If among Dylan devotees, and you feel your position threatened, move the conversation along with one (only one is necessary) of the following:-

1) Did He (always speak of Dylan with a capital 'H') ever record 'Love Is Just A Four Letter Word'?

2) Did the "Judas Shout" occur at Manchester or London in 1966?

3) Postulate that – as his eyes altered colour in the interim – He died in the 1966 bike crash.

4) Demand to know if He wrote 'The Weight' (it is wise to mention 'The Ballad Of Easy Rider' in this context).

5) Provoke an argument by stating, either (a) you felt you got good value for money at the Isle of Wight, or (b) you thought Renaldo & Clara was really good!

6) Say you always preferred (over 30s) Donovan (under 30s) Billy Bragg anyway.

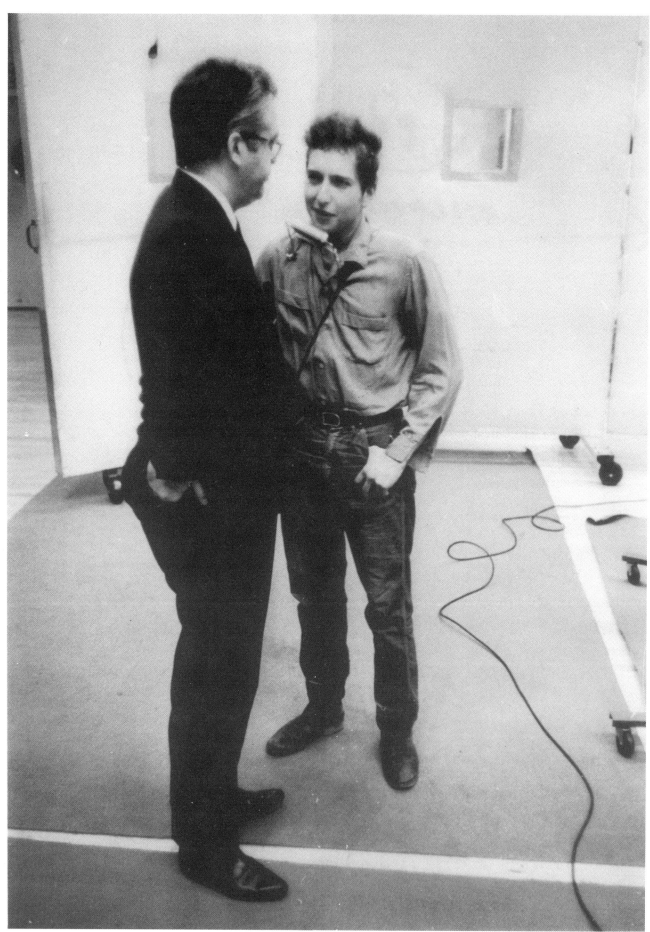

With his manager Albert Grossman at his first recording session

INTRODUCTION

"Gemini: chaos likely . . . Moon messages emphasize 'here and now' rather than the future . . . Be on the spot with ideas . . . The moonrays are conflicting, create tension, nerves. Relaxation attempts are failed. Annoyances (unforeseen but highly significant) will occur. Be prepared to revise plans." *Evening News astrologer Cullen Moore, 26/27 May 1966.*

"Judas!" They say that Bob Dylan recoiled, stung, incredulous, after that accusation; like someone they said, who had just received an electric shock. Inside of the Gothic gateau of the Royal Albert Hall that night in the late May of 1966, Bob Dylan ended his slow, snaking journey to Golgotha.

"I don't believe you . . . you're a LIAR . . . play it fucking louder". With that, Bob Dylan spun on his Cuban heel, slammed it down, and led his band into a scorched-earth version of 'Like A Rolling Stone', before quitting touring for seven years.

That legendary May 27th show at London's Albert Hall in 1966 was Dylan's final concert before the bike crash which gave him the breathing space he needed. The moment, preserved on the poorly pressed vinyl of a thousand different bootlegs, remains the most pivotal, accusatory moment in rock history. After that "Judas" shout there was no going back, only forward into the unknown.

What was it that had so inflamed the unknown voice? Why did he feel so personally betrayed by one who was, after all, just a rock star? He was not alone, the slow handclapping during those momentous 1966 shows with his electric band signalled the frustration and alienation of many of the people who had been so wholeheartedly behind Dylan during his four-year career. In mitigation, back then the equipment was primitive, the acoustics primaeval, the determination unexpected. But to hear Dylan's response ("I don't believe you . . . ") is to share his conviction; stung into retaliation by months of audience antipathy, that hostility had only confirmed his determination to pursue, as he had always done, his own vision.

There has never been such a confrontational moment in rock history, it is unlikely there ever will be. No one figure could ever again inspire such devotion as Bob Dylan, no modern audience feel so betrayed. The gunfight at the Albert Hall has entered the annals of rock history, because that night in May 1966, Bob Dylan was rock 'n' roll.

Dylan laid the foundations of rock's conscience, he is the medium's most quoted lyricist, he is rock's poet laureate; his influence awesome. Yet despite being one of the most written about and endlessly analysed characters of his time, his impact is still under-rated, largely due to his own belligerence and tenacity.

Convenient flaming death in 1966 would have seen him comfortably enshrined as perhaps the greatest ever rock martyr; but trenchant and irascible, Dylan still causes irritation and exasperation, awe and incredulity in equal measure. Above all, after nearly 30 years in a career which stands unequalled in rock, he persists.

The tenacious refusal to lie down wearing his crown of thorns is an essential part of Dylan's mystique. He is in the unenviable position of having been the focus of attention for all his adult life, but despite occasionally retiring winded from the arena, he remains a gladiator, always willing to return to face the raised thumbs or catcalls from the crowd. But even this was not enough for his audience, they have elevated the feisty old fellow to a curious position, somewhere between Elvis Presley and Mahatma Gandhi.

Dylan's most widely perceived image may be that of a sackcloth and ashes poet, purging with his dirges, a grim-faced Guthrie relic of the 60s – but that is to overlook the humour, which was surely an equal constituent of his success. 'Times They Are A-Changin'' may be dutifully dusted down by sub-editors as the anthem for periodic seismographic youthquakes, but its creator was as likely to be found gleefully taunting the prevalent pop styles and more significantly carrying this style through to his dealings with the press and public. For a long time the public image of a pop star had been as Trilby to some managerial Svengali, but Dylan was the puppet who cut the strings and watched them flutter in the wind. Dylan's refusal to be like a butterfly pinned down in the display case of the 60s, saw his career fluctuate madly, but whilst often maddening and irritating, his determined inconsistency is also part and parcel of his appeal.

To hear Bob Dylan sing is to feel the pulse of the

times, to study his lyrics is to gauge the confused and confusing snail's trail of a generation, to look at Bob Dylan's career in detail is to follow the course of recent history; a history that he helped to shape as much as it helped shape him. That's quite a burden for any artist, for a human being it may be an intolerable weight.

His refusal to be bound by the established rules saw him create his own ground rules which the rock culture still largely continues to adhere to. Dylan didn't merely interpret and influence the times he helped change; he became fused inseparably to them. His persona became a symbol of those times, conjured up to evoke the end of an era. When during Philip Kaufman's 1979 film *The Wanderers*, Karen Allen drifts into a Greenwich Village club to hear 'Bob Dylan' sing 'The Times They Are A-Changin'', we know that this moment represents the loss of innocence which came in the wake of the Kennedy years. To see Ron Kovic's brother falter through the same song in *Born On The 4th Of July* is to identify the exact instant that a generation changed its way of thinking. But Dylan's impact, far from being fixed fossil-like in 60s rock, has seeped down through the years and whether they were conscious of it or not, has touched everyone who followed after.

If Dylan is not noticeably changing anything now, there are still plenty of stethoscopes hovering over his heartbeat. Bob Dylan impressed himself onto a generation, an industry, a movement; the time spent

charting that impact is rewarding for anyone with even the remotest interest in the development of popular culture. Dylan gave rock music a voice, he made rock matter again and he took risks like they were necessities. Between 1962 and 1968 he redrew the map; anything after that was a bonus.

The battle for the soul of Bob Dylan has raged for nearly a quarter of a century, with dozens of different Mephistopheles each claiming possession; whether it's the folk/protest establishment of 1963, A.J. Weberman's coyote filchings, Stephen Pickering's theory that Dylan is simply "the most important poet in Jewish history" or Ralph J. Gleason's assessment of him as "the first poet of the juke box". Dylan collects 'firsts' like rosettes at a gymkhana: the first to make the lyrics of a pop song matter, the first folk-rocker, the first to throw the concept of the three-minute song out of the window, the first rock poet to be embraced by the literary establishment, the first rock star to consistently wear sunglasses indoors, the first victim of the rock bootleg, the first established rock artist to allow a cinema verité portrait to be made - and released. The first one to be later the last.

Bob Dylan has refused to play the game or adhere to any rules, he has destroyed guidelines and blazed his own. If his recent works have produced confusion and vexation in his followers, there is still some comfort to be gained from one who has endured so many deaths and rebirths. He has viewed rock through a glass darkly, and has himself been viewed through smoked glass, which never allows a clear vision. That opacity has been simultaneously exhilarating and frustrating. For over a quarter of a century now, Bob Dylan has been the donkey onto which we try and pin our own tails; and as we all know, the tale's the thing.

Dylan's influence is pervasive even today, not directly but through the distillation of him which is now part of the rock culture. Anyone who picks up an instrument and rails against anything, whether in a tiny Croydon folk club or a Los Angeles stadium is paying his dues to Bob Dylan, even if they can't stand Dylan's voice and have never owned any of his albums. Dylan has become a part of popular mythology, has given us plenty of jokes and helped us cry a few tears. He was

FOOTNOTE: As with so many Dylan-related events, confusion reigns: the weight of evidence now suggests that the "Judas Shout" actually occurred at Manchester's Free Trade Hall 10 days before the final show of that controversial 1966 tour. Many, though, still claim to have been at the Albert Hall when the accusation was hurled, probably because the torrent of bootlegs in the early 70s cite the source as the Albert Hall. Whatever and wherever, it remains the cynosure of that extraordinary tour.

At the Kalvoya festival 13 June 1990

some kind of man, and what is so genuinely encouraging about Bob Dylan after a lifetime in the eye of the hurricane, he still is.

Nearly a quarter of a century on from that watershed Albert Hall confrontation, Dylan was back in London to continue what he called his "never-ending tour". During February 1990 he was in residence for six nights at London's 3,000 seat Hammersmith Odeon, it was the smallest venue Dylan had played in the capital since 1965. But it was more out of a sense of "foolish duty" than desire that I went along. Dylan, for me after all, hadn't cut the mustard in concert for a long, long time.

Too often during his British appearances in 1984, 1987 and 1989, Dylan coasted. The devotees reported with wide-eyed enthusiasm: "That's the first time he's ever played 'Positively 4th Street' live". So what? It still sounded like any one of half a dozen slap dash renditions of something that could be anything. Too often during those concerts, I felt like Somerset Maugham (the 'Just Like Somerset Maugham Blues'): the writer was an on-set guest watching Spencer Tracy tackle the transformation scene in the 1941 Dr *Jekyll & Mr Hyde*. Tracy poured every creative ounce into the metamorphosis, only to hear Maugham lean across and ask the director sotto-voce: "Which one is he supposed to be now?"

So my hopes for Dylan that February were about as high as a fly's forehead. Immediate comfort was gained from the size of the venue, for too long rock had become a spectator sport, but for remote spectators, armed with binoculars. As the artist took to the distant stage, the binoculars were raised until the scene resembled the bridge of a battleship during an Exocet attack ("a million faces at my feet, but all I see are dark eyes"). Here, at least, you'd be able to witness the blood, sweat and tears.

The closeness lent flesh to the myth, substance to the phantom, and buoyed by that intimacy Dylan duly delivered. Backed by a three-piece band, Dylan savaged the songs with a venom and bite which suggested that he too found something of merit in them. He played them with such fire that they weren't thrown like cursory bones to the pariah dogs, but reformed and relived. Maybe it was the fact that he could see beyond the first 30 rows, glimpsing the faces of the people who've kept him in work for the last quarter of a century. Maybe it was the wheel creaking full circle, maybe the time was just right. Whatever the reason, the 20 songs in that Tuesday night show were enough to make me realise again just what the hell I *was* doing there.

For once there was a genuine two-way traffic, the adulation washed over the footlights, and from the stage came back a genuine warmth and delight. Middle aged men reacted like Brosettes as Dylan's glance fell on them, the stalls swayed at every facial tic and myopic gaze. Here was real empathy, here was epiphany, here was where all the good times had gone.

Close up, it was hard to reconcile the boyish idealism of 'Song To Woody' with the craggy faced troubadour onstage, but from that fresh-faced first album of nearly 30 years ago, Dylan now had the experience to sing 'Man of Constant Sorrow'. Here was a performance which spanned the teenage adulation of Dylan's first professional song, to Woody, and concluded with an atmospheric 1989 'Man In A Long Black Coat'. With the band in tow, Dylan built up a righteous head of steam for 'Masters Of War' and kicked mighty ass for 'Stuck Inside Of Mobile'. The distant rolling thunder of 'Ballad Of Hollis Brown' swelled and roared, 'It Takes A Lot To Laugh, It Takes a Train To Cry' detoured to Southside Chicago for a slow, steamy electric blues.

The harmonica was whipped out, and greeted like a fond, familiar, asthmatic uncle. Solo, Dylan gave an inspired reading of 'Boots Of Spanish Leather', fluid and melodious, rekindling fires of adolescent passion and parting. Legs akimbo, jacket glittering, hand flailing over solo guitar, Dylan recast 'Blowin' In The Wind'. By asking "How many years must a people exist before they're allowed to be free?" Dylan had made a thousand troubadours ask a million unknown people the same question. I felt the same sensation of wonder as the eight-year old I sat next to watching *Batman*: as the Caped Crusader made his first onscreen appearance, he helpfully whispered to me in awe "That's Batman!". Face aglow, I found myself thinking that Tuesday night at Hammersmith: "That's Bob Dylan! And he's singing that song he wrote all those years ago, 'Blowin' In The Wind'".

As the end of that memorable evening hove into view, the quartet lumbered into 'Like A Rolling Stone', the song that has become the 'We'll Meet Again' of the Woodstock generation. And for the first time in so many years, and after how many hundred performances, it seemed that the author sensed what we had known all along: that it was a good song then, and it's a great song now. It's a fact which had seemed to slip Dylan's mind in performance on too many occasions in the past.

In a performance which helped re-establish Dylan in my mind as a major force, one of the most intriguing moments came during a song Dylan had so often used as little more than an encore lullaby. Along with 'Forever Young', 'Knockin' On Heaven's Door' was Dylan's cosy valediction, a song used to ease the crowd out the doors humming an old favourite while the drifter made his escape. However the 1990 version offered a précis of Dylan's whole career, beginning as

a stately acoustic, it swept through four-on-the-floor rock 'n' roll and culminated in a genuine spiritual assertion. It was an all too rare, and therefore precious, moment of Dylan pacing a song, rather than relying on aimless metal thrash or grungy solo strumming.

That Tuesday night, I found myself warming to Bob Dylan, the man. I mean, we all know he's the spokesman of his generation, poet of the juke box blah, blah, blah. But here was a spritely father, pushing 50, living out a lifelong ambition to join Little Richard. Here he was, splintered knees bent with the rhythm, his guitar strung at crotch level, the blind as a bat squint, the quirky smirks, that bargain bin voice. Jesus, I thought, what keeps him up there?

Why does he persevere with all this at an age when most men would settle for pipe and slippers in front of the fire? What's he got left to prove? The answer I think, is that this "never-ending tour" is the only way Bob Dylan knows to communicate with his audience.

His video ventures have proved unsatisfactory, his record sales stacked next to, say, Paul Simon's are negligible. No one ever sees his paintings, his prose remains unread. But as rock enters its fifth decade, Dylan just has to go out there and work hard at getting his music across to an audience.

Alongside the diehards who know every nuance and phrasing trick in his voice, every line from every performance of every song better than he does, this audience always includes a new generation come fresh to his work, curious to see for themselves this wizened relic of rock's Mount Rushmore. Under the stage lights, Dylan dips into a repertoire which encompasses hundreds of his own songs, as well as sorties into Country & Western standards, blues, R&B, folk, gospel. Here on the concert stage is where the legend springs to life.

There he was, clunking his way through 'It's All Over Now, Baby Blue'. No great guitarist he, shambling through the song, giving it his best shot. Somewhere along the line, ol' Bob got a little bit confused, and began one verse with the words of another. No big deal, governments didn't tumble, but I could sense 3,000 people sucking in their breath simultaneously, consulting their own mindbound copies of *Lyrics 1962 - 1985* and all coming to the same split-second decision: BOB GOT IT WRONG! And Bob knew he did too, and Bob knew that we all knew, and Bob thought fuck it, and carried on clunking away.

So I found myself thinking this is really weird. Bob Dylan really doesn't need to look back, that's what his public does for him. Why keep a diary when thousands of people know your own past better than you do? They keep his diaries for him ("Uh, 6th of January 1971? Think you'll have found yourself on the phone

At the recording sessions for Freewheelin' 1962

to A.J. Weberman there, Bob, at one point exclaiming: 'Oh fuck, man, Jesus'!") With such pedantic Boswells dogging Dylan's footsteps for most of his adult life, its a small small wonder that Dylan is mistrustful, and has kept the myth burning while the life is in other hands.

Onstage at Hammersmith, I kept coming back to the man, not merely gazing at the idol ("Gosh, here I am sharing the same room as Bob Dylan!"). Just revelling in the freedom he obviously relished. Over the years, we've all watched the masks tumble and fall, and seen them replaced by a drawer full of other masks, but here we were seeing the real him at last, watching the blood of performance pour onto those much-loved tracks. Watching that spritely performance I got the nearest I suppose I'll ever get to understanding what it's like to be Bob Dylan. (That's always one of the top priority categories for Dylan bores, (1) If you met him, what's the first question you'd ask Dylan? Or (2) I wonder what it's like being Bob Dylan? Or (2a) I wonder what it's like having Bob Dylan as a father? Or (2b) I wonder what it's like having Bob Dylan as a father-in-law?) . . .

Up there was the man only 10 years younger than my father-in-law, rocking out with abandon, fronting a three-man rock 'n' roll band. For a recluse and an enigma, Bob Dylan has led a public life. There is an evident need to perform, to justify to himself his own existence, to rationalise all the nonsense. That was the man I found so endearing, the man who had taken all those risks, who had single handedly taken pop music by the lapels, shaken it, and made it grow. He'd infused the teenage form with adult wisdom. He'd rocked and rolled, suffered the slings and arrows of outrageous fortune, had dined off the fortune of a torrent of royalty cheques. He's been hosannaed and damned; he straddles an incomparable body of work, yet remains determined to keep pushing onwards and upwards. And here he was, still at it, the rolling stone outlaw, the fully rounded man with so many sides, rockin' out with abandon. There has to be a story worth telling there I thought . . .

On the second gospel tour 1 November 1980

CHAPTER

1

Zigman Zimmerman quit the Black Sea port of Odessa in 1907 to settle in the town of Duluth, Minnesota, which huddled in the northern reaches of that promised land whose liberty lady welcomed untold millions of European refugees. The Russia he left behind was riddled with anti-semitism and the Czarist pogroms were to continue unabated right up to the outbreak of World War I, which was to lead within three years to the overthrow of the Romanov dynasty.

A further, unimaginable terror engulfed Stalin's Russia barely a month after Zigman's latest grandson, Robert Allen, came into the world on May 24th 1941. By the spring of that year, Hitler's empire stretched from the English Channel to the borders of Russia, from the Baltic to the Mediterranean, a terrifying new order which he vowed would rule for a thousand years. To a cowed world on the evening of June 21st 1941, that vow looked set to ring horribly true. The Führer's pact with communist Russia in 1939 reassured his generals that they would not have to repeat the military recipe which had ensured their defeat in the first Great War, by fighting a war on two fronts. By 4am on the morning of June 22nd however, their complacency was shattered, as Hitler's megalomania saw him launch Operation Barbarossa, the world's largest military operation whose aim was the subjugation of the USSR before the winter snows.

Hitler's regime was already bathed in evil, but the bestiality of the Nazis reached new heights following Barbarossa. In his definitive history *The Holocaust*, Martin Gilbert wrote: "From the first hours of Barbarossa . . . a new policy was carried out, the systematic destruction of entire Jewish communities . . . In advance of the invasion of Russia, the SS leaders had prepared special killing squads . . . which set about finding and organizing local collaborators, Lithuanians and Ukranians, in murder gangs, and were confident that the anti-Jewish hatred which existed in the East could be turned easily to mass murder. In this they were right". Of an estimated Jewish population of 80,000 in Odessa prior to Barbarossa, Gilbert documents at least 70,000 being butchered.

The full scale of the Holocaust was not realised until the first liberating troops emerged dazed and sick from the charnel houses of Auschwitz, Dachau and the other death factories which fuelled the Third Reich. Half a lifetime later, Robert Zimmerman was not alone in pondering the Almighty's absence from the camps. Mere words, even those as harrowing as 'Holocaust', 'Genocide' and 'Shoah', can never fully convey the systematic massacre which constituted the Nazis' Final Solution; even the survivors were stained by guilt at having experienced such horrors and remaining alive.

In the immediate post-war years, Europe reeled like a famished refugee, aimlessly and blindly groping for some restoration of order, for some semblance of life which recalled the old ways, before the continent was devoured by the salivating foulness of Hitler and his regime. Denied their home, the Jews perforce looked to America, and sought comfort from those who had already found a home there.

The Zimmermans quit Duluth in 1947, all the young Robert claims to remember of it was the plaintive wail of the foghorns. A lifetime later, after years of municipal indifference, plans for a 'Bob Dylan Drive' in Duluth were mooted. On the patchwork quilt of those united states, Hibbing lay nestling next to the Canadian border, windswept and a long way from the main trade routes. It wasn't an easy place to grow up, but then is there anywhere on earth that is?

The child is allegedly the father of the man, and so when maturity brings fame or infamy, inevitably the early years are endlessly sifted for clues, for indications of future greatness. Bob Shelton has written eloquently of the young Robert Allen Zimmerman, of the early Hibbing years, of the unremarkable parents' day poems, of the *Classics Illustrated* comics piled high and the old records which the teenager jived to, of the claustrophobic bonds which bound the young Robert and so many of the other small-town war children who later manned the barricades of the 60s. They all seemed to feel that there simply had to be more to life than Hibbing . . . or Dartford or Liverpool, and couldn't wait to quit as soon as they were of an age to go "as there ain't nothing there now to hold them".

By the end of the 40s, CBS Records, appropriately for this tale, had introduced the first 33rpm Long Playing Records and around 250,000 new television sets

Hibbing, Minnesota

were being brought into American homes every month. With an unexpected second-term Presidency, Harry Truman was leading the nation to post-war prosperity whilst setting an unhealthy precedent by involving American troops in SE Asia during the Korean War.

Reminiscing, Dylan told Cameron Crowe of the country he came from as a teenager: "America was still very 'straight', post-war and sort of into a grey-flannel suit thing, McCarthy, commies, puritanical, very claustrophobic and what ever was happening of any real value was happening away from that . . . "

The 50s have yet to take on the patina of the 60s, but it was those years that formed the backdrop for the psychedelic explosion of the 60s. In 1950, *Life* magazine asked the youth of America to name its heroes and heroines, and the youth replied with a list led by Franklin Roosevelt, Lincoln, General MacArthur, Roy Rogers and Doris Day! But conformity and complacency are the very foundations on which rebellion is built, and under Eisenhower, America was throughout the 50s, a cosy and comforting edifice ripe for change.

With the news that former ally Russia had the atom bomb in 1949, America fell victim to the incipient 'reds-under-the-bed' paranoia of Senator 'Tail Gunner Joe' McCarthy. The senator-from Minnesota's next door state of Wisconsin - stomped and bludgeoned his way to national infamy, but not before causing immeasurable harm to many innocent people. As a senator, McCarthy had been a disaster, with even the hawkish Republicans finding him an embarrassment, he needed a cause, something - anything - to keep his name in the headlines. In desperation, one afternoon during January 1950, McCarthy finally found his cause.

It was in the normally cosy surroundings of the Ohio County Women's Club in Wheeling, West Virginia that McCarthy waved a sheet of paper which he claimed was a list of 205 known Communist Party members active in the State Department. The list was as much a product of the blustering Senator's imagination as his war-time record had been, but for the ensuing four years McCarthy's hectoring style, persecution and victimisation spread like a cancer across an America which was otherwise in the ascendant.

The nationwide prosperity didn't bypass Hibbing, but its very isolation ensured a provincialism that was only breached by the first assault of mass media. In the Depression-ridden 30s, radio was the great new communicator: from the ominous propaganda broadcasts of Hitler's rapidly expanding Third Reich to FDR's "Fireside Chats" and down-home concerts from Nashville's Grand Ol' Opry. The amazing power of radio was perhaps most graphically illustrated by the precocious 22-year -old Orson Welles in his infamous 1938 *War of the Worlds* broadcast which convinced large segments of the nation that Martians were making their own territorial demands here on earth.

By the 50s, the hold which the cinema exercised over its enormous audience and had taken for granted for over 20 years, was beginning to loosen. The 30s had seen the inexorable rise of the Hollywood Dream Factory, pumping out production-line escapism as surely as the Ford factories. The irrepressible Marx Brothers' brand of anarchy highlighted the follies of the times while Fred & Ginger elegantly swanned down to Rio. Busby Berkeley's phantasmagoric dance numbers wouldn't have shamed one of Albert Speer's stage-managed Nuremberg rallies and perky Shirley Temple was the nation's sweetheart, by doting on a daughter that didn't need to stand in line for food queues, movie audiences were able to escape for a few precious hours.

The television set was now an accepted fixture in many American homes and the inhabitants of the box soon became as familiar to householders as their next-door neighbours. Lucille Ball, Milton Berle, Ed Sullivan and that endless list of cowboy heroes recreating a Wild West where villains conveniently wore black hats, men such as Bronco, Cheyenne, Rowdy, Maverick, Wyatt, Hopalong, and of course Matt Dillon - whose *Gunsmoke* lurched on into the record books for an incredible 20 years.

But for all its pervasive power, television didn't quite break the movies' stranglehold during the 50s. Reading between the grainy, black and white lines on their sets, even that first impressionable generation of devotees had an inkling that the medium wasn't capable of producing proper stars. The real stars still came every week in Todd-AO technicolour to the movie house, and in the safe warm fug of the cinema, before heads tilted back and eyes squinting through a haze of smoke, these stars loomed over the auditorium, filling the screen and the imagination of their disciples.

The icons of the 30s, Gable, Cooper, Flynn and

New York City 1962

Bogart still towered, but they were of course showing their lines by the 50s and the tribes were gathering at the gates, their fresh faces filling the screens. Montgomery Clift battled against the face of America – John Wayne himself – in 1948's *Red River* and a confused John Garfield represented rebellious decency in 1947's *Body And Soul*. All the while, the archetypal rebel figure was braced to take on the establishment although the head-on collision would not happen until 1952 when Marlon Brando brought the Method to Hollywood, and snarled, scratched and smouldered his way through *A Streetcar Named Desire*.

Throughout the early 50s Brando established himself, with a handful of definitive performances, as the face of the moment. Before Elvis Presley's knockout, Brando was a contender, the first viable role model for disaffected youth who had no heroes of their own on TV, radio or record. The phenomenon reached apotheosis with 1953's *The Wild One*. Brando was the sneering, contemptuous biker at the head of a gang of Hell's Angels who terrorised a small American town; for many parents it was an all too accurate portent of the encroaching cockiness of youth, and such was its malodorous potency that it was officially banned in Britain until 1968! For all its faltering plot and artificial dialogue, the film is worthwhile for one exchange between Brando and the sheriff's daughter: "What are you rebelling against Johnny?" "Waddya got?" It's a line Bob Dylan could have been born to say, and

savour.

By the mid-50s though, with an Oscar already under his belt, Brando was leaving his adolescent audience behind as he disappeared under make-up to become Napoleon and Mark Anthony. Down South, another pivotal creature of the 50s was scraping off mannerisms and conformity; on July 5th 1954, Elvis Presley was goofing around in Memphis' Sun Studios. At the end of that first session with Scotty Moore and Bill Black, producer Sam Phillips can be heard exulting at the conclusion of the rebuilding of Bill Monroe's 'Blue Moon Of Kentucky' "Hell, that's different. That's a pop song now, nearly 'bout". A fortnight later, Elvis' first single, 96 seconds of Arthur Crudup's 'That's All Right, Mama' was heard on regional radio stations, while the world outside Tennessee carried on, blithely unaware of the incalculable impact simmering within the body of "the kid with sideburns".

A thousand miles north of Memphis, such sounds went unheard but in 1955, 14-year old Robert Zimmerman made his pilgrimage to Hibbing's Lybba cinema to see the film debut of James Dean in Elia Kazan's film of the last third of John Steinbeck's *East Of Eden*. Dean's impact on a world as yet unprepared for Elvis was spectacular but *Eden* was the only one of his three films to be premiered during his lifetime. In September 1955, just a fortnight after he finished filming his third feature *Giant*, Dean died in his Porsche on Highway 46, just outside Paso Robles. Dean's

Two handbills for Dylan's first professional appeareances in 1961

influence on the teenage Zimmerman was enormous, as it was on millions of teenagers all around the world. In later years, Dylan wrapped up his 1986 tour in Paso Robles, and following a 1988 show in Indianapolis, Dylan made a midnight flit to Dean's hometown of Fairmount, Indiana. He also spoke enthusiastically about tracking down actress Bette Treadville - who played the barmaid in *East Of Eden* - for an unspecified film project.

To a generation hemmed in by strict orthodoxy, James Dean offered a vivid, gigantic symbol of freedom, of unorthodoxy. The beauty of his unlined face, frozen forever aged 24 and enshrined in two of the 50s' greatest and most evocative films is in itself a myth which rings down the years. Dean himself said "If a man can bridge the gap between life and death. I mean, if he can live on after he's died, then maybe he was a great man". By this definition, Dean was a very great man: over 30 years from his death, his image is everywhere. He is commemorated in song by Phil Ochs, Bruce Springsteen, Lou Reed, The Eagles, Mick Jagger, Madonna and Billy Joel; his acting style can be detected in the work of Robert De Niro, Dennis Hopper, Sean Penn, Matt Dillon; his look is endlessly, painstakingly evoked in advertisements; he has become the icon of an era, all the more poignant because his talent, which bordered on genius, was distilled in only three films.

Each successive generation has adopted Dean, and down the years that surly, incandescent image endured, the faltering growing pains of the youth that would not, could never grow old. But more than a mere Peter Pan, Dean managed to embody all the angry, incoherent sense of rebellion youth feels on its wayward journey to maturity; and lines - like lines from Dylan songs of the next decade - still echo: "You're tearing me apart . . .", "Talk to me please, mother"; and the images endure: Dean 'crucified' before a kneeling Liz Taylor in a publicity still from *Giant*, Dean stalking the streets in his striking red windcheater in *Rebel*, Dean hunched in his pullover riding the rails at the opening of *Eden*. Perhaps most telling, the image of Dean and Brando in the only known picture of them together: visiting the set of Dean's debut film, while filming *Desiree*, his none too successful costume drama, Brando is relaxed and smiling in the company of an admiring Julie Harris and companionable director Elia Kazan, while Dean hovers on the edge of the group, his eyes avoiding the camera, like a frightened fawn.

Actor Martin Sheen, a diehard Dylan fan who prepared for his role in *Apocalypse Now* by endlessly playing 'Knockin' On Heaven's Door', wrote in 1984: "Dean was a genius at a time when one was needed. There were only two people in the fifties; Elvis Presley who changed the music, and James Dean who changed our lives. Nothing really happened again until Bob Dylan came along - and Dylan himself was influenced by Dean. If you can imagine the strength and influence Dylan had in the sixties, that's what Dean was to the fifties. When I was a young actor in New York, there was a saying that if Marlon Brando changed the way actors acted, James Dean changed the way people lived." Without pushing the point, it might be added that Dylan changed the way people thought.

Hibbing contemporaries of the teenage Zimmerman recall Dean's impact on their group, they felt an immediate identification with the character and image Dean projected in his three films, and the young Robert could personally identify with the man's myopia. Only six years after Dean's death, while Robert Allen Zimmerman was buried alive in Hibbing, Minn., Bob Dylan began emerging as a separate character, hipspeaking to his cohorts and attempting to fashion an image as durable as Dean's: "Hey man, you oughta see some picture of me . . . Ummm, I look like Marlon Brando, James Dean or somebody . . .".

James Dean's flaming death in 1955 had given youth its first martyr but that same year gave them a most unlikely looking new idol, the avuncular Bill Haley, whose 'Rock Around The Clock' hit Number 1 that May. The halfway year of the decade proved to be a watershed for the country. Senator McCarthy had been driven off the scene the year before when his futile efforts to prove the Army was riddled with Communist sympathisers finally revealed the idiocy of his witch-hunt, but not before many good and true citizens had been humbled by the blustering Wisconsin Senator's truculence. Lillian Hellman defiantly stated "I cannot and will not cut my conscience to fit this year's fashions", while the towering figure of Paul Robeson railed at the House Un-American Activities Committee (HUAC) "You are the non-patriots, you are the UnAmericans and you ought to be ashamed of yourselves!" Charlie Chaplin was hounded out of America, while folk singer Pete Seeger conducted himself with rare dignity during this most unseemly episode of post-war American history.

Way up on the windswept Canadian border, the deep South of America seemed like a foreign country where things hadn't changed much since the Civil War and where Jim Crow politics still held sway. South of the Mason-Dixon line, if you were white, you were back in the territory of *Gone With The Wind*, surrounded by magnolia blossom and mint juleps, where or'nry niggers kept their place, and white supremacists enhanced theirs. Down South, the Civil War wasn't yet history, it was a part of everyday life. During his American lecture tour of 1888, Oscar Wilde encountering a Confederate Colonel remarked on the beauty of the moon and was surprised by the response: "Ah, but you should have seen it before the war". In the aftermath of the war, the Ku Klux Klan - who take their name from a corruption of the Greek 'kuklos' meaning circle - was first formed, it resurged during the 50s, harassing not only negroes, but Catholics, Jews, anything or anyone in fact who was anti-"the American way of life"; and for American, read white, Anglo-Saxon, and Protestant.

Racial stereotyping in the South was as deeply ingrained as its mule-headedness about progress. Lynchings of negroes were an accepted fact of life and the fiery cross of the Klan was still a familiar sight halfway through the 20th Century. In 1954 the Supreme Court had outlawed segregated schools, but the progressive whims of a bunch of Northern liberals carried little weight in the entrenchedly racist strongholds of Alabama, Mississippi and Carolina. During the watershed year of 1955, two events bookmarked the foulness of the system and offered the first real hope of altering it. That August, in Greenwood, Mississippi Emmett Till, a 14-year-old negro, was murdered by three rednecks, who were later acquitted by an all-white jury. In Montgomery, Alabama in December, a black 42-year-old seamstress called Rosa Parks unbalanced centuries of entrenched racism when she refused to give up her seat to a white passenger on a city bus.

It was Rosa Parks' courageous determination to remain seated which led to the year-long bus boycott by the city's black population and propelled a 26-year-old black clergyman called Martin Luther King onto national and international platforms. The Montgomery boycott laid the foundations for King's national Civil Rights movement, clearly modelled on Gandhi's principles of passive resistance which had helped liberate India from the British Raj nearly 10 years before.

The Civil Rights movement was only one thread in the tapestry which threatened to wholly alter the world during the mid-50s. Fellow travellers of Kruschev's Russia were bitterly disillusioned by the Kremlin's brutal crushing of the 1956 Hungarian uprising; Suez saw any vestige of Britain's imperial ambitions vanquished. Angry young men had plenty to be angry about, and John Osborne's *Look Back In Anger* and Jack Kerouac's *On The Road* sounded the first, and most memorable shots in what was to become a fusillade. Kerouac, apotheosis of the Beats, heralded real opportunity and freedom in his best novel. The sense of awe and discovery, of shaking off the shackles of conformity and restricting attitudes of middle America were a revelation to those bound by the security and cherished values which Kerouac kicked against.

1959 Hibbing High School yearbook photograph

There was something in the air that period of time, and for once it was something tangible, something which could be snatched out of the air, even in remote Hibbing, far, far away from the activities depicted by Kerouac, far from the grim realities of the struggle bitterly being fought out in the South. It was a sound which traversed the world, we know it by many names now, but then, baby, that was rock 'n' roll.

'Hibbing was a good ol' town . . .'

CHAPTER

2

By 1956 America seemed like a country split so many different ways; the left and right divisions of the McCarthy era were slowly receding into memory, the fissures now were up and down. When L.P. Hartley so memorably wrote "the past is a foreign country, they do things differently there" he could have been talking about the Confederacy, alien and a century behind, a nation stalked by the "ghost-robed Ku Klux Klan". Finally, after years of largely passive suffering, the blacks had found a spokesman and champion in Martin Luther King, who was starting to bring their struggle to the attention of the world.

In the wake of the invention of the teenager, emerged the first real generation gap. There was a gulf appearing between the old and young, the title of one of Lawrence Ferlinghetti's early poems - 'Tentative Description of a Dinner to Promote the Impeachment of President Eisenhower' - showed how wide it was. But the real wedge came in the shape of 21-year-old Elvis Presley, the first properly threatening rock 'n' roller (the only threat posed by Bill Haley the year before was the possibility of being smothered by his good nature). But whichever side of the generation gap you were on, you couldn't ignore Elvis during 1956 - he was at Number 1 in the charts for six months of the year, and in the sneering, smouldering dynamo that appeared on national television, youth found an idol to replace James Dean. The young Bob Dylan was only one of the many who were mesmerised by Elvis - other devotees like John Lennon, Paul McCartney, Bruce Springsteen, Paul Simon and Elton John have testified to that searing, earth-stopping moment when they first heard Elvis. That first entreaty not to step on his blue suede shoes, the danger evoked by the drumming on 'Jailhouse Rock', the menace implied by checking into 'Heartbreak Hotel' . . . any one of a dozen chilling moments, frozen as if in aspic, captured on those early Elvis records. In 1978, Dylan told Bob Shelton that so closely was Elvis linked to his own adolescence, that his death in 1977 was one of the few occasions he had ever ventured back to that foreign country. Later, Dylan would speak again of that impact: "Hearing him for the first time was like busting out of jail. I think for a long

time that freedom to me was Elvis singing 'Blue Moon Of Kentucky'".

It was a sense of freedom others revelled in and celebrated, across the borderline in 1959 the Hawks were pummeling audiences with fiery rock 'n' roll, in Liverpool the Quarrymen toyed with skiffle (Britain's DIY equivalent of rock 'n' roll) while in El Cerrito, California, John Fogerty led the Blue Velvets on their first, faltering steps.

But there were other strange and memorable sounds in the air . . . They came across the dark, the lycanthropic dark outside the bedroom, carried on unseen waves across the planet; weird, unearthly sounds, transported as if by magic, pumped out by frenetic disciples charged to spread the Gospel, shuttered in their tiny studios, crouched beneath the mighty sprouting mast which carried their words and sounds across state boundaries.

They came to the young Robert Zimmerman, transports of delight: listening to that stuff, you could be anybody. Those voices, floating from the stratosphere, down through his radio and into his brain, permeating his mundane existence, voices drifting over mountains and whipping across plains, over frozen lakes and tall trees, drifting down trash-filled alleys, an electric whiplash, the spark of something which once it had lit, started a conflagration which would sweep all before it. On the ether came the sounds, the radio waves oscillated round the planet, the cycles lodged in the ears of a generation who received their Pauline conversions through electric modulations.

In a world now comfortable with new technology, which at the flick of a switch can conjure up alien sounds, languages and noises, world music and state of the art pop in an electronic magnet, it is perhaps hard to recall just how alien and affecting those remote voices and primitive instruments could sound plucked out of the air - distinctive echoes like Leadbelly, Big Joe Turner, Little Richard, Odetta, Jimmie Rodgers, Johnny Ray, Robert Johnson, Johnny Cash, The Weavers, Hank Snow, the Everly Brothers, Chuck Berry, Hank Williams, Buddy Holly, Gene Vincent, Johnny Ace . . . a random litany that helped shape the boy into the man. Odd lines from those singers lay

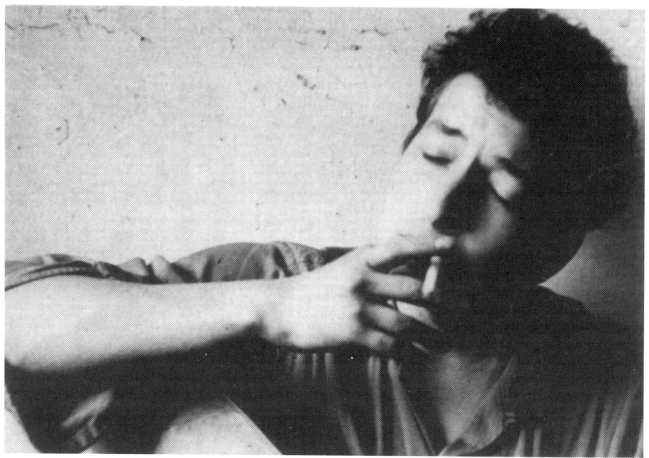

New York City 1962

dormant in the boy's subconscious, to be sifted out years later. The influences which shaped Bob Dylan's musical direction were diverse and durable, of all the rock icons of the 60s, Dylan's musical lineage was the most eclectic - folk, blues, Country, rock 'n' roll, rockabilly, Gospel, Western Bop all tumbled into a rich jambalaya which simmered and bubbled throughout his career.

The sights and sounds of that time are like a bell struck in a tunnel, its echo carrying on down the years. The aspirations and desires of the young Zimmerman were likely no more than those of the average teenager of the 50s, those which Eddie Cochran detailed on 'Teenage Heaven': phone in your room, shorter hours in school, a Coupe de Ville (with dad footing the bill) and "staying up at night and seeing the big city lights". But it was lone voices which reached out and seared: the aching delta blues of Robert Johnson (who Dylan remembered many years later in the dedication of *Writings & Drawings*), the nervous pop of Buddy Holly, who the young Bob religiously sought at the Duluth Armory only 48 hours before Holly died. There was the rockabilly "blue guitar" of the young Johnny Cash, the ebullience of Little Richard uttering rock's coded clarion call "awopbopaloobopalopbamboom" carefully locked against parents; there was the self-inflicted grief

of Johnnie Ray, who was the first singer to make a real impression on the 15-year-old Bob and there was his "first idol" - Hank Williams, the purest purveyor of white man's blues.

Hank had been dead over a year by the time of Bob Zimmerman's barmitzvah in 1954. He towered over Country music, becoming its first superstar, his plaintive, aching voice seemed to live the songs he sang, "moanin' the blues" he called his distinctive, lonely vocal style - 'I'll Never Get Out Of This World Alive', 'I'm So Lonesome I Could Cry', 'I Heard That Lonesome Whistle', 'Weary Blues From Waitin'' and the chilling 'Lost Highway', with its stark opening line depicting the singer as a "rolling stone" on the lost highway, a line which Bob Dylan was not unfamiliar with.

Hank's songs spoke volumes to those whose sole source of entertainment (and frequently education) was the radio, not for nothing was Hank known as "the hillbilly Shakespeare", but as is often the case, there was a dichotomy between the man and his art, Hank spoke movingly for the dispossessed and lonely, but as a human being he could be difficult. Hank broke hearts, upset the Nashville establishment and rarely slept two nights in the same bed; a recurring back injury drove him to seek solace in drugs and alcohol, all of which helped make him a prickly character. Joe Ely told me of the janitor at Lubbock's Cotton Club who couldn't resist sneaking a glimpse into Hank's suitcase while he was onstage performing: "What was in there was a roll of wadded up $20 bills, a bottle of bourbon and a .45."

Life on the road in those days of the late 40s was hard, and it was a lonely death in the back of a limo on the way to yet another show which awaited Hank Williams on New Year's Day 1953. A radio broadcast on Nashville's WSM (ironically on '*The Health & Happiness*' show) near the end of his career has him sounding as weary as his alter-ego Luke The Drifter; but without Hank Williams' contribution, C&W would

still be a regional phenomenon for farmers, hick music for hillbillies, and any appreciation of Bob Dylan has to find accord with occasional sidekick Kris Kristofferson when he sang 'If You Don't Like Hank Williams, You Can Kiss My Ass'! Even when hailed himself as "the poet laureate of young America", Dylan was still acknowledging his debt to "the hillbilly Shakespeare".

"In 1955, when rock 'n' roll was showing its first stirrings, church attendance was at an all-time high in America. Between 1940 and 1958 there was an increase from 64.5 million worshippers to 109.6 million. There was social kudos attached to being a church member,

New York City 1962

middle-class morality and respectability were framed by it . . . " wrote Steve Turner in *Hungry For Heaven* (Virgin, 1988). That craving for conformity was a constituent factor why rock 'n' roll cut such a swathe through middle America; those denizens of high culture, the North Alabama White Citizens Council declared: "Rock 'n' roll is part of a pest to undermine the morals of the youth of our nation. It is sexualistic, unmoralistic and . . . brings people of both races together". Any deviance from the norm in the Eisenhower years was likely to raise an eyebrow, cocking a snook was one thing, but rock 'n' roll, why that was just one step away from anarchy.

If toeing the line was the acceptable face of middle America, Little Richard chainsawed it, and with a flamboyance that was unique. Even Chuck Berry, the most literate of the early rockers, had presented an acceptable figure, apart from his awkward tendency to duckwalk; Elvis could croon with the best of them, even Buddy Holly was a bespectacled Texan kid who was polite to Ed Sullivan, the Everly Brothers were good ol' Kentucky boys . . . but Little Richard Penniman, he really did seem to pose a flaring threat to the American way of life. Parents scratched their heads over lyrics which - if they could decipher them - sounded suggestive, Richard flouted authority with every gesture.

Fleetingly moving through the ranks of teenage

On the steps of the Folklore Center 1961

rock groups like the Golden Chords and Elston Gunn & His Rock Boppers, Bob Zimmerman found himself aged 18 and quitting school, there he is, puppy fat swathing those soon to be familiar gaunt features, bright eyed and full of promise among the class of '59, with his stated ambition in the High School Yearbook "To join Little Richard"!

The rock 'n' roll animal had sunk its teeth deep into Robert Zimmerman and in the ensuing years, which saw him emerge from his chrysalis as Bob Dylan, the venom of that bite continued to course through his veins: his first CBS single, after all, was to have been 'Mixed Up Confusion', a healthy slab of 50s-sounding rockabilly, while on his debut album the traditional 'Highway 51' is begun by the same guitar figure which ushered in the Everlys' 'Wake Up Little Susie'.

In the confusion that surrounded the birth of Bob Dylan, just before the umbilical chord which connected him with Robert Zimmerman was finally severed, there occurred one of those close encounters which makes any study of the history of rock 'n' roll so fruitful. February 3rd, 1959 was "the day the music died", when Buddy Holly, Ritchie Valens and the Big Bopper all perished in a plane crash on their way to another show. Such was the demand for the services of pop stars – hell, reasoned the promoters, the kids'll never know the difference between 'em anyhow – that acts were needed urgently to bolster the now tragically depleted roster of the ill-fated Winter Dance Party. Dion & The Belmonts were hastily drafted in as bill-toppers and at The Moorhead Armory in Minnesota the night of February 3, Robert Velline – who had at one stage included Bob Zimmerman in his band – made his stage debut as Bobby Vee.

Endeavouring to give his orthodox adolescence more colour, Dylan claimed he had played piano on Vee's debut single 'Suzie Baby' in 1959. Ironically Vee was one of the squeaky clean pop idols who emerged during the post-Elvis, pre-Beatle rock 'n' roll drought, but was soon blown away by the tempest which followed Dylan and The Beatles in 1964. Vee recalled that as a pianist, Zimmerman "played great – in the key of C!" Saxophonist Bobby Keys though, had a different memory: as a member of Vee's band in the late 50s, he told Robert Greenfield that he remembered "a kid called Eldon Gunn" (sic) with a penchant for Hank Williams' tunes being rejected by Vee.

Short of any Elston Gunn or Golden Chords tapes turning up on the bootleg market, we have to conform, and accept Bob Dylan's eponymous 1962 album as his recorded debut. But all that was a long way in the future, in the meantime our hero set his sights no higher than the University of Minnesota in Minneapolis: no headful of ideas driving him insane, rather a jumble of influences rattling around, a thrift shop figure, keen to seek out the city's Beat quarters, enlightened by Kerouac and Hank Williams, inspired by Elvis and Little Richard, he may have been confused about how it all would affect his future, but at least he had a name.

CHAPTER
3

Dylan Thomas had been dead for six years by the time Robert Zimmerman hijacked his name. In his revealing biography *Dylan Thomas* (Penguin, 1977), Paul Ferris writes of the poet's Christian name: "'Dylan' was an obscure figure from the 'Mabinogion', the Welsh medieval prose romances. As a noun the word means 'sea' or 'ocean'. In the 'Mabinogion' Dylan makes a brief appearance when Math the son of Mathonwy challenges Aranrhod, who claims to be a virgin, to step over his magic wand. 'A fine boy-child with rich yellow hair' drops from her as she does so. Math . . . calls him Dylan, and the child makes for the sea, his natural element".

Bob Dylan has strenuously denied taking his surname from the poet, acknowledging a familiarity with his work, but nothing else. "I did more for his name than he ever did" the singer vainly claimed, adding that he just "plucked it out of the air" when applying for a gig at the Ten O'Clock Club in Minneapolis. The rumour-mad years of the early 60s had Dylan himself citing an uncle (an old family name etc.) as his source, while some unkind critics had the uncouth youth pillaging that Western stalwart Matt Dillon for inspiration. More recently and with a scrupulous attention to detail, the indefatigable Ian Woodward (Mycroft Holmes to Bob's Sherlock) was on the trail of an otherwise forgotten 50s' folk singer called Dylan Todd.

Dylan Thomas' best known work, *Under Milk Wood* had been premiered on BBC Radio in 1954, and in the years since his death a cult had developed which frequently overlooked the quality of the man's work, concerning itself more with the prodigiousness of his alcoholic intake; one thing the two Dylans have in common is a willingness to "rage, rage against the dying of the light". Rock trivia buffs will know of Dylan Thomas' several other contributions to the culture: Paul Simon namechecks him on 'A Simple Desultory Philippic', King Crimson's *Starless & Bible Black* took its title from *Under Milk Wood*, while one of Frankie Goes To Hollywood's final singles 'Rage Hard' echoed the refrain of Thomas' poem 'Do Not Go Gentle Into That Good Night'. In 1988, George Martin produced a lavish musical version of *Under Milk Wood* which included contributions from Mark Knopfler, Elton John and Tom Jones, while John Cale's album *Words For The Dying* (1989) featured his orchestral adaptations of four of Thomas' poems.

It was in the Bohemian quarter of Minneapolis that 'Bob Dylan' first began performing and the name certainly looked better on a marquee than Zimmerman - something Ethel Merman had recognised 30 years before when she dropped the 'Zim' from her surname. There are those who soar high blessed with memorable names from birth - mean to say, you couldn't imagine Marlon Brando as a grocery clerk. In rock, staccato surnames such as Jagger, Marley, Lennon resonate, but Punk was not so easily satisfied, Tom Verlaine, Sid Vicious and Rat Scabies invented their headline-grabbing surnames; Elvis Costello was deliberately provocative in the aftermath of the King's death, whereas the fact that Gary Glitter could have been the leader of the gang as Larry Lurex is surely only of interest to his dwindling fans. Bob Dylan fell off his stool laughing when he learnt that Ramblin' Jack Elliott was christened Elliot Adnopoz, but that was Bob Dylan laughing, Robert Zimmerman wouldn't have seen the joke.

So, the kid had a name, and with the adoption of an alias, he also felt free to colour in the background of his new persona. "M'name's Robert Zimmerman, I'm the eldest son of middle class Jewish parents from Minnesota, like to play some songs of Okie drifters and negro slaves for y'all", hardly packed the punch of Dylan the Drifter, shifting from state to state, bouncing round orphanages like a pinball. From very early in his career, Dylan understood the importance of myth-making as well as Oscar Wilde who once remarked: "What is true in a man's life is not what he does, but the legend which grows up around him. You must never destroy legends. Through them we are given an inkling of the true physiognomy of a man". A new name meant freedom from the past and from now on the teenager only had eyes for the future, but he needed a road map.

The first 'folk' singer Dylan admitted made an impact was Odetta, whose magnificent bluesy singing conveyed the suffering and indignity of black slaves on her debut album in 1956, and who later went on to record an entire album of Dylan songs. Always one to acknowledge influences, Dylan dedicated 'Tomorrow Is A Long Time' to Odetta when she attended one of his Japanese concerts in 1978.

Woody Guthrie's autobiography *Bound For Glory* first published in 1943, documented his years drifting through a land choked by the Great Depression, writing a thousand songs about what he saw, castigating landlords and faceless bankers, those who - with the swish of a fountain pen - could make whole families homeless. Woody sang of the power of the trades unions which could bind "we the people" together, his songs came from the heart and poured from that heart as blood from a severed artery. 'This Land Is Your Land', 'Jesus Christ', 'Grand Coulee Dam', 'Pastures Of Plenty', 'Ramblin' Round', 'Pretty Boy Floyd', together formed a tide as urgent as that of the Columbia River. Woody could communicate directly with a song like 'Jesus Christ', summon up anthems like 'This Land Is Your Land' (written as a socialist response to Irving Berlin's ubiquitous 'God Bless America') or effortlessly contour the sublime poetry of 'Grand Coulee Dam': "In the misty crystal glitter of that wild and windward spray . . . ".

Woody was called a folk singer because he played the guitar and sang of contemporary events in a jagged, frazzled voice as dusty as the roads he'd travelled; as he wrote in the 1965 collection of his writings *Born To Win*: "I say that folk music and folk songs, folk ballads are just now getting up onto their feet, like Joe Louis after a couple of sad knockdowns . . . As long as we've got wrecks, disasters, cyclones, hurricanes, explosions, lynchings, trade union troubles, high price and low pay, as long as we've got cops in uniform battling with union pickets on strike, folk songs and folk ballads are on their way in".

Many besides Bob Dylan were touched by the permanence and pertinence of Woody's songs back then. During his 1980/81 world tour, Bruce Springsteen who was well on his way to becoming the biggest white rock star on the planet, made a point of including Woody's 'This Land Is Your Land' in every show. He told an interviewer at the time: "I sing that song to let people know that America belongs to everybody who lives there: the blacks, Chicanos, Indians, Chinese and the whites". Springsteen has also admitted that one of the three books he'd ever read for pleasure was Anthony Scaduto's biography of Bob Dylan, later acknowledging that Dylan "was the guy who made it possible to do the things I wanted".

To say that Woody Guthrie 'influenced' Bob Dylan is only to hint at the effect of the punchy little singer on the fledgling folk singer. Dylan's embracing of Woody Guthrie was wholehearted and devout, the same way that five years later many would embrace Dylan as influence and eminence-gris. Dylan wrote that Woody was his last idol, whose strength lay in his "shatterin' even himself/as an idol." Woody's influence on Dylan was devastating, he was a great communicator who wrote of what he devoutly believed, fought hard against what he knew was wrong and then rusted tragically away in a New York hospital, withered by Huntington's Chorea.

Woody's genius lay in the directness of his communication - he posed questions, supplied answers, stole from older songs and entered the mainstream of American popular music with his own simple melodies. He sang for children, for dispossessed farmers, for committed anti-fascists, for those of every colour; he damned capitalism, espoused communism, hated racism and loved kids. Ideologically and politically, Woody had been on the right track from his birth in Oklahoma before World War I; as a husband and father, Woody was as feckless as a tumbleweed, as careless as he was otherwise caring. He couldn't keep an appointment to save his life and treated his wives appallingly, but from that mass of contradictions shone the bright essence of the human spirit, a brightness only dimmed by his tragically prolonged death on October 3rd 1967.

Dylan's first original recorded song was entitled simply 'Song To Woody' and during the early years of his career, Dylan became Guthrie, endlessly performing his songs, shaping his own in the style of Woody's, adopting his image, clutching at his style, recasting himself again, this time in the role of Woody Guthrie. He made pilgrimages to see the dying Woody in hospital and the night Guthrie died, Dylan got on the phone to his manager Harold Leventhal to pledge his commitment to any planned tribute, and in January 1968, his appearance with The Band at Carnegie Hall for Woody's memorial Concert marked his return to the world after the 1966 bike crash.

During Dylan's spectacular attempt to rediscover America during its Bicentennial, each night of the Rolling Thunder Review ended with everyone assembled onstage to sing 'This Land Is Your Land'. To look at the cover of Dylan's third album *The Times They Are A-Changin'* is to see a direct descendant of Woody Guthrie, the stark, black and white face of a writer who had stalked the country, standing up for what was right and singing out against what was wrong. Though in typical Dylan doubleplay, the pose also recalls Roy Schatt's classic portrait of James Dean which graced posters for 1957's *The James Dean Story*.

To commemorate the 20th anniversary of Woody's death, BBC radio mounted a four-part series in which Dylan admitted that at the beginning of his career he was "like a Woody Guthrie jukebox". A quarter of a century after he had been so fired by his first acquaintance with Woody's work, he also tried to define what was so special about Guthrie: "He had a particular sound, and besides that, he said something that seemed to be needed to be said . . . There was an innocence, you know, to Woody Guthrie. I know that was what I was looking for. Like a lost innocence or something, after him, it's over . . . ". Despite Dylan's avowed Guthrie influence, he has rarely gone officially on record to testify, the three Guthrie songs he performed in January 1968 did appear four years later on *A Tribute To Woody Guthrie/Part One* and in 1988 Dylan contributed, along with Bruce Springsteen and U2 to *Folkways: A Vision*

Shared, an album which celebrated the music of Guthrie and Leadbelly.

Woody's most immediate impact on the teenage Zimmerman was as a magnet, which drew him away from Minneapolis, away from the state of Minnesota where Robert Zimmerman would be laid to rest, and to draw Bob Dylan out onto the highway to snake down to New York City.

The timing was perfect, along with Hibbing, the 50s also lay behind him; and whilst decades aren't necessarily the best arbiters of eras or styles, it is not without significance that Bob Dylan arrived in New York just as the 60s were drawing breath.

Ann Arbor, Michigan

Dear Editor:

I visited Woody Guthrie again during the Christmas holidays—I stayed as long as I could, singing and playing a lot of Woody's songs, and some new ones as well. Woody really enjoyed the songs; the interns told me that they hadn't seen him sit down and listen for such a long period of time in years, and that these visits helped considerably. And yet, Woody gets few visitors: his wife comes when she can, but she has to support the family; some of his friends used to drop in occasionally, but few of them have come in some time. I visit Woody when I can, but I'm out here in Michigan for eight months of the year. I'm appealing to you folk-singers and folk music listeners, friends of Woody's, people who have heard him sing, and those who just know his songs, to come up and sing for him. It's hard to get to him, I know; Dr. Glenn, who is in charge of that particular ward, is very wary of visitors and fearful of any publicity, not really understanding the respect that folk music artists and listeners have for Woody. And it is heartbreaking to see Woody as he is now; the disco-ordination has hit most heavily in his arm and throat. so that he can hardly talk, and can't write. The interns affection-ately call him "Ramblin' Wreck," and the des-cription is tragically fitting. But still, the now-gray hair is as curly-wild as ever, the deep eyes have the same old blaze, and Woody is still Woody in spite of everything. He still loves to hear the old songs and the new ones, the voices of friends, and news of this "better world a-comin'." He needs visitors, contact with the outside world, above all the songs. Hard though it is to reach him and sad as it is to see him, remember that he wrote more than a thousand fine songs for us, and he needs our help now. He's at Brooklyn State Hospital, Reception Hall, in Ward #3. It's not too hard to find him; I've done it. I ask you who sing Woody's songs—in Washington Square, in coffee houses, on records, or just for yourselves—go and sing for him. It helps.

Leslie Fish

Letter from Sing Out!

West 4th Street in the snow in 1961

CHAPTER

4

Bob Dylan made it to New York in late January 1961, and spent some time drifting round the city before hitting Greenwich Village that February. Only four days before, John F. Kennedy had been inaugurated as the 35th President of the USA, proclaiming: "Let the word go forth from this time and place . . . that the torch has been passed to a new generation of Americans . . . one unwilling to witness or permit the slow undoing of those human rights to which this nation has always been committed . . .".

The sort of torch-bearer he had in mind was busy soaking up the ambience in Greenwich Village which boasted clubs where you could hear the best jazz and listen to Lenny Bruce pushing back the barriers. These were the streets where Mark Twain, Edgar Allan Poe, Henry James, Herman Melville and John Reed had walked, and the area was now experiencing some sort of golden age as the artistic hub to which the hip gravitated. This is how Liam Clancy recalled it to me when we spoke over 20 years later: "It was a certain sort of spontaneous combustion. It's a thing that happens round the world at different times. It happened in Paris in the 20s, when Hemingway was writing, a mini-renaissance. It moves from place to place, and there are people who try to find out where it's going to happen next, to follow it. But you can't control it, you can't predict it".

Dylan's first year in the Village polarised opinions: critics saw him as little more than a Guthrie clone, shamelessly ripping off the wasted Woody cloistered uptown. Others tolerated him, recognising his infatuation as that of a besotted youth, some even claim to have spotted the nascent talent and speak of a star in the ascendant. Hindsight certainly alters perspective, what is certain though is that he didn't go unnoticed.

Dylan was only one of dozens of struggling folk singers who had flocked to the Village during the last years of the Eisenhower administration and the bright beginning of Kennedy's new frontier, all were keen to make their mark, because folk was where it was at.

It is one of rock history's axioms that the period between Elvis' Army discharge in 1960 and the arrival of The Beatles in 1963 was one of its most fallow. The late 50s and early 60s did throw up their fair share of great pop records: 'Speedy Gonzalez', 'A Picture Of You', 'Johnny Remember Me', anything by Eddie Cochran and most of Cliff's stuff of the period will always find a place in my heart. But rock had become pop, threat had become pose, passion had become novelty and while cheap music retained its customary potency, and it was a good enough time to be young, there was no unifying factor, no sense of the community that the mid-50s had boasted.

Folk alone seemed to offer some sort of purity and passion, commitment and concern over pop's frivolity and fashion. Authenticity was venerated but not everyone could be a grizzled bluesman or dustbowl balladeer but if you could fake it, hell that was almost as good. There was certainly a vacuum to be filled, Bryan Hyland's 'Itsy Bitsy Teeny Weeny Yellow Polka Dot Bikini' didn't seem quite the clarion call that Little Richard had sounded five years before. What was needed, was what later became known as a role model. On his release from the Army, Elvis became a virtual prisoner of the Hollywood film studios, though, with good behaviour, he might get time off from *It Happened At The World's Fair*. Substitutes proliferated, pick'n'mix pop stars like Fabian, Frankie Avalon, Bobby Vee, Bobby Rydell and Tommy Sands grinned obligingly and twitched to order. Bob Marcucci, who was Fabian and Frankie Avalon's manager, simply told his partner: "We need some idols", and watched them roll off the production line.

The Bob Dylan who was scuffing round the Village at that time had one characteristic that everyone agreed on – he was a great listener; he picked up songs, tunes, politics from everyone. Liam Clancy told me: "He was a teenager when he came to the Village, and the only thing I can compare him with was blotting paper. He soaked everything up. He had this immense curiosity, he was totally blank, and he was ready to suck up everything that came within his range". Maybe this is what singled Dylan out; he was not without talent, but then neither were Patrick Sky, Eric Andersen, Tom Paxton, Phil Ochs, Peter LaFarge and David Blue, but always it was scrawny, pilfering Bob Dylan on whom the hosannas were heaped.

With the second and third albums, came irrefutable

evidence of a rich talent in the process of maturing and developing, but how many of the few who bought Dylan's debut could have predicted quite such a future? The crowds that filled the Gaslight or Folk City, Cafe Lenna or the Cafe Wha? were by no means convinced. We can try to imagine what his impact would have been back then, but with the distortion of hindsight it's hard to think of acclaimed talents such as Dylan, The Beatles or David Bowie beginning anywhere. It may be tempting to assume they arrived fully formed at their moments of triumph, but there are those who crowded into Wallasey ballrooms, Greenwich Village folk clubs and the Beckenham Arts Lab, who were there at the beginning. "Take care of your memories . . . for you cannot relive them". It is to Bob Shelton's eternal credit that he recognised that raw, hungry talent in Bob Dylan when he saw an early gig at Gerde's Folk City. Of course, we'd all like to think that we too would have spotted that precocious, fledgling talent, hindsight has the comforting ability to prove yourself right, but to have seen it then . . .

On the tapes which survive from those pre-*Bob Dylan* days, there is an appealing, edgy energy as Dylan runs through the Woody Guthrie songbook, borrows from old blues shouters, pillages Hank Williams' repertoire, borrows from Big Joe Turner and in short, keeps everything that's owed. But there are some, just enough, fragments which indicate a talent about to burst, not as a writer, that is still in the future, but as an interpretive singer. Over a quarter of a century later, there remains an engaging zeal in Dylan's handling of 'Sally Gal' or 'Stealin'', and a certain dues-paying intensity on 'Rocks & Gravel' and 'Cocaine'. There is the pleasure of hearing a raw 20-year-old at the beginning of his career tackling '(I Heard That) Lonesome Whistle' and trying to match the pain of Hank Williams at the end of his life. Here is the nervous near-teenager gamely trying to convince an audience that he is a 'Man Of Constant Sorrow'. We know now that Dylan never lived the life he claimed, but he sounded like he did, and in the face of such conviction one can almost forgive the falsehoods.

The two outstanding performances from those distant days are 'Black Cross' (aka 'Hezekiah Jones') and 'No More Auction Block'. These performances are filled with gravitas, Dylan truly seems to become the character and convinces the listener with his grizzled credentials, a young singer sounding just like the black and white Henry Fonda of *The Grapes Of Wrath*.

'Auction Block' began life as a post-Civil War negro spiritual, celebrating the freedom won by that four-year war, and praying that never again will human beings have to endure the indignity of being auctioned like cattle. In other performances of this period, anxious to emphasise his integrity and commitment, Dylan often sustains a note to the point of irritation ('Rocks & Gravel'); on 'Auction Block' though the trick of sustaining actually works, somehow helping to convey the degree of indignity and suffering endured by slaves and the celebration of liberation. Pete Seeger later recognised the melody of 'Blowin' In The Wind' as a free adaptation of 'Auction Block', so the song obviously held a deep appeal for the young Dylan.

It was the blessedly unclassifiable Lord Buckley who, a year before he died in New York, recorded 'Black Cross' on his 1959 *In Concert* album, claiming to have learnt the monologue from "Paul Newman's beloved grandfather". Richard Buckley was born in 1905, and became a monologist of mark, pre-empting Mort Sahl and Lenny Bruce with his trick of milking sacred cows dry and use of black jazz argot. In Buckley's irreverent hands, Shakespeare is transformed into 'Willie The Shake', and Mark Anthony's celebrated speech opens "Hipsters, flipsters and finger-poppin' daddies, knock me your lobes!" For Woody Guthrie, Jesus Christ was a fully paid-up member of the Wobblies, for Buckley he is 'The Naz', one cool cat, who prefaced miracles by asking "What's de matter wit-choo baby?".

'Black Cross' is an attempt to grasp the blind hatred of the lynch mob, Buckley speaks of Hezekiah Jones, "black as the soil he was hoeing" and slowly, eloquently builds up the picture of a dignified, self-educated man with noble principles, who, when accused of not believing in anything, by "the white man's preacher" replies "Oh yes I do . . . I believe that a man should be beholden to his neighbour, not for the reward of Heaven or the fear of Hellfire" only to be met with the unanswerable retort: "But you don't understand – there's a lot of good ways for a man to be wicked!", and Hezekiah is hung "as high as a pigeon . . . 'cos the sonofabitch never had no religion!".

Dylan performed the song regularly over a period of two years, and his handling of it on the recordings which survive is rarely short of stunning, swiftly and strikingly conjuring up the gnarled character of Hezekiah and the bigoted preacher. Buckley's performance is striking enough, but he was well into his 50s, Dylan was barely 20. Hearing his voice break as he narrates how they "hung Hezekiah . . . high as a pigeon" is an astonishingly dramatic moment, all the more so given the tender years of the performer. The monologue became a Dylan perennial of the period, indeed in an interview with Izzy Young towards the end of 1961, when asked about his views on religion, Dylan quotes whole chunks of 'Black Cross' verbatim in his reply: "Got no religion. Tried a bunch of different religions. The churches are divided, can't make up their minds and neither can I. Never saw a God, can't say until I see one".

The folk songs which Dylan in common with so many of his Village contemporaries endlessly plundered, had been in circulation for centuries. Originally the province of European peasants with no access to print, the songs had been passed down orally, plot variations adopted by different regions. Walter Scott and Robert Louis Stephenson were aficionados of the traditional ballads, but it was during the 19th Century that collectors such as Francis Child started seriously to chronicle them. Child's exhaustive five volume *English & Scottish Popular Ballads* was compiled between 1882-98, and stands as the source for many songs popularised during the American folk revival of the late 50s and early 60s. The genealogy of individual songs is often fascinating, to take one example, 'Barbara Allen' which Dylan regularly performed during his early days in New York (and still does to this day) was for Samuel Pepys "a perfect pleasure" to hear sung in the London of 1666, and hundreds of variants of it were sung in Europe and later taken to America. A western pioneer wrote of the song that it was "a favourite cowboy song in Texas before the pale faces became thick enough to make the Indians consider a massacre worthwhile!".

This was the rich heritage which Dylan now absorbed; his Woody Guthrie infatuation of the period also led him to perform ballads like 'Jesse James' which Woody had discovered on his travels. Folk music was in the public domain, so any young performer who was lucky enough to have a contract could simply put 'Trad. Arr . . . ' after the song and claim the royalties. Dylan used regularly to perform such traditional songs as 'The Cuckoo Is A Pretty Bird' and 'Omie Wise' before he found his own style as a writer, but even afterwards the indebtedness to the folk tradition remained, assimilated into his own work by a process of osmosis. The tune of The Clancy Brothers' stirring account of an 18th Century Irish highwayman 'Brennan On The Moor' soon found a new home in Dylan's account of a philandering gambler 'Rambling Gambling Willie', while his 'Ballad Of Donald White' borrowed its tune from the traditional 'Peter Amberley'.

Over the years, in areas of popular music as diverse as jazz, folk and rock 'n' roll, there have frequently emerged two camps: the purists and the innovators or experimenters. The purists believing that the original version of a song or style was sacrosanct, whether it was a 400-year-old Scottish ballad or the traditional jazz of Beale Street. The folk ballad purists maintain the belief that if an extant version has survived the centuries intact, then that is how it should be performed. This attitude was prevalent in New York during the early 60s and even persists today. Hence the telling joke

about how many folk singers it takes to change a lightbulb: 17! One to change to the bulb, and 16 to sing about how good the old one was! And Billy Bragg moaned about folk club organisers in the 80s who still hark back to the good old days of the 30s - the 1830s!

The folk revival had received a tremendous boost from Woody Guthrie and Cisco Houston, and The Weavers had had a great run of hits during the 50s with their singalong versions of Leadbelly's 'Goodnight Irene' and the traditional 'On Top Of Old Smokey', but Pete Seeger's 1955 refusal to name names to HUAC saw him effectively blacklisted for six years and brought the golden age of The Weavers to an end. It took the crew-cut charm of The Kingston Trio to turn 'folk' into a truly national craze when their version of the 19th Century ballad 'Tom Dooley' reached number 1 on the pop charts in 1958, opening the doors to the thousands of guitar-clutching, weekend beatniks with a headful of 'folk' songs who swarmed in their wake.

The purists were naturally outraged at what they saw as a contamination of their sacred tracts, but the experimenters found this attitude inexplicable and continued to exploit songs in the public domain with

Handbill for the first solo New York concert

THE FOLKLORE CENTER

Presents

BOB DYLAN

IN HIS FIRST NEW YORK CONCERT

SAT. NOV. 4, 1961   8:40pm

CARNEGIE CHAPTER HALL

154 WEST 57th STREET • NEW YORK CITY

All seats $2.00

Tickets available at: The Folklore Center
                                        110 MacDougal Street
    GR 7 - 5987   New York City 12. New York
                                        or at door

relish. Talking to Cameron Crowe in 1985, Dylan remembered: "There was a clique, you know. Folk music was a strict and rigid establishment. If you sang Southern Mountain Blues, you didn't sing Southern Mountain Ballads. If you sang Texas cowboy songs, you didn't play English ballads. It was really pathetic . . . If you sang folk songs from the 30s, you didn't do bluegrass tunes or Appalachian ballads. It was very strict. Everybody had their particular thing that they did. I didn't much ever pay attention to that. If I liked a song, I would just learn it and sing it the only way I could play it . . . ". Dylan's attitude was not simple irreverence, it was a recognition of his ability to assimilate and utilise a tradition to his own ends; "I could sing 'How High The Moon' . . . and it would come out like 'Mule Skinner Blues'" he said much later. The traditionalists though stuck to their guns and the British electric folk bands Fairport Convention and Steeleye Span encountered their wrath later in the decade. As late as 1982, the division still festered on and Bruce Springsteen got it in the neck from the other side who considered his acoustic album *Nebraska* to be a betrayal of his rock roots, while The Pogues attracted incredible antipathy from died in the wool folkies for their irreverent retelling of traditional folk songs in the late 80s.

Soaking up the heady musical brew New York had to offer, making pilgrimages out to Greystones Hospital to talk and sing to Woody Guthrie, cultivating an air of mystery about his past, the Bob Dylan that survives from that period, on tapes, bootlegs and through personal recollections, was a determined young hustler. The dogged intensity of his performances however also survives, a committed young minstrel, determinedly ploughing through his set of Guthrie songs, blues hollers, blue yodels and talking blues to largely uninterested audiences. His guitar playing was just sufficient to carry the melodies, the harmonica punctuations frequently distract rather than focus attention on the song, there is indeed an almost comic element in the troubadour's torment, the cherubic youth singing in a scratchy voice of pain and suffering which he obviously had not experienced. Knowing now where he went, we pay painful attention to these fumbling first steps and listen intently for that first hint of the profuse talent which lay ahead, but what was most apparent then was an endearing monotony, a diligent determination as Dylan ploughed doggedly through his many songs of injustice.

What first drew attention to the precocious Bob Dylan was the harmonica playing, which led to his first paid engagement in a recording studio. Singlehandedly Harry Belafonte had fostered attention on the calypso craze, and for his 1962 album *Midnight Special* he needed a harp player to blow on the title track, which is described on the sleeve notes thus: "This album started with a lonesome harmonica player, playing his heart out in a shanty on a hand-me-down harmonica . . .". The song had been discovered by Leadbelly who first heard it during a spell in a Texas prison in the early 20s: the inmates legend had it that if the light of the Midnight Special out of Houston shone on a prisoner, then he would soon be freed. It remains one of the pre-rock 'n' roll era's most formative songs, later memorably recorded by Creedence Clearwater Revival and Paul McCartney.

The album also included a version of Paul Clayton's 'Gotta Travel On' which Dylan subsequently recorded on *Self Portrait* and much later Belafonte worked with his former harp-player on USA For Africa's 'We Are The World' single in 1985. But back in June 1961, Dylan though delighted at the opportunity to blow his heart out on the album, found himself unable to cope with Belafonte's determination to get just the right sound on each song, and ended up only appearing on the album's title track. Dylan's evident proficiency on the harp however saw him appear on albums by veteran blues singer Victoria Spivey and Texan folk singer Carolyn Hester prior to the release of his own first album in 1962.

Dylan never had the patience for such perfectionism in the studio as can be seen in his work from that early experience with Belafonte right up to the messy *Down In The Groove* (1988). Even in the studio, Dylan relies on the spontaneity of early takes, the results can be shambolic, but at best they capture some of the vitality of a live session. Dylan's determination to retain the shaggy spontaneity of recording is one way he keeps in touch with his roots in the technology obsessed studios of the 80s. One imagines the relish with which Phil Spector anticipated producing Dylan: "He's never been produced", the first Tycoon of Teen complained. While we're still waiting for a full Spector/Dylan collaboration, much of the critical praise heaped on *Oh Mercy* (1989) attested to Daniel Lanois' sympathetic production.

Occasional harmonica sessions and poorly paid gigs were barely steps on the ladder, and certainly weren't enough to "shoot lightning through the sky in the entertainment world" which by 1961 was a cumbersome, conservative thing. Heralding the launch of the CBS label in Britain in 1962, a breathless report in the *New Musical Express* announced that the label would boast albums from Steve Lawrence & Eydie Gorme, Johnny Mathis, Andy Williams, Don Costa and Doris Day. There was no mention at all of the 21-year-old whose vigour had so impressed the label's John Hammond and led to his debut album release in March 1962.

PRICE - 35¢

BROADSIDE # 6, LATE MAY 1962 BOX 193, CATHEDRAL STATION, NEW YORK 25, N.Y.

BLOWIN' IN THE WIND
by BOB DYLAN

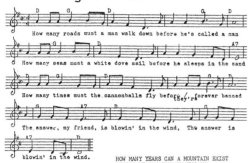

How many roads must a man walk down before he's called a man

How many seas must a white dove sail before he sleeps in the sand

How many times must the cannonballs fly before they're forever banned

The answer, my friend, is blowin' in the wind, The answer is

blowin' in the wind.

HOW MANY YEARS CAN A MOUNTAIN EXIST
BEFORE IT'S WASHED IN THE SEA
HOW MANY YEARS CAN SOME PEOPLE EXIST, BEFORE THEY'RE ALLOWED TO BE FREE
HOW MANY TIMES CAN A MAN TURN HIS HEAD, AND PRETEND HE JUST DOESN'T SEE
THE ANSWER, MY FRIEND, etc.

HOW MANY TIMES MUST A MAN LOOK UP, BEFORE HE CAN SEE THE SKY
HOW MANY EARS MUST ONE MAN HAVE, BEFORE HE CAN HEAR PEOPLE CRY
HOW MANY DEATHS WILL IT TAKE 'TIL HE KNOWS THAT TOO MANY PEOPLE HAVE DIED
THE ANSWER, MY FRIEND, etc.

© Copyright 1962 by BOB DYLAN

First publication of 'Blowin' In The Wind'

BROADSIDE #20

PO Box 193 Cathedral Sta., NY 25 NY

FEBRUARY, 1963
35 cents

MASTERS of WAR
by BOB DYLAN
Illustrated by Susie Rotolo

Copyright 1963 BOB DYLAN

Come you masters of war —,

You that build all the guns

You that build the death planes—

You that build the big bombs

You that hide behind walls— You that hide behind desks, I just

want you to know I can see thru your masks.

You that never 've done nothing but build to destroy
You play with my world like it's your little toy
You put a gun in my hand then you hide from my eyes
And you turn and run farther when the fast bullets
fly.

Like Judas of old you lie and deceive
A world war can be won you want me to believe
But I see thru your eyes & I see thru your brain
Like I see thru the water that runs down my drain.

CONT'D →

Broadside publication of Masters of War with illustrations by Dylan's girlfriend, Suze Rotolo

The withdrawn promotion edition of the Freewheelin' Bob Dylan

CHAPTER

5

The *New York Times'* folk critic Robert Shelton first spotted the nascent talent of the young Bob Dylan during a performance at Gerde's Folk City; and it was Shelton's eulogistic review in September 1961 which brought Dylan to the attention of John Hammond. Hammond was already a venerated figure in the music industry, his standing further enhanced by his bringing not only Dylan but also later Bruce Springsteen to CBS. Hammond intuitively recognised a certain something in the abrasive, plagiaristic kid.

With a meagre recording budget of $402, *Bob Dylan* slipped unnoticed into a popular music world which was busy fêting clean-cut kids like Cliff, Eden Kane and Mark Wynter. Dylan's album is a useful souvenir of his stage set around that time, but the only original compositions were the autobiographical 'Talkin' New York' and 'Song To Woody' his homage to Guthrie. As a debut it contained conviction and vivacity, but lacked any real indication that, as Shelton's sleeve notes promised, Dylan was "bursting at the seams with talent".

Though now revered as a songwriter, it was as a singer that his initial impact was felt. Bob Dylan did for popular singing what Marlon Brando had done for screen acting: he introduced the Method to rock 'n' roll. The classic rockers of the 50s had brought a verve and fervour to their performances, Buddy Holly's hiccuping vocals had captured all the nervy energy of teenage romance, Little Richard's frenzy was orgasmic, Elvis' sneering vocals had trumpeted rebellion, but the smooth and insincere teen idols of the early 60s only perfected an anodyne singing style which limited their appeal to the pre-pubescent market. Only in the marginal areas of C&W, folk and blues was there anything approaching authenticity and honesty, but the audience for these musical styles was still often regional or limited to converts (Johnny Cash's gravelly crossover hits didn't start rolling in until 1963).

Despite the scant evidence of writing ability offered on Dylan's debut, there was a distinctive, novelty sound to his singing. Dylan's singing was rarely comfortable, he tortuously extended lines and phrases, but could peremptorily snap others. His singing style was dramatic, cloaking himself in his characters. Today

it may sound mannered and the humour cumbersome, but at the time there was something fresh and original in his treatment of an old chestnut like 'Pretty Peggy-O', having wrested it from the saccharine sanctuary of the Scottish balladic tradition, he gnawed at it like a starved pariah dog. Already on this first album, Dylan's singing can evoke lone voices floating over penitentiary walls, the plaintive echo of a hobo riding freight trains up and down the spine of the country or forbidden pleasures resonating in a New Orleans brothel. The voice already seems aged with experience and waiting for the visit to "God's golden shore", but is still belied by the youthful face staring wryly from the album cover. While it may not have been apparent to the tiny nucleus of Dylan fans of the period (around 5,000 of them bought the album on its release), there was something bursting out of that cap atop the curly headed baby.

As a songwriter, what was so surprising about Bob Dylan's growth was his prolificity, the quantity and quality of material was breathtaking, and to put his talent in some sort of perspective, you have to consider the marketplace he was pitching into during 1962.

Folk music was enjoying a revival, but aside from the success of The Kingston Trio, had yet to make any sizable impact on the pop charts; because of that, few publishers were interested in having folk songwriters on their books, the real money still lay with hits on the pop charts. With the 50s breakthrough, rock 'n' roll had become a global business, Iron Curtain governments may have expressed their distaste for this latest capitalist conspiracy and Europe had witnessed seat-slashing Teddy Boys and rioting youths at performances by visiting American rock groups, but by the end of the decade, rock 'n' roll had established itself as a major contributor to the economy, and as such was welcomed.

With little more than youth and näiveté on the performers' side, the cynicism and greater experience of their managers and publishers ensured that there was plenty of give and little take. The Beatles, for example, were guaranteed only one old penny for every record sold when they signed their Parlophone contract in 1962, split between themselves and manager Brian Epstein! Johnny Rogan in his exhaustive survey of pop management *Starmakers & Svengalis* (Macdonald, 1988) showed that by 1964, after three Top 10 singles including a US number 14, the Nashville Teens had made the grand sum of £585.12s.4d. each on sales approaching 1 million records!

Of course 'Tin Pan Alley' still had its stranglehold on pop; in Britain it was geographically situated off London's Charing Cross Road along Denmark Street, where the music publishers clustered, and in America around Times Square, Manhattan and the Brill Building.

Of the first generation rock 'n' rollers, Eddie Cochran, Sam Cooke, Buddy Holly and Chuck Berry had been unusual in writing much of their own material; with the early 60s' quest for singers whose looks - we'd now call it style - mattered more than the content of their songs, professional songwriters were called upon to supply the market. In Gerri Hershey's memorable *Nowhere To Run: The Story Of Soul Music* (Pan, 1985), the flavour of those days is captured: "Jerry Leiber and Mike Stoller were easily the most successful team of that era . . . They were the best and most prolific of a new breed of songwriting and production teams. In the high-speed pop market, they were the pit crews, leaping out to change a bass line, a horn pattern, a lyric, to clap hands and sing backup, if need be, to complete a session and drop a tune into the groove of the moment". Other "pit crews" of the time included Gerry Goffin & Carole King, Barry Mann & Cynthia Weil, Ellie Greenwich & Geoff Barry, while fledgling talents such as Paul Simon and Neil Diamond were also gaining experience. In Detroit, Motown's Hit Factory, exemplified by Holland-Dozier-Holland and Smokey Robinson were hitting full stride.

"Unlike most of the folk songs written these days in Tin Pan Alley, this wasn't written there, this was written somewhere down in the United States . . . " intoned Dylan in 1963. Over 20 years later, he expanded this conviction to Cameron Crowe: "I didn't know it at the time but all the radio songs were written at Tin Pan Alley, the Brill Building. They had stables of songwriters up there that provided songs for artists. They were good songwriters but the world they knew and the world I knew were totally different. Most of all the songs, though, being recorded came from there... Anyway, Tin Pan Alley is gone. I put an end to it . . . ".

FOOTNOTE: For convenience in looking at the development of Bob Dylan as songwriter, I have decided largely to follow the song sequence of *Lyrics 1962-1985* (Jonathan Cape, 1987). Though some Dylanologists have criticised it for allegedly wayward chronology and its placing of *The Basement Tapes* is admittedly haphazard, it was nevertheless authorised by Dylan and at least offers a useful guide to his progress.

That is a sweeping statement for anyone to make, the only person capable of making it seem credible is Bob Dylan. The Beatles were loosening Tin Pan Alley's noose in England with their first recordings in late 1962, but their first album of all original material still lay two years in the future. It is interesting to note that on July 9th 1962, the same day that Dylan was in CBS' New York studios laying down 'Blowin' In The Wind', The Beatles were performing at St Helens' Plaza Ballroom, energetically roaring through a repertoire revolving around R&B standards, new Motown and showbiz smoochers like 'Falling In Love Again' and 'Besame Mucho'.

Precisely where Dylan drew his songs from can never be known, the composer himself has successfully covered his tracks. During the early days there are obvious sources: his early ballads of Emmett Till and Donald White drew directly on newspaper and television reports. Other songs composed around the time of his debut and second album cast the composer in the role of the hard traveller, the drifter, the rambler, the highway bum, drawing on his assumed experiences on the road. The songs are sung with such conviction that few would doubt the singer's credentials, and even with the benefit of hindsight, we appreciate the skill of the deception.

Dylan's genius in those early days lay in the immediacy of his response to situations, his eye for a telling image, the ability to offer what seemed like mature reflection within the format of a popular song. A good example comes with one of his earliest and most mature songs, 'Let Me Die In My Footsteps' (actually scheduled for inclusion on his second album, but frustratingly still officially unavailable). By this stage, Dylan had outgrown the pervasive Guthrie influence, while retaining Woody's insistence that this land is your land.

The fallout shelter madness which embraced America during the 50s came with Russia's rapidly increasing A-bomb programme, years ahead of US intelligence estimates. Around $3,000 could get you a 'Mark I Kidde Kokoon', which included a three-way radio, air blower, clock, first aid kit, generator, chemical toilet and radiation charts, ideal for a family of five to spend up to five days underground. Such examples of free range capitalism predictably avoided the moral fallout; where did a citizen stand - in the event of nuclear Apocalypse - on how to handle his less far-sighted neighbours who might also wish to shelter? Even clergymen suggested that firearms could be used, in a Christian sense, to repel unwelcome boarders. 'Let Me Die In My Footsteps', from its imaginative title, ruminates that the final dignity left in a world that crazy was to die on your own terms, and majestically invokes the scope of the nation in the last verse with "let every state in this union seep down deep in your souls" before the mushroom cloud envelops it all.

Many of those early songs identified with society's victims, whether named (the brutally and needlessly murdered Emmett Till) or unnamed ('Man On The Street', 'Only A Hobo', 'Poor Boy Blues'). Recognising the division, Dylan asked at the conclusion of 'The Ballad Of Donald White': "Are they enemies or victims/Of your society?". There is no doubt that Dylan's sympathy lay with the victims, those bludgeoned to death by racists or dying through disinterest; he railed against trains travelling "with a firebox of hatred and a furnace full of fears", recognising the rapidly worsening situation in the Deep South. In the lyrically impressive, but poorly performed 'Long Ago, Far Away' (which pre-empted the far more serious consideration of the subject in 'With God On Our Side') Dylan tried to come to terms with the dark side, the underbelly of a society which, on the surface had everything going for it: surely with the prevailing liberalism of the Kennedy administration, the consumer boom, the New Frontier, things must be getting better, they cannot be returning to the bloody Roman amphitheatre or slavery of "Lincoln's time", can they?

Those early songs have Dylan speaking with the singleminded arrogance of youth, of a world starkly divided into issues of black and white, he clearly feels that a world barely born must be able to better itself. Dylan's indignity and compassion still shines through in those early songs, but he was also quick to realise that irony and satire could be equally effective weapons. The talking blues was another weapon culled from the arsenal of Woody Guthrie, and employed on 'Talkin' John Birch Paranoid Blues', in Dylan's hands it could be withering. The real John Birch had been a headstrong army Captain, killed on a Chinese hillside in 1945; even his commanding officer recognised that "militarily, John Birch brought about his own death" at the hands of Chinese communists, but that hadn't stopped his name being hijacked by extremist right wing elements in America. In Dylan's song, he satirizes the only "true American" as the odious George Lincoln Rockwell, leader of the American Nazi Party, and develops acute paranoia by spotting Reds everywhere, a teasing rejoinder to those who climbed aboard McCarthy's bandwagon.

In the dirge-like 'John Brown' there are the obligatory parents passing on the glories of war to the young only for them to discover its true horrors, while 'Ain't Gonna Grieve' is a throwaway blues-based tune, notable for the first use of the line "We're gonna notify your next of kin . . ." which was used to greater effect in later years on 'This Wheel's On Fire'. 'Ballad For A

Friend' inaugurated the theme of lost innocence more fully explored on 'Bob Dylan's Dream' while 'Farewell' (with its melody of 'The Leaving Of Liverpool') was a standard ballad of leaving which caused untold frustration many years later, when it was widely bootlegged as the mythically elusive 'Farewell Angelina'.

Songs were bursting out of Dylan, he didn't have time to hone or perfect anything, they just poured out, and others were left to do the polishing on glossier cover versions. Such prolificity meant that not all could hit the high standards of folk poetry and unerring disquiet of his best works. Perversely, few of the original songs written and recorded between his first two albums were ever officially released, and the bulk remain unavailable to this day.

Following the release of his first album, Dylan was now fully immersed in the burgeoning New York radical movement, acclaimed by Robert Shelton, hailed by the up and coming and already established folk scene, lionised by the left, Dylan seemed to be everywhere, soaking up, distilling and spewing out songs. With the launch in early 1962 of *Broadside* magazine, which provided a focus for the radical musical movement, Dylan along with Tom Paxton, Richard Farina and Phil Ochs, gained a less ephemeral platform for his catalogue of songs.

Through his girlfriend Suze Rotolo's work on behalf of the Congress Of Racial Equality (CORE), Dylan was inevitably sucked into the drama developing in the Deep South, where the Freedom Riders were courageously challenging the long established and deeply rooted racism. The Kennedy administration at least seemed to be trying to come to terms with the two nations the USA had become, but change was slow, especially when pitted against the entrenched bigotry of Governors like George Wallace of Alabama who defied the government's ruling on the desegregation of Southern schools and campaigned with the rhetoric of intolerance: "From this cradle of the Confederacy, this very heart of the great Anglo-Saxon Southland . . . I draw the line in the dust and toss the gauntlet before the feet of tyranny. And I say: Segregation now! Segregation tomorrow! Segregation forever!".

But troops were marshalling to fight against such blind hatred, and they needed songs to sing to unify them. In Martin Luther King the black community had found a dignified and powerful spokesman and few who remember those times can hear 'We Shall Overcome' sung without registering real emotion at the memory of what was achieved and equally how much remains undone. But new songs, new rallying cries were needed.

The common criticism of Dylan's best known 'protest' songs of that period was that they posed questions, but offered no answers. What often goes unappreciated is how badly those questions needed to be asked at that time. The answers seem obvious: discrimination against people on the grounds of gender or colour is wrong; this planet's obsession with weapons that can destroy it while ignoring the disease and famine which blight many of its inhabitants is stupid 'and illogical; that a world where the rich grow richer while the poor grow even poorer is immoral and can be changed. But what was needed then was a forum to air those questions and let them be heard by as many people as possible. That was the challenge Bob Dylan accepted, and by one of those curious circumstances which pepper history, his was the voice which was heard, his were the songs which asked the questions most strikingly, his was the platform around which the disaffected clustered.

Who is to say that if Dylan had not been singled out, contemporaries like Phil Ochs and Tom Paxton could not have plugged the gap? Their songs of the period were certainly drawn from the same well of indignation as Dylan's, their consciences moved by the same injustices. It was Bob Dylan though who brought a lyricism and poetry to popular music, but he also provided a focus at a time when clarity was needed. That focus was largely provided by 24 lines Dylan penned in a café on MacDougal Street early in 1962.

The first the world outside of Greenwich Village folk clubs knew of 'Blowin' In The Wind' was when it appeared in the May 1962 issue of *Broadside*. One of the earliest recorded versions surfaces on the bootlegged *Finjan Club* album, recorded that July. Although it has been widely rumoured that the performance was actually at the Village's Gaslight most experts agree that the source was this Montreal night club. Wherever the location, the dates can be corroborated, and it is a confident performance of what probably remains Dylan's single best known song. Amidst tentative interpretations of the traditional 'Hiram Hubbard' and 'Stealin' as well as his own 'Emmett Till' and 'Footsteps', Dylan introduces the young song as something which he hopes says "a little more than 'I love you and you love me and let's go over to the banks of Italy and we'll raise a happy family, you for me . . . and me for me . . .'". The audience, sounding like 16 bored Canucks, is muted, unaware that they were among the first to hear a little slice of history.

The song is irrevocably, inextricably linked to its time. It has surfaced in various shapes and forms in Dylan's hands over the years, even being sung by a smartly dressed composer and friends at 1986's Martin Luther King gala, but the starkest and simplest version, the young composer and his deadly guitar is still the one which causes many to wipe away a tear for all the questions which remain unanswered, and also for their own lost youth.

Although it did not surface on an album until May 1963, the song immediately pushed Dylan to the top of the class; I love Dave Van Ronk's comment to the composer "Hey man, you're really getting into something with those songs. Welcome to the 20th Century!". From now on, the only limitations to Dylan's talent would be self imposed. But first there was some unfinished business to attend to, which saw

Dear Editor:
    I am a girl of 14 who bought an issue of SING OUT! for the first time...and was rather upset to find the many letters in opposition of Bob Dylan. True, Dylan is sloppy, dirty, and ugly, and he doesn't have the voice that one might expect of a successful folksinger, but he is still, by far, my favorite...

                                    Sincerely,
                                    Name Withheld
                                    Ithaca, N. Y.

Letter from Sing Out! 1962

the troubadour drift across the ocean to a London bracing itself to swing. TV producer Philip Saville, who later went on to direct British television's finest achievement of the 80s, Alan Bleasdale's *The Boys From The Blackstuff*, had spotted Dylan performing in Greenwich Village, and thought him perfect to play 'Bobby the Hobo' alongside David Warner in a BBC TV Play For Today, *Madhouse On Castle Street*. He lured Dylan, without too much difficulty, to London at the end of 1962. In the end, Dylan delivered himself of one line, his own 'The Ballad Of The Gliding Swan' and half a minute of 'Blowin' In The Wind', which prompted the TV critic of *The Listener* to write of "the young American folk singer said to have been brought over for the play, (who) sat around playing and singing attractively, if a little incomprehensibly".

England was in the midst of its worst winter this century, which did little to endear the capital to the visitor. Whilst here, Dylan did his blotting paper act, soaking up much of the rich British folk revival. Martin Carthy who was at the forefront of this renaissance, spoke to me about Dylan's trips to Britain in December 1962 and January 1963: "Throughout the 60s he was the only one; individual writers have produced the odd nice thing, but none of them had that sort of grinding fire. I first met Dylan in 1962 when he used to come and sing at the folk clubs - he was always very well received. He was doing one or two traditional things, like the stuff on his first album, you know, 'Pretty Peggy-O', which he did as a joke because a lot of American performers had made records, and the studio technicians thought they knew what a folk song was. The story Dylan told was that he was in the studio doing all his own stuff and the bloke said 'Hey man, why don't you sing a folk song?' And Dylan said 'What sort of folk song?' 'Oh, you know, a folk song like "Pretty Peggy"' - because every folk singer always did that song! So Dylan says 'Yeah, I know "Pretty Peggy"', and he goes up and goes chung, chung and makes it up on the spot!

"He was a good bloke, but a very private bloke, didn't like to mess around. He laughed a lot, then he was very quiet . . . He liked to talk and we just got friendly. He's got a natural blotting paper mind, but perfectly open about it, if he heard something he liked he'd ask you about it. When he wrote the song ('Bob Dylan's Dream' on *Freewheelin'*, the melody of which came from Carthy's version of the traditional 'Lord Franklin') he was fascinated by the tune, by the feel of it; so rather than sing the song he'd try and write down what he felt about it, what it conjured up in him, which wouldn't necessarily be a traditional song. It was a crucial period for Dylan. You listen to *Freewheelin'* and *The Times They Are A-Changin'*, and between those

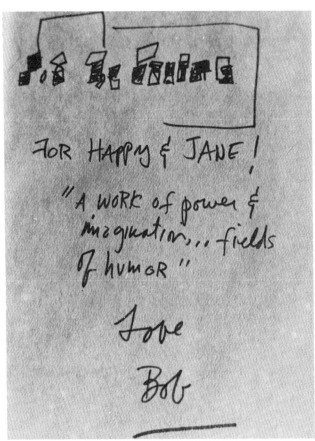

Inscribed copy of Tarantula, dedicated to Mr and Mrs Happy Traum

two records he came to England, and the difference is just amazing. His singing is a lot more florid and the tunes become very lyrical. I remember when I first heard *The Times They Are A-Changin'*, I thought 'Oh yes, you've been to England, you've learnt a lot!'"

London also provided Dylan with another opportunity to crop up almost undetected on record. Richard Farina and Ric Von Schmidt were also in London, and in the "maniacal gilded rooms of the Hotel de France near the South Kensington tube station" plans for an album were hastily put together. *Dick Farina, Eric Von Schmidt, Ethan Singer . . . and occasionally Blind Boy Grunt* was recorded in the basement of Dobells record shop in Charing Cross Road over two nights in mid-January 1963. 'Blind Boy Grunt' was an alias Dylan had previously used in New York, and he supplies harp to five tracks and can be heard croaking back-up vocals on the Rev. Gary Davis' ubiquitous 'Cocaine'. The album is not surprisingly a ramshackle effort, liberally fuelled by red wine, with 'London Blues' as its most representative track.

Sporadic and generally ill-received appearances at folk clubs around the town did little to warm Dylan to the capital. London, by and large, was not yet ready to welcome Blind Boy Grunt with open arms, and settled down instead to free itself of the freeze and brace itself for Beatlemania.

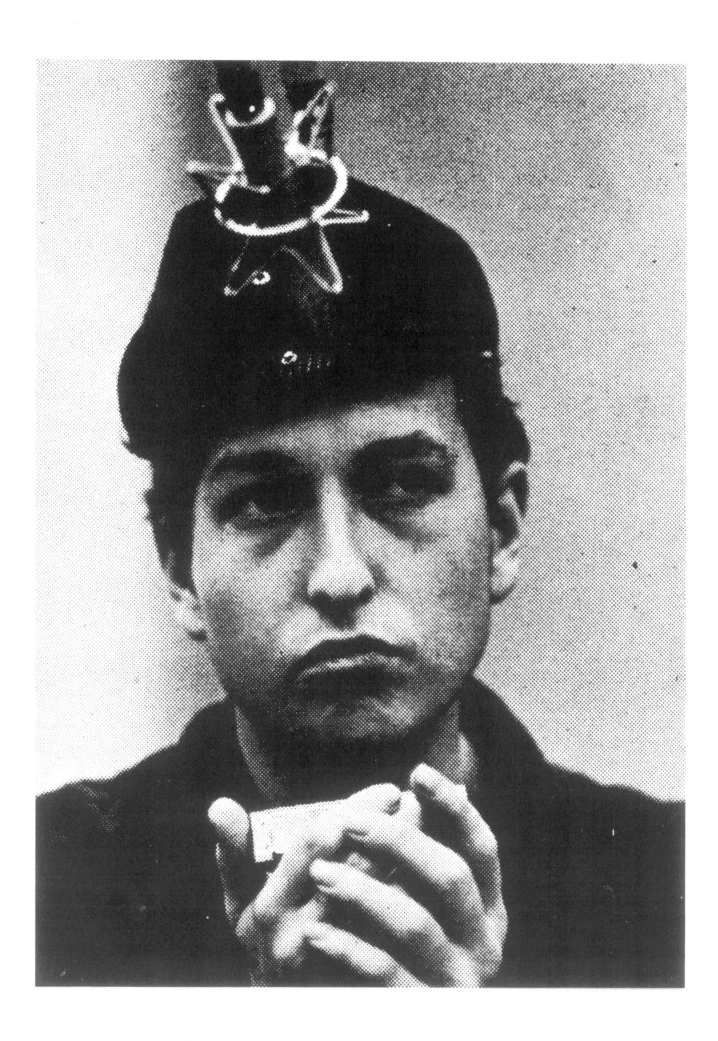

CHAPTER

6

Rarely has there been such a quantum leap between a debut album and its successor. In barely over a year, a young plagiarist had been reborn as a songwriter of substance, and his first album of fully realised original material got the 60s off their musical starting block. With the release of *The Freewheelin' Bob Dylan*, in May 1963, the 22-year-old singer-songwriter stood in an unprecedented glare of attention and the shadow he cast spread itself over the rest of the decade.

Although other albums by dint of their nostalgic qualities cause the listener to remember, rarely has one album so effectively reflected the times which produced it. *Freewheelin'* spoke directly of the concerns of its audience and addressed them in a mature and reflective manner. It mirrored the state of the nation, it spoke with optimism of the promise offered by Kennedy's Camelot, it shone its light into the darker areas on the underside of that hope, it dealt with prevalent pop fashion, it spoke with the irreverence and optimism of youth but balanced that with the eerie wisdom of experience.

The Cuban missile crisis of late 1962 had seen the world precariously balanced on the brink of Armageddon, to say that the world faced war as the Russian ships sailed towards the American blockade gives no indication of the crisis faced. Since 1945 there had been many wars, but Cuba was the first opportunity for mankind to appreciate the awesome power of the weapons which would now be used. Hiroshima and Nagasaki 17 years before had seen a destruction unleashed which had rendered the cities into dust, by the 60s the scale of the weapons had multiplied. Cuba faced off a young and untested American President against a bluff and truculent Soviet Premier. There was an almost audible sigh of relief throughout the globe as the Russian ships avoided the blockade, and it looked as though the world did have a tomorrow. That second chance was not to be wasted, and the buoyancy following Cuba was global.

On civil rights, though supportive, the President and his brother Robert the Attorney General, were slow to act. But events were fast coming to a head: the courage of the Freedom Riders in the South, the eloquence of Martin Luther King and the boorish intransigence of the South's white leaders proving too volatile a combination to be ignored. Kennedy biographer John H. Davis wrote of the

brothers in *The Kennedy Clan* (Sidgwick & Jackson, 1985): "It was obvious to many that they lacked a sense of Southern history, had no idea how deep-rooted the racial problem there was. It was not, as they had imagined, a small bush that could easily be spaded up, but a giant oak with a hundred massive roots reaching deep down into centuries-old soil".

Civil rights was the issue which united Northern liberals with the Southern blacks, and this was the struggle tackled by Dylan on 'Blowin' In The Wind' and 'Oxford Town'. The Cuban crisis hung like a Damoclesean sword as the world realised just how close to extinction it had become, and this Dylan tackled on 'A Hard Rain's A-Gonna Fall', taking a wider perspective than he had on 'Footsteps'.

The whole album is that of a young man finding his own voice, the derivative Dylan of the year before had been replaced by a far more original and thoughtful spokesman of his times. There is also the voice of a man telling tales of himself and his love, of his background (real and imagined), with verve and wit, satire and sombre purpose. The album became a focus for disaffected youth, whether lamenting their lost innocence as captured on 'Bob Dylan's Dream', asking the questions that needed to be asked on 'Blowin' In The Wind' or reflecting on the scope of 'Hard Rain'.

Contemporaries of Dylan in New York around this time recall him in the midst of an avalanche of songs. They poured from him ceaselessly, inspired variously by newspaper reports, television news of events in the South and the brinkmanship of Cuba; despite the nervous uncertainty of the future and the confusion of the past, Dylan managed to instil some sense of order into the chaos in his wealth of songs. Frustrated by the delays surrounding the release of his first album, Dylan had poured everything into his second, but even before the dust had settled, he was already the most talked-about songwriter in the country. Dylan had zeroed in on headlines like a sniper, recreating them as bullet-thoughts in his songs.

It was his ability to tackle major issues within the format of a popular song which found Dylan at the centre of attention. The liberal and left wing causes in New York were delighted to have found such an eloquent spokesman, young activists identified with his image of drifter and his irreverent dress and hairstyle, while old guard leftists rejoiced that here was someone directly addressing the issues of his time as Woody Guthrie had done a generation before. But it was the young record buyers, disillusioned by the pap pouring out of their radios (full of 'Rock-a-Day Johnnies' singing trite and insincere love songs) who embraced Dylan in numbers which saw the start of his ascendancy. For many, the intensity and honesty of 'Girl From The North Country' and 'Don't Think Twice It's All Right' were a revelation; the whimsy and pointed satire of 'Talkin' World War III Blues' and 'Bob Dylan's Blues' essential conversation pieces. Lines were endlessly plucked and repeated over cups of coffee and pitchers of beer. Tentatively, Dylan's words were making their first impression.

Dylan's attacks were far reaching and relentless, his targets widespread. 'Masters Of War' raged against soulless arms manufacturers, and nothing in pop had matched Dylan's vindictiveness in hoping for "the Masters" premature death and following their funeral "in the pale afternoon". In the context of the album, 'Oxford Town' was a surprisingly flippant look at the plight of James Meredith, a negro who tried to enrol at the all-white University of Mississippi the day after Kennedy's inaugural speech, only to be greeted by the same old blind obstinacy and bigotry and a riot which left two men dead.

The self-confidence of the young Dylan was reflected in the fact that two of the album's songs included his name, and that the album's final song, the exuberant 'I Shall Be Free', has him advising the President on domestic policy. That Dylan's name was never far from the headlines was ensured by Peter, Paul & Mary's dignified cover of 'Blowin' In The Wind', which reached number 2 on the American charts in July 1963.

That July was a pivotal month for Dylan, and gave a wider public the opportunity to view the fledgling phenomenon. Concerned liberals and leftists were determined to do what they could to improve the lot of the blacks, and getting them to vote was the first step on the ladder: of approximately 5 million blacks in the South at the time barely 2 million were registered as voters. On July 6th Dylan appeared alongside Pete Seeger and Theodore Bikel at a voter registration rally in Greenwood, Mississippi where he sang a new song: 'Only A Pawn In Their Game'.

Dylan's appearance in Mississippi gave the lie to those who saw him as an opportunist, riding to his early success on the suffering of the blacks and the coat-tails of the folk-protest movement. Later, there were others who, whilst vociferously castigating Dylan for moving away from 'protest', accused him of having callously used the protest movement as a bandwagon for the furtherance of his own career. These critics have failed to recognise the composer's very real empathy with underdogs like Donald White,

Hattie Carroll and Emmett Till and the communities of "countless . . . accused" victims who populate his songs to this day. His 1971 single 'George Jackson' was a spontaneous response to the bloody murder of the 'Soledad brother', while 1974 saw Dylan appear at a benefit concert in New York for the victims of the Chilean coup and his recognition of the plight of the jailed boxer 'Hurricane' Carter in 1975 focused attention. The 1988 'Human Rights Now!' tour on behalf of Amnesty International adopted Dylan's 'Chimes Of Freedom' as its unofficial anthem. Throughout his career, Dylan has identified causes and in his songs cut through the mask of dogma to the heart of the matter.

While Woody Guthrie and Pete Seeger willingly endorsed Dylan's songs, recognising their importance in raising the political consciousness of generally disaffected youth and Broadside welcomed every new song which tumbled out of him, Dylan was not writing to a formula, he was genuinely inspired by events happening around him and was already gaining a perspective on them which his contemporaries could only struggle to match.

The end of July saw Dylan hailed by 46,000 fans at the Newport Folk Festival. Newport 1963, was the moment which saw the baton finally pass from Guthrie's generation to Dylan's. The festival was a unifying event (unlike Newport '65, which was the folk revival's most divisive moment). The young crowds flocked to see Dylan, his gaunt features were everywhere, his painful thinness seeming to cast him as the movement's ascetic figurehead, no luxuries for him, sackcloth and ashes were his garb. Elvis had defined rock 'n' roll style for the 50s, the 60s had yet to produce its style – The Beatles were still waiting in the wings – but although for folk musicians anything approaching an act was anathema, in its own way, Dylan's image was as important as his songs.

Dylan was young, his Brillo-pad hair was already beginning its eternal circle, his voice, though it couldn't be called attractive, was light years away from the pop crooners and their gelled image, a fact which imbued him with authenticity and a perceived inability to conform or kowtow. Dylan was embraced by a youth which had little or no interest in 'folk', but who responded to the image. They began to listen to the singer whose cracked voice seemed to speak for them and slowly they began to understand the importance of the issues which they were only belatedly starting to recognise.

The songs though, were making Dylan's name in other circles: they spilled from him as from a printing press, his feet barely seemed to touch the ground but his hands were constantly hammering the typewriter keys and the results were soon being used as weapons in the struggle. While the bulk of his output comprised the rallying cries which soon became clarion calls, Dylan could still prove his fluency in the pure folk tradition, 'Seven Curses' is a Dylan composition but has all the hallmarks of a traditional ballad, and his performance of it reveals a sensitivity and respect for the narrative tradition unique in that period of his creativity.

Newport '63 concluded with Dylan, Joan Baez, Peter, Paul & Mary and the black acapella group The Freedom Singers linking arms for an emotional 'We Shall Overcome'. Few who witnessed the event could doubt that the fulfilment of that shining optimism would soon replace the rhetoric. The young folk singers and the largely youthful audience who attended that festival believed themselves to be in the vanguard of real change. No one doubted Dylan's commitment to the inexorable march then, he was indeed the standard bearer. More recent global events such as Live Aid and the Nelson Mandela 70th Birthday Concert, have shown how irrevocably linked rock and politics now are, but it was not always so. Back in 1963, the idea of popular music being allied to political action or even social comment was unheard of; the idea of other stars of the '63 vintage (Freddie & The Dreamers, Frank Ifield, Kathy Kirby) being anything more than just popular singers on their way to that ultimate showbiz goal of becoming an "all-round entertainer" is fatuous. But the first seeds of the pop–politics alliance were being sown back then by Bob Dylan.

The apotheosis of the folk and civil rights movement came with Martin Luther King's March on Washington on August 28th 1963 (coincidentally, the same day that one William Zanzinger was sentenced to a mere six months in prison for the murder of black maid Hattie Carroll). Dylan serenaded the crowd of 400,000 with 'Only A Pawn In Their Game' (an uneasy choice, given that in it he justifies Medgar Evers' white assassin as being also a victim of the rotten system). Peter, Paul & Mary sang 'Blowin' In The Wind' and Martin Luther King shared his dream with the world "even the state of Mississippi, a state sweltering with the heat of injustice … will be transformed into an oasis of freedom and justice. I have a dream that my four little children will one day live in a nation where they will not be judged by the colour of their skin but by the content of their character". It was one time when, united against the common enemy of racism and inequality, the white liberals and the oppressed blacks felt a bond stronger than bigotry.

As his reedy voice reached out over the throng, and while taking in the enormity of the gathering, Dylan could not help but be moved, but he had his doubts. Anthony Scaduto in *Bob Dylan* (Abacus, 1972) reports the singer glancing towards the Capitol Dome querying "Think they're listening? No, they ain't listening at all".

They were listening, but not understanding. Attorney General Robert Kennedy held a meeting around this time with Jerome Smith, a CORE representative who as a Freedom Rider had suffered at the hands of southern bigots and spoke to Kennedy of the growing militancy amongst blacks, who in the face of constant intimidation and the continuing violence of the Klan and White Citizens Councils, were fast tiring of King's non-violent philosophy. Concluding his historic speech, Martin Luther

Rich Brute Slays Negro Mother of 10

By ROY H. WOOD

BALTIMORE — Mrs. Hattie Carroll, 51, Negro waitress at the Emerson Hotel, died last week as the result of a brutal beating by a wealthy socialite during the exclusive Spinsters' Ball at that hotel. Mrs. Carroll, mother of 10 children, was the deacon of the Gillis Memorial Church. She died in the hospital where she had been taken after being felled from blows inflicted by William Devereux Zantzinger, 24, owner of a 600-acre tobacco farm near Marlsboro, Md.

Mrs. Carroll was one of two waitresses whom Zantzinger struck with a wooden cane at the society affair. He first struck at Mrs. Ethel Hill, 30, Negro waitress who was cleaning a table near him, then, without being restrained by any of the other members of the social register present at the white-tie affair, he strode to the bar and rained blows on the head and back of Mrs. Carroll who was working there. The cane was broken in three pieces.

At this point other hotel employes called the police.

Mrs. Carroll was taken to the hospital, where she died from internal hemorhages.

As police were taking Zantzinger down the stairs from the ballroom, his wife, one of the socially prominent Duvall family, leaped from the landing and struck a policeman, who had to be hospitalized with a leg injury.

A Negro bellman at the hotel reported that earlier in the evening, Zantzinger struck him across the buttocks with his cane.

Zantzinger's father is a member of the state planning commission in Maryland. Others of his relatives in the Devereux family are prominent in politics here.

The judge who released Zantzinger on bond has already permitted his attorney to claim that Mrs. Carroll died indirectly as a result of the attack rather than directly.

There is speculation here that attempts will be made to get Zantzinger off with a slap on the wrist.

Recently a "cat burglar" caught in the wealthiest section here, Guilford, received a 99-year sentence. He never once committed violence.

Original newspaper report which inspired the composition the 'Lonesome Death of Hattie Carroll' 29th August 1963

King had quoted the words of an old negro spiritual: "Free at last, free at last!". In a *New Yorker* article at the time, James Baldwin also noted the mood of change and challengingly quoted another less conciliatory spiritual: "God gave Noah the rainbow sign/No more water, the fire next time!"

For "one brief shining moment" there had been a cohesion, but now the unity was splintering. Kennedy's Civil Rights Bill was due before Congress in 1964, when it was confidently expected he would be elected for a second term. But the government's growing involvement in Vietnam and the increasing impatience of blacks at home would finally see the flood giving way to the fire. Dylan was striding ahead, already questioning the validity of the movement whichhad elected him their figurehead;one of his songs of the period spoke of the lie that life was black and white, nothing was ever to be that certain again.

BOB DYLAN

Exclusively on Columbia Records

"In his first album, accompanying himself on guitar and taking an occasional whooping break on the harmonica, Dylan plunges into Negro blues, plaintive mountain songs, updated Scottish tunes and sardonic folklike pieces of his own composition. He adapts his sound and phrasing to the varying needs of the material, but throughout he is unabashedly himself. Among his other accomplishments, Dylan is expert in the 'talking blues' popularized by Woody Guthrie, a friend and major influence."
Nat Hentoff, <u>The Reporter</u>, May 24, 1962

"Resembling a cross between a choir boy and a beatnik, Mr. Dylan has a cherubic look and a mop of tousled hair he partly covers with a Huck Finn black corduroy cap. His clothes may need a bit of tailoring, but when he works his guitar, harmonica or piano and composes new songs faster than he can remember them, there is no doubt that he is bursting at the seams with talent."
Robert Shelton, New York <u>Times</u>, September 29, 1961

CL 1779 / CS 8579 Stereo

WATCH FOR HIS NEW ALBUM TO BE RELEASED SOON

One of the earliest advertisements for a Bob Dylan record

CHAPTER
7

For Bob Dylan, the pace during 1963 was breakneck. His opinions constantly sought by journalists keen to tap into what the youth of America was thinking, his lyrics had impressed themselves onto many minds, his concert appearances noted for the fervour of the audience response, his name was reverentially intoned from the concert platforms of Joan Baez and Peter, Paul & Mary, his attitude was becoming increasingly abrasive as he was expected to have answers on tap to all the tricky questions posed by the times.

Dylan was typecast as "the voice of a generation", as Holden Caulfield had been in J.D. Salinger's *The Catcher In The Rye* during the 50s. The book had become a parents' Bible for those trying to understand the first generation of teenagers: "What does a boy. . . think and feel about his teachers, parents, friends and acquaintances? Why does he want to break away from his social and domestic environment? Why is he so mixed up?" asked its blurb. Salinger's book concludes with some advice for Dylan – who around this time was tipped to play Holden in an unrealised film of the book – "Don't ever tell anybody anything. If you do, you start missing everybody."

Dylan himself was full of questions he couldn't answer about the validity of the songs he was singing, their actual use and application, his role in the 'movement', the inadequacy of the response to its fragmentation and not least how 'Bob Dylan' could develop. Aretha Franklin remembered a summer '63 CBS Convention to Gerri Hershey, and seeing Dylan ill at ease amidst the executives and only happy stalking up and down the beach alone: "Believe me, neither of us knew where we were headed then. 'Cause neither of us was what you call – ah – mainstream!"

One constant throughout a turbulent career has been Dylan's unwillingness and inability to compromise, and he certainly had no intention of going mainstream, but he couldn't help it if the stream started meandering towards him. While his third album, which was to become the cynosure for a generation, was being recorded in New York – *The Times They Are A-Changin'* would not be released until early 1964 – Dylan had found a haven of serenity on the other side of the country. Staying at Joan Baez's house at Carmel in

California, he managed to escape the turbulence of New York, and there wrote two of his finest ever songs: 'When The Ship Comes In' which would appear on his next album and 'Lay Down Your Weary Tune' which did not officially appear for over 20 years.

'When The Ship Comes In' is among the most exceptional works of the period, but it remains one of Dylan's most under-rated songs. Written prior to Kennedy's assassination, it perfectly captures the buoyant optimism which accompanied his administration. While the title track of '*Times*' became the unifying anthem, 'Ship' offered fascinating rhythmic connotations, audacious rhymes, and a beacon of hope that the meritocrats who made up the ship's crew would overcome the sterile faceless bureaucrats, who were still wiping the sleep from their eyes, unable to comprehend the rising tide of optimism. As such the song was an appropriate choice – though sadly marred by an inept interpretation – for Dylan's Live Aid set 20 years later.

'Lay Down Your Weary Tune' is a song on a far broader scope (Bob Shelton called it "his first withdrawal song"). Dylan stands "unwound" beneath the enormity of the sky, beside the vastness of the ocean, while leaves, branches, rivers and breezes play a symphony, and how he must have welcomed the "cryin' rain", singing like a trumpet, asking for no applause, just a troubadour singing his songs, without recourse to audience or acclaim. It is a supremely religious song, like William Blake able "To see a World in a grain of sand/And a Heaven in a wild flower/Hold Infinity in the palm of your hand/And Eternity in an hour". The frailty of Dylan's performance and the intensity with which he infuses the song make it a perfect epitaph – one which I'd welcome on my tombstone. That Dylan was capable of writing such a magnificent song, even at this early stage in his career, is a testament to his development as a writer; though not to release it was an indication of the contrariness which would be a constant source of frustration in later years.

The world was stunned by the sudden, shocking murder of John F. Kennedy in Dallas that November and an era drew tragically to a close. Much has been written of The Beatles' immediate success in America during February 1964, elaborate theories abound that Beatlemania (always so much more virulent in America) was the product of a nation's spontaneous outpouring of grief in the aftermath of the Kennedy assassination. Whatever the truth, there is no doubt that if The Beatles symbolised the exuberance of American emotion, Bob Dylan had already become the conscience. While The Beatles offered escapism, Dylan provided reflection, while the Fabs provided anthems for the good times, Dylan offered eloquent ballads for the underdogs.

The stark black and white cover of *The Times They Are A-Changin'* was a statement in itself – here was someone not abasing himself before the Moloch of the media, here was an ascetic poet with no time for the glitzy trappings of showbiz. Serious and dedicated, the Dylan in his Okie workshirt whose eyes avoided the camera seemed to be the human embodiment of authentic folk-protest, a feeling enhanced by listening to the 10 dry and humourless songs contained therein. Dylan was like one who bore the burdens of the world on his frail shoulders, suffering for the sins of mankind.

The album's title track is a very polite protest, (senators, congressmen and parents are asked to "please" stand aside) but the widely quoted refrain of "don't criticize what you can't understand" rang true. While 'Times' was a reflection of the change, providing a commentary rather than an impetus, other songs in the collection dealt with specific injustices, the needless and cruel murder of Hattie Carroll, the sad and pointless death of Hollis Brown, the devastation of whole communities in 'North Country Blues', the prevalent agnosticism of 'With God On Our Side'.

The album showed how adept Dylan had become at viewing the whole ('God On Our Side') or focussing on specifics ('Hattie Carroll'). While earlier epic songs, such as 'Hard Rain' (which showed his developing interest in the works of Rimbaud and Brecht) had dealt in poetic abstracts, 'With God On Our Side' was nothing less than the ambitious re-telling of American history, concluding with Judas' betrayal of Christ. The questions posed by Dylan in that song had never been heard in popular music before, the scope of his questioning was magisterial.

Even the album's 'simpler' songs raised questions which had previously gone unasked, the pleading intensity of 'Boots Of Spanish Leather' was well beyond the province of labelmates like Andy Williams or Johnny Mathis, while the dignified retreat evinced by 'Restless Farewell' would not be matched by the Beatles or Rolling Stones for another three years. 'North Country Blues' had the feel of a traditional ballad, but the sense of community it evoked, created a yet to be equalled contemporary resonance. Bruce Springsteen recognised this in the final verse of his 1984 song 'My Hometown' (from *Born In The USA*) which eerily recalls Dylan's song.

'Only A Pawn In Their Game' takes as its starting point the murder of Medgar Evers, but develops from there to consider far wider and more complex issues. Evers, the local leader of the National Association For The Advancement Of Colored People (NAACP) who had advised James Meredith to enrol at the University of Mississippi, was murdered outside his home by a white sniper, and because of his status as a former soldier was buried in Arlington Military cemetery just five months before JFK. Dylan's song is a curiously ambiguous response to the murder, refusing to blame Evers' murderer but instead castigating the system which encourages the white trash who lord it over the blacks, simply because they're the only people they can look down on. Few would deny the dehumanising nature of such a system, but nevertheless one wonders how the relatives of the murdered Evers' reacted to the song. However in the current climate of racism in rock, with racist rants coming from the hard rock of Guns N' Roses and rap's Public Enemy, it is worth restating Dylan's continued abhorrence of racism, and listening again to his early songs which spoke out so eloquently against it.

On the album's shortest song 'One Too Many Mornings', Dylan displayed his commensurate grasp of lyric and melody. "Crossroads of my doorstep" is a magnificent line, poignantly and economically describing the many directions a young life can take. In the final verse Dylan sings "You're right from your side/I'm right from mine . . . " ; his vision was expanding beyond the simple voice/guitar/harmonica fusillade, and setting his sights over the horizon, tuned into the sounds inside his mind.

★ ★ ★ ★ ★

As Cameron Crowe wrote in his sleeve notes to *Biograph*: "It is now almost a casual observation in the works of pop and rock historians that 'Bob Dylan changed the face of popular music' . . . ". It is a sweeping claim for one man; but it happens to be true. The mechanics of that change over two tumultuous decades are still fascinating and much of the continued interest in Dylan can be traced back to the changes he instigated at this time.

Like Dylan, The Beatles' musical heritage went far beyond their contemporaries; their championing of Chuck Berry, Buddy Holly, early 60s Motown and all-but forgotten rock 'n' rollers of the 50s like Arthur Alexander and Larry Williams was crucial. It was The Beatles "bringing it all back home" in 1964 which reminded young Americans of their largely forgotten rock legacy. Dylan has been widely reported as the man who turned the Beatles on to marijuana in the stately rooms of Manhattan's Del Monico Hotel, but his influence on the Fabs was more than a night of reefer madness during August 1964.

George Harrison is quoted by Derek Taylor in his engaging memoir *It Was Twenty Years Ago Today* (Bantam, 1987): "The day Bob Dylan really turned us on was the day we heard his album, *The Freewheelin' Bob Dylan*. Right from that moment we recognised some vital energy, a voice crying out somewhere, toiling in the darkness. When we actually met him in '64 it had a certain effect on us, but I think the seed was already sown by the album." Paul McCartney concurred: "Dylan was a big hero. We admired him a lot. We'd all liked his early talking blues and he was entering now in the mid-sixties a very poetic period. We liked him because he was a poet, far out, a friend of Ginsberg, on the same road as Jack Kerouac."

But The Beatles' political and philosophical impact would not be felt for some years to come; it was the single figure of Bob Dylan who did transform pop music, and that transformation couldn't help but affect The Beatles and all the other groups of the first "British invasion" of America. To imagine the world of popular music without Bob Dylan is inconceivable, a world shackled to the simplistic sermons of Jan & Dean, the music hall antics of Herman's Hermits, the teenage angst of Paul And Paula, a world full of one-hit wonders with nothing to worry about but where their next hit single was coming from. Pop's complacency was the prey Dylan was stalking, and he was doing it largely alone.

Solzhenitsyn wrote that "one word of truth will outweigh the world" and in 1985 Dylan admitted: "I always thought that one man, the lone balladeer with the guitar could blow an entire army off the stage if he knew what he was doing." That has become one of the music industry's constants, and strangely, considering all the new technology available, it has never been truer than in rock today. A balladeer alone onstage, with nothing but a guitar and no place to hide, is exposed and has only the strength of his song for an ally; but the isolated minstrel is a powerful image and can form an immediate rapport with the audience.

From that initial point of strength Dylan, of course, moved through phases which saw him fronting bands of increasing size (in crucial tandem with The Band, but with the Rolling Thunder community as the largest), yet even now in concert, it is frequently solo Dylan performances which receive the loudest applause. This is not simply the audience's delight at nostalgic retreats, audiences do enjoy old songs – for one thing they know the old songs – but they also welcome the sight of the balladeer battling against the odds. T-Bone Burnett told me of his early admiration for Dylan, forged during their Rolling Thunder acquaintance; "To see him out there alone, odds of 10,000 to one, that was something to see."

A promotion photograph for Fender Instruments, who sponsored Dylan's tours in 1965/66.

By early 1964, with only two albums of original material to his credit, Dylan had already hewn out an audience and proved that ideas of unexpected weight and complexity could be tackled in the format of the popular song. He would continue to grow and expand – particularly during that extraordinary burst of creativity during 1965/66 – but by the age of 23 he had already proved his capabilities.

In the fashion of all things, once Dylan had paved the way, the imitators and disciples flocked in his wake, flooding through gates that Dylan had singlehandedly forced open. In its retrospective on the decade, *Life* magazine wrote that Dylan "set a musical style for the 60s by giving new life to the ancient tradition of the wandering troubadour. Creating a folk music for his contemporaries and the age. Dylan wove themes of social protest and love and nostalgia into lyrics that both enchanted and stung – sometimes simultaneously."

His triumph was not only in the substance of his songs, Dylan's singing was an equally iconoclastic weapon. Primitive double-tracking had given many pop singers of the period a syrupy sound, but there was no escaping the harsh rasp of Dylan, that very harshness implying an honesty which pop had previously lacked. His rudimentary guitar playing acted simply as a foundation for the lyrics, but his harmonica-playing added a trampolining edge which helped illuminate the words.

There was also the Dylan 'attitude'. Biographers have spoken of his abrasiveness increasing along with his popularity and the well documented fiasco of Dylan's acceptance of the Tom Paine Award in late

At the Savoy Hotel, London April 1965

1963 – when he shocked the older audience by seeming to compare his feelings to those of Lee Harvey Oswald – was insensitive, but it also displayed an honesty which couldn't be disguised by silky PR sheen. That honesty was becoming more open in the increasingly abstract interviews Dylan granted, the high-flight surrealism of the electric years left most fans and journalists baffled at the time, but the Dylan of this period was a still young (if old sounding) man, finding his feet, finding his voice. It wasn't Dylan folding deckchairs on the Titanic; it was a talented, assertive poet, refusing to take the world at face value, trying to balance a spirit level on quicksand.

From ad-libbing in Hibbing with The Golden Chords only a few years before, having his horizons widened by Woody Guthrie, having his attention focused by Odetta, Josh White, Pete Seeger, by 1964 Dylan was well versed in all manner of heady influences. While still with girlfriend Suze Rotolo in New York, Dylan had watched attentively as she worked on productions of plays by Bertolt Brecht, which gave Dylan yet another dimension for his songwriting: impressed by the scope and sweep of Brecht's writing for the stage, Dylan adopted some of the techniques for his longer songs (specifically citing Brecht's structure in 'The Black Freighter' as his inspiration for 'Hattie Carroll'). Brecht was not a name to be lightly tossed around in pop circles, Dylan was an early proselytiser – although later both The Doors and David Bowie would record his 'Moon Of Alabama'.

Pitched into the chowder too, was Arthur Rimbaud the French Symbolist poet, whose wild, daemonic poems were written in an incredible five-year-burst, which ended before he was out of his teens. Rimbaud ran away from home in 1869 at 15 and spent most of his teenage years on the road, spitting out black and vehement poems; to Dylan his image as a Woody Guthrie of the Third Republic had a certain piquancy. Critics have particularly cited Rimbaud's influence on Dylan's 'A Hard Rain's A-Gonna Fall' and in 1974 he was namechecked on 'You're Gonna Make Me Lonesome When You Go'. But it was Rimbaud's disgust at the world he was born into which exercised such a dark fascination, his ability to recognise what had ended when he voluntarily ceased writing, which struck a chord in Dylan. Rimbaud 's simile in his 'Evening Prayer' "like an angel in a barber's chair" wouldn't have been inappropriate in Dylan's 'She's Your Lover Now'.

Dylan also found much which appealed in the works of Brendan Behan, whose play *The Hostage* so impressed him in 1963, while the melody of 'With God On Our Side' came from his brother Dominic Behan's song 'The Patriot Game'. Many years later

On the streets of New York City 1964

there was a spirited correspondence instigated by Dominic Behan over Dylan's utilisation of traditional melodies, conducted in the letters pages of *The Guardian* during 1984. In the revealing conversation reported in *Hot Press* in 1984 between Dylan, Bono and Van Morrison, Dylan spoke of his affection for Behan's 'The Old Triangle', a haunting ballad set in a prison cell, as well as evincing an affection for other traditional Irish singers like The Clancy Brothers and the McPeake Family (whose arrangement of 'Wild Mountain Thyme' Dylan had featured at 1969's Isle of Wight concert). Soaking up these invigorating new influences, Dylan's horizons were expanding yet further, and so were his targets.

In the gardens of the Savoy Hotel April 1965

If the vintage of Dylan '63 had been verging on the sparse, full-bodied but demanding, then Dylan '64 already had a much fuller, richer flavour. His was the hip name to drop. In his account of The Beatles' progress *Love Me Do*, published in 1964 and the only Beatles book John Lennon spoke of with any affection, Michael Braun reports seeing Dylan's first album in the group's hotel suite in Paris; by the end of that year, after meeting the Fabs, Dylan's influence can be detected, particularly in Lennon's writing. It is impossible to imagine either 'I'm A Loser' or 'Baby's In Black' from *Beatles For Sale* appearing without Dylan.

Dylan's response to The Beatles was also enthusiastic, and the mutual admiration between the two pioneers of pop was boosted by the fact that they all knew they were Kings. But for Dylan, "uneasy lies the head that wears the crown"; while The Beatles' very existence was enough to inspire untold thousands of groups in Britain, Dylan was preparing to distance himself from the movement which had held him in reverence. On the basis of only two albums over a two-year period, Dylan had found himself precariously posed as a leader, a position he could comfortably have held by producing a steady series of rallying cries - it is important to consider just how easy that would have been for him. The old pop adage is that once you've tapped the mother lode, you drain it dry, and the sales of '*Freewheelin*'' and '*Times*' must have assured him that this was the right direction. The easiest course of action would have been to remain the Pope of Protest, zeroing in on the issues of the time, writing a song about them and then settling down to count the royalties. You can imagine music biz moguls of the time dreaming up titles for Bob - 'The Times They Are A-Changin' Cha-Cha', 'The Ballad Of Martin Luther King', 'A Hard Rain's A Gonna Fall Rhumba'. But one constant of Dylan's career has been a wilful determination to follow his lonely muse, wherever it may take him.

It is perhaps hard now to envisage just how all-pervasive and influential Bob Dylan's position was at the beginning of 1964. With rock's increasing fragmentation, the idea of a single figurehead today is inconceivable, but back then - before pop videos, without the tabloid press' muckraking obsession with pop stars, with no corporate sponsorship - a star who could articulate the aspirations and concerns of his contemporaries was a rare and sought-after commodity. Dylan's move towards greater introspection and the switch away from songs which acutely reflected the times, thus caused much concern amongst those who had championed him as a leader, and there were many who deeply resented Dylan's refusal to keep writing what he now called "finger-pointing" songs. The entrenched folk-protest world of *Broadside* and *Sing Out!* were also concerned about the new songs Dylan was performing, particularly the complex wordplay and atmospherics of 'Chimes Of Freedom' and 'Mr Tambourine Man' during 1964. If these were rallying calls, then the rally would be held in the swirling confines of Dylan's imagination.

The public change came about largely due to Dylan's appreciation of what The Beatles were achieving within the pop format, but another indication of where he could go came with the success of The Animals' second single 'House Of The Rising Sun', which gave them a British and American number 1 single during the summer of 1964. The single was already a British hit while Dylan was recording his fourth album over two nights in New York that June. The first imprint on the folk-rock landscape is widely believed to have been made by The Byrds with their electric reworking of 'Mr Tambourine Man' in 1965 and certainly their closeness to Dylan and systematic plundering of his canon was substantial. However it is to The Animals that one should defer for leading the way. Their first single 'Baby Let Me Follow You Home' was a pop rewrite of Dylan's 'Baby Let Me Follow You Down' from his 1962 debut album, although the group's musical mastermind, Alan Price, claimed the group took their inspiration from Hoagy Carmichael's 'Baby Don't You Tear My Clothes'. Dylan had also memorably included 'House Of The Rising Sun' on that first album, even though The Animals' bassist Chas Chandler recalled seeing Josh White perform the song in Newcastle as early as 1957. Searching for a potential second single, producer Mickie Most opted for 'Can't You Hear My Heartbeat' (later a hit for Goldie & The Gingerbreads); Chandler, however, stuck out for 'Rising Sun', and so in 35 minutes at a cost of £4.10s., they cut the landmark single which helped shatter the two-minute stranglehold and acted as a sign post which Dylan was swift to follow.

Although their best work with Alan Price over the subsequent 18 months produced some classic singles and Price was to be one of Dylan's regular visitors during his 1965 British tour (as seen in *Don't Look Back*), The Animals never again achieved the heights reached by that second single. With Price, and with Eric Burdon - arguably the finest white blues singer Britain ever produced - The Animals had proved that there was room for authenticity in rock singles. The band's eventual decline was one of the saddest in the annals of British rock. I have long felt that the Newcastle quintet's pivotal role in suggesting the possibilities of a folk-rock fusion has been consistently underestimated, their contribution seeming always to be overshadowed by that of The Byrds. A tip of the hat is also due in the direction of The Searchers who made their own gentle folk-rock excursion on Malvina Reynolds' 'What Have They Done To The Rain' in late 1964 and whose hallmark jangling guitars and close harmonies were a strong influence on the developing Byrds.

The "something" that Bob Dylan had learned "over in England" - which had listeners baffled on his 'I Shall Be Free Number 10' and caused Dylan to chuckle - was the sound of The Animals tearing into 'House Of The Rising Sun'; for his followers though, it would not be a laughing matter!

The electric rhythms which would so fascinate Dylan during 1965 were already apparent on *Another Side Of Bob Dylan* released in August 1964. His melodies - particularly on 'Spanish Harlem Incident' and 'To Ramona' - would not be fully realised and embellished until the following year, but you can hear him beginning to play with phrasing and yearning to try his songs out against a fuller background. The restrictions of the folk movement were not simply ideological: musically too it was felt that the only 'authentic' accompaniment for their versifiers was the guitar, the acoustic guitar, fripperies such as the electric version were disdained; purity could never be allied to a Rickenbacker.

Years later, Paul Simon spoke of the same musical short-sightedness he encountered during the recording of *Graceland*: "It's as if you wanted to say to Ray Charles: 'Where do you get the nerve to sit there playing that 18th Century European instrument'? You know, it's an absurd idea".

At the end of his third album Dylan sang of saying farewell and not giving a damn. It was that singleminded sense of purpose and youthful arrogance which buoyed him, percolated through his fourth album and which found full voice during 1965. *Another Side Of Bob Dylan* saw the Dylan humour back on board, the angst of *Times They Are A Changin'* found sanctuary in the soaring 'My Back Pages' and 'Chimes Of Freedom', while the skittish 'All I Really Want To Do', 'I Shall Be Free No.10' and 'Motorpsycho Nightmare' conveyed the shades of grey which Dylan felt he could no longer deny.

'To Ramona' is wistful and wise, 'Spanish Harlem Incident' is swirling and atmospheric, and as in so many of his love songs, Dylan though conveying universality, imparts his own individual experiences. Nobody was writing love songs like that, the nuances and cadences of love, its subtleties, had gone unreported and unrecalled in popular song. That pertinence can be found on 'I Don't Believe You': the sensuality of kissing a mouth all "watery and wet", the detailing of a doomed relationship, to be confounded by the punch line of pretending that you've never even met (Al Stewart and Lloyd Cole obviously recognised the scenario when they covered the song). The churning autobiography of 'Ballad In Plain D', graphically details the breakup of his relationship with Suze Rotolo and casts her sister Carla as the villainess - the "parasite sister" - for whom Dylan had no respect. In later years, Dylan publicly regretted writing the song, but some sweet revenge was apparently obtained 20 years later, when the lavish 10 album bootleg collection *10 Of Swords* (put out to counter CBS' official *Biograph* retrospective) was compiled by Carla Rotolo, Chairperson of the PSA (Parasite Sisters Anonymous!). 'It Ain't Me Babe' helped revitalise Johnny Cash's career, gave the Turtles a hit and absolved Dylan of any blame in a relationship by denying that he was involved.

For the old guard, there was little to seize hold of, the anthems were limited to only two songs: 'Chimes Of Freedom' and 'My Back Pages', both of which dealt in vagaries and seemed to be distancing Dylan from any involvement when commitment was required. 'Chimes Of Freedom' at least had a promising sounding title, but what was all this about "starry-eyed and laughing ..."?, there was no room for laughter here, now. Who were these "disrobed faceless forms of no position"? Where were the lines addressed to mothers and fathers, senators and congressmen?

The turmoil Dylan felt was most acutely demonstrated by 'My Back Pages', a song full of lies and confusion, mutiny and jealousy, with a chorus of cumulative wisdom from a 23-year-old resignedly recognising that "I was so much older then/I'm younger than that now".

This smacked of someone moving away; it was in fact the echo of somebody already gone.

ROYAL FESTIVAL HALL
(General Manager : T. E. Bean, C.B.E.)

JOHN COAST

presents

BOB DYLAN

in his first public London Concert

Sunday, May 17th 1964 at 3 p.m.

Programme 1/6

CHAPTER
8

"I define nothing. Not beauty, not patriotism. I take each thing as it is, without prior rules about what it should be". *Bob Dylan, 1966.*

From now on, it was out of his hands anyhow. Definition and defamation; divinity and duality were all assigned to Dylan. He was just the messenger, he just happened to be there, that's all.

While Elvis Presley was recording 'Milk Cow Blues' in Sun's tiny Memphis Studios in 1954, just as the slow black, sloeblack blues starts lurching, he calls to Scotty Moore and Bill Black, "Hold on fellas, this don't move me . . . let's get real gone . . . " And that is where Bob Dylan was going in 1965.

In tandem with The Band, Dylan re-invented rock 'n' roll, snatching the vengeful snarl of the 50s and forging it on the anvil of his own intense vision. As with so much of Dylan's life at this period, confusion surrounded the simplest facts. Who forged the initial connection between Dylan and The Band (better known around Canada as The Hawks, rockabilly singer Ronnie Hawkins' backing group)? Was it John Hammond's son, John Hammond Jr, or a Canadian secretary in Albert Grossman's office Mary Martin? Whoever made the recommendation, it was obviously strong enough to send Dylan out to Somers Point, New Jersey to witness the band in action. The head-on collision between Dylan and The Band was shattering: the wiry fluency of Robbie Robertson's guitar, the alternately funereal and joyful keyboards of Garth Hudson and Richard Manuel; all buoyed Dylan's steely vocals.

It was a two-way process, The Band's years on the road prior to working with Dylan had honed their act to precision, and the collaboration provoked some of their best playing. Multi-instrumentalists to a man, in the cloistered confines of the Big Pink basement, their arcadian images rubbed off on Dylan, and steered him in the direction of *The Basement Tapes* and *John Wesley Harding*. In tandem, during the first half of 1966, they took on the world: that tour was the most divisive in rock's short history. Controversy was not unknown in rock, however this time the criticism came not from parents, but from contemporaries who came in their thousands to boo!

There weren't any maps for where Bob Dylan was going; nobody sat him down and pointed out the fiscal advantages of fusing his lyrics to a rock beat. You couldn't learn to write '4th Time Around', there wasn't a correspondence course for 'Desolation Row'. Hindsight, of course, lends a different perspective: if The Beatles were the ultimate 20th Century fairy tale (four poor lads leave home, take on the world, and win) then Bob Dylan's career between 1962 and 1965 seems positively Biblical - a journey from the Garden of Eden to the East of Eden. Dylan's body of work during the 14-month period during 1965/66 stands unequalled in rock's 30-year history. In substance, style, ambition and achievement, no one has even come close to matching *Bringing It All Back Home, Highway 61 Revisited* and *Blonde On Blonde.*

It is not just that Dylan invented 'folk-rock' in that period, it is not just that the 34 songs on those albums redefined rock. Into that staggeringly fertile period must be added one-off singles like 'Positively 4th Street', 'Can You Please Crawl Out Your Window' and 'If You Gotta Go . . . ', as well as such magnificent 'lost' songs as 'Farewell Angelina' and 'She's Your Lover Now'. The workload alone was backbreaking. Here were some of pop's most affecting love songs, most audacious efforts and ambitious achievements. It is not just that Dylan's work during that period led to the maturation of music . . . It is as much to do with the fact that he had the audacity to attempt it, and the arrogance to achieve it.

This is the period of which contemporaries and later critics have been most scathing, accusing Dylan of wilful obscurity, pointing out the excellence of earlier rock poets (notably Chuck Berry) and querying exactly what Dylan was about with these surrealist songs.

His champions from the folk days were equally scathing, suspecting that Dylan's willingness to jump aboard the rock bandwagon was purely commercial. Of the critics, Nik Cohn was amongst Dylan's harshest, opining "In my own life, The Monotones have possibly meant more in one line of 'Book Of Love' than Bob Dylan did in the whole of *Blonde On Blonde!*" Mind you, Cohn did relent in his 1969 book *Pop From The Beginning* when he wrote: "his effect on pop remains enormous: almost everyone has been pushed by him, Beatles, Stones, Hendrix, Cream, Doors, Donovan, Byrds - almost everything new that happens now goes back to his source. Simply, he has grown pop up, he has given it brains". Cohn also admitted in 1988: "Bruce Springsteen? Ugh. The worst. I listen to his lyrics and think, God, if I'd known this was coming I would never have been so hard on Dylan!"

Certain artists in rock do leave their imprint on a whole decade. Elvis' pomaded rebellion of the 50s, Bowie's androgynous eclecticism and Springsteen's full-throated rock 'n' roll revivalism in the 70s; Prince's cut-up funk and bravura pilfering in the 80s. For the 60s, The Beatles may have stylised the period, but the decade's authentic substance was that of Bob Dylan. The mistake that rock critics and historians make is in insisting that 'Desolation Row' is a better song than 'Book Of Love', or trying to use 'Like A Rolling Stone' to prove the inferiority of 'Tracks Of My Tears'. They are all fibres in rock history, integral parts of a gloriously rich and varied whole.

Dylan's genius - and I don't use the word lightly - lay in identifying and appreciating the many disparate strands, in drawing on rock 'n' roll, folk, country and pop and coalescing them. Whether acoustic voice of conscience, Rimbaud with a Rickenbacker or C&W crooner, he elevated the language of the street into poetry, filching slang and distorting cliche to wring more and fresher meaning from them. He shattered Tin Pan Alley's stranglehold and enabled the existence of the singer-songwriter, which despite its many later aberrations was a crucial factor in the development of rock culture. He had done it once by 1963, by 1965 he was set to shatter further preconceptions.

In the face of all this achievement and forging of new paths, it is often forgotten that Dylan's first love had always been rock 'n' roll, as early as 1962 he had made tentative electric recordings of 'Mixed Up Confusion' - released as his debut single but quickly withdrawn - and 'Rocks & Gravel'. In his work during 1965/66 he was simply pursuing that first love which he thought had been lost.

It was as much as anything Dylan's arrogance during the transition which so infuriated fans and critics. In none of his interviews did he explain just why he had undertaken this treacherous path, at no point did he admit any sense of himself as traitor, even going so far to deny his role as leader. When he sang "But I can't think for you/You'll have to decide" on 'With God On Our Side', Dylan's concern was equally with his audience's preconceptions as with Judas' betrayal of Christ. Dylan's was an arrogance fostered by his own belief in his talent and fuelled by the reverence with

which his work had been greeted up to that point.

If you bought a Beatles album at that time, you knew what you'd get: 12 or 14 immaculately crafted, three-minute love songs; Stones fans welcomed another album of R&B standards with nascent Jagger/Richard pop songs to flesh it out; albums by Herman's Hermits, Freddie & The Dreamers, The Dave Clark 5, all contained just what their public wanted, and then some more of the same. Dylan didn't seem to care what his fans wanted - as always he was doing what he wanted regardless, and that put a lot of backs up.

He was tampering with the very format of pop music, switching coats from Okie workshirt to Carnaby Street modern, singing songs about 68-year-old women claiming to be 54, about parking meters and handle-less pumps, about master thieves and paralysis. His albums featured songs that rambled on for 5, 7 even 11 minutes. He was, in short, unpredictable and uncontrollable. In his thoroughly entertaining autobiography *Rock Odyssey: A Chronicle Of The Sixties* (Hutchinson, 1984) Ian Whitcomb recounts meeting the hapless manager of Freddie & The Dreamers at the height of Dylan's 1965 folk-rock fusions, who complained "It's that Bob Die-lon man. The bloke's really killing our Freddie!". In The Rock Olympics, Dylan was tackling the Pentathlon while everyone else was still hop, skip & jumping.

Such chutzpah was bound to attract enemies, what was so surprising was their virulence. There is a certain sort of self-indulgent delight to be found in criticising an album in the comfort of your own home, to carry that dislike through to the concert hall and boo takes perverse pleasure a step further. The film *Eat The Document* briefly interviews fans outside the Albert Hall after the confrontational 1966 show; they explained their displeasure along the lines of "Well it was rubbish, I came along expecting to see a folk singer and heard all this rock 'n' roll rubbish." Flash forward 13 years to fans being interviewed outside one of Dylan's Born Again shows: "Well it was rubbish. I came along expecting to see a rock 'n' roll singer and heard all this Gospel rubbish!". I figure anyone who can antagonize all of the people, all of the time, must be doing something right!

Now of course we can bask in the smug conviction that we'd have been there applauding Dylan's 'defection', we would have recognised the innate quality of the music he was making with The Band, we also like to think that we too would have had Bob Shelton's intuition at that 1961 performance and prophesied the rise. Hindsight's a wonderful thing. Mike Sharp was at the legendary Albert Hall concert in 1966, and puts his finger on that sense of shock: "There were people I recognised from the Pete Seeger concert

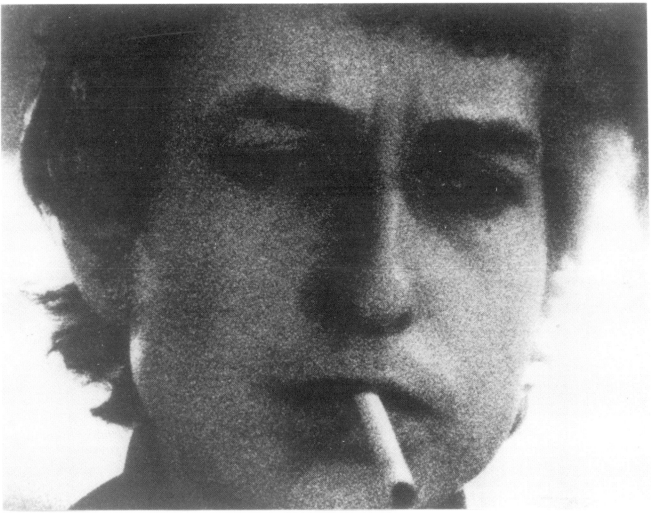

In Don't Look Back on the 1965 British tour

at the Albert Hall a couple of weeks before, who would come along to see Joan Baez sing every time she performed, diehard folkies, and they were outraged when all this equipment started filling up the stage. It almost seemed like a personal insult!"

In The Band, Dylan had found his perfect foil. The Band gave rock music a John Ford vision of America at a time of immense confusion and widespread rejection of traditional values, together with Dylan they were unbeatable. Marlon Brando once told Robbie Robertson: "The two loudest things I've ever heard are a freight train going by and Bob Dylan and the Band!". Of that watershed 1966 tour, Robertson later recalled: "Can you imagine what it was like for us? Our job was to get on a private plane, fly somewhere, get off and go and play. People booed you. You got back on the aeroplane and fly somewhere else. You get off and play - people booed you. We thought 'Jesus this is a strange way to make a living'!"

Fleeing from the persuasive "lies that life is black and white", Dylan was now exploring the rainbow. Few can forget their experience of hearing 'Like A Rolling Stone' for the first time, it was like everything before had just been a rehearsal and this was the real thing. In the best fairy story tradition, the song begins with the familiar "Once upon a time . . . " before steamrollering all that had gone before and spiralling onwards through outrageous rhymes and metre, lyrics flung like accusations, affronting yet compelling, that age-old fascination which lures unwary travellers right to the heart of darkness.

Rock, for all its liberalism, can be as inflexible as protocol, and there seemed to be little room for Dylan and his wayward odysseys, but surprisingly they were selling; new fans were voting with their feet, and his songs hurtled up the charts. His was the name on people's lips and The Byrds' truncated but catchy 'Mr Tambourine Man' was echoing round the world. Dylan found himself followed by Sonny & Cher and Barry McGuire, Simon & Garfunkel and Donovan, all the disciples who tapped into the folk-rock vein while Dylan transfused it. For all their oblique, elliptic lyrics, even at the time there seemed to be much wisdom contained in those songs of his: "Don't look back", "Don't follow leaders", "They say sing while you slave..", "Let me forget about today until tomorrow",

Press conference on arrival at London Airport April 1965

"Strike another match, go start anew", "How does it feel . . . ?", "Something is happening, but you don't know what it is", "Everybody must get stoned", "He not busy being born is busy dying . . .", "When you ain't got nothin', you got nothin' to lose . . ." As Clive James later wrote: "For an entire generation, Dylan *was* language".

In their zeal to scream "Sell Out", critics concentrated on the sackcloth and ashes Dylan had left behind and his infuriating unwillingness to explain just why he'd taken the rock 'n' roll route, any 'explanation' was cloaked in a surrealism that sounded like it had stepped off the set of a Marx Brothers movie. For me, at least half Dylan's appeal anyhow has been his sense of humour although this element has been overlooked in most estimations of his work. Like soothsayers sifting through the entrails ("the boiled guts of birds"), critics search for the MEANING: THE DEEP INNER MEANING of his songs. Bob Dylan? Something about the wind blowing, times changing, tambourines playing, mothers bleeding, stones rolling, says the man in the street. But running alongside the minstrel of misery has always been a quixotic satirist.

His sense of humour was one of the factors which helped Dylan keep his head during those frantic, fecund months. Pinned against a wall by "a million invisible people", jeered when he performed, met with blank incomprehension as he persevered with what he was doing ("I'm always trying to stay one step ahead of myself, and keep changing with the times, right. Like that's my foolish mission" he later said). It wasn't that

people were missing the point, they weren't listening, and were busy disseminating misinformation about someone who failed to fit into their view of the world of music. There is little doubt that around the time of his greatest fame, when he became an international pop phenomenon during 1965/66, Dylan's brusqueness, arrogance, mistrust and frequent boorishness made him not a very nice person to be near. He eschewed old acquaintances, and perhaps understandably assumed that everyone was after him for something (Michael Jackson said 20 years later "My idea of your average person is someone in a crowd running after me trying to tear my clothes off").

Mistrusting the motives of the people he met, he usually went on automatic attack. But comfortable or not, people kept coming back for more. The Beatles could always be relied on for witty quips, the Stones could always piss against another garage wall, but while none of The Fortunes, the Rockin' Berries or Sam The Sham & The Pharaohs seemed to have the answer, Bob Dylan did, and was endlessly pursued for it. As Herman Melville wrote in *Moby Dick* for Ahab: "That inscrutable thing is chiefly what I hate". Dylan's inscrutability has seen much mixed up confusion.

Suddenly it's 1970. There's a dance in Norbury in SE London, and the headline act are Eire Apparent. There is much excitement at this as Eire Apparent's recent album has been produced by Jimi Hendrix! In the anticipation leading to their set, I wander to the toilet and observe a piece of graffiti: "The sun's not yellow, it's chicken! Bob Dylan, 1965". Now there's someone who enjoys a good joke I thought, not the Bob Dylan I recognised. The Bob Dylan I was familiar with was the one Bernard Levin had pinned down in his memoir of the 60s *The Pendulum Years* (Pan, 1970), the man who "sang in the tones of a medieval flagellant charging the sins of mankind with responsibility for the ravages of the plague . . ."

Exposing any 'joke' invariably destroys it, the high watermark music of the period aside, Dylan's dress, attitude and caustic wit shaped the 'Bob Dylan' who bestrode the rock scene during 1965/66. In song, Dylan's humour could be cumbersome (the one-gag idea of 'Motorpsycho Nightmare' is soon exhausted, while the early talking blues quickly palled). But Dylan's irreverence was buoyed by the keenness of his satire. The press conferences were a hoot. It had been Dylan's attitude as much as anything which helped revolutionize pop music and enabled it to develop into a whole separate rock culture. Prior to Dylan, journalists were figures to be courted, their help coveted by struggling artists, but in Dylan's company they were mocked and taunted, forced to question themselves and confront their own limitations. "I'm only as good as the questions I'm asked", Dylan said in 1966. In Dylan's hands, the freewheeling press conferences of 1965/66 were absurdist affairs, with Dylan hopping, dancing and dodging like a bantamweight, refusing to be pinned down, categorized or analysed.

REPORTER: Who are your favourite performers? I don't mean folk, I mean general.

BOB DYLAN: Rasputin . . . Charles de Gaulle.. . the Staple Singers.

REPORTER: How do you get your kicks these days . . . ?

BOB DYLAN: I hire people to look into my eyes, and then I have them kick me.

REPORTER: And that's the way you get your kicks?

BOB DYLAN: No. Then I forgive them. That's where my kicks come in.

It was all more Groucho than Karl. There was plenty to laugh at then, Dylan deals with the best known painting in the world on 'Visions Of Johanna', he explains the enigma of a smile which has haunted the imagination for centuries thus: "Mona Lisa musta had the highway blues". In Dylan's hands, Abraham's response to God's dictate that he must sacrifice his only son is: "Man, you must be puttin' me on!". There's the slapstick farce of "They asked for some collateral, so I pulled down my pants." Brother Bill's biggest thrill would be to die in chains, so Bob kindly sends out for "some pillars and Cecil B. de Mille". There was a waspish wit at work here. He was seeing the absurdity of the world and holding up a mirror so the world could see it too. Some of it was clumsy, some of it was

as incomprehensible as the dance steps to Shirley Ellis' 'The Clapping Song', but a lot of it, like all the best humour, held an element of truth which exposed the farcicality of a world inhabited by riot squads, drainpipe sniffers, superhuman crews, insurance men and calypso singers.

The sleeve notes of *Bringing It All Back Home* and *Highway 61 Revisited* are sly and revealing, putting on and putting down as well as putting up with, the staccato prose style which would later become *Tarantula*. But what people still wanted from Dylan was THE TRUTH, they wanted answers not tongue-in-cheek put-ons or satiric shafts. His message? Easy: "Keep a good head, and always carry a lightbulb." That celebrated exchange produced the joke "How many Bob Dylans does it take to change a light bulb?" "Just the four: one to turn the electricity on and off, one to change the bulb, one to deny he'd changed it and one to reveal in interview that it was somebody else's idea to change it!". In the cut and thrust of interview, Dylan kept the phantasmagoria rolling: "What does protest mean to

Press conference in Los Angeles December 1965

you?" "It means singing when you really don't want to sing". More "What are your songs about?" "Some are about 11 minutes long, others five or six". He gave great copy, and when asked if he had a good quote replied: "If I had a good quote I'd be wearing it".

The press conferences gave Dylan another stage on which to perform. While he might not have made a living as a stand-up comic, Dylan elevated the pop star press conference. Today, when a major star graces a press conference with his fleeting presence, it's usually to justify tour sponsorship. In Dylan's hands, the brief encounters between artist and journalist became verbal duels.

Such was Dylan's high profile, that he in turn provided an easy target for humourists. Tom Lehrer's 1965 'The Folk Song Army' left little doubt as to its target: "The tune don't have to be clever/And it don't matter if you put a coupla extra syllables into a line/It sounds more ethnic if it ain't good English/And it don't even matter if it don't rhyme, 'scuse me, rhyne"! In the 70s, Neil Innes' 'Protest Song' was clearly modelled on acoustic Dylan, complete with performer falling asleep during tuneless harp solo and the rejoinder "Ladies and gentlemen, I've suffered for my art – now it's your turn!". The National Lampoon parodied electric Dylan with "The spangled dwarf in his bow tie/The infantry that don't ask why . . ." before admitting "Well, I guess it's time for my boot-heels to be wanderin' . . ."!

If 1966 was all-out war, 1965 was a series of feints and skirmishes. The Newport Folk Festival which had embraced Dylan so reverentially in 1963 and 1964, gave him an openly hostile reception in 1965 when he brought out the Paul Butterfield Blues Band to back him. Newport '65 was where the backlash began, his audience and contemporaries felt a sense of betrayal, that Dylan's electric rerouting was an affront, a snub to all they held most dear.

Liam Clancy who was at that year's Festival relished observing the furore, but found himself profoundly moved, telling me: "It was obvious that he was stoned, bobbing around the stage, very Chaplinesque actually. He broke into 'Tambourine Man' and I found myself standing there with tears streaming down my face, because . . . I saw the butterfly emerging from the caterpillar. I also saw, for the first time, the immense value of what the man was about. When he sang 'my ancient empty street's too dead for dreaming', I knew it was about Sullivan Street on a Sunday . . . I suddenly realised that this kid – who had bugged us so often – had emerged into a very major artist".

Tom Lehrer called 1965 "a nervous year, people have begun to feel like a Christian Scientist with appendicitis!". Others too were appreciating Dylan's

impact during 1965, in a "frivolous afterthought" Kenneth Tynan proposed a National Theatre pantomime that Christmas, venturing Dylan as Peter Pan, Joan Baez as Wendy and the Rolling Stones as the Lost Boys!

All this give-and-take comedy couldn't disguise the wealth of quality material which poured unbounded from the composer, to him it was all wine from the same vat, but even in his determination to qualify each song, Dylan couldn't help but appreciate the quality of 'Tambourine Man', 'Like A Rolling Stone' or 'Desolation Row'. To the millions who had bought The Byrds' version of 'Tambourine Man' – which only included the second verse and endless choruses – Dylan's full version came as a revelation, a moody, meandering epic, weary and resigned, it displayed his acute eye for a telling image and consummate ability to find just the right word.

Endlessly dissected, imaginatively interpreted, Dylan's music from this period has undergone as much analysis as Woody Allen, as indeed it should for there is a wealth of imagery and source material to draw upon. What Dylan was singing about seemed a lot more interesting than what was being taught in classrooms to impressionable teenagers. I'm sure I wasn't alone in thinking that if Bob Dylan was singing about F. Scott Fitzgerald, Ezra Pound and T.S. Eliot, I should be reading them. If Dylan felt Ma Rainey could be equated to Beethoven, then that was good enough for me. Just trying to cope with the concept that "Inside the museums, Infinity goes on trial" was heady stuff.

It was Dylan's scope which stunned at this time, namechecking T.S. Eliot in the penultimate verse of 'Desolation Row' was no bravura namedropping – the verse owed an open debt to the conclusion of Eliot's *Love Song Of J. Alfred Prufrock*. In the same way that Eliot's *The Waste Land* in 1922 attempted to clarify the chaos and disillusionment immediately after the First World War, 'Desolation Row' ambitiously attempts to chart the flux of America during the mid-60s.

Given the plethora of material, it is extraordinary that Dylan's eye for detail remained so acute. He admitted three years later that he was "pumping out" songs around this time, but instead of opening the sluices, what tumbled out were crystal visions; difficult certainly, occasionally incomprehensible, but nonetheless invigorating and spellbinding. To hear that aching, aged voice, battling against the rising tide of electric backing, pouring his heart into ideas that even he didn't fully understand or appreciate was a memorable experience.

Squinting through the miasma, one could appreciate the compactness and aptness of his hazy visions: on

'Queen Jane Approximately' the moaning bandits appropriately laying down their bandanas was spot-on, just the titles were enough to set you alternately chuckling and questioning. Why does it take a Train to cry? Why was Queen Jane only an approximation? What were Tom Thumb's blues? Why only temporarily like Achilles? What was the blind fear of being Stuck Inside of Mobile with the Memphis blues again?

Given the huge output, there were invariably some images and metaphors which missed the mark and Dylan's juxtapositions occasionally grew wearisome, his song titles deliberately misleading; but by steadfastly ignoring interpreters, Dylan tossed them more meaty bones which added further levels of ambiguity and misinterpretation.

It was hearing the language of the streets - lyrics which echoed real life conversation in a pop song - which was so invigorating. On '4th Time Around', a weary revisit to The Beatles' 'Norwegian Wood', the protagonist "gallantly" proffers his "very last piece of gum" - 'gallant' is what Arthurian knights did for a living, chewing gum is urban and contemporary, by deft juxtaposition Dylan combined the two. Amongst all the displaced Phantoms of the Opera, Ophelias, Casanovas and Romeos on 'Desolation Row', we find Cinderella standing "Bette Davis style". The landscape he evoked on 'Mr Tambourine Man' was easily visualised, the limitless "circus" sands, the Gothic romanticism conveyed by the "foggy ruins of time". 'Gates Of Eden' had good and bad in equal measure, but Dylan's imagery in the sixth verse is vivid, weeping "to wicked birds of prey/who pick up on his bread crumb sins"; the idea of birds of prey feasting on petty, "bread crumb sins" is a novel and striking one. It was like hearing Lewis Carroll rewritten by Kafka.

Much of it, of course, did not go beyond deliberate obfuscation, like Joyce finally finishing *Ulysses* with the cheery cry of "There, that'll keep the scholars busy for centuries". Scholars found much to attack Dylan with in that wilful obscurity. There were, of course, faults, not everything Dylan did during that manic period during 1965/66 had the stamp of genius. There was dead wood aboard, like the interchangeable bluesy riffing of 'Outlaw Blues', 'On The Road Again', 'From A Buick Six' or 'Pledging My Time'. Lyrically too, Dylan would juxtapose real people with myth, fairy tale and history, often to little real effect. The "philosophies" of that period frequently sprung from simple contradictions, living honestly "outside the law", speaking like silence and so on. The real pretentiousness of rock poetry though sprang from others' pens, those who took their cue from Dylan, but lacked his fluency and vivid imagination.

What critics during 1965 overlooked was Dylan's great affection for the rock medium: it wasn't just his puckish humour which had him christen Smokey Robinson "America's greatest living poet", it was his genuine astonishment that none of the government had been to Harlem's Apollo Theatre. It was with true fondness that he performed Ricky Nelson's 1958 hit 'Lonesome Town' on tour in 1986; it was with real pride that he recounted Elvis' recording of his 'Tomorrow Is A Long Time' as his favourite cover; in 1974 Dylan spoke of singers like Buddy Holly and Johnny Ace transcending nostalgia.

Noel Coward's endlessly quoted remark about "how potent cheap music is" is appropriate, but from that cheapness, further, wider horizons can be glimpsed. The common mistake in interpreting Dylan - and trying to separate him from the rock and folk cultures which produced him - is that taken together it all falls into place, Hank Williams can stand next to Little Richard, lining up alongside Arthur Rimbaud, Lord Buckley, Herman Melville, Paul Verlaine, Paul Robeson, Lenny Bruce, Little Anthony & The Imperials, Odetta, Josh White, Robert Johnson, Bertolt Brecht, Wilson, Kepple & Betty. They can take you so far, from then on you're on the road alone, with a road map and a headful of ideas for company. If Dylan 'taught' a generation anything, it was to go their own way, to think for themselves, to not follow leaders, not to "sing while they slave" if they're bored witless, to explore everything, to put it all into the journey. "Try everything once" said Master of the King's Musick,

Performing at a workshop at the Newport Folk Festival July 1965

Arnold Bax, "except incest and folk dancing". Bob Dylan tutored us in the joy of travelling.

Old fans felt *Blonde On Blonde* to be little short of contemptible, both in attitude and its success. Here was Dylan apparently courting The Beatles' crowd with pop pap like 'I Want You' and 'Rainy Day Women . . .' The package has a strong claim to being rock's first double album (confusion surrounds the release of Frank Zappa's debut for The Mothers Of Invention, *Freak Out*, which was truncated for its British release and which one reliable rock encyclopedia has down as an August 1966 release, three months after *Blonde*). The hazy photo of Dylan on the cover reflected the brown feeling of the songs, with its hero out of focus, the songs too came across as blurred and even more elliptical than before. His mouth set in vengeful retribution, the songs were alternatively dark and brooding and playfully outgoing.

Blonde On Blonde had mysteries abounding even before you played it. The title was a cryptonym for 'Bob'! Of all the bibliophiles who have scrutinised Dylan's reading habits, I haven't found any mention of his fondness for P.G. Wodehouse, so it's unlikely that Dylan had any knowledge of the following passage: "Like so many substantial Americans, he had married

young and kept on marrying, springing from blonde to blonde like the chamois of the Alps leaping from crag to crag". The record sleeve was the only one to feature actress Claudia Cardinale, who had been elevated as the ideal, unattainable screen goddess in Fellini's 1963, *8 1/2*.

Dylan's decision to be the first rock act to record in Nashville, Tennessee - the "buckle of the Bible belt" - was in itself a landmark. Twenty two years before Dylan, Eddie Arnold had started a tradition by recording in Nashville and the city had soon become the home of Country music. By the early 60s, The Nashville Sound, typified by the lavish use of strings and backing vocals, smooth steel guitars and popularised by producers Billy Sherrill and Owen Bradley, was a recognisable force, but recognised only by aficionados of Chet Atkins, Tammy Wynette, Loretta Lynn and George Hamilton IV. Nashville pumped out a stream of easy listening C&W. For fans of the growingly complex move of rock to a higher strata, Nashville epitomised all that was risible in popular music. Dylan recording there gave it a seal of approval, like so many of his moves at the time; where Dylan led, others flocked.

On the album's finest song, 'Visions Of Johanna', Dylan sings that "the country music station plays soft", and he was listening, but such was the pressure on him he had little time to pay real attention. He spoke some years later of the Nashville musicians playing cards in the studio while he wrote the songs to flesh out the album. Al Kooper remembered: "Dylan had sketches of most of the songs, but he completed the bulk of the writing there in Nashville, most of it in the studio. When he felt like writing or rewriting, everyone would repair to the ping-pong tables in the canteen. Sometimes, in the case of 'Sad Eyed Lady Of The Lowlands' or 'Visions Of Johanna', he would sit in there for five hours without coming out and just play the piano and scribble." That "scribbling" between card games and ping-pong, gave him the pop hits he coveted with 'I Want You' and 'Rainy Day Women . . .', but also the haunted landscapes of 'Sad Eyed Lady . . .' and 'Johanna'.

Dylan was poised on the brink, a year earlier Phil Ochs had eerily written: "One year from now I think it will be very dangerous to Dylan's life to get on the stage . . . he's gotten inside so many people's heads - Dylan has become part of so many people's psyche, and there's so many screwed-up people in America, and death is such a part of the American scene now . . . It's not that everybody sits there listening to him with a single-track mind. Dylan has managed to convene a very dangerous, neurotic audience together in one place . . . it's because of this very neurotic audience . .

(that) Dylan has got to be careful, and that is why he'll have to quit singing".

With all the inevitability of a Greek tragedy, Dylan's bike crash of July 1966 looked like the final act. Comparisons with James Dean flashed up and as someone once wrote, you couldn't go anywhere in Europe during 1967 without meeting an American tourist whose sister was working in the drug clinic where Dylan was detoxing or the hospital where he was undergoing plastic surgery. With so much achieved during the preceding months, Dylan couldn't keep up the (almost literally!) breakneck pace. It was at his instigation that rock music had realised its almost limitless potential, but while contemporaries flailed away at works of incredible pretentiousness and pomposity which he had made possible, Dylan fell silent, reacquainting himself with his roots, the joys of traditional music, the honesty of Woody Guthrie. The disciples were still there, devoted and inspired, but leaderless, rudderless. If a week is a long time in politics, Dylan's 18 months' absence in rock terms seemed like a lifetime.

If the back wheel hadn't locked on his motorcycle that midsummer day in 1966 constitutes one of rock history's great "What Ifs . . . ?". (What if Raymond Jones hadn't walked into Brian Epstein's record shop in 1961 and asked for a record by The Beatles? What if Keith Richard hadn't spotted Mick Jagger carrying a pile of Chuck Berry LPs on a Victoria-bound train? What if David Bowie had never read William Burroughs? What if Bruce Springsteen had never learned to drive?..). By late 1966 Dylan would have played Shea Stadium and been on a par with The Beatles in commercial terms, he would have carried on at the same crippling pace: a bootleg album from an April 1966 concert in Melbourne has him sounding at the end of his tether, the songs squeezed out like blood from a stone. In plain view, he would surely have felt compelled to try and match *Sgt Pepper* with some madly ambitious concept, to have costumed himself like some psychedelic pierrot or simply have frazzled up with drugs.

Without that bike crash there wouldn't have been any *Basement Tapes*, Woodstock wouldn't have become the cynosure of the rock hemisphere, there'd have been no Country-Rock and the thunder would never have rolled. But the wheel did lock, it didn't catch fire, its passenger just languished in the basement of a house known ungrammatically but effectively as 'Big Pink' while rock music underwent its craziest caperings.

If Dylan's life was a film, the afternoon of July 30, 1966 is where it would end: a long, circling helicopter shot over the mangled motorcycle, the smoke curling black into the sun, the crumpled body lying still, his Medusa-hair coiling like a wreath as the final credits roll on the sunny stillness .

Bob Dylan's 25th birthday party, Paris, May 24 1966

On stage at the Sydney Stadium April 1966

CHAPTER
9

"Using a blowtorch on the middle of the candle is less aesthetic than burning it at both ends, but more people see the flame" wrote Richard Farina of Dylan prior to his Woodstock sojourn. As he recuperated in Woodstock, if it had been in his nature, Dylan could have looked back with pride and satisfaction on just what he had achieved. His folk-rock fusion of 1965 had led to the many excesses of 1967 and by the time he disappeared, Dylan had become the yardstick by which pop was measured. With Dylan in abeyance, his acolytes were free to over-indulge themselves in the vacuum his departure had created.

Sensing that Dylan's absence would be prolonged and that there wouldn't be a new album in 1967 to fulfil his contractual obligations, CBS rushed out a workmanlike *Greatest Hits* in March. Although his record sales had already been escalating, with *Bringing It All Back Home* selling over 500,000 in the States and doubling the sales of *Another Side, Greatest Hits* went on to become Dylan's best selling album of the decade. But while he never enjoyed the real commercial success of The Beatles, Dylan's influence on the music of the 60s cannot be measured in units shifted.

Though publicly invisible we now know that Dylan was far from idle during his time away from the spotlight. Much of the year was spent in arduous basement recordings with The Band and in October he flew to Nashville to commence recording *John Wesley Harding*. But it was ironic that while absent that his influence was most strongly felt: his presence could be sensed like Banquo's ghost at a rock 'n' roll feast when the rock culture reached its apogee during the frenetic summer of 1967. The soundtrack for that year was 'A Whiter Shade Of Pale', 'San Francisco' and *Sgt Pepper* (Dylan shared with Dion the distinction of being the only pop singers featured on the cover), none of which would have been feasible without Dylan.

Despite the naïveté of the period, there was undeniably an air of optimism, perhaps this was the herald of the new dawn. There was full employment, the economies of Britain and America were strong and there were a baffling new series of alternatives on offer (life/newspapers/music/sex/drugs). During the plethora of 60s' anniversaries, it has become fashionable from the vantage point of the 80s to mock and deride the idealism of that earlier decade, but the real achievements remain considerable. The gradual erosion of racial barriers, a healthy distrust of establishment and authority figures, the seeds of the women's movement and the awareness of ecology, the growth of the peace movement, the politicization of pop and as a consequence, the younger generation's willingness to challenge whatever had gone before, a widespread and enduring raising of public consciousness.

Rock was growing increasingly complex, like a child trying to prove to its parents that it could act grown up, rock music felt that three-minute singles were kids' stuff; what really mattered were 'statements' which reflected the writers' concerns and which their audience could respond and relate to. The fact that the bulk of these statements were self-centred, drug-induced and largely incomprehensible, seemed at the time to be of little consequence.

The limited release during 1967 of the film *Don't Look Back* reminded fans of the Dylan of two years before and helped perpetuate the enigma. While rock rampaged on an orgy of self-indulgence and florid excess, Dylan remained silent, but even that silence helped spread the dust of rumour. On learning that Dylan had left New York, pilgrims made the journey up to Woodstock to try and learn the 'truth' from his lips. Sara Dylan wearily admitted to Larry Sloman: "I'm so used to them. I mean we get a Christ every six months coming up to our house . . . We even got a John the Baptist last year!" He was writing a novel, reading the Bible, he was writing the Bible and reading a novel! In fact, Dylan was largely concentrating on what he did best.

The Basement Tapes were rock 'n' roll's equivalent of D-Day; its best kept secret and a formidable assault when apparent. While American rock music was flowering wild in a colourful explosion, Dylan and The Band were getting back to its roots. While the rock world publicly vented its spleen on parents and leaders, Dylan was privately singing about parental fidelity. While George Harrison was testifying that life went on within and without you, Dylan was taking his potatoes down to be mashed. While Mick Jagger was

Arriving in Brisbane, Australia April 1966

2,000 light years from home, Dylan was bracing himself against a towering tree with deep roots. While Jim Morrison was working out his Oedipal complex, Dylan was bemoaning the cruelty of children to parents. While the Strawberry Alarm Clock were singing about 'Incense & Peppermints', Dylan was concerned with a chauffeur with "a nose full of pus".

Pop stars now felt confident enough to tackle 'Teenage Operas', they could hear the grass grow, were grateful to be dead, could touch the sky and spend a lifetime watching the hole in their shoe letting in water. But while all this cosmic capering was going on, Bob Dylan was singing about eskimos, burning wheels, million dollar bashes, clothes lines; in short, odds & ends. What makes the *Basement Tapes* such a unique body of work is the sheer size and scale: over 150 songs were estimated to have been laid down during that four-month period up in Woodstock, which works out at about 10 finished songs a week - more songs in those months than during Paul Simon's whole 30-year career! Their impact if released at the time is incalculable, with rock teetering on the edge, the tapes could have drawn it back to a centre.

The fact that Dylan could let his hair down on these fragments and finished songs had to do with the fact that none were ever intended for release. Although *Melody Maker* had spoken of the tapes' existence in late 1967 (citing titles such as 'If Your Memory Serves You Well', 'Ride Me High' and 'I Shall Be Relieved') the first official hint of their existence came on a demo tape sent out by Dylan's publisher in 1968, from which Brian Auger took 'This Wheel's On Fire' and Manfred Mann culled 'Mighty Quinn'. There was something about Dylan's song, inspired by the 1960 Anthony Quinn eskimo drama *The Savage Innocents*, which tells of how eskimo culture is corrupted by among other things rock 'n' roll, that appealed to people, despite the fact that when the eponymous eskimo does arrive after all that waiting, everybody immediately wants to go to sleep. It also provided the name for a Newcastle group in 1988, the title of a 1989 film and a Manfred Mann number 1 British hit in 1968. In 1969, Dylan spoke fondly of Manfred Mann's covers of his songs, but in 1970 Mann admitted "The whole thing with Dylan is really a big myth. None of us have ever met him. It's just a business thing where his publisher sent a tape to us".

It was of course the furtiveness, the secrecy, the

wait, which gave the tapes their legendary status. They finally became available – as *Great White Wonder*, rock's first bootleg – during 1969 and there was such an illicit pleasure in listening to Dylan let his hair down, it was like eavesdropping on the decade's most influential composer, almost hearing the creative wheels turn. After the original batch had been in wide underground circulation for some years, CBS and Dylan eventually relented by releasing in 1975 – a sticker entitling them *The Historic Basement Tapes* – a patchy double album of the 1967 sessions. By 1986 though, a whole new trove was being bootlegged, more rich waters from the bottomless well which had only been tapped 20 years before – although we have still to see the pork chop rock 'n' roll of 'Even If It's A Pig, Part I and II' on record. The gradual reel-to-reel revelations of the Basement Tapes occur in much the same way that new novels and short stories of Hemingway and Scott Fitzgerald continue to surface years after their death.

The second batch of Basement Tapes were even more revealing in the glimpses they gave of how Dylan and The Band set about creating their music. The melody of 'One Single River' was later used for 'Open The Door Homer' and in the middle of a magnificently haunting rendition of 'Hills Of Mexico', Dylan cuts it short muttering about wasting tape! Here are songs which spanned his career to date, 'Young But Daily

On the Johnny Cash Television Show June 1969

At the Woody Guthrie Memorial Concert, New York, January 1968

Growing' had been part of the set at his first public concert in New York in 1961. Curtis Mayfield's 1965 hit for The Impressions, 'People Get Ready' – which surfaced again later in *Renaldo & Clara* – was aired, as was Hank Williams' 'The Stones That You Throw'. There were also some alternative takes of familiar songs from the period, which somewhat belies the legendary spontaneity of the sessions.

As with so many other things, Dylan gave the world its first rock bootleg, but as usual, he started the torrent. In a major article on bootlegging in February 1970, *Rolling Stone*'s headline ran: "Bootleg: The Rock & Roll Liberation Front?" It reported CBS' lawyers pinpointing the originators of *Great White Wonder* as a pair of draft-dodgers who'd split to Canada with their profits, where they apparently opened a strictly legitimate petrol station!

Bootlegging is now a worldwide industry, but Dylan – because of his reluctance to acknowledge any one performance as definitive by committing it to vinyl – is still among its most sought after artists, with an estimated 1,000 titles available, now including CD bootlegs. Tapes of Dylan's answerphone message, of his rant against garbologist A.J. Weberman, even of his address to the 1965 CBS sales conference, have all flooded onto the market. It's hard to believe that over

On the Isle Of Wight August 1969

20 years after the original sessions, fans would still be sifting through illicit tapes, trying to match titles to songs and sympathising with producer Tom Wilson as he tries to log another title from 1965: "'Alcatraz To The 9th Power' . . . that's what you told me when you left!". There was even a spate of Italian pressings during the 70s which featured such Dylan classics as 'Lady Down Your Weart Tune' and an advert on the back offering the six album set of Benito Mussolini's collected speeches!

Amongst all the fripperies and flippancies of the tapes, there were miraculous moments of music. Spontaneous and shaggy, 'Tears Of Rage', 'Too Much Of Nothing' and 'I Shall Be Released' are among the most mature and considered works Dylan has ever written. With the newly discovered experience of parenthood and something approaching domestic bliss, he was able to view the world from a different perspective. Freed from the madness and rigours of the road and the increasingly confrontational concerts, these were wry and rueful glimpses into the composer's state of mind. Also in there was that sly humour which is inseparable from Dylan. 'Clothes Line Saga' pre-empted Watergate, 'You Ain't Goin' Nowhere' is veranda singing from Kentucky, 'The Mighty Quinn' is full of appealing contradictions, 'Goin' To Acapulco's melody is an early version of 'Tears Of Rage'; while 'Yea! Heavy and a Bottle of Bread', 'Lo & Behold' and 'Don't Ya Tell Henry' are no more than engaging fripperies, but made all the more endearing by their evident spontaneity. However the influences are still as diverse as ever: 'Get Your Rocks Off' includes a trip to Blueberry Hill, while the Vivian in the chorus of 'Too Much Of Nothing' has been suggested as T.S. Eliot's first wife Vivian, who succumbed to the oblivion of madness.

On songs like 'Apple Suckling Tree' the good humour spills out like cider, just good time music, amazingly suggesting that the man who had spent so much time agonizing on 'Desolation Row' could really be happy now under an apple suckling tree. It was that feeling of a privileged glimpse, the off-the-record record, which gave Dylan fans a conspiratorial unity. The morality of it all was not yet in question, never before had an audience glimpsed behind the mask of their idol, until then all that had been allowed was the carefully prepared patina the artist wanted seen, but here was Bob Dylan, undeniably warts and all.

Parallel to their work on the tapes, The Band were preparing their debut *Music From Big Pink*, the release of which in 1968 gave the myth to Woodstock as the artistic hub of the rock universe. The 1969 Woodstock festival actually took place at neighbouring Bethel in upstate New York, but such was its allegiance to Dylan and the Band, that the festival took its name from the community they'd made their home. Far from street fighting men, Dylan and The Band now gave the image of contented family men, new frontiersmen whose idea of a good time would be to gather round on a chill winter night before a crackling open fire for a few choruses of 'Shall We Gather At The River'.

In 1987, Robbie Robertson spoke of his songwriting in a mood which evoked the feel of his work with Dylan 20 years before: "I need the plains, that little house out there with one light on – that's what drives me nuts, I gotta know about this". This was the territory of the Big Pink house and the tapes recorded in its basement. Dylan's singing had never sounded more wise, a sense of gravitas was in his voice during the sessions' more sombre moments. In truth Dylan's absence was a hectic time for him, with four months mixing up the medicine in the basement with the Band and three separate trips to Nashville to record his next album, but the break did at least free him from the spotlight of public scrutiny for a much needed intermission.

The return of Bob Dylan to the public eye came during a blitz in January 1968. The release of *John Wesley Harding* was kept deliberately low key in the wake of the excesses of his rock contemporaries: the packaging alone a slap in the eye for any satanic majesties who might have been watching. Just a Polaroid snap of a slyly grinning Bob, a Woodstock neighbour and Purna and Luxman Das of the Bauls of Bengal troupe (it is not without coincidence that the Stones' 1968 album *Beggars Banquet* was their most Dylan influenced, while the Beatles' double set of the year *The White Album*, was their deliberate 'back to the roots' effort; once again Dylan's shadowy presence could be detected).

Anyone expecting to revisit the haunted pastures of *Blonde On Blonde* had a shock in store on their baptism of *John Wesley Harding*. John Peel gleefully announced a preview of the album one Saturday afternoon on Top Gear and I can remember sitting avidly awaiting more trips with the ghost of electricity in tow, but being struck instead by the winsome acoustic opening of the title track and the homely poesy which imbued the album. 10 of the 12 songs are strict three-verse ballads, one of the exceptions being 'The Ballad Of Frankie Lee & Judas Priest'. Jimi Hendrix transported 'All Along The Watchtower' to Armageddon later in 1968, while 'I'll Be Your Baby Tonight' became a staple of many crooners' repertoires. Simple the album may have been, but never simplistic.

The songs sounded deceptively straightforward to those used to the maze Dylan had inhabited before the crash, but they enabled fans to stock up with a veritable

Performance, Isle Of Wight August 31st 1969

thesaurus of new Dylanisms: "He was never known to make a foolish move", "There must be some way out of here", "Nothing is revealed", "No martyr is among ye now" . . . While firmly denying his past, Dylan was busy shaping his role for the future. But any 'role' was difficult to detect in his new album, the songs were folksy fables, clean cut against a stark backdrop of bass, drums, lightly strummed acoustic guitar, piano and occasional pedal steel. For clarification, Dylan offered on the sleeve notes that "The key is Frank", which helped a lot.

What made *John Wesley Harding* even more difficult to appreciate at the time, was that 1968 was a year of chaos: Martin Luther King and Robert Kennedy fell victim to assassins' bullets, students were taking to the streets in Paris, Berlin and London; the Parisian students' slogan perfectly captured the mood of the times: "Be Realistic. Demand The Impossible!". The Yippies tried their best to disrupt the Democratic Convention in Chicago, only to collide head-on with Mayor Daley's police. In Ireland, the first stirrings of the non-violent Catholic civil rights movement took to the streets, while in Czechoslovakia Alexander Dubcek's 'Prague Spring' was crushed beneath the wheels of Russian tanks. More than at any other time during the 60s, the youth movement was looking for leaders, but there was no encouragement from Dylan – he was tired

of being a leader and anyway, 'I'll Be Your Baby Tonight' hardly had the anthemic qualities of 'The Times They Are A-Changin''.

John Wesley Harding, perhaps because it is one of Dylan's most enigmatic albums, amply rewards frequent returns; its very starkness and the plaintive quality of the songs mean that it can be revisited with none of the embarrassment of the psychedelic excesses of that period. The album wasn't hitching itself to any movement, as ever, Dylan was leading from the front.

During his isolation in Woodstock, Dylan had cropped up at concerts by Northumbrian traditional singer Louis Killen and Johnny Cash, re-establishing his roots. But his first official concert re-appearance took the drifter all the way back home, when he was announced as one of the guests at the Woody Guthrie Memorial Concert to be held in New York in January 1968. It was the world's first glimpse of the new Dylan. Gone was the familiar electric halo of hair, instead there was a chubbier, shorter haired, wispily bearded figure, fronting The Band. Together they played with muted energy, like some exceptional skiffle group, rocking out on 'Grand Coulee Dam'. That was the first record I ever bought, an old pink labelled Pye 78, by Lonnie Donegan - the King of Skiffle's nervous treatment of one of Woody Guthrie's best songs - and here a decade later was Bob Dylan tackling it. The sound and look of

Bob Dylan at the beginning of 1968 was a remarkable transition from the turbulent pop star of 1966.

As the decade he epitomised swung to a close, Bob Dylan stood back and took stock. While new bands like Chicago pompously dedicated their second album "To the Revolution" and CBS' official advert in the Isle of Wight festival programme boasted "The revolutionaries are on CBS", while Lennon sat on the fence and couldn't decide whether to be included in or out of his 'Revolution' and the counter-culture (in part thanks to 1969's *Easy Rider*) became a hugely marketable commodity, Dylan's utterances seemed largely unremarkable. His last recorded statement of the decade was 'Tonight I'll Be Staying Here With You' on *Nashville Skyline* in April 1969, the spokesman for a generation, the poet laureate of young America throwing his troubles out the door. They would remain there for some time.

In the 60s' "selling out" was the ultimate insult (today it seems a pre-requisite for pop success). While the first full blooming of the counter culture was generally held to be Woodstock in 1969, Dylan chose instead to appear across the Atlantic at the first Isle of Wight festival, where his controversial hour-long set was loudly raspberried. The performance even caused

a question to be asked in the House of Commons, Marcus Lipton MP asking whether Dylan's five-figure fee for a mere 60-minute performance "was not a powerful incentive for workers to accept income restraint"! The music press had gone round chasing its tail promising superstar jams with The Beatles, Blind Faith, Stones, Uncle Tom Cobbley & all. It was certainly an event, guests included John and Yoko, George and Patti Harrison, Elton John (better known as Pinner's Reg Dwight back then), Jane Fonda, Steve Winwood and Terence Stamp. The official Musicians Union 'exchange' for Dylan and The Band were Marc Bolan's Tyrannosaurus Rex.

Of the actual performance, too much was expected. The 200,000 devotees who went "To help Bob Dylan come and sink the Isle of Wight" wanted the fire and brimstone, the tormented fiery shaman; what they got was a white-suited singer backed by his friends, crooning his way through a few old favourites, glad to be on the Isle of Wight and looking forward to visiting the home of Alfred Lord Tennyson. The crowd also got a lovely, weaving version of the McPeake Family's 'Wild Mountain Thyme' (aka 'Go Lassie Go', also recorded by Joan Baez, The Byrds and Van Morrison). There were also frail and haunting solo versions of 'It Ain't

Recording Self Portrait in Nashville May 1969

Me Babe' and 'To Ramona', but these were largely overlooked in the the frenzy of chasing THE EVENT! In that weekend's *Evening Standard*, astrologer Katrina wrote: "GEMINI: You may be keeping rather in the background today, but all the same you will be busy skilfully engineering people and circumstances along the lines you have in mind"! Such was the fascination with Dylan's first headlining concert in three years that Sandie Shaw even released a single with the refrain "Wight is wight/Dylan is Dylan".

At the desultory press conference prior to the festival, Dylan was asked if he had "a personal message for the kids of today." Pausing, the spokesman for his generation sagely replied "Take it easy and do your job well", anyone that earnest couldn't pose a real threat. As for the Bob Dylan who opened his soul to Jann Wenner in the November 29th 1969 issue of *Rolling Stone*, a magazine which after all took its name from his 1965 song and was to feature him on a further 10 covers . . . Well you couldn't ask for a chummier compadre, ol' Bob didn't have a bad word to say 'bout anybody, even Toby Thompson who'd been digging around Hibbing looking for clues about the young Bob Zimmerman was equivocally dismissed as a "boy with a lot to learn". Bob "always liked" Ray Stevens, Joe South, Otis Redding, John Lennon, was surprised that Albert Grossman was such a difficult character, laughingly confused Smokey Robinson with Arthur Rimbaud, asked Jann if he'd got the right person here: "A youth leader? . . . I mean there must be people trained for this job you're talking about" and guilelessly of his recordings: "Boy, I wish you could've come along the last time we made an album". Why sure Bob, love to.

Plans for hitting the road were discussed, ace guitarist James Burton had been approached by Dylan (who fondly remembered his picking for Ricky Nelson) to go on a three-month US tour during 1969, but Burton was already committed to sessions and live gigs with Elvis in Las Vegas. That same issue of *Rolling Stone* carried a report of Kerouac's funeral, a review of Led Zeppelin's watershed second album, the announcement of the Supremes split and an account of Paul McCartney's "death", many felt it also contained the obituary of Bob Dylan.

Dylan's wholehearted espousal of Country & Western on his 1969 *Nashville Skyline* followed The Byrds' landmark album *Sweetheart Of The Rodeo* in August 1968. It was during Gram Parsons' brief time with the group that Roger McGuinn had become fascinated by the possibilities of a country-rock fusion. This was only a minor diversion for The Byrds, but with the Flying Burrito Brothers and Emmylou Harris, one which Parsons pursued to the end of his short life.

Dylan had fond memories of C&W giant Johnny Cash's championing of his early work, when Cash was undoubtedly one of CBS' biggest stars. Cash also came to Dylan's defence when Dylan switched from "finger-pointing" songs in 1964. Dylan was a regular visitor to the Cash household while he was in Nashville – a fact Cash recalled on his 'Songs That Make A Difference' from the 1990 *Highwaymen II* – and made a rare television appearance on Cash's 1969 special. The two men spent time in Nashville recording in February 1969 and the tapes of those sessions reveal a relaxed and smooth sounding Dylan backed by Cash's Tennessee Three. The two croon through old standards such as 'Mountain Dew', a couple of Jimmie Rodgers blue yodels, rock 'n' roll classics like Carl Perkins' 'Matchbox' and Elvis' first single 'That's All Right Mama'; it's good ol' down-home stuff, with Johnny urging "Yodel one more time for me, Bob". However only one song from these sessions was ever officially released. The Dylan-Cash duet of 'Girl From The North Country' on *Nashville Skyline* was the first time that Dylan had ever re-recorded one of his own songs (another indication to critics that he was running short of ideas). Perversely, 'Girl From The North Country' is one of the weakest of the Cash-Dylan duets, in particular, there's a lovely rolling version of 'One Too Many Mornings' which would have fitted much better onto the finished album.

To find Dylan in the company of Cash, a known supporter of President Richard M. Nixon, seemed to many like sacrilege, to hear them singing together and appreciate Cash's influence on Dylan's Nashville album almost heretical. Dylan had obviously sold his soul to 'the Establishment' and was out for bucks, keen to tap into the lucrative AOR/C&W market of the late 60s. This was 'selling out' with a vengeance. The apparent flippancy and lightheartedness of Dylan's C&W album also managed to ruffle more than a few feathers, it seemed as if Dylan was embracing the very establishment that he had railed against during so many of his formative years.

The parochialism of the allegedly liberal rock establishment found much to carp at with Dylan '69. Having wrestled him from the clutches of the diehard folkies, the rock 'n' roll fraternity now found him defecting to the bosom of Nashville and all its redneck values. The fact that Dylan had cited Hank Williams, Jimmie Rodgers and Hank Snow as formative influences all along was overlooked. Nashville was rhinestone and patented insincerity, it lacked the purity of intention which rock espoused, it detracted from the growth of the alternative community rock was building. For all their loudly vaunted liberalism, the rock critics were showing themselves to be as doctrinaire as their 'opponents'.

Hindsight of course reveals the sagacity of Dylan's move; along with *Sweetheart Of The Rodeo*, *Nashville Skyline* helped pave the way for the 'Outlaw Country' movement of the mid-70s, when Waylon Jennings and Willie Nelson broke Nashville's monopoly on country music and took C&W back to its roots, infusing it along the way with a bold authenticity and much needed contemporary edge. Gram Parsons' two solo albums of the early 70s helped make many more people aware of the possibilities of the sincere avowals of Country music. Anticipating the furore which his own equivalent of *Nashville Skyline* would cause over a decade later, Elvis Costello's 1981 album of classic C&W songs *Almost Blue*, boasted a cover sticker "WARNING: This record may bring out a violent reaction in narrow-minded people".

Dylan's *Nashville Skyline* was a pleasant, light and brisk album, his rasping voice had mellowed to match the contented, wispily bearded singer on the album cover - the smile says it all. The album's best known song is 'Lay Lady Lay', originally intended for the 1969 film *Midnight Cowboy*, Dylan, however, had been late delivering it and the producers opted instead for Nilsson's version of Fred Neil's 'Everybody's Talkin'. Dylan also offered the song to the Everly Brothers; Phil Everly told me that they were playing New York's Bitter End in 1969 when Dylan came backstage after their performance, and, asked if he had any songs for the brothers, he began singing 'Lay Lady Lay', Phil thought the chorus ran "lay across my big breasts" and figuring that would scupper any airplay, the brothers graciously declined the song!

Certainly your mind could stay in neutral while the album played, there weren't any fighting poets or rolling stones here, instead a distillation of the sweet and plaintive C&W sounds the young Dylan remembered from his adolescence. The album proves Dylan able and adept at utilising archetypal Country clichés, with 'One More Night' as its most delightful song, but otherwise you tend to believe the composer when he said that he could turn out songs in his sleep; they're engaging little things that he happens to pin down.

Thus the 60s came to a close. The most golden post-war era, the glittering Swinging Sixties, when pop singers became as important as Popes. It has become fashionable to knock the idealism and näiveté of the era from the vantage point of the ruthless 80s. The 60s were flawed, there was a lot of terrible music, self-indulgence and whimsicality, it was fun though. Dylan looking back on the decade, likened it to "a flying saucer (which) landed . . . that's what the 60s were like. Everybody heard about it but only a few really saw it". At the dawn of the 70s, Richard Neville portentously wrote: "(Dylan) helped open the eyes of a generation. Nothing would close them now". As we enter the 90s, those eyes aren't closed, they're just trapped behind designer shades; idealism and heart tidied away into a bulging Filofax.

The notorious garbologist A J Weberman

CHAPTER

10

It began with the breakup of The Beatles and ended with the death of the Sex Pistols' Sid Vicious, bookends on the 70s. If the 60s were the party everyone claimed, the 70s were the hangover. Musically the decade wasn't kickstarted until Punk in 1976, otherwise the music scene was on a pacemaker. Increased commercialism and a nervous looking over the shoulders at 60s' leaders left much of the early 70s barren. The early years of the decade were characterised by the blandness of The Osmonds, The Carpenters and Dawn, while 'Glam Rock' ("rock 'n' roll with lipstick on" according to John Lennon) was pantomime fare in the hands of Gary Glitter, The Sweet and Slade. There were of course occasional classic singles to keep things from ossifying completely, but by and large things were in a parlous state. Even the overwhelming success of the most striking single of the early 70s, Don McLean's 'American Pie', was largely due to its nostalgic symbolism. After the excesses and experimentation of the late 60s, the early 70s were characterised by restraint and formularised pop.

Rather than looking forward, people looked back to the stars of the 60s to lead them. The Stones were exiled from Main Street, The Beatles were clawing their way through the courts, Elvis was in his gaudy heyday in Las Vegas, Simon & Garfunkel had split up, Creedence Clearwater Revival - who had offered so much promise - were no more, Eric Clapton was trapped in the self-destructive spiral of heroin addiction, The Who (after their triumphant 1971 *Who's Next*) were trapped in the morass of the unrealised *Lighthouse* project. Of the new acts, Led Zeppelin were steamrollering across America, David Bowie was revelling in his role as a "leper Messiah", Bruce Springsteen was tentatively sending out greetings from Asbury Park, Pink Floyd were growing increasingly ambitious and remote, Motown was running off production-line hits, Elton John was camping it up as rock's Liberace . . . and Bob Dylan all but disappeared from public view for the best part of three years.

Tired of being typecast as the spokesman for a generation which during the Nixon years was becoming increasingly fractured, annoyed at the proliferation of bootlegs, Dylan now set out to explore the possibilities of myth-destruction. He certainly seemed to have succeeded with the release early in 1970 of *Self Portrait*. As a public suicide note for the Bob Dylan of the 60s, the double album is one of rock's most successful iconoclasms.

For eight years Dylan had displayed a consistency which dwarfed his contemporaries, as an idol he towered; the late 60s and early 70s however seemed designed to display his feet of clay. The desire for rock idols to shatter their own myths has been well documented. The polarisation displayed by Lennon and McCartney in their debut solo works is of interest: Lennon throwing himself into wholehearted catharsis with '*Plastic Ono Band*', which renounced both The Beatles and Zimmerman, while McCartney contented himself with a home-grown and undeniably charming album, all his own work but much under-rated, when all the public wanted were variations on 'The Long & Winding Road', fully formed ballads not rock doodlings. From Dylan, they wanted either questioning protest songs or introspective enigmatic meanderings. What they got and definitely didn't want, was Bob Dylan singing 'Blue Moon'! Advocates of *Nashville Skyline* could at least excuse that album as an attempt to reach the white working classes, as Ralph Gleason said in his review of the album : "This is the kind of language used by the guy who wrote 'the ghost of electricity howls in the bones of her face', then you have to ask why is he using this language? You have to ask what objective he has in mind".

Self Portrait found fewer apologists and even the passing of time has done little to improve the album's standing. Despite claiming authorship of many of the album's songs, which were widely held to be in the public domain or else light-fingered rewrites, Dylan declined to include them in either the 1973 or 1985 collections of his lyrics. In London, for example, at his debut British concert in 1990, Dylan's *Oh Mercy* producer Daniel Lanois pointedly introduced 'In Search Of Little Sadie' as "an American folk song". The album displayed the shoddier aspects of his Isle of Wight performance of the preceding year and you wondered - if it really was a 'self portrait' - why the influential songs of Woody Guthrie, Hank Williams, Robert

Johnson and Leadbelly were so notably absent?

Was Paul Clayton's 'Gotta Travel On' included out of remorse? Dylan had lifted the melody for 'Don't Think Twice It's All Right' from the traditional 'Who'll Buy Your Chickens When I'm Gone', which Clayton had unearthed. Although the song was in public domain, many felt at the time that Dylan should have credited Clayton as the source - he had after all cited Martin Carthy's version of 'Lord Franklin' as the source melody of 'Bob Dylan's Dream'.

Was there really such a paucity of new songs that Dylan had to record two versions each of 'Alberta' and 'Little Sadie'? Could Dylan finally have run out of steam? Otherwise what was the justification for including lacklustre instrumentals like 'Woogie Boogie' and 'Wigwam'? Was it genuine admiration for Paul Simon's finest song 'The Boxer', which prompted Dylan to record it, or was it another snide aside? Simon himself hadn't been slow off the mark knocking Dylan and there is a school of thought that 'The Boxer' is about Dylan. The sheer quantity of material ensured that there were some highlights, Dylan's sensitive handling of 'Belle Isle', 'Copper Kettle' and his Everly Brothers tribute 'Take A Message To Mary' were notable, while 'Let It Be Me', the rumbustious reading of 'Days Of '49' and the driving 'Alberta No.2' also stood out.

The faults of the album were manifest, but more importantly it revealed - really for the first time - the fallibility of Bob Dylan. After a career which had gone straight along the fast lane, Dylan was now crawling along the inside track being overtaken by all and sundry. *Rolling Stone* dispatched no less than 12 writers to undertake a hatchet job and there was a general feeling that the set should more appropriately have been called 'Self Assassination'.

Later on Dylan claimed that he regarded *Self Portrait* as his own bootleg. He was vexed and frustrated at the deluge of bootlegs which had followed 1969's *Great White Wonder*, tapes and poorly pressed albums were available documenting his entire career, from fledgling 1961 performances in a Minneapolis hotel room and his 1963 Town Hall concert in New York, to studio out-takes and live cuts with The Band. Dylan later likened the phenomenon to "phone tapping", but such was his prolificity and his constant changing of lyric and arrangement, so great the frustration of hearing a song in concert which would never appear on record, that bootlegging Dylan had inevitably become big business. The bootlegs reached a mass market, the audience who had grown up alongside Dylan's official releases. What the pirates brought was

access to the private Dylan, or more particularly, the early Dylan who had reached barely thousands rather than the millions who now constituted his audience. But infuriated by what he saw as an invasion of his privacy, angry at the public release of records intended solely for private purposes, *Self Portrait* was intended to call the bootleggers' bluff.

The fact that people could be so upset by a record was proof – if any were needed – of Dylan's continued stature; such a public fall from grace though was unprecedented and made fans wonder just how Dylan would cope with the ensuing decade. It was now widely acknowledged that he couldn't be pigeonholed and the swiftness and luminescence of his best work had shown that he had forgotten more than most would ever know; but his first record of the decade raised innumerable questions and supplied precious few answers.

The scorn which greeted *Self Portrait* obviously rankled, but it also suggested that the rock culture still badly needed a leader, and the only person remotely qualified for that role was Bob Dylan. For half his career Dylan has been in the highly contradictory position of trying to teach his followers not to follow leaders. Like Brian in the Monty Python film he challenges his slavish followers with "You must all learn to think for yourselves" only to have them chorus "Yes Master, how must we learn to think for ourselves?" It is difficult enough to recruit followers, to stop them following poses a whole new set of problems.

Dylan's work could be a starting point for many fruitful voyages of discovery, into music, poetry, art, politics, responsibility. That his best work even caught the interest of academics more attuned to Milton or Blake was a cause of great satisfaction to those who felt that rock had long merited treatment as an independent art form. Ralph Gleason wrote: "Dylan's impact is comparable . . . in terms of concepts and additions to the language, only with Shakespeare and the Bible". While Professor Christopher Ricks was to later admit: "I'm not so besotted with Dylan's genius not to know that not all of his best work is perfect. He's only as good as Shakespeare, who had a lot wrong too!" Now the genre's most quoted and respected lyricist found his work coming under the microscope of academia, an interest which burgeoned during his years of silence in the early part of the 70s.

Each new album from rock deities was now greeted reverentially by the press and the lengthy expositions pioneered by *Rolling Stone* had become the norm. With Dylan in abeyance, new albums by James Taylor, The Moody Blues, Crosby, Stills, Nash & Young and Joni Mitchell were the chariots which bore the messengers, and boy they really did bore. Elvis Costello told Bill Flanagan of his attitude around this time: "There were

two types of rock 'n' roll that had become bankrupt to me. One was 'Look at me, I've got a hairy chest and a big willy!' and the other was the 'Fuck me, I'm sensitive' Jackson Browne school of seduction. They're both offensive and mawkish and neither has any real pride or confidence".

But there was still one more surprise left in the locker. October 1970's *New Morning* had a genuine Dylan self portrait on the cover and the whole album spoke of taking stock. The back cover showed a painfully young Dylan alongside Victoria Spivey and welcomed back Al Kooper – who had contributed the hallmark organ sound of 'Like A Rolling Stone'. It painted a picture of Dylan's domestic bliss, surrounded by kids, salmon streams and memories of Elvis Presley (the gipsy settled in his Las Vegas hotel), while recording the honorary doctorate Princeton had conferred on Dylan that June. The rural serenity apparent on 'Time Passes Slowly', 'Sign On The Window' and 'Winterlude' was comforting, after the years of torment, it was encouraging that Dylan could welcome a bright, new morning.

The album was wildly overpraised, on its release the normally cautious Ralph Gleason thrilled "We've got Dylan back again". But far from becoming public property, Dylan was going private again. The period between *New Morning* and *Pat Garrett & Billy The Kid* was the longest gap in his recording career to date, but for a recluse Dylan remained in evidence. Still eschewing his expected 'role', he cropped up as session pianist and harp player, donated songs to friends, and appeared as a surprise guest at concerts. But all this was viewed through opaque glass, no clear picture was to emerge for the best part of four years.

It was during the low profile years of the early 70s that the Dylan myth industry went into overdrive. Chinks in his armour had been spotted in the most recent albums, but nevertheless with the widespread release of the 1965 documentary *Don't Look Back*, the publication of the first in-depth biography by Anthony Scaduto, the proliferation of bootlegs documenting every facet of his career and his own provocative refusal to comment, Bob Dylan was news.

The screenings of *Don't Look Back* gave an insight into the frenzy under which Dylan was creating during those frenetic mid-60s' years, churning out songs in hotel rooms, on planes and in cars, dealing with unimaginable pressures but coping with the madness with a necessary acerbity ("God, I'm glad I'm not me" says Dylan early on in the film). It still stands as the best rock film ever, because it details the development of rock's most influential artist during the period of his greatest work. 'Fly on the wall' films can err towards frustrating self-indulgence, but the honesty of *Don't Look*

As 'Alias' the printer's assistant in Pat Garrett & Billy The Kid, 1973

Back sees it stand undated. On its revival in London during 1983 a friend came out from seeing it and marvelled of Dylan "I didn't know anybody was that cool!"

Don't Look Back just happened to be there at the right time, and through its detailing of frenzy, creation and conflict, provides us with a permanent document not only of Dylan circa '65, but also of rock's changing face. Director D.A.Pennebaker said in 1983 that the idea for the film had "been in my head for a long time. Not necessarily about Dylan, but about an artist trying to stay on top of an extraordinary talent in the face of adulation and disapproval . . . That seemed like a film worth making. All it needed was finding the right person at the right moment. A film for history: perhaps instead of history". Dylan, to his credit, let the film out as it stood: a far from flattering portrayal of himself, as irascible, temperamental, falling in and out of control. It is hard to imagine anyone sanctioning such a revealing portrait today. With such vignettes, Dylan gave revealing glimpses of what he later called "the blood behind the myth (creating) the art".

On the film's video release in 1988, Pennebaker recalled its subject: "He had to be extraordinary where most of us settle for just being adequate. *Don't Look Back* is about the sixties, and the man who got us through them. Bob Dylan is more than just a folk singer touted by the record industry, more than the songwriter whose poetry is the only kind many of us remember, more than the Kerouac-kid who haunts our best writing. He is the force that blew us out of one era and into another . . . he remains the influential voice of our times". Pennebaker also shot miles of footage of the turbulent 1966 British shows with The Band and regrets bitterly Dylan's refusal to sanction their release, calling them "extraordinary concerts and wondrous music . . . of much greater historical importance". Aside from a heavily edited hour, which surfaced briefly as *Eat The Document*, Dylan retains the rights to this footage.

Rumours of Bob Shelton's definitive biography filled the air, but Scaduto's was the first book to effectively lift the mask. It revealed Dylan as manipulative but provided another valuable insight into the artist. Dylan's cooperation ensured the book's readability; it nailed down some myths, it gave the lie to others, it also gave his audience a welcome opportunity to look back at Bob Dylan's achievements at a time when his future was nervously unpredictable.

Such was the music press' lack of commitment to the development of rock in the decade that they found themselves looking back over their shoulders, only able to make judgements by comparison, thus every act of promise became either "the new Beatles" or "the new Dylan". In 1981, critic Greil Marcus submitted a list of "The New Dylans", six of whom were Bob Dylan! Marcus's list reflected 70s' obsessions and also included Bruce Springsteen, Steve Forbert, Elliott Murphy, John Prine, Kris Kristofferson, Bob Seger, Paul Simon, Loudon Wainwright III, Neil Young, John Denver, Arlo Guthrie, Don McLean, Bob Marley, Randy Newman, David Ackles, Tim Buckley, Tim Hardin, Phil Ochs, Mark Knopfler, David Blue, Ian Hunter and Marc Bolan!

Of them all, Springsteen was the most obvious "successor", largely because he had been discovered in 1972 by John Hammond who 10 years before had championed Dylan. Hammond told *Crawdaddy*: "When Bobby came to see me he was Bobby Zimmerman. He said he was Bob Dylan, he had created all this mystique. Bruce is Bruce Springsteen. And he's much further along, much more developed than Bobby was when he came to me". The Springsteen/Dylan comparisons were further fuelled in 1973 by Springsteen's first single 'Blinded By The Light' which obviously owed a debt to Dylan's 'Subterranean Homesick Blues' of eight years before. Mind you, Dylan had used the song structure of Chuck Berry's 'Too Much Monkey Business' for his song, a format Elvis Costello also adopted for 'Pump It Up' and which Andy White hijacked on 'Religious Persuasion'.

The spate of "new Dylans" in the 70s was a testament to his standing in the rock community. Such was the interest and speculation engendered by Dylan's absence, that fans and critics would pounce on anything which might provide an insight, a glimpse behind the shades. Sometimes it was hardly worth the effort. When his only novel *Tarantula* was finally published in 1971, it read like a collection of amphetamine sleeve notes hastily bound together on a typewriter lacking capital letters on the roads of excess. The enigmatic title could well have come from a section in Kerouac's *On The Road*: "I was all set except for a great hairy tarantula that lurked at the pinpoint top of the barn roof. Terry said it wouldn't harm me if I didn't bother it . . . I made love to her under the tarantula. What was the tarantula doing?" What indeed! *Tarantula* is worth dipping into but not slaving over. There is periodic black humour: "john wayne might've kicked cancer, but you oughta see his foot", wisdom: "hitler did not change history. hitler WAS history" and the perseverance of Dylan's opaque philosophy of the mid-60s: "compared to the big day when you discovered lord byron shooting craps in the morgue with his pants off . . . and he offers you a piece of green lightbulb and you realize that nobody's told you about this and that life is not so simple after all".

As an artist hailed for his lyrics, it is strange that at

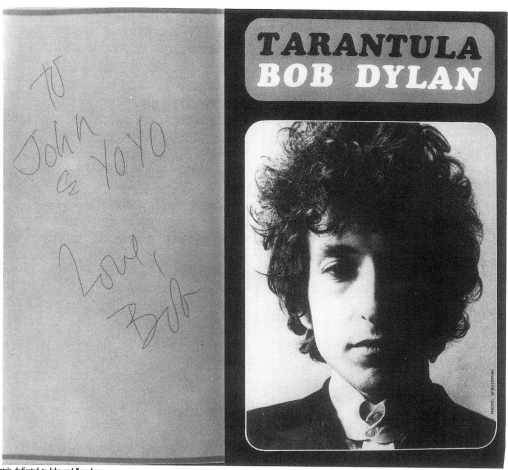

An inscribed copy of Tarantula dedicated to John and Yoyo Lennon

this time none of Dylan's albums had ever had the lyrics printed on the sleeve, even though it had become something of a craze in the wake of *Sgt Pepper*. The only two Dylan albums to boast sleeve lyrics are 1990's *Under The Red Sky* and 1985's *Empire Burlesque*, ironically an album which finds him rhyming "moon" and "June". Understandably, the publication in 1973 of *Writings & Drawings* provoked enormous media interest. At last you could see what he'd been singing all those years, marvel at his inability to pronounce the word 'mirror', remain puzzled by what an "onion gook" was and be dazzled by the audacity of his rhymes. The collection ended optimistically with the lyrics of 'When I Paint My Masterpiece', cunningly implying that "the best is always yet to come". As for the drawings, well don't give up the day job . . .

Few rock stars could withstand the scrutiny which Dylan was undergoing. The bootlegging craze, while providing invaluable patterns in the shaping of his career and insight into the development of his art – charting the progress from Robert Zimmerman to Bob Dylan – washed both dirty and clean laundry in public. At least with Dylan there was something worth bootlegging. No collection of rock history can be complete without the '66 Albert Hall show, and its frustrating unavailability led to further accusations

flying towards Dylan, although his record company's stick in the mud attitude was underestimated. There was nothing static in Dylan's career, so anything which provided stasis was welcomed, the likes of self-styled "garbologist" A.J.Weberman spoke loftily of "liberating" Dylan material (arrogantly assuming that he could also "liberate" Dylan himself!) Weberman's obsession was a further testament to Dylan's stature, which other rock star's dustbin ever merited such academic dissertation?

Dylan's standing ensured a fan following which bordered on the unhinged. A century before, Oscar Wilde had pleaded "Oh Lord, save me from my disciples" – a sentiment Dylan understood only too well. For many, he is a canvas on which to paint our own self portraits, a painting by numbers – and we never did learn which No.12 & 35 ever were! It's not even about Bob Dylan, or rock 'n' roll, it's a journey through the maze, with Dylan as the thread. We take something from his work, and try to impress our own order on his chaos. On the cover of an early issue of the Dylan magazine *The Telegraph* was part of a letter: " . . . that's the odd thing about Dylan; he reduces me almost to the level of a screaming groupie, anxious for details about what he eats for breakfast and for the latest photograph of him, and at the same time, inspires me to a contemplation of the most crucial questions about life and art . . . ”

During his life, Dylan has been the subject of endless books, articles and theses, a play was mounted during the mid-80s in America on his "life and works". He has spent so much of his time dodging asinine questions ("Don't you have an important philosophy for the world?" "I don't drink hard liquor, if that's what you mean!") that it's a miracle he didn't simply fold up his tents and steal silently away. People who sound like they'd be happier inside some institution dog him; fanzines devote space to "the necklaces worn by Dylan during the 1978 tours", treat his every word and utterance as though hewn in stone and quiz him in person as though he were the holder of the sacred truth. "Jeez, how come nobody asks Kris Kristofferson/Neil Diamond/Billy Joel questions like that?" he regularly retorted.

During the 70s even his answerphone message was widely bootlegged. Tapes circulate of studio warm-ups, soundchecks; fans sift for "the nightingale's code" version of 'Visions Of Johanna' and transcribe Dylan's onstage raps for circulation. In 1982 New York hosted the first 'Bob Dylan Impersonators Contest'; the 1986 event saw 300 turn up to enter in one of four categories - 'Folk-Protest', 'Post Motorcycle Accident', 'Born Again' and 'Free Style' - like some bizarre replicant Olympics. With the burgeoning new technology Bob Dylan even became available on computer software: "You simply put a question to Dylan on the computer and the program finds a correlative answer in one of his songs!"

For all the doors Dylan opened, he closed others. A letter from *The Telegraph*: "The Respondent has an obsessive interest in poetry and Bob Dylan. The respondent frequently attends concerts and poetry readings and undertakes a life-style of anti-social hours and pursues these major interests away from the home to the exclusion of the Petitioner and causing her distress". (Are the majority of Dylan fans middle-aged men who sit with furrowed brows each looking for their own sad-eyed lady and asking "can you cook and sew, make flowers grow"?) What was it about this man that inspired such obsessive devotion? Why did he sear where others only grazed?

Part of it, of course, was Dylan's refusal to stick to the guidelines of what is expected of a "rock star"; who else would record a magisterial body of work throughout a 25-year career - and then refuse to release it?

The morality of bootlegging has been discussed far and wide; many true fans would argue that they own everything official anyway, diligently buying substandard official albums whose royalties bolster the composer's coffers. Artists are of course deprived of income, and lose the right to veto the release of material which they consider substandard; but many would argue that the availability of certain crucial performances and unreleased studio material add immeasurably to their knowledge and appreciation of an artist. Scholars welcomed Ezra Pound's annotated *The Waste Land,* with the aid of computers Joyce scholars have revised *Ulysses* again and again until they had a definitive edition, with the aid of cut scenes and hitherto unavailable footage Thames TV's series *The Unknown Chaplin* gave a vivid and fascinating insight into Chaplin's creativity.

From Dylan collectors, the plaintive cries of "Why can't he release . . . " are constant, and indeed it is little short of criminal deprivation to be denied 'I'm Not There', 'Blind Willie McTell' and dozens more. One can only assume that at his death, his 50th birthday or whenever he's good and ready, these and all the other gems will officially surface, in the meantime there is the samizdat of bootlegging.

Dylan seems to be as aware as anyone of the value of what he has kept hidden. The release in 1972 of *More Bob Dylan Greatest Hits* gave just a hint of what was there: the double set tantalisingly included three reworked songs which had originated at the time of *The Basement Tapes*, as well as 1963's haunting solo 'Tomorrow Is A Long Time'; hearing the song now, it sounded a lifetime ago. Also officially available was 'When I Paint My Masterpiece', which The Band had included on their 1971 *Cahoots* album; inexplicably though Dylan's version excluded the splendid bridge: "Sailin' round the world in a dirty gondola/Oh to be back in the land of Coca-Cola!". It was to be a further 13 years before Dylan trawled the Augean Stables of his back catalogue for *Biograph*, but typically, it was what he perversely left out that helped fuel the rumour-mongers and turn casual fans into diehard collectors.

The reclusive Dylan was a willing participant at the August 1971 Madison Square Garden concert organised by George Harrison to aid the refugees in Bangla Desh. Overshadowed now by 1985's Live Aid, Bangla Desh was rock's first attempt at raising money for the Third World on a grand scale, while endeavouring also to raise public consciousness about the suffering in the newly born state. The roar of delight when Harrison brought on "a friend of us all" was effusive and incredulous. Dylan diligently got on with his set, delivering a surprising selection of his classic songs to the delighted crowd. The subsequent triple album of the event went on to win a Grammy award as 'Album Of The Year'. The notoriously conservative Grammy establishment had hitherto ignored Dylan's contribution to popular music; as far as they were concerned 1965's 'Record Of The Year' was Herb Alpert's 'A Taste Of

Honey' while 'Song Of The Year' went to 'The Shadow Of Your Smile'! *Sgt Pepper* was the first rock album to be honoured and Dylan was to wait until 1979 before receiving a Grammy in his own right - oddly as a singer rather than a composer.

Showing that he could still be moved by events, Dylan's 1971 single 'George Jackson' was written in angry response to the murder of the black activist only days before. Like John Lennon, it looked as if Dylan was going for singles with the immediacy of newspapers, the single proved a one-off but was nonetheless sincere. As usual with Dylan, it provoked a controversy, dividing the rock world into those who felt he was bandwagon-jumping and supporters who welcomed his return to protest. There could be no winning, but plenty of equalizing.

The mythologizing of Bob Dylan continued apace in his absence. In 1969, The Hollies became the first group to record an entire album of Dylan songs although the album saw Graham Nash quit the group because he felt they were trivializing the composer's work. Joan Baez's double *Any Day Now* in 1968 had displayed what a fine interpreter of Dylan's work she was, and she was later to address Dylan directly in song with the facile 'Song To Bobby' and the touching 'Diamonds & Rust', however on the *Diamonds And Rust* album (1975) Baez's impersonation of Dylan's singing style on 'Simple Twist Of Fate' was strictly Bobby Davro. In 1972, arising from the ashes of McGuinness-Flint, the legal-sounding Coulson, Dean, McGuinness, Flint cut *Lo & Behold*, an imaginative album of mainly Basement Tapes era Dylan songs.

Dylan had also cropped up in other people's songs, John Lennon invoked 'Ballad Of A Thin Man's "Mr Jones" on The Beatles' 'Yer Blues', while David Bowie - on his best album *Hunky Dory* in 1971 - had included 'Song To Bob Dylan', requesting Dylan's return to "the Movement". In the same way as Dylan himself had addressed Woody Guthrie in his first original song, Ralph McTell repaid the compliment on his 'Zimmerman Blues'. The Who addressed him in 'The Seeker', as did Rick Nelson's 'Garden Party', while Don McLean cast him as " the Jester" in 'American Pie'. Not every invocation was flattering though, in 1990, Everything But The Girl, on their *The Language Of Life* album included the track 'Me And Bobby D': "You tell the world, 'be free, love life'. Tell me, is it true you beat your wife?" The group's Tracey Thorn commented: "It's disillusionment with the male preserve of the hippy mentality. The whole idealisation promoted by everybody from Dylan to Kerouac is a boys' lifestyle, and a lot of those boys had women waiting at home for them. Which is the perfect lifestyle. Go out on the road and be wild for a year, then come home to

your wife. Must be brilliant!" The 'Dylan As Misogynist' boot had also gone in with a vengeance in 1979 when Tony Parsons and Julie Burchill had corruscated Dylan: "'Is Your Love In Vain?' moves as breezily as a slug with a limp, a verbose Andy Capp cross-examining a potential hausfrau to ensure she's everything a woman should be. Virgin Mary, Mona Lisa, Jeeves the Butler and Mom!"

The "seems like every time you turn around" Dylan school had plenty going for it well into the 80s. The 1988 debut album from the Red Hot Chilli Peppers included a cover of 'Subterranean Homesick Blues' which featured the engaging couplet "The good God willin'/We'll bebop to Bob Dylan". The 80s also saw Young Turks such as Aztec Camera, Falco, Nick Kamen and Stan Campbell cover Dylan songs, while other new acts like U2, The Jeff Healey Band and Edie Brickell got plenty of mileage out of venerated Dylan originals.

Slowly too, Dylan was being taken away from rock by the scholars, who saw in his work a reflection of the turbulence America had undergone during the 60s. Treatises, theses, all kinds of odds'n'ends, were generating another type of industry. Many were published, but they met largely with public incomprehension. Predictably the man who sparked off such an industry remained silent, or if commenting at all, scathing: "you can twist anybody's words" Dylan said in 1985, "but that's only for fools and people who follow fools." The circumstance and motivation for many of his songs forgotten, he had little interest in those who ceaselessly sifted through his works. With so much still to do, there was so much to forget.

That didn't stop the growing army of Dylanologists, like Professor Terry Shute, Regius Professor In Absentia at the University of Delacroix, who recently completed his Doctoral Thesis on 'Visions Of Hispidity In The Record Sleeves Of Bob Dylan', an excerpt from which I gratefully reproduce here:

"...which makes my central contention that there is a direct link between the quality of Dylan's music and the amount of facial hair he disports on the relevant record jacket. Leaving aside the debut album, (Lusk in his *The Firstborn: Biblical Sacrifices In Literature* [Yale, 1947] cites Hubbard's footnotes to Till's foreword to Winter's *Isaac's Error* [Princeton, 1937]: "We take the firstborn as the mistake, the mutant which must be cast out, spurned, remaining unappreciated in any consideration of what follows.") I follow the herd that insists all of Dylan's records from 1962 to 1966 feature a face devoid of filamentous substance, and that that wilful disregard for hirsuteness reflects the inherent quality of the music.

"I have speculated elsewhere ('The Lonesome Death Of Bob Dylan, July 30, 1966' [*The Village Echo*, 1972]) that the face we see on record sleeves from *John Wesley Harding* onwards is not Bob Dylan, but for the sake of convenience I will accept that the figure is him and pursue my argument thus: Dylan's first post-crash record has a simpler, starker sound, but the cover portrait, showing straggly, desperate attempts at a beard, is a Polaroid photograph, the very symbol of the ephemeral. Dylan's weakest album to date is *Nashville Skyline*, and there he is on the cover, smiling, proffering his guitar as a sacrifice and bearded; bearded in his den I suggest. This is a playful Dylan, smiling, knowing that the songs are his weakest yet: contemptuous, but masking that contempt behind his beard . . .

"*Self Portrait* has a 'self portrait' by Dylan on the cover, the painting is, of course, clean shaven, suggesting a return to the 'old' persona. Dylan however persists with the beard on the inner sleeve photographs, this may be in part a reaction to the scars inflicted by the suicide attempt of August 1966 (Op.cit.), but significantly there are more photographic representations of the artist on the sleeve of *Self Portrait* than on any other work in the canon (9 here compared with *Blonde On Blonde*'s 7) and here he is bearded in every one. Nine Dylans, only 3 less than the Disciples; all are bearded, all appear on the sleeve of his worst record ever. *New Morning* is irrefutable proof of my thesis, here we have the Yin and Yang of the dichotomy. On the cover a bearded Dylan stares unflinching into the camera's lens, but on the back sleeve, the youngest pictorial record on record Dylan has provided and he too stands unflinching, staring at the camera - clean shaven! . . . As for *Pat Garrett*: the only Dylan album to date not to feature Dylan on the cover or inner sleeve, but with credit given to three photographers (only one less in number than the Horsemen of the Apocalypse!) *Planet Waves* of course, features no picture of Bob Dylan as this record is not by Bob Dylan . . .

"Crinosely, *Blood On The Tracks* offers purity; no hint here of hispidity: clean shaven, Dylan delivers his most substantial testament of the decade, without the benefit of any woolly facial lineament. His purpose obfuscated, we are denied substance until 1975's *Desire*, a compromise. As Professor Francis Lee has pointed out elsewhere ('40 Red White & Blue Shoestrings: The Numerology of Bob Dylan', unpublished) "*Desire* is the fifth album in a suite all of which feature Dylan's profile on their respective covers. In addition, each side of the recording - with the sole and significant exception of side two - features five songs, it was released in 1975, exactly halfway through the decade, and pivotally five is exactly half of ten: significantly only one less than the

'11 Outlined Epitaphs' Dylan had written exactly *eleven* years before."

"The constant, repetitive display of profile is, according to Hassidic Dylan scholars, the poet's device for affirming his own Jewishness. But returning to *Desire*, we are confronted by the beginnings of a beard; the unshaven Dylan, as if uncertain of the album's qualities, certainly laughs Dylan to us: 'It is better than *Dylan*, but it is not as good as the album I haven't made yet which will not feature me bearded.'

"I would like to quote Professor M. Quinn from his definitive work 'Skeleton Keys In The Rain: Bob Dylan's Harmonica Holders' (unpublished): "We know nothing. We come into this world knowing nothing. We leave this world knowing nothing. During our lives here we learn nothing. Nothing is taught to us and we teach nothing . . . .In conclusion, if Dylan has taught us anything, it is that you can never have too much of nothing."

★ ★ ★ ★ ★

The cachet of having Bob Dylan on your record was considerable during his missing years. Doug Sahm, Roger McGuinn, Barry Goldberg and Steve Goodman all benefited; the latter from a piano player impishly hiding behind the pseudonym 'Robert Milkwood Thomas'. Rumours, as usual, filled the air, but though still held in reverence, something altogether more substantial was to be hoped for from Dylan during the 70s. It came rather unexpectedly, from director Sam Peckinpah, who managed to coax the reluctant 32-year-old in front of the cameras for his elegiac western *Pat Garrett & Billy The Kid* in 1973.

Billy is one of the cinema's perennial outlaw favourites and Dylan's friend Michael J. Pollard, who shot to fame as C.W. Moss in *Bonnie & Clyde*, had portrayed him in 1972's *Dirty Little Billy*. It was Pollard, who while filming *Hannibal Brooks* in 1968, experienced difficulty when called upon to mow down some Nazis with a machine gun - an idea which repelled the pacifist in him, only to be urged by director Michael Winner "It's easy Michael, just imagine they're all Dylan-haters!"

On screen, *Billy the Kid* has held a fascination for film makers since the silent era; clean-cut cowboy Roy Rogers improbably pitched his stetson into the arena in 1939 and by 1966 there was even *Billy The Kid Meets Dracula!* The Kid is the second most filmed Western character, the 44 films made about him exceeded only by the 47 featuring Buffalo Bill. One of the most interesting expositions was the 1958 Gore Vidal-scripted *The Left Handed Gun*, which had Paul Newman as a psychologically unstable Billy, a role originally intended for Dylan's early hero James Dean.

Peckinpah selected Kris Kristofferson to play Billy only after Waylon Jennings had reputedly declined the role because "it showed Billy as a basically decent symbol of the West, while I found him to be something of a retarded, bloodthirsty juvenile delinquent!" Although he was still working as a janitor in CBS' Nashville studios when Dylan was cutting *Blonde On Blonde* there in 1966, Kristofferson had since proved his acting prowess – alongside Gene Hackman in 1972's *Cisco Pike* – and with a selection of best-selling Country albums to his credit, was also being touted as one of the "new Dylans" of the period. The gaunt James Coburn was selected as the avenging sheriff Pat Garrett, and the rest of the cast were drawn from the Western stalwarts Peckinpah had used to great effect in his earlier films – familiar faces such as Slim Pickens, Chill Wills, Jack Elam and Harry Dean Stanton.

Peckinpah intended *Pat Garrett* as a sweeping, stately testament to the old West, to friendship and betrayal, to entrenched values, the spirit of the new frontier and the inability of outlaws like Billy to compromise with the changing times. As Garrett, Coburn exemplified the spirit of change, bowing down to the "businessmen from Taos" who wished to hasten those changes. The film is the dark side of 1969's *Butch Cassidy & The Sundance Kid*, the most successful Western ever made. Peckinpah too had enjoyed commercial success in 1969, with the bloodily brilliant *The Wild Bunch* which also dealt with a gang's tragic inability to accept the inevitable changes, and while subsequent films such as *The Getaway* and *Straw Dogs* had also been successful, none had matched his majestic vision of the West. *Pat Garrett* was intended to exemplify that feeling once more.

Both Garrett and William Bonney were treated as myth-figures in the film, Peckinpah's image of Billy the Kid becomes clear early in the film, finding himself the only survivor of a Garrett ambush the Kid surrenders, his arms held out horizontally, a Christ-figure offering himself up for crucifixion. Peckinpah's protagonists are in the style of John Ford characters, and the film echoes with one of the last lines of Ford's 1962 classic *The Man*

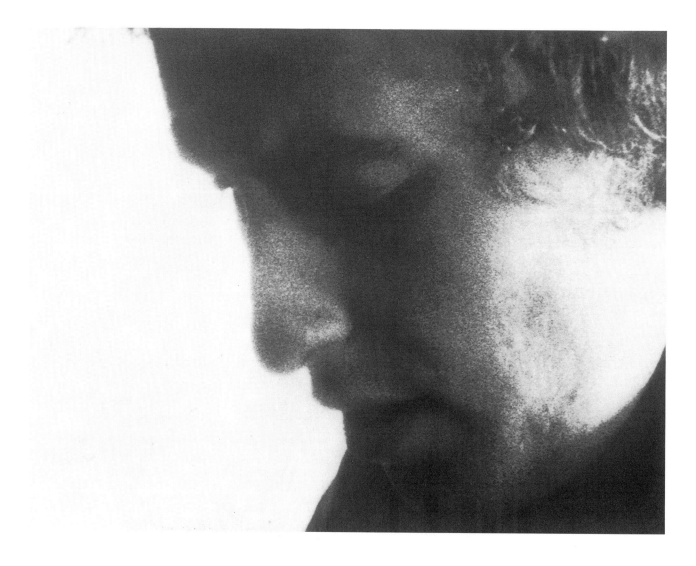

Who Shot Liberty Valance delivered by the cynical newspaper editor: "This is the West. When the legend becomes fact - print the legend!"

The director's final cut of the film ran close to four hours, intended as a sprawling epic along the lines of Sergio Leone's *Once Upon A Time In The West*. Unfortunately Peckinpah was too much of a maverick, and found himself, like his film's protagonist, fighting the businessmen and their desire to change and alter his vision. The Hollywood moguls butchered Peckinpah's film, with the chief culprit rumoured to be one Alfred Garcia and Peckinpah's next film after Pat Garrett was entitled *Bring Me The Head Of Alfredo Garcia!*

Among the miles of finished film which ended up on the cutting room floor were many which contained the genesis and development of Dylan's character - the aptly named 'Alias'. The filming had anyway been a very frustrating experience for Dylan, as with his work for Harry Belafonte a decade before, he couldn't comprehend Peckinpah's painstaking perfectionism on set, endless re-takes did little to foster good relations between the two men, although the finished soundtrack album was dedicated to the director.

Dylan's soundtrack album was the perfect accompaniment to Peckinpah's visuals. Even in its truncated form the film contained many memorable images and eloquently stated scenes, which Dylan's music ably enhanced. Indeed the scene in which Slim Pickens sits down to die by the riverside at dusk, while 'Knockin' On Heaven's Door' plays softly in the background remains one of the cinema's most perfect syntheses of music and image. Whilst writing a novel about Billy the Kid, Texan writer Roxy Gordon drove endlessly across Billy's terrain of eastern New Mexico between Clovis and Fort Sumner, using the Dylan soundtrack as a background, he later wrote of the album: "It was mournful and the past has always been . . . mournful for me. It's gone and I'm sorry it's gone - sorry I can't somehow keep it for real the way I've kept it in my mind . . . the feel is right - a dark, Catholic, Spanish kind of atmosphere - a sound as dark and lonely as the place".

As a soundtrack, Dylan's music for the film was near perfect; as his first album of original material in three years it was an anti-climax, although as with much of his work, time has leant it a patina it lacked on release. While the three versions of 'Billy' on the album are obviously similar, they are sufficiently different to be treated as separate songs; 'Billy 7' is particularly notable, the singer in weary, reflective voice, pondering the end of the old ways and taking us back to the there persona of early songs where he was cast as a rambler and a drifter. The song concludes in the same beautifully understated tone: "Maybe you will find yourself tomorrow . . . spending the time that you borrow/ figuring a way to get back home". For many however, the album's highlight was the haunting ballad 'Knockin' On Heaven's Door', which worked sufficiently well, even out of context, to give Dylan his biggest hit since 'Lay Lady Lay', which coincidentally had also been written for a film four years before. In that year's Oscars though, Dylan's contribution was totally overlooked, the 'Best Original Song' award going to Marvin Hamlisch for 'The Way We Were'.

The painstaking restoration of David Lean's 1962 *Lawrence Of Arabia* which was acclaimed on its release in 1989, started a vogue for Restored Movies. One which had been crying out to be restored from the cutting room floor was *Pat Garrett*. Its editor, later turned director, Roger Spottiswoode duly delivered a recut version, which was hailed on its cinema release. All that was actually new was a black and white prologue (reprised as an epilogue) showing Garrett's death, but in the process of re-editing from various prints, the familiar vocal version of 'Knockin' On Heaven's Door' was replaced in the 1989 film by a less striking instrumental.

His contract with CBS expired, Dylan was now free to switch labels, but not before some blood money was extracted by his old label. *Dylan* released in late 1973, was CBS' clumsy attempt at blackmail. Culled from studio warm-ups from his 1970 sessions, the album remains a landmark in a record company's misrepresentation of one of its leading artists. Dylan lethargically crooning through Elvis Presley standards such as 'Can't Help Falling In Love' and 'A Fool Such As I', along with the stilted version of 'Spanish Is The Loving Tongue' and a macabre cover of Joni Mitchell's 'Big Yellow Taxi', all managed to make the album quite the shoddiest ever package with Dylan's name on it.

It was not without irony that Dylan entitled the official souvenir of his 1974 tour with The Band *Before The Flood*; it was his first album for Asylum - Island in the UK - and he was anticipating a flood of tour bootlegs, and a further flood of CBS sanctioned cash-ins like Dylan. There did seem to be a vindictiveness to CBS' approach; this of course would have been the ideal time for a thoughtful, reasoned series of releases - including perhaps the complete 1966 Albert Hall concert and some of the material which eventually surfaced on *Biograph* over 10 years later - but instead was a heavy-handed hint that if Dylan persisted with his defection, then seriously flawed and sub-standard albums such as *Dylan* would flood the market. A journalist friend recalls being in New York at this time and dining with CBS executives who were hungry for the "new Dylan" now that the old one had so peremptorily upped and left. Springsteen was still too much of an unknown quantity back then, so the execs had singled out Kris Kristofferson, whose sales were encouraging, and were seriously considering a campaign to market him as being to the 70s what Dylan had been to the 60s. In the meantime they were quite willing to carry on pumping out albums like *Dylan* in the hope of pressurising Dylan back into the fold again.

Dylan though had other plans. *Planet Waves* was cut late in 1973 in a three-day burst with The Band and drew fulsome praise from critics who hailed it as Dylan's best album in five years. Robertson's edgy guitar recalls his work on *Blonde On Blonde* while the lyrical feel has Dylan looking back to his childhood, reflecting on the nature of love and commitment, and includes the hymnal 'Forever Young' as a legacy to his children. There is a cohesion to the album which much of his work since the bike crash had lacked. In the 70s, Dylan was no longer required to be the role model which the 60s had cast him. Nobody listened to him now as a leader, simply as a survivor - and one of the few genuine legends the rock world still had. Now Dylan was mirroring the concerns and anxieties of a fresh decade, the feelings of those who had survived the 60s and gone on to flourish: *Planet Waves* is an album of substance from the most eloquent of those survivors. "Back to the starting point . . " claimed Dylan in his vivid sleeve notes.

This was to be the beginning of a new era; with the increasing corporate chicanery of the record companies, many rock bands now felt that having their own record label was a virtual necessity if they were to regain the freedom of artistic control over their own work; it also gave them the opportunity to nurture new acts and express the independence which had been such a hallmark of the 60s. Both the Rolling Stones and Led Zeppelin had formed their own labels during the 70s, but neither had used them as anything much more than a clearing house for their own product. Dylan envisaged his 'Ashes & Sand' as a way of getting his own releases out quickly and directly to his fans, but also hoped to use the label as an umbrella for bringing to public attention meritorious acts he felt were worthy of wider attention. The first of which was to have been Groucho Marx lookalike Leon Redbone, the mysterious sandpaper-voiced singer who popularised forgotten songs of the 30s and 40s. But while *Planet Waves* attracted the sort of media attention that only a Dylan album could, Ashes & Sand was stillborn, although the name did appear on the video sleeve of *Don't Look Back* in 1988.

Planet Waves was rightly praised for the economies of its verse and playing. The album's two major songs, 'Dirge' and 'Wedding Song', proved that Dylan had lost none of his lyrical inventiveness, although a line like "in this age of fibreglass I'm searching for a gem" was clumsy. Dylan sang of "the naked truth" as the only purity, a quality which was being frequently overlooked as President Nixon lied his way into the Watergate morass and out of The White House. 'Wedding Song' is one of the most desperate love songs ever recorded, its intensity is frightening, while 'Never Say Goodbye' remains one of Dylan's most gloriously nostalgic songs with one of his warmest vocals on record. The consistency of the album, the interplay between Dylan and The Band and the "promise that it showed" were a glorious beginning to the year which saw Dylan right back in the public glare. After years of evasiveness and mystery, the lone balladeer would at last return to bind his spells, with myth and a band behind him, the future was bright ahead; eight years since their last tour together, Bob Dylan and The Band were back on the road again.

Backstage at Folk City October 1975

CHAPTER
11

Like a juggernaut, the Dylan/Bandwagon rolled across North America. Nixon had fallen, his successor Gerald Ford never did manage to stick around long enough to fart and chew gum simultaneously. The 1973 Yom Kippur war had resulted in the oil crisis, which presaged the austerity of the decade. The community of the 60s regrouped itself at tribal gatherings, rock festivals just got bigger and bigger: 1973's Watkins Glen with The Band, Grateful Dead and Allman Brothers had drawn 600,000 devotees, putting it in the record books as the biggest ever. Rock bands devastated America like barbarian hordes, destroying hotel rooms, holding court in ever larger stadia; they brought a BIG sound to rock 'n' roll, it didn't really matter who was onstage as long as you could be deafened by the PA and blinded by the light. It was The Event which mattered, the words were simply what was carried along by the electricity. Rock music, from being the reflector of the times, was no longer representative; it had become a get-rich-quick vehicle, growing ever more remote and hyperbolic – for all its glitter, it was fool's gold that was being mined.

The news that Dylan and The Band were hitting the road, seemed to give some focus to it all. Dylan's weren't just songs, they were anthems, and where better to hear anthems than with up to 20,000 fellow travellers? The news that in January 1974 Dylan was to undertake his first full tour in eight years was enough to make it THE Event. Promoter Bill Graham was inundated with ticket requests – among those in attendance were Warren Beatty, Cher, Paul Simon, Shirley MacLaine, Jack Nicholson, Yoko Ono, Joni Mitchell, Joan Baez, Ringo Starr, Carole King, Governor Jimmy Carter, along with about 600,000 others who were the lucky ones out of an estimated 5 million applicants. With a gross of around $5,000,000 it became the biggest rock tour to date; with 40 dates in 21 cities, it became the blueprint for much of what was to follow. Welcomed by deliriously happy fans and ecstatic critics, the tour was a triumph. However, looking back over 10 years later, Dylan expressed doubts: "We were cleaning up, but it was an emotionless trip". It didn't seem that way at the time though, here was a chance to see the legend – the man who turned

The Beatles onto marijuana! The man who had asked "how many roads". Mr Tambourine Man himself! This was history in the making.

From an 80-song repertoire, Dylan and The Band played a punishing three-hour set each night; dipping into his back catalogue the first song on the tour was the obscure 1963 'Hero Blues', long gone ago Dylan. There were other surprises too, 'Desolation Row' was played only once, appropriately in St Louis, the birthplace of T.S. Eliot. 'Just Like Tom Thumb's Blues', 'The Ballad Of Hollis Brown' and 'She Belongs To Me' were also disinterred and the prescience of Dylan's line from 'It's Alright Ma . . .' about the President of the United States standing naked elicited the tour's biggest cheers. Amidst all the old favourites, the battle cries, the folk-rock fusions, the seamless playing of The Band, came the unknown 'Except You' a dramatic solo reading of an exceptional song; so new there wasn't even room for it on his most recent album, nor his next album, nor the one after that . . . just another one of those uncollected treasures that litter the attic of Dylan's mind. At Dylan's end will lie his beginning, and middle, like the last scene of *Citizen Kane*, with the reporters sifting through the contents of Xanadu - the mansion piled high with the detritus of Kane's life - trying to piece together what made the man; I often think that Dylan's 'Xanadu' will be a warehouse lined with untold miles of unmarked tapes.

Like the frenetic years of the mid-60s, Dylan gave his usual elusive interviews, seeming amazed at the media interest, but feeling that the time was right for him to reclaim his territory. Twelve years into a career that threatened to take on astonishing new directions, the tour's official vinyl souvenir, the double *Before The Flood* was his first official live album. Part of the success of that 1974 tour was the simple, unalloyed pleasure of seeing Dylan back performing again, particularly in tandem with The Band: those most sympathetic accompanists to his music who had been there at the genesis and had shared in some of Dylan's finest moments.

Unfortunately the album didn't quite live up to its promise. There was a speedy necessity in Dylan's delivery of his best known songs, a pugilistic approach, shouting the lyrics as if to ensure that everyone in the vast arenas could hear them. The aggressive delivery, though arresting, robbed the songs of any nuance or subtlety, a predictable result of stadium rock. He was barking the words into the microphone, snapping at the songs like an irritated terrier, but there was little of the sense of discovery that there would be in future journeys. It was as if it were enough for Dylan simply to be there, singing his songs; the actual delivery was almost immaterial. By and large, the people who flocked along to the 1974 shows were too young to have booed eight years before and there was a willingness to accept whatever Dylan had on offer; that should have been a change for the better, but the music seemed to suffer from the absence of antagonism, tending to rely on former glories instead of punching ahead to new ones. But it was enough, Dylan was back, and the omens were that he was far from finished.

He didn't of course need to do any of this, while financially he had never enjoyed the cumulative success of Paul Simon or Paul McCartney, his songs were still very much in the marketplace, and healthy royalty statements alone would ensure a comfortable income for life. Dylan though had sensed an emptiness in the state of rock, a sprawling behemoth had replaced the lean, supple animal of promise. It was surely more than a sense of "foolish duty" which made him want to undertake the 1974 tour, and while the financial aspects were of course an incentive, others had been floated before him previously and been refused; perhaps it was as much as anything a question of timing. Sensing that he needn't be a spokesman for anybody but himself now, that the pressures had been alleviated; Dylan finally felt free to pursue a vision, a career, a life of his own.

The 1974 tour was a watershed, behind him lay the years of silence and neglect which had hitherto constituted the 70s, but with The Band in tow he had vanquished some ghosts, raised just enough hackles - rumours were circulating that all profits from the tour were going to militant Jewish organisations - and evened things out. The tour had been a triumph, but on his terms: now people were sharing his idea of what music could be about, unlike 1966 when they had been so disparate. In the immediate future lay obscure outlines which would involve the blood-letting catharsis of his most acclaimed album of the decade and collecting together a bunch of gipsy minstrels to go looking for America.

Throughout his career Dylan had made foolish moves, frequently, flagrantly and in public. Often though he had been so far ahead of the rest of the flock that he lapped them; he seemed to have an unerring instinct at gauging what was right, and equally important,

when it was right. He was an endlessly fascinating figure during the mid-70s, when as so often happened during his career, there simply wasn't anyone to touch him.

The singer-songwriter vogue which had enjoyed enormous acclaim during the early 70s, had shot its bolt when it was discovered that its purveyors didn't have the answers either: if anything they seemed even more confused than their audience! To his credit though, Neil Young went his wayward way, refusing to conform to his audience's expectations. Bruce Springsteen was beginning, with his third album *Born To Run* in 1975, to find an authentic voice, although he admitted in 1987: " . . . when I went into the studio to make *Born To Run* I wanted to make a record with words like Bob Dylan that sounded like Phil Spector but . . . I wanted to sing like Roy Orbison". Ironically the Dylan's fellow Traveling Wilbury Orbison had turned down Dylan's demo of 'Don't Look Twice, It's Alright' in 1963. David Bowie was going through the ch-ch-changes which would characterize his whole career and the solo careers of individual Beatles had been largely anti-climactic. There was a vacuum, and once again - as in 1963 - it looked like Bob Dylan was set to fill it. Rock music has, by and large, a short memory. Idols are swiftly sacrificed on the altar of success, when the public tires of them and moves off in search of newer, cheaper, quicker thrills. For substance, there is an occasional glance back over the shoulder, but venerated figures, the old contemptibles, are expected to keep pace, "you're only as good as your last album" is the music biz truism.

With *Planet Waves* Dylan was back, the success of his tour had seen him fêted, and once again in plain sight, his next move was keenly anticipated. In the same way that newspapers had their Kremlin Watchers on call for every subtle change and nuance in the Politburo, the music press had their Dylan Watchers to keep the inscrutable singer-songwriter under constant scrutiny as he approached his mid-30s. If Dylan didn't grant interviews, then they interviewed his garbologist or his childhood friends, they were trained to detect any slight change of direction, any switch of allegiance, to be first with the news about what Dylan was going to do next. Omens to his future were to be found in his past, album covers were pored over for clues - was that really The Beatles upside down in the tree on *John Wesley Harding*? Why had he worn the same old brown jacket on four consecutive covers? The rumour-factories worked 24-hour shifts, lyrics were sifted for consistency, finding none, that very inconsistency had to prove something! With Dylan, face value meant naught, confusion was all.

Such media speculation was only fuelled by their

On the road again with the Band January 1974

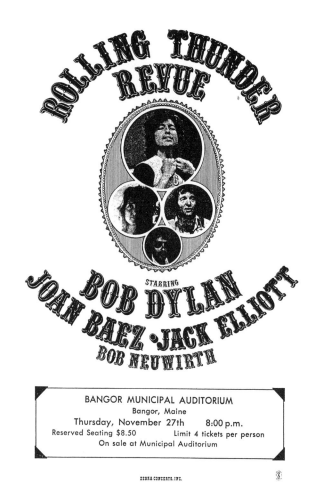

ROLLING THUNDER
REVUE

STARRING
BOB DYLAN
JOAN BAEZ · JACK ELLIOTT
BOB NEUWIRTH

BANGOR MUNICIPAL AUDITORIUM
Bangor, Maine
Thursday, November 27th   8:00 p.m.
Reserved Seating $8.50   Limit 4 tickets per person
On sale at Municipal Auditorium

ZEBRA CONCERTS, INC.

Rolling Thunder Revue handbill 1975

subject's innate reluctance to talk, although if you were lucky enough to talk to Dylan in the mid-70s, the answers were reasonably comprehensible. But while there was little of the role-playing or surrealistic put-ons, Dylan was always guarded in his responses, for like Peter Sellers, Dylan could be anyone to everyone, it was only as himself he found difficulties in communicating.

Dylan's legacy was apparent as the 70s progressed: "If you seek his monument – look around you". Mott The Hoople had plundered the handbook of Dylan vocal intonations and imagery, singer-songwriters toted their guitars and bared their souls. New bands like Starry Eyed & Laughing and Judas Priest had even named themselves after Dylan songs, while genuine up and coming talents like Tom Waits adopted Dylan's style and verbal dexterity although they borrowed little else.

Acolytes and contemporaries freely acknowledged Dylan's swingeing influence, Jackson Browne admitted: "I didn't take notice of anything until Bob Dylan". Little Feat's Lowell George remembers meeting Dylan during 1978 and commenting on the quality of Browne's work, the next time he saw him, Dylan's room was strewn with Jackson Browne albums. Paul Simon admitted that Dylan "made it possible for a whole group of lyricists to come onto the scene. I just think we wouldn't be there if it wasn't for Dylan". Leonard Cohen in the 70s called Dylan "the only genius of rock"; Pete Townshend: "Dylan's triumph, I suppose, was to demonstrate that you didn't have to stick to a song structure". Van Morrison simply said: "Dylan is the greatest living poet", while John Fogerty in 1986 was eulogistic: "Did the idealism of the 60s have any impact? Hey, we got rid of Nixon and the war's over! If you really want to hang it on one guy, you could say that Bob Dylan ended the war and got Nixon kicked out. Bob Dylan turned a lot of heads by writing politically . . . He certainly turned John Lennon's head. He turned my head". Appropriately it was Fogerty who came up with rock's best evocation of Watergate in his lines "The light at the end of the tunnel/Was nothin' but a burglar's torch". Joe Strummer spoke to me in 1988 about his 'conversion' in 1970: "I don't think anyone's touched him lyrically, or the sound of those classic albums, they floored me".

Everywhere during the early 70s, the freedom of expression in rock music was largely due to Dylan: the Californian bonhomie of The Eagles, the Rimbaudesque bacchanals of 'punk' poetess Patti Smith, the Outlaw Country of Waylon & Willie, the wilful obscurity and image manipulation of David Bowie, the masterly pop punnery of Ian Dury, the *Blonde On Blonde* sounding worldwide smash of Cockney Rebel's 'Make Me Smile', the *Another Side Of . . .* feeling on Leo Sayer's 'Long Tall Glasses'. Olivia Newton-John's singalong 'If Not For You' and Bryan Ferry's mannered but engaging 'A Hard Rain's A-Gonna Fall' kept the royalties coming in and even Lindisfarne's Geordie good-time folk-rock was overseen by longtime Dylan producer Bob Johnston.

Just a random sift through any record collection displays Dylan's influence – the Bee Gees' first single, 1967's 'New York Mining Disaster 1941' owed a strong structural debt to 'Ballad Of A Thin Man' two years before; Steely Dan's debut album in 1973, *Can't Buy A Thrill* took its title from a line on 'It Takes A Lot To Laugh, It Takes A Train To Cry'. Lyrically, Jimi Hendrix's third single of 1967, 'The Wind Cries Mary' sounded like it had been soaked in circa '65 Dylan, with lines like: "A broom is drearily sweeping, up the broken pieces of yesterday's life. Somewhere a Queen is weeping; somewhere a King has no wife". While the Rolling Stones most lascivious single, 1969's 'Honky Tonk Women' relished Dylanesque wordplay when Jagger sang: "she blew my nose and then she blew my mind". You simply could not have imagined David Bowie writing a song with a title like 'Unwashed And

Somewhat Slightly Dazed' without Dylan having written 'Just Like Tom Thumb's Blues', or Warren Zevon calling a song of his 'Accidentally Like A Martyr' without Dylan having proved you can be 'Temporary Like Achilles'.

By that time, Dylan's influence was more than just a barometer of pop taste or a clearing house for cover versions, a world without Dylan would have meant no *Astral Weeks* or *Forever Changes*, no *Ziggy Stardust* or *Never Mind The Bollocks . . .*, no *My Aim Is True* or *The Joshua Tree* - just rock mutants, "creatures void of form".

The myth was given fibre and substance with the release in January 1975 of *Blood On The Tracks*, hailed by many as not only Dylan's finest album of the 70s, but one of his greatest ever. The recording of such a pivotal album was extraordinarily chaotic, emphasising once more Dylan's impatience with the actual process of recording. The original sessions in New York, featuring Eric Weissberg's Deliverance - named after the John Boorman film to which he contributed the music, including the hit single 'Duelling Banjos' - were scrapped, and a scratch band put together in Minneapolis immediately after Christmas 1974 to re-record five songs.

In shorthand, the Dylan of the 60s spoke out, while the 70s' model worked from the outside in. A popular poet's greatness lies in the public's response to his work; while the circumstances of composition may be hazy and the actual meaning confused, the words must strike a responsive chord in the audience. But it's an audience which is inconsistent, sometimes coming to his work years after the writer has delivered it; a song which for him is a diary entry from times long gone, may on paper lie desiccated. On record however, the timbre of the singer's voice developing with the years and the music evoking an atmosphere, combine to breathe life into the words. Dylan's vocal style is one of rock's most idiosyncratic and malleable from the uncomfortable dustbowl balladry of the early albums and the tentative rock outings, to the full blooded dark mystery of 1966, the pedal steel plaintiveness of the C&W years and the swaggering 'go for it' abandon of *Planet Waves*.

Such is Dylan's position in pop that he looms over rock music from 1963 onwards, every fledgling singer-songwriter and many more besides, owe him a debt. During the past quarter of a century therefore, new converts have constantly been coming fresh to Dylan's work. While there are those who recall the plaintive, questioning of 'Blowin' In The Wind' or the electric maelstrom of 'Like A Rolling Stone' with clarity as that first moment when they heard Dylan; there are others who have come only recently to the songs which have been a part of the fabric of rock music for 20 years and more. Many new converts were not even born in the

60s and come to Dylan only when they read of their latest idol citing Dylan as an influence.

Dylan's notorious reluctance to slave over a song in the studio has ensured that most of the finished songs are early takes and he never relied on fashionable technology, endless overdubs or lengthy remixes, so the albums themselves retain all their freshness. For novitiates there is the joy of tracing back the thread or more haphazardly picking out albums; of realising the extraordinary richness that awaits them. Whatever has drawn them to Dylan, there is a challenge posed by his songs, which though passed down the years like a baton leave themselves open to reinterpretation by each ensuing generation.

The songs remain constant, the audience expands or dwindles, but each new generation brings to them their own ideas and search for explanations. The convenient way for Dylan to avoid fresh interpretation of his songs, to avoid the questions being asked, is to retire from the public eye, but he refuses to accede to the easy way out and is still to be found out there, failing in public one moment, gloriously succeeding the next. Always inconsistent: that's the Dylan dichotomy!

The internal angst of much of *Blood On The Tracks* struck a responsive chord at the time. Whinging self-pity has little place in art, but reasoned examination of personal failure and defeat is another thing entirely. Songs about redemption and salvation were here in abundance; that Dylan felt able to commit them to record is a key to his eternal popularity. In the face of enough negative criticism to lay low the most dedicated professional, he stood bloody but unbowed. 'Shelter From The Storm' has all the hallmarks of a Luis Bunuel film, the futility of purpose, the villagers gambling for clothes and bargaining for salvation, waiting for a Godot who turns up! The strength of the album lay in songs such as 'Shelter From The Storm', 'Tangled Up In Blue' and 'Simple Twist Of Fate'; they are among Dylan's most pliable and rewarding songs and would continue to be performed for much of the next decade in many and various guises.

'Lily, Rosemary & The Jack Of Hearts' is a good example of just why Dylan still mattered in the mid-70s; he was a whole pack of cards himself, he'd been the King and the Joker, he'd held the dead man's hand of aces backed with eights, he'd been dealt winning hands and thrown them away and at other times he had managed to bluff his way through with nothing at all in his hand. The song was full of western stereotypes (the drunken hanging judge, the hooker with a heart of gold, the town's big shot) and had a driving story tinged with mystery: I remember the first time I heard it, I was convinced the second line spoke of "a Dylan in the wall", which seemed somehow appropriate.

92

Such was the richness of the song's narrative, that Dylan approached scriptwriter John Kaye (who later wrote the 1980 film of Hunter S. Thompson's chaotic *Where The Buffalo Roam*) to turn the nine-minute song into a feature film. Kaye duly delivered a script, but as with so many other Dylan projects, it has since lain dormant.

Buoyed by the triumphant reception of his last two albums and the success of his tour with The Band, Dylan was refired, reborn, and the period 1974-78 was amongst the most prolific and rewarding of his career. Yet again, Dylan threw away the rule book and by redefining what a star of his magnitude could achieve, reinforced his position as the genre's most influential figure. Recognising the stagnation of the scene, Dylan had blitzed with The Band in 1974 and asked his new audience "How does it feel?" By the summer of 1975 there was another question to be asked: "Is it rolling, Bob?"

Ten years before, in his determination to bring the Vietnam war to a conclusive end, President Lyndon Johnson had inaugurated the saturation bombing of North Vietnam, reasoning that constant bombing by the American fleet would bring the North Vietnamese to their knees, begging for mercy. The campaign was christened 'Operation Rolling Thunder'. By 1975, with the Vietnam war concluded only two years before, the name came to Dylan in a dream and with it a determination to let the thunder roll as America geared itself for its Bicentennial celebrations. To Larry Sloman, Dylan spoke of a period of reflection in Corsica which presaged the Rolling Thunder Review: "I was just sitting in a field overlooking some vineyards . . . and that's when it flashed on me that I was gonna go back to America and get serious and do what it is that I do, because by that time people didn't know what it was that I did. All kinds of people, most people don't know what I do, only the people that see our show know what it is that I do, the rest of the people just have to imagine it".

Rolling Thunder required a powerful imagination of those not privy to its power. Open-mouthed, those unfortunates in Europe read in the music press of the maverick carnival that was cutting a swathe through North America towards the end of 1975. Dylan back on the road after barely a year away; Dylan and Baez sharing the same microphone, Bruce Springsteen bopping with the blues backstage, picking up passengers like Joni Mitchell, Ringo Starr, Mick Ronson and Roger McGuinn. And here was the crunch: Rolling Thunder wasn't going for the big stadia, ploughing the same furrow as the other giants, Dylan was taking rock back to its roots, he was back in the liberation business.

The 1975 leg of the tour was one of rock's most audacious steps. The guerilla minstrels prowling round America, poised to strike, left the establishment powerless, because as the terrorists they had to make the first move. This at the time when rock was Big Business, Peter Grant's heavy-handed tactics with American promoters had seen Led Zeppelin enshrined not simply as the biggest rock band on the planet, but setting new financial horizons which would become industry standards. By 1975 they were smashing box office records which The Beatles had been expected to hold inviolate. To book Zeppelin, promoters had to accept a meagre 10% instead of their customary 50% of the gross. 10% of a Zeppelin gross though was still enough to keep most promoters in the ball park, including Jerry Weintraub, then handling Elvis' Messianic concert tours and later to look after Dylan. Peter Grant met Dylan at a party to mark the conclusion of the Rolling Stones' 1972 tour: "Hello I'm Peter Grant, I manage Led Zeppelin", to which Dylan retorted: "Hey man, I don't come to you with my problems!"

The Rolling Thunder Review was to press the pause button on all that madness. Sneaking up unannounced, the review would hit town like a circus and pitch its tent in local halls, with precious few details of the concert emerging prior to showtime. The clandestine nature of the operation and the deliberately low profile press was a direct antithesis to the 1974 tour, and few of the fans who were lucky enough to witness the 1975 shows could believe that it was actually Bob Dylan up there, with his "Bob Dylan mask on", singing all the songs which had been passed down to them as almost sacred texts: 'Hard Rain', 'Times They Are A-Changin'', 'Hattie Carroll', 'It Ain't Me Babe' and dozens more over the sprawling three-hour shows. For someone reckoned to be the most elusive character in rock music, Bob Dylan was proving astonishingly accessible.

The thunder had begun rolling long before the review's official opening at the War Memorial Auditorium in Plymouth, Massachusetts in October 1975. Dylan was ubiquitous around Greenwich Village during that summer, sifting through the furnace of 1975 for the embers of 1962, catching gigs by Phil Ochs and Ramblin' Jack Elliott, checking out Patti Smith and Television's Tom Verlaine, fusing the old to the new. Mott The Hoople's Ian Hunter recalled to Pete Frame how he saw Dylan perform songs from what became the *Desire* album in the Village during the summer of 1975: "He was singing 'Joey' laughing and winking all the way through it - as if it was the most preposterous satire imaginable. His tongue was almost bursting through his cheek!" Dylan was playing in a restaurant next to the Other End as part of his plan to check out talent in the Village to enrol in the band for the review. One of the recruits was David Bowie's erstwhile guitarist Mick Ronson, no big Dylan fan at the time according to Hunter who was working with the guitarist: "He reckoned Dylan couldn't sing . . . he wasn't into the Greenwich Village vibe at all . . . until I took him down there and he realised that things were happening".

Bobbing up at a Folk City birthday party for owner Mike Porco, at various clubs around the Village, at a San Francisco charity concert with Neil Young, with childhood buddy Lou Kemp on board, Dylan was raring to go. Half-formed ideas filled his head, of a film, of shows quite unlike any the country had seen, but over-riding it all was the desire to get the fires burning again. It was a time of change, the colourless Gerald Ford was soon to be deposed by former Georgia governor Jimmy Carter, who had met with Dylan during the 1974 tour, and was later to quote some of Dylan's lyrics from 'Song To Woody' in his 1976 inaugural address. Carter was to offer a Democratic hiatus in the uninterrupted Republican presidencies of Nixon, Ford, Reagan and Bush. His was to be a low-key Presidency, his idealism tempered by the exigencies of political life; but for all his näiveté, Carter did take a strong stand on human rights and introduced a strong welfare programme at home. But it was to be another Carter that attracted Dylan's attention and gave the Rolling Thunder Review its focus.

Rubin 'Hurricane' Carter had been imprisoned for murder in 1966. For years he had eloquently attested his innocence and his plight moved Dylan, who saw in Hurricane another victim with whom he could identify. His 'Hurricane' single was direct and confrontational, in it the judge and jury who had convicted Carter, were accused of racism and the song mounted an impassioned

With Sara and Joan Baez in Renaldo and Clara 1975

indictment of the judicial system unmatched since 'Hattie Carroll'. The boxer's shadow hung over the review, and gave it one of its most memorable moments, The Night of the Hurricane at New York's Madison Square Garden in December 1975.

Whether it was the new and vital fusing of his past with his present, the identification with Hurricane Carter, or whether the anonymity of the Review had freed him from the worst aspects of being 'Bob Dylan'; whatever the reason, Dylan sang with an impassioned eloquence during those early shows, savagely plundering his back catalogue for inspired and dramatic readings of some of his best known works, as well as delighting in the urgency of the new songs from *Desire*. He seemed to have found a sense of time and place in the community which constituted Rolling Thunder.

For Dylan it was an opportunity to relocate his past and pay homage to some of the ghosts which had haunted him as a youth; and how appropriate to be searching out for America in the months leading up to the orgy of patriotism which would surround the Bicentennial in July 1976. In November 1975, in tandem with Allen Ginsberg, Dylan made a pilgrimage to Jack Kerouac's grave in Lowell, Massachusetts. Impassive behind shades, Dylan stood over the small plaque, pondering on the tragedies of that talented, temperamental writer's life. The most loquacious of 'The Beat' writers and the one who best captured that amphetamine frenzy of life 'On The Road', Kerouac however lived the experiences vicariously: it was the turbulent and troubled Neal Cassady who went out and did it, Kerouac who had the gift to capture it on paper. But by the end of his short 47 years, he had become a sad, shambling figure, living in tense proximity with his mother in their Lowell house. Towards the end of his life, Kerouac spotted a young girl reading a copy of his best known book on a beach and shambled up to introduce himself: but the girl just thought he was some incoherent old drunk and the police came and took him away. The writer who gave freedom of expression to a generation lay, in peace at last, observed by his spiritual descendant. Dylan had survived his own trials and tribulations, had escaped the demons which had dogged him, and during his country's birthday, found himself "reborn and then mysteriously saved".

The search for freedom embodied by Rolling Thunder produced two books: Larry Sloman's compelling account and Sam Shepard's pretentious tome; one tragically misconstructed album - *Hard Rain* was a dismal souvenir of the wealth of material and possibilities offered by the tour - and one film *Renaldo & Clara* which captured some of the chaos and confusion which had been so productive. But while the concert footage was among the finest ever shot, the pretentious sub-Bergman confrontations were at best tiresome and better left to Woody Allen and at worst revealed a self-indulgent side of Dylan which until then he had kept firmly under control.

The truncated two-hour version rightly concentrated on the music, but the four hour version was simply an embarrassment, giving Dylan critics more welcome ammunition. While the star/director/producer/writer was right in saying that movie audiences had got lazy by the late 70s, dutifully shuffling into a series of undemanding box office smashes which would have been truly empty vessels without their lavish special effects, budgets, Dylan's alternative wallpaper movie hardly offered any real salvation.

It began promisingly with symbolism enough for the most ardent Dylanologist: a masked figure takes to the microphone singing 'When I Paint My Masterpiece', implying . . . well, pretty much anything really. This was Dylan saying you ain't seen nothing yet, this was a Bob Dylan saying this isn't the Bob Dylan, truth hides behind the mask; ambiguities abounded - but really none were worth exploring.

As with many rock films in which self-indulgence runs amok (Neil Young's *Journey Through The Past*, McCartney's *Broad Street*, Prince's *Cherry Moon*), a disciplined director and scriptwriter could have given the sprawling morass a shape, the form it so desperately needed.

What was so frustrating about *Renaldo* was that it shirked so many possibilities. Here was Dylan, undeniably one of rock's most charismatic performers, tapping a rich musical vein and showing social purpose he hadn't even attempted in a decade; on the road with a motley crew of musicians, poets and painters, reaching out for audiences which had lain undisturbed for much of the 70s. On the eve of the Bicentennial, with a country eager for change, Dylan was pounding through sets which brimmed with commitment and urgency, ready and willing to journey back to a past he had all but disowned. The possibilities for a first-rate documentary in the hands of D.A. Pennebaker, or an impressionistic piece from, say Robert Altman, were enormous; instead, the only sad souvenirs of the revitalised Dylan during the Rolling Thunder period are the rarely played *Hard Rain* and the widely avoided *Renaldo & Clara*.

To the sympathetic Jonathan Cott, Dylan said the film was "about . . . naked alienation of the inner self. . . integrity . . . the fact that you have to be faithful to your subconscious, unconscious, superconscious". It's also "about" Bob Dylan clumsily trying to confront his own myth, through a four-hour farrago of half-truths, illusions, pretentious confrontations, rampant self-indulgence and philosophy going off at half-cock. As a myth-shattering vehicle, *Renaldo & Clara* is a cinematic

Self Portrait - at least *Tarantula* had a few jokes!

A chance meeting with Roger McGuinn's occasional songwriting partner Jacques Levy, provided another strand to be added to the fibre of the Rolling Thunder era. The two meshed to such an extent that neither can recall precisely who wrote what on *Desire*. Dylan certainly had the bones of 'Isis' and 'Romance In Durango', but during a burst at Levy's Village apartment and a further collaboration at a rented house in East Hampton, the back of *Desire* was broken. Levy remains the most sympathetic and consistent collaborator, they fitted together like fingers in a glove, but true to form, Dylan never again worked with Levy.

Still Dylan fanned the fires. A frantic rush in a New York studio produced *Desire*, which would become his best-selling album. Some of the freneticism of Rolling Thunder was captured and there were echoes of many Dylans on the finished album: the Tex-Mex influences picked up while filming *Pat Garrett*, the stark confessionals of *Another Side Of . . .*, the freewheeling fantasies of *Highway 61*, all tied to a richer instrumentation and Dylan's voice playing off against the exemplary female backing singers. There was a breezy Dylan on 'Mozambique' (the colony had celebrated its independence from Portugal in July 1975), the pensive and brooding 'One More Cup Of Coffee', an outlaw blues seething with passion while 'Black Diamond Bay' crackles with Dylan's eye for detail, only to be upturned by the concluding verse which reveals it is only an item on the TV news, and the narrator had no plans to go there anyway! The album bookends are 'Hurricane' Dylan's impassioned plea for the release of Rubin Carter (who was eventually freed in 1985, and currently lives in Canada) and 'Sara' on which Dylan pleads with his wife not to leave.

There is a richness and density to the album which had Dylan hitting three great albums in a row (there was also the bonus of *The Basement Tapes* made officially available in mid '75). He was hitting his stride as he hadn't done since 1965/66 and there was no sign of the fervour abating. The second leg of Rolling Thunder snaked through America during April and May 1976 and produced the TV concert *Hard Rain*, notable for a wondrous Dylan/Baez duet on Woody Guthrie's poignant 'Deportees'. Rolling Thunder II had the outlaws looking more menacing than before, swaggering under bandanas, confident enough that this land was their land that they dispensed with the song as a climactic anthem, finishing usually with Paul Clayton's 'Gotta Travel On' - implying there was still plenty of territory to be covered.

In November 1976, helping The Band bring it all home again in San Francisco - when their glittering

Last Waltz wrapped up 16 years on the road – Dylan stole the thunder from the galaxy of stars in attendance and provided the film of the event with its highlight. The official departure of The Band seemed to mark the end of something which had begun a chaotic decade before, now Dylan had the flexibility to work with all manner of diverse musicians and was facing hosannas with every outing. But although the hostility had gone, the restlessness was still apparent.

Three years of virtually uninterrupted touring and recording meant it was time to take a break and 1977 was a year of unusually low profile for Dylan. Much of the year was spent editing the endless miles of *Renaldo & Clara* footage ready for the film's official release in January 1978 and despite the desperate pleas contained on recent albums, his wife of 12 years filed for divorce during 1977.

For Dylan it was a year spent largely in absentia, but his prolificity had only been matched by the diversity and quality of the music and performances he had produced of late, and even diehard fans now allowed him time off for good behaviour.

The triumphs were, of course, tempered with criticism. The second leg of Rolling Thunder smacked of money-making opportunism, while Dylan's virtual deification of gangster Joey Gallo left a sour taste. For all the inherent quality of his recent work, there had been a feeling that some of the songwriting was Dylan By Rote, recycling familiar images and characters with little enthusiasm – 'Meet Me In The Morning' and 'Isis' strike me as lacklustre for example. Occasional weaknesses, though, were overlooked in the welter of striking new material.

With the increasing availability of new technology and the sheer number of shows between 1974 and 1976, came a wealth of Dylan bootleg material to saturate the market and console the fans. Dylan was back at the peak of his profession. Due to a complex legal battle, Bruce Springsteen – the only possible pretender – had been unable to go into the studio to follow up his triumphant *Born To Run*, and Dylan had proved again that he was more than capable of meeting every other challenge hurled his way.

He was really the only one. Other giants of the period were coasting on former glories, their very remoteness at odds with Dylan's eagerness to see the face of his audience. The underground had been painlessly absorbed into the mainstream, with mega-bands like the Stones, Led Zeppelin (who in 1975 had steamrollered through 'In My Time Of Dyin'', claiming the song as their own!), Genesis, Pink Floyd, Yes, and stars like Rod Stewart and Elton John growing increasingly remote and rich. There didn't seem to be any alternative to the bloated pomposity of rock music

by the beginning of 1977, while Dylan took a break. But during 1976, the first generation to have grown up away from the shadow of the 60s were finding frenzied voice, and what they had to say didn't make for comfortable listening to anyone over 30.

From the Hard Rain television special filmed at Fort Collins Colorado, May 23rd 1976

From the photographic sessions for the sleeve of the 1976 album Desire

BOB DYLAN IN D.A. PENNEBAKER'S CLASSIC

DON'T LOOK BACK

X3 POSTERS 01-739-5352

d for the film's reissue in 1984.

4. Filming Hearts Of Fire, Hamilton, Ontario, October 1986.

5. Rotterdam, 4 June 1984.

HYPNOTIST
COLLECTORS

JEAN-LOUIS DREAU
ROBERT SCHLOCKOFF

DONT L
A Film and Boo

DYLAN

Bob Dylan

Damer i regn

Spellbinding

Bob Dylan

Le risposte nel vento in formato poste

KNOCKIN' ON
DYLAN'S
DOOR by the authors of
ROLLING STONE
magazine

BOB DYLAN
APPROXIMATELY

A Midrash

A Portrait of the Jewish Poet
in Search of God

STEPHEN PICKERING · Chofetz Chaim Ben-Avraham

NEW MUSIC
MAGAZINE

Bob Dylan
compleet
Alle songteksten

Folk-Rock: The Bob Dylan Story
50¢
The first! The one and only
by Sy and Barbara Ribakove
DYLAN
The explosive new film starring Bob Dylan, Fiona, and Rupert Everett
Hearts
Fire
A beautiful singer... the two men who love her... the seduction of fame
LARRY MILNE
A novel based on the screenplay by Scott Richardson and Joe Eszterhas
Song and Dance Man
The Art of Bob Dylan
by Michael Gray
A ROLLING STONE BOOK
editora brasiliense
MIT FÚJ A SZÉL
BLOWIN' IN THE WIND
Tempo ritrovato
Feltrinelli
ROBERT SHELTON
VITA E MUSICA DI
BOB DYLAN
Rowohlt
CONCLUSIONS ON THE WALL
NEW ESSAYS ON BOB DYLAN
EDITED BY ELIZABETH M THOMSON
$2.95
MORROW PAPERBACK EDITIONS
Bob Dylan
A RETROSPECTIVE
Edited by Craig McGregor
12.98
bob dylan
by
daniel kramer
BOB DYLAN

7. Making the video for 'Emotionally Yours', 22 August, 1985.

8. Making the video for 'Emotionally Yours', 22 August, 1985.

9. USA tour, 1978.

Spalding
BOB DYLAN
BOB DYLAN & THE BAND
HALL 1966
Real Cuts At Last
& Jelly Roll
BOB DYLAN
DYLAN
OUTFIDELS
FRIENDS
Dylan
Boy

11. With Roger McGuinn, Wembley Arena, 16 October 1987.

12. With Joan Baez, Hamburg, 31 May 1984.

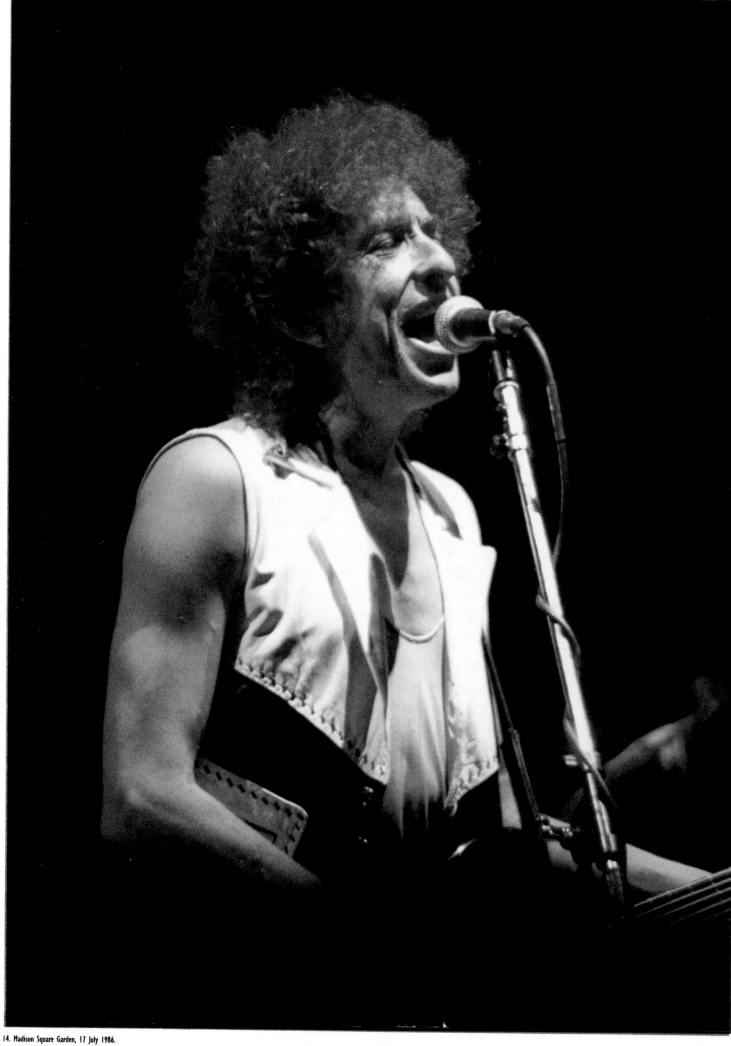

14. Madison Square Garden, 17 July 1986.

15. Making the video for 'Emotionally Yours', 22 August, 1985.

16. With Mick Taylor, Brussels, 7 June 1984.

17. Woodstock, June 1966.

19. With Keith Richard, Live Aid, Philadelphia, 13 July 1985.

20. With Robbie Robertson and Levon Helm of the Band, January 1974.

21. Copenhagen, 10 June 1984.

22. Hamburg, 31 May 1984.

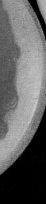

24. Dublin, 3 June 1989.

S. Hartford, Connecticut, 11 July 1986.

26. San Francisco, 18 November 1980.

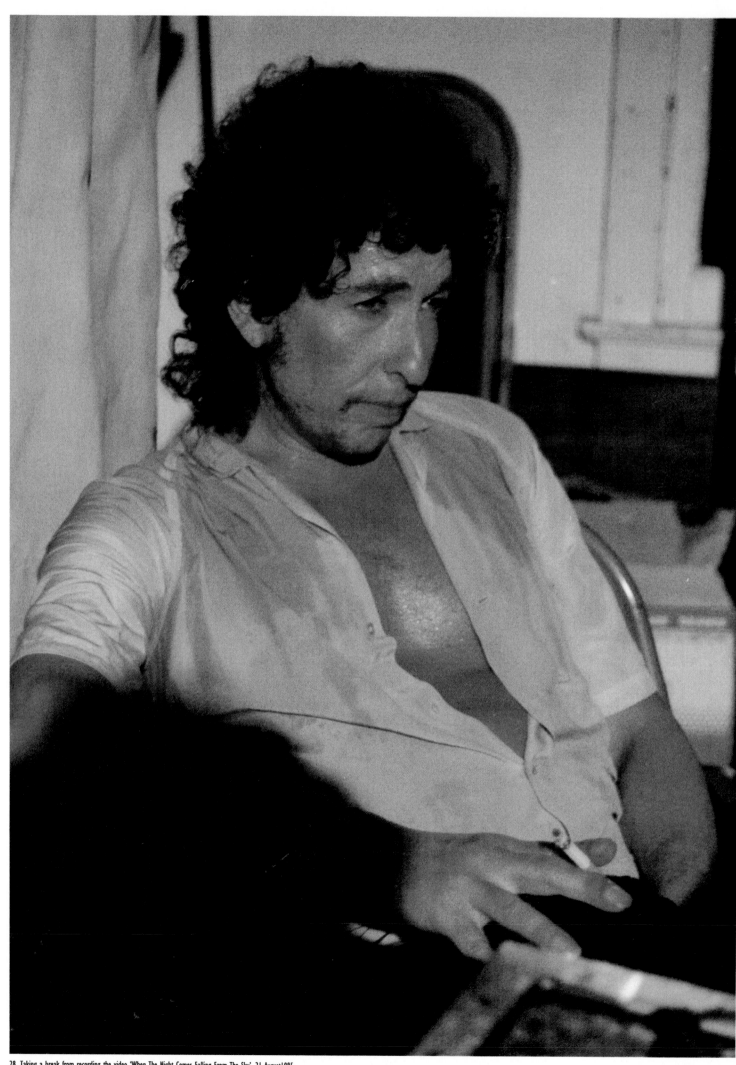

28. Taking a break from recording the video 'When The Night Comes Falling From The Sky', 21 August 1985.

29. With Kenny Aaronson, Santa Barbara, California, 7 August 1988.

30. Boyhood home, 2425 East 7th St.,Hibbing, Minnisota.

31. Rome, 20 June 1989.

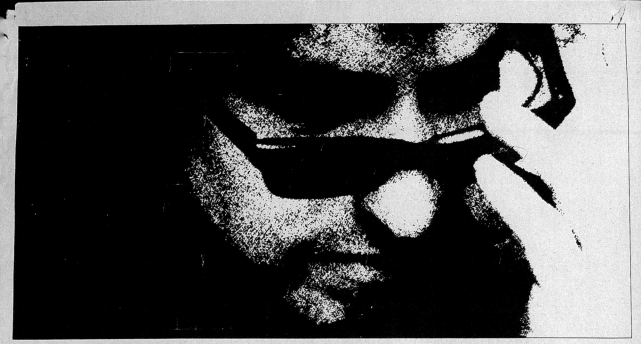

Desire   86003

Street Legal   86067

Blood On The Tracks   69097

Budokan   2 record set 96004

Bringing It All Back Home   62515

Greatest Hits   62847

Another Side   32034

More Greatest Hits   2 record set 67239

Bob Dylan   32001

Blonde On Blonde   2 record set 66012

DYLAN

34. With Dave Stewart during the making of 'Emotionally Yours', 22 August 1985.

THE TELEGRAPH
SPRING 1986

THE TELEGRAPH
WINTER 1986

TELEGRAPH 22
SUMMER 1985

THE TELEGRAPH
SUMMER 1986

THE TELEGRAPH
AUTUMN/WINTER 1986 25

THE TELEGRAPH

THE TELEGRAPH
SUMMER 1987

36. Mannheim, Germany, 18 July 1981.

37. Basel, Switzerland, 2 June 1984.

BOB DYLAN

CHAPTER
12

"We decided to start our own group because we were bored with everything we heard. In 1974 there was nothing to listen to anymore. Everything was tenth-generation Led Zeppelin, tenth-generation Elton John, or overproduced, or just junk. Everything was long jams, long guitar solos. We missed music like it used to be before it got 'progressive'. We missed hearing songs that were short and exciting and . . . good! We wanted to bring the energy back to rock & roll."

Joey Ramone.

"We're the flowers in the dustbin. We're the poison in your human machine We're the future, your future."

The Sex Pistols.

While punk took its first faltering steps in New York with The Ramones' debut at CBGBs in August 1974, the Molotov Cocktail of the movement exploded in England. The impact of the Sex Pistols was seismographic, not since The Beatles had any one group inspired so many others. Within weeks of the Pistols' first dates in late 1975 and early 1976, literally hundreds of bands were inspired by this Go-For-It brand of rock 'n' roll, the very antithesis of the remoteness practised by the established rock elite. The bulk of the punks paid lip service to no one; the only acknowledged influences were, if pushed, Iggy Pop and the Stooges or The New York Dolls. With the revisionism which so characterises any new movement in rock, anything beforehand was blown away.

Life of course isn't that simple: Graham Parker & The Rumour tipped their hat to Van Morrison and the '66 model Dylan, Ian Dury's Blockheads combined music hall razzmatazz with the acutest English rock writing since Ray Davies. But the very business of Punk was destruction, therefore anything which smacked of the 60s was vetoed, songs were snarled through in three minutes, direct imagery was employed in the lyrics, audiences no longer needed to look up to the bands who were now filling the stages of pubs and clubs around the country, punk was taking rock back to its roots. The bands were the same age as their

audience, the 'message' was simply that anyone could do it, the songs spoke of contemporary issues, "the sound of the Westway", not waves from Topographic Oceans. Why worship anyone just because he can play the guitar for 25 uninterrupted minutes? Why bother spending aeons, like the Moody Blues, in search of the lost chord? Just master three simple chords and the world was yours for as long as you wanted!

The punks seemed wholly uninterested in what had gone before. "No more Beatles, Stones or Elvis in 1977" snarled The Clash on '1977', but significantly Dylan's name was missing from the litany. Prior to his emergence as the New Wave's most durable and articulate songwriter, Elvis Costello was playing round the folk clubs as D.P. Costello and 'Knockin' On Heaven's Door' was never far from his repertoire. As he hit his stride in 1978, Costello's work recalled Dylan at his best: the linguistic gymnastics, the acute eye for a telling image, the wordplay and creative control over his own destiny bore close comparison to Dylan a decade before. Of the new bands of the time, Dire Straits were among the older sounding, and Mark Knopfler's vocal styling owed a debt in equal parts to J.J. Cale and Bob Dylan. Tom Robinson made a point of including 'I Shall Be Released' in his sets, altering the lyrics to deal with the case of George Ince - indeed it was Robinson's championing of the song which led to its adoption by Amnesty International as their official anthem. The most important British post-Punk movement came with Jerry Dammers' 2-Tone label and it was The Specials, who after the election of Margaret Thatcher in 1979, spotted the new relevance of 1965's 'Maggie's Farm' and made it a British Top 5 hit in 1980 .

In one of the earliest Punk retrospectives, the *NME*'s 1978 supplement 'The Book Of Modern Music' wrote: "Dylan remains a mysterious and compelling figure and one of the few artists to enter rock 'n' roll middle age with any semblance of dignity". At a time when venerated figures of the 60s were being constantly reviled, this was high praise indeed.

With Elvis dead and buried, John Lennon and Paul Simon in the middle of their five-year isolations and the Stones courting the lucrative disco market, with

On stage in Göteborg, Sweden, July 11 1978

Elton John's engaging brand of rock becoming more and more like pantomime and other venerated figures ducking below the parapets to shelter from the Punk onslaught, there were few rock icons left to court the contempt of the New Wave. But true to form, Dylan chose 1978 as the year to undertake his most comprehensive world tour to date, which saw his position as rock's most important figure go unchallenged.

In his largest permanent band to date, Dylan boasted saxophonist Steve Douglas, one of rock's most acclaimed 'back room boys' who had worked regularly on Phil Spector's epic wall of sound records in the 60s. The cherubic violinist David Mansfield was there, along with Rob Stoner and Steven Soles he was one of the few survivors from the Rolling Thunder era and went on to form the under-rated Alpha Band with T-Bone Burnett. Bob Marley's enthusiasm for Dylan's work was repaid by a shuffling reggae re-arrangement of 'Heaven's Door' and a call and response back-up trio, which recalled Marley's own I-Threes.

It was Dylan's most ambitious and comprehensive tour to date. It was the first time that audiences outside North America had been able to see him in over a decade, and the reviews from Japan, Australia and Europe were adulatory. Perhaps made complacent by acquaintance with the 1974 tour with The Band and the Rolling Thunder Review, the American notices ranged from restrained to hostile. American critics felt the fact that Dylan had rehearsed a 29- song show which aimed for a comprehensive overview of his 16-year career smacked of 'Selling Out'. Bob Dylan "treasuring" an Elvis Presley recording of 'Tomorrow Is A Long Time' was one thing, but Dylan emulating The Vegas Elvis in a spangled jumpsuit was quite another. Las Vegas after all was the hollow tooth in the mouth of the American Dream.

The shows were Dylan's first mainland British dates in 12 years and the anticipation could not have been keener. After encouraging reports from the Far East leg of the tour early in 1978, the first of the six sold out shows at Earl's Court was the highlight of the musical year. Britain had missed out on the '74 tour, had not witnessed Rolling Thunder, and heard only tantalising rumours of Bruce Springsteen's four-hour shows, and was ready for Dylan to come and reclaim his crown. As the shadowy figures took to the stage that first night on June 15th the excitement was tangible; for many, myself included, this was the first opportunity to witness Dylan in the distant flesh. The wiry halo of hair was a giveaway, but it proved to be Mansfield, then Dylan took the mike and that familiar nasal voice echoed across the cavernous hall, and the past came to reclaim the future.

That first night held a series of frustrations. As it was the first time, I wanted the live versions to duplicate the records I had lived with all those years; it was only on my second visit that I appreciated how much work Dylan had put into re-arranging his songs. The easy option, of course, would have been a quick canter through the Greatest Hits catalogue, but Dylan had chosen to face up to the present and reinvent those songs in a style more relevant to the late 70s.

It was almost enough just to be in the same room as him, each spoken word from the stage was received reverentially in the hall – I remember when Dylan dedicated 'To Ramona' "To Ramona, who's here tonight", and thousands of heads twitched trying to pinpoint the elusive heroine of 14 years before. "I've waited my whole adult life for this moment" said a friend as the band swung into 'Like A Rolling Stone', and for many, those nights were an opportunity to reflect on what had gone before, but also to contemplate a future in which Bob Dylan still played a positive role. The veiled threat that Dylan had gone Vegas simply failed to materialise.

The release of *Street Legal* immediately prior to the London shows was further cause for jubilation. Here was a Dylan back in full control, the enigmatic excursions through 'Changing Of The Guards' and 'Senor', the powerful wordplay of 'No Time To Think' and 'Where Are You Tonight?', the throaty blues of 'New Pony' and the almost hit single 'Baby Stop Crying'. The album's back sleeve baffled British fans, who couldn't understand what the bug-eyed comedian

With Ginsberg in Renaldo and Clara 1975

Marty Feldman had to do with Bob Dylan until they learned later that – in the best tradition of American entertainers – it was not the comedian at all, but Dylan's accountant! The triumph of those British shows which culminated in July's mammoth Blackbushe festival, lay not so much in seeing Bob Dylan back performing with a zeal and commitment none of his contemporaries could match, as in the fact that he was patently not a 60s' relic relying on former glories but was keen to meet the expectations of a new audience eager to familiarise itself with his work.

It was Dylan's willingness to confront his own past which helped make those 1978 shows so memorable. The way that he would reinvent familiar old songs, altering the perspective on 'Simple Twist Of Fate' and stripping down the otherwise throwaway 'I Want You' to transform it into a stark, brooding plea. He acknowledged Hendrix's seething, apocalyptic reworking of 'All Along The Watchtower' in his own concert reading and took 'One More Cup Of Coffee' from its Mexican origins to treat it as a smouldering slab of gris-gris. 'Love Minus Zero' became as fresh as a *Street Legal* song and he seemed genuinely curious when he asked "How does it feel?" to his audience during that tour. It was the rare and encouraging sight of a performer taking risks when none were really needed, or given his known intransigence, expected.

It was that restlessness which was so encouraging, there was little on the album to imply contentment or sustained happiness; it is one of life's cruel clichés that only out of turmoil does great art arise, and certainly the emotional turbulence of Dylan's own life during the 70s was matched by a commensurate quality in his work. There was always an edgy unwillingness to stand still in Bob Dylan, that reluctance has long been part of his infuriating ability as an artist. Many may wish he had stayed in the crazy capering vacuum of 1965/66, but a large part of Dylan's appeal is the sheer frustration which is an inseparable part of it. How could anyone who had written songs as good as 'Abandoned Love' or 'Up To Me' or 'Except You' choose not to include them on his next albums? That is what makes Dylan such a 'collectable' artist on bootleg. His unwillingness to stay in any one place helped foster the myth, his uncanny ability to stay one foot ahead of the pack was another ingredient in the mythologizing of the man – wherever rock went, Dylan's calling card could usually be found!

Bracing himself for his third decade as a performer in the public eye, there was much to look back on with satisfaction, but again part of Dylan's appeal was his refusal to look back, which always gave fans hope for the future. Even as rock was undergoing its most fundamental alteration since The Beatles, there was still

room for Bob Dylan.

The 1978 shows were not only a triumphant return, they were affirmation of a fiery genius which had refused to be tamed. As the Sex Pistols and The Clash marched with daemonic energy and irreverence towards their no future, their safety pins and chains clanking in disharmony, they gave rock 'n' roll a relevance: an infusion curiously matched by a revitalised Bob Dylan. Much as they were at odds, the two marched strangely in unison, but as the 70s drew to a close, their paths would soon, dramatically separate.

The second gospel tour November 1980

CHAPTER
13

For the 60s' generation, who had come to believe that the power of rock 'n' roll could change things, the 70s came as a bitter disappointment. Those they had elected via record sales didn't have the answers, and the real world tightened its grip. The 70s saw Nixon's White House come to resemble Hitler's bunker as paranoia and deceit took hold. The Indian Summer of Jimmy Carter's Presidency was replaced by the diehard conservatism of Ronald Reagan, who won a sweeping victory over Carter in 1979, the same year which in Britain saw the Iron Lady win her first general election. The transatlantic alliance was now in the hands of two of the most extreme conservative politicians of the post-war era. The era summed up by Robert Lowell in his poem 'Day by Day': "If we see light at the end of the tunnel/It's the light of the oncoming train!"

Dylan's role during the 70s had largely been as an observer not an activist and mercifully the 'Dylan As Leader' crew had dwindled. The strength of his vision was not impaired, but the balance offered by maturity had put an end to his finger-pointing days. The real protestors of the decade were all the young punks, who like Dylan a decade before had few answers to offer, just questions which needed asking. The more articulate of the punks saw the dualities of the time and recognised the inherent injustices of Thatcherism and Reaganomics, but such was the innate conservatism of the period that most people were more concerned about getting jobs than the morality of the "sing while you slave" system.

Tom Robinson and Elvis Costello sang against the incipient neo-fascism of the late 70s, The Clash rocked against racism and railed against class. Their sentiments and rage were heartfelt and contemporary, their voices were couched in the language of Bob Dylan. The times they had a-changed and to his credit Dylan had changed with them. But while being spokesman for a generation had been a full-time job, playing godfather to the next one wasn't nearly so time consuming and allowed Dylan plenty of time for new and interesting hobbies.

For Dylan, if a thing was worth doing, it was worth doing in public. "An artist is never off the record" he told Bob Shelton. And so it came to pass that even his most ardent fans were baffled by the release in 1979 of *Slow Train Coming*. It was the year of Elvis Costello's *Armed Forces* and The Clash's *London Calling* and Dylan's album lay uneasily alongside these demonstrations of punk's maturation. The Specials' early releases indicated the positive aspects of 2-Tone the same year, while Dylan's inexorably slow train only displayed its dogmatism.

Coming from someone who had taught tolerance and iconoclasm at degree level and whose constant message was change and the vital necessity of independent thought, Dylan's 'Born Again' period of the late 70s stands as by far the most bewildering of his career. Until then, however mercurial he seemed, there had been a thread running through the changes, but his devotional zeal of 1979-81 was greeted with incredulity by his fans. Dylan had always eschewed the eternal isolation of the recording studio as a sanctuary to hone and perfect his material: even on vinyl he preferred spontaneity. He refused to let his songs own him and was quite happy to develop or regress in full public view. "If it doesn't come naturally, leave it" sang Al Stewart once, and that was how Dylan viewed songwriting. By and large he had carried his audience with him throughout the decade, but for many the parting of the ways came with the release of his first album of "Inspirational" music.

The images of Christ betrayed by Judas' kiss, hanging on the cross at Golgotha and rising after the third day have obsessed writers and artists down through the centuries and religion and religious imagery had played a substantial role in Dylan's writing from the very beginning. Early songs such as 'Long Ago, Far Away' dwelt on the crucifixion, 'Quit Your Low Down Ways' evinced an early agnosticism, which was dwelt on in more detail at the conclusion of 'With God On Our Side' and the rich imagery of 'When The Ship Comes In' drew heavily on the Old Testament. 'Lay Down Your Weary Tune' was positively hymnal, while 'Gates Of Eden' dwelt in the territory of Cain and Abel, and the fourth verse of 'It's Alright Ma' dealt scathingly with the increased commercialism of organised religion.

Biblical characters were frequent travellers on

With Joan Baez at Peace Sunday, June 6 1982

Highway 61, but then so was everyone from Jack the Ripper to Ezra Pound! The years of *The Basement Tapes* had seen the contemplative 'Sign On The Cross', while *John Wesley Harding* which Dylan called "the first Biblical rock album", was steeped in the language of the Old Testament, the 'other' John Wesley being the founder of Methodism. 'The Ballad Of Frankie Lee & Judas Priest' dealt with the duality of Dylan's belief back then, "The big house, bright as any sun", could just as easily be a brothel or a church, 'Eternity' can easily be mistaken for 'Paradise' and it was only with God's help that the drifter was freed from his absurd, Kafkaesque trial. *New Morning* contained the tongue in cheek 'Three Angels' and the hymnal 'Father Of Night'; *Planet Waves* was populated with angels, martyrs and the devotional 'Forever Young'.

In 1974, Dylan spoke of being relieved of his crown of thorns and sighting the "lone soldier on the cross", while 'Up To Me' from that time spoke of the complexity of the Sermon on the Mount. On 'Oh Sister', Dylan purposefully speaks of a higher spirit, while the dichotomy the man felt was apparent in hindsight on the last two verses of 'Where Are You Tonight'? By 1976, in his engaging interview with *TV Guide*'s Neil Hickey, Dylan was speaking of God in Blakeian terms "I can see God in a daisy. I can see God at night in the wind and rain. I see creation just about everywhere. The highest form of song is prayer. King David's, Solomon's, the wailing of a coyote, the rumble of the earth. It must be wonderful to be God!"

The successes, both critical and commercial, of his work during 1978 should have brought Bob Dylan a sense of satisfaction and tranquillity, but there was a restless, surging spirit loose, which was only reconciled by Dylan's attendance at Bible study classes and the tangibility of Christ in his life. The swiftness and zealousness of Dylan's conversion left his fans bereft and his detractors hooting with laughter. The general mood of disbelief that year was nearer to Ian Dury singing that "The hope that springs eternal, springs right up your behind" than Bob Dylan's proselytizing! It was the intolerance displayed in *Slow Train*'s lyrics which was so uncomfortable and incomprehensible. Throughout Dylan's previous work there had always been a choice. He was the man whose thought-provoking lyrics urged tolerance, sympathy and compassion, who had singlehandedly freed pop music from its shackles: to be lectured by Bob Dylan was an incongruous and disquieting experience.

The view from Dylan's pulpit had the world divided into those who were devoutly behind the teachings of Christ and those who opposed them. "You either got faith or you got unbelief, and there ain't no neutral ground" was how Dylan summarised the situation. This from the man who had become renowned for his appreciation of the manifold shades of grey, the man who first identified the "lies that life is black and white". The feelings of betrayal were compounded when his first 'Born Again' shows, in California in November 1979, rejected all the previous, secular material, to concentrate solely on material from the *Slow Train* album and new songs from his forthcoming religious album.

It was precisely because Gospel can be one of popular music's most invigorating and uplifting styles that Dylan's conversion was so disheartening; his performances at those shows and the material which constituted the *Slow Train* and *Saved* albums was desultory and dispirited. If this was the Born Again Bob Dylan, then God help us all! Dylan was eager to renounce all that had gone before, anything tainted by commercialism and disbelief was anathema to him. He was returning to the sackcloth and ashes prophesying purgatory with no time off for good behaviour and no good times, now was the time to renounce all your sins and the time was now!

It was not that his fans doubted Dylan's sincerity or his desire to be saved, but at the time the Moral Majority and the Christian Right were in the ascendant in America, and the very thought of Bob Dylan allying himself to a movement which substantially helped to elect Ronald Reagan and breathed hellfire and damnation on those who did not share their beliefs was too much to take on board. There was also the natural reluctance his audience felt at being force fed a diet of Dylan's religious beliefs, which allowed no room for doubt or questions.

That he managed to make Gospel sound so joyless was his failing, he could have carried his audience with him – rock audiences have thrilled to the uplifting gospel of The Jessy Dixon Singers and the Mighty Clouds of Joy; even Bob Marley's devout Rastafarianism became accessible because the music was so elevating, a New Testament delight in the resurrection and the power of good which Christ harnessed. Dylan's gospel was strictly Old Testament, dour and damning.

Dylan's was a masochistic baptism; by purging himself of the sins of the flesh, he felt that his soul was washed clean, such purgatory wasn't meant to be comfortable. Anyone else would have checked in to some spiritual Betty Ford Clinic, to emerge reborn, but Dylan had an urgent need to convey his spiritual rebirth. It had been a bare eight months which saw him transformed from a born-again rock idol to Born Again Christian. The singer's single-minded sense of purpose may have been redeeming for himself; for his public it was chillingly alienating.

The antagonism he aroused was as Bob Shelton wrote, a result of "mistaking his role of misunderstood combatant for past similar roles in which he was simply running too far ahead of the consciousness of his audiences". Many sympathised with Dylan's personal revelation, but were concerned by his identification with a stern and unforgiving Deity, rather than the God of love and forgiveness.

The actual musicianship and production of *Slow Train Coming* ranked it as Dylan's best sounding album to date. Veterans Jerry Wexler and Barry Beckett gave the album a gloss which helped compensate for the startling lyrics. Wexler and Beckett had been working with Dire Straits on their breakthrough second album *Communique* in 1979, which helped foster the relationship between Dylan and long-time fan Mark Knopfler, and he and Straits' drummer Pick Withers were enlisted for the sessions. "I was hugely influenced by him about the age of 14 or 15" Knopfler told *Guitar Player*, "going round to girls' houses, drinking 75 cups of coffee, smoking 90 cigarettes and listening to *Blonde On Blonde* 120 times!".

Knopfler was exuberant at the prospect of working with his hero; to John Swenson in 1983 Knopfler said of Dylan: "He had such a hard time, being deified. He knew what he was, and it wasn't God. He's just a very spiritual, poetic . . . gentleman". This was a view shared by Eric Clapton who confirmed to Roger Gibbons: "I always saw Bob as religious. Always a deeply religious, moral, humanitarian type of person" adding "I think the born-again thing was blown out of all proportion. Bob goes through changes. Sometimes he's a heavy drinker, sometimes dry. Sometimes he's into dope, then not. He can disappear with a car-load of Mexicans. No phase is the final one".

The finished album did undoubtedly have its musical merits, 'Precious Angel' rolls along with a determination and sense of time and place, 'Slow Train' burns with a quiet fire while 'When He Returns' is imbued with a fervour and simple devotion which is touching. 'I Believe In You' benefits from a chord structure based on 'Smoke Gets In Your Eyes', but the sermonising hectoring of 'Gotta Serve Somebody', 'Gonna Change My Way Of Thinking', 'When You Gonna Wake Up?' and 'Do Right To Me Baby' is trying, and Dylan's spiritual 'Dr Dolittle' on 'Man Gave Names To All The Animals' is just plain embarrassing.

If Dylan's slow train picked up few passengers, *Saved* had them cashing in their tickets and fleeing the station in droves. From its ragged cover through to the dour delivery of the songs, it antagonised people in a way no Dylan album had done since *Self Portrait*. I remember the album on sale at the 1980 Dylan convention in Manchester, boasting a sticker along the lines of "Warning. Do not buy this album unless you own every other Bob Dylan album!" It was an uncomfortable album to listen to, with only the gritty 'Pressing On' and the serene 'In The Garden' displaying any balance between the spiritual and artistic. Dylan came across as a fire and brimstone Elmer Gantry, with the fires of hell as his final destination, and he sounded like he was looking forward to the trip!

Saved was when even Dylan diehards drifted off to pastures new. It was the man's attitude as much as anything which alienated supporters, he breathed intolerance, railed against his audiences about the borrowed time they were living on, hounding against the temptations of the flesh and the illusory nature of temporal life.

What made this period doubly difficult was Dylan's wholehearted embracing of the very letter of the Bible, which saw homophobic rants from the man who had breathed tolerance with his every breath. It was a revivalist meeting, but with little joy coming across the footlights. During those early Born Again shows, Dylan further antagonised his audiences by refusing emphatically to play any songs from before his spiritual reawakening. It was all very dry and humourless, for so many years Dylan had denied his role as a leader, yet here he was now preaching from the pulpit. He did at least recognise the dilemma when he addressed the crowd in Nebraska in January 1980: "Years ago they used to say I was a prophet. I'd say 'No, I'm not a prophet'. They'd say 'Yes, you are a prophet'. Now I come out and say 'Jesus is the answer'. They say 'Bob Dylan? He's no prophet!' They just can't handle that!"

With a pastor as a regular member of the road crew, a blithe dismissal of everything that had gone before and the only olive branch offered being to take Jesus into your life, the period 1979-81 was a difficult one for admirers. Only the year before Dylan had been offering a choice between "Lincoln County Road and Armageddon", but by the end of the decade, there was no choice. Greil Marcus resented Dylan's use of religious imagery: "not to discover and shape a vision of what's at stake in the world, but to sell a pre-packed doctrine he's received from someone else".

Steve Turner, in his highly readable account of rock's search for redemption *Hungry For Heaven*, wrote of Dylan's Born Again experience: "His conversion . . . was uncomfortable for most because initially he forsook the symbolism, although not the subject-matter, of his earlier songs and laid it on the line in unembroidered challenges . . . It was understandable why he did it. He'd been converted, he had something to say and he had an audience. He was overtaken by the new truths before they'd had time to sink from his head to his heart and work their way into his life and actions".

On receipt of his first ever Grammy, for his vocal on 'Gotta Serve Somebody', Dylan told the Grammy crowd that his Born Again lyrics were an integral part of his music now, removing them "would be like separating the eyes from the nose, the foot from the ear". Leonard Cohen may well have had Dylan, and the conflicts he was facing, in mind when he sang in 1988 " . . . everybody knows that you're in trouble. Everybody knows what you've been through, from the bloody cross on top of Calvary to the beach at Malibu".

The third album of the Born Again period, 1981's *Shot Of Love* effected the reconciliation between the art and the belief, most notably on 'In The Summertime'

On stage in Toulouse, 21st June 1981

and 'Every Grain Of Sand', two of the finest songs Dylan has ever created. The album marked a return to roots, the producer on the title track was none other than 'Bumps' Blackwell - long-time producer of Sam Cooke and Little Richard - and with that collaboration, the rock 'n' roller from Hibbing came halfway to realising his graduation ambition "to join Little Richard". He later said of Blackwell: "even though he only produced one song, I gotta say that of all the producers I ever used, he was the best, the most knowledgeable and he had the best instincts . . . " While the finished album was the most rewarding since *Street Legal*, it could have been a monster: the magnificent 'Caribbean Wind' - a driving, relentless, seething vision, conjuring up the Titanic's fateful voyage and the hellhounds which haunted Robert Johnson, while the singer himself stands on the abyss - was recorded at the same sessions, as was the pounding 'Groom's Still Waiting At The Altar', which recalled the swaggering organ-dominated *Blonde On Blonde*-era Dylan. Despite the baffling exclusion of these two sterling songs, the finished album was a substantial achievement.

With 'Summertime' and 'Sand', Dylan returned to an awesome contemplation of the world that God had created, which he had so successfully used on 'Lay Down Your Weary Tune'. 'In The Summertime' is a beautifully benign, reflective piece, driving to a higher gear in the second verse, as Dylan sings "We cut through iron and we cut through mud/Then came the warning that was before the flood", the determination of the pilgrim on his journey through the Slough of Despond to the serenity of eternity and redemption. It is the humility of 'Every Grain Of Sand' which makes it such an uplifting song, humility was not an emotion one had come to associate with Bob Dylan, but here, through its six stately verses, the writer has come to accept his place in the scheme of things, taking his key from William Blake's 'Auguries Of Innocence' ("To see a world in a grain of sand . . . "), his humble appreciation is spellbindingly conveyed in one of Dylan's most affecting vocals. The songs also benefited from two of the composer's most lilting and beguiling melodies.

With a zealous desire to bear witness, Dylan toured with a large band that reflected his current state of mind. The six London shows at Earl's Court in June 1981 could not avoid being compared to the triumphant shows at the same venue only three turbulent years before, but more immediate comparisons were made with Bruce Springsteen, who had just finished a spectacular run of shows at Wembley Arena. These were Springsteen's first British dates since the disastrous 1975 tour and British fans who had for years been frustrated by the rumours of his action-packed

Stockholm, 8 July 1981

spectaculars elsewhere in the world weren't disappointed. Springsteen poured everything into those six shows, and even his harshest critics came away concurring with the widely held view that he was now rock's premier live performer.

In contrast, Dylan's shows were largely lacklustre. Despite some energetic readings of songs from his Born Again trilogy and flawless solo versions of old favourites (even dipping back over 20 years for the traditional 'Barbara Allen') there was still little enough to delight in. Dylan's performances were arbitrary and defiant: Take me as I am or let me go, seemed to be the message, with the old songs thrown in as a sop. Even on his new religious material Dylan lacked fervour and fire, which made their relentless repetition very disheartening. Dylan evidently had experienced something which profoundly altered his life and was understandably keen to relay it to his audience, but the music with which he reflected that experience was curiously uninvolving and unmoving.

Dylan's tribute to Lenny Bruce which he performed regularly on that tour, was somehow superficially trite and yet sincerely moving. Back in June 1964, Dylan had signed a letter to the authorities protesting about the continued police harassment of Lenny Bruce, not

Paris, 1 July 1984

surprisingly it had little effect and Bruce's friend and admirer Phil Spector felt that the comedian's death in 1966 was the result of "an overdose of police".

The 80s were not kind to Bob Dylan. With the evidence that his diehard Born Again period was waning, Dylan withdrew and took stock. His record sales were disappointing, but then Dylan's impact and influence have never been equated to sales: Whitney Houston's 1984 debut album shifted 14 million copies alone, while Michael Jackson's *Thriller* has sold more copies than all of Bob Dylan's albums put together, and then some.

Here was someone whose influence stretched way beyond the facile Top 40 but who had never gone on to enjoy the commercial success of many of his contemporaries. When the Stones started touring during the early 80s, the T-shirt sales from their LA show alone, amounted to over $1 milion. But Dylan's commercial zenith had come long ago during 1965/66 when songs such as 'Like A Rolling Stone', 'I Want You' and 'Rainy Day Women' were substantial hits, since then it was strictly one-offs like 'Lay Lady Lay' and 'Knockin' On Heaven's Door' which had brought Dylan into the charts. On their initial release, his albums were still swiftly sought by the devout, but they soon dipped down the charts.

The myth though lived on despite the music. His influence had been so all pervasive that he was still revered; but the widespread feeling was that his best work was long since gone. With rich irony, those who had plundered the Dylan style soared past him. As a composer, Dylan need never worry, constant royalties flood in as each succeeding generation finds something of substance in his songs; their timelessness ensuring constant covers such as the 1980 TV-promoted *It Ain't Me Babe* which had Bryan Ferry, The Tremeloes, Jimi Hendrix, Johnny Cash and half a dozen others' hit versions of Dylan songs. The infinitely superior double 1989 collection *The Songs Of Bob Dylan* collected together rare covers from Sam Cooke, Carl Perkins, Elvis Presley and Judy Collins.

Bob Dylan cover versions would make a book in themselves, ranging from actor Sebastian Cabot's extraordinary ham readings of familiar Dylan compositions, including 'Who Killed Davy Moore' through to Marlene Dietrich's 1965 'Blowin' In The Wind' which was credited to Dylan/Bradtke. Thatcher's 1979 electoral victory, inspired new versions of 'Maggie's Farm' from the Blues Band and The Specials. With Them, Van Morrison cut a gutsy 'It's All Over Now, Baby Blue', the Alpha Band weighed in with a breezy 'You Angel You' and Rod Stewart, Fairport Convention and Jimi Hendrix have recorded small but perfectly formed canons of Dylan songs. Indeed, the very act of covering a Dylan song was in itself a statement, whether overtly commercial - such as Olivia Newton-John or Eric Clapton's singalong 'Knockin' On Heaven's Door' - or hoping that by being seen as pinching a Dylan song, some of his lustre would lend itself to inferior artistes.

The general consensus though, was that as he blew past 40 in May 1981, the man himself had shot his artistic bolt. Having taken rock by the throat and shaken it, Bob Dylan was now hanging grimly onto its coat-tails. The status quo had been swiftly re-established despite all that Punk had threatened, and the 2-Tone movement had been little more than a flash in the pan; The immediate post-Punk legacy was a reaction against its deliberate ugliness and howls of despair. Enter the New Romantics, lightly tripping and boasting a new brand of Thatcherite, escapist, innately conservative pop. The rock hierarchy re-asserted itself: the 80s saw Bowie back with a vengeance on his 1983 Serious Moonlight tour, the Stones were offering periodic hints that this could be their last tour, so if you wanna see the legends in action, you'd better get there quick, while Genesis inexplicably became bigger than ever and Bruce Springsteen took a short detour en route to becoming the man at the top to produce his 1982 acoustic album *Nebraska*.

Springsteen was proving himself to be Dylan in reverse: although John Hammond had originally envisaged him as a singer-songwriter in the Dylan mould, Bruce was a died- in-the-wool rocker, but with *Nebraska* he caused a similar sort of furore as Dylan had when he "plugged in" nearly 20 years before. With pop's detours down the dead end streets of style and fashion, by the mid-80s only Elvis Costello showed the dogged determination which had characterised Dylan's haphazard odyssey during the 60s.

Costello never stayed in one place long enough to be pinned down, following his most assured album *Trust* with the C&W *Almost Blue*, recording and performing with such legends as George Jones and Tony Bennett, touring with masochistic regularity and scouring every imaginable source for material. Songs poured from him in a torrent, some recalling the vindictiveness of 'Positively 4th Street', many endlessly questioning the status quo, others just contemporary classics - 1982's 'Shipbuilding' for example, gave us the refrain which would come to symbolise the Thatcher years: "diving for dear life when we should be diving for pearls". Costello's ear for epigrammatic copulets recalled Dylan at his peak, as a composer he revelled in puns and stretching metaphors until they snapped.

While in 80s' argot, anticipation of new Dylan 'product' was muted, an appreciation and respectful cognizance of his role remained, and halfway through the selfish 80s, there came a general nostalgia for the colouful 60s, and all its rich symbols. Rumours were soon growing thick on the grapevine that the next Dylan album was to be the "return to form" which every decade produced, he'd done it before, he could do it again. Such was Dylan's unpredictability that any album could quite conceivably herald a return to form.

He himself has always maintained that he could make *Blonde On Blonde* tomorrow and no one would appreciate it.

When it became known that Mark Knopfler was in charge of overseeing the comeback – after Frank Zappa and Giorgio Moroder had been discarded – it aroused more than a *frisson* of interest. Dire Straits had started their inexorable spiral of success at the beginning of the

Wembley Stadium, 7 July 1984

decade, and 1982's *Love Over Gold* saw them established as one of the world's biggest draws. Coincidentally it was an album which contained more than a tip of the hat towards Dylan's influence, 'It Never Rains' reprised the organ-grinder from 'I Want You', while Knopfler's lyrics suggested a healthy diet of mid-60s' Dylan. In January 1983, Dylan approached Knopfler to produce his next album, and the two spent a month in the studio slaving over what eventually became *Infidels*, although originally Dylan had ruefully entitled it, *Surviving In A Ruthless World*. The only predictable thing about Dylan was his unpredictability, and true to form this new, much touted album was largely a disappointment.

Knopfler is known as a sympathetic producer (witness his later work with Aztec Camera and Willy DeVille), and as a Dylan fan of long-standing it was a dream come true, but - as is sadly too often the case with Dylan's work - much of what constituted the very best from the sessions was left off the finished album. Most notably absent was the magnificent lament 'Blind Willie McTell', a weary contemplation of mortality. Also excluded was the ragged but searing 'Julius & Ethel', a bar band reflection on the fate of the Rosenbergs. Executed in 1953 for selling atomic secrets to the Russians, theirs was a cause which had united the left (the night they were killed, James Dean sat up reading and re-reading Oscar Wilde's 'The Ballad Of Reading Gaol') and the song again displayed Dylan's sympathy for and identification with the victim.

Instead of these were slotted in such grumpy songs as 'Union Sundown' which found Dylan sounding increasingly middle aged and grumbling about the misused power of American trades unions and the fractious 'Neighbourhood Bully'. Knopfler's original production and mixes were far more suitable than the version which surfaced, he spent a month coaxing some of Dylan's most atmospheric vocals from the singer. Amongst the songs which did emerge, 'Jokerman' the lyrically adept and evocative opening track, was strong, as were the quietly compelling 'I & I' and the wryly caustic 'Sweetheart Like You' - surely only Dylan would think of placing a sweetheart "in a dump like this".

There was certainly much to like on *Infidels*, as there had been on *Shot Of Love*, but as a 'comeback' it never got off the starting blocks. *New Musical Express* grudgingly wrote: "His new album is lead review this week because of *Highway 61* and *Blonde On Blonde*, not *Planet Waves*, *Street Legal* or *Shot Of Love* . . . The sad thing is that even if he could recapture his old glory it wouldn't make much difference; pop is now too diffuse, too cynical, too won't-get-fooled-again restricted . . . this is one reason why Elvis Costello, whose best work compares with pre-'66 Dylan, has

Madrid, 26 June 1984

never come close to attaining his mythic status".

Clearly something was needed, it looked like even God had let Dylan down. The restlessness which sent him ramblin' through the world was not the urgency of 20 years before, older demons dogged him now, and for once it looked as though his muse, which had after all been a constant companion on that road, had left him. While the work just passed muster, there was little real inspiration behind it. The real frustration though, lay in listening to yet another 12-bar blues variation or unconvincing reggae shuffle, when there were gems like 'Blind Willie McTell', 'Lord Protect My Child' and 'Julius & Ethel' languishing in vaults. Somewhere we knew, there were songs like 'Angelina' (which managed to rhyme 'subpoena' and 'Argentina' with its heroine's name), but what we got instead was 'Neighbourhood Bully'! There was also much to infuriate in his infrequent live appearances, for too long Dylan had got by on big band versions of his greatest hits and an over-reliance on a trio of backing singers, which tended to render every song similar.

At least the 1984 tour got back to some sort of basics, with a stage band drawing on British rock veterans. There was also a frequently inspired choice of material (including a masterly reworking of 'Tangled

Up In Blue') and a dip into rarely heard songs such as 'Tombstone Blues'. Dylan never regards songs as finite, finished creations, in his hands they are malleable, in performance pliant, sometimes with only a vestige of their origins remaining. But having a pub band playing 100,000 seater stadia didn't do much for Dylan's reputation.

His Wembley show had good and bad in equal measure, he showed himself still willing to take risks, but the under-rehearsed element was shoddy in the extreme. Too often Dylan in performance replaces sensitive interpretation with bluster, while nuance and subtlety are sacrificed to ill-natured temerity. Van Morrison elbowing his way to the microphone for a dark and brooding 'Baby Blue' was outstanding, but too much was made of the European Dylan/Baez duets, as if their simply being onstage together again would signal a return to the buoyancy of the 60s. By her own admission Baez was totally out of step with the music of the 80s, and her old frictions with Dylan – which were recounted with relish in her 1988 autobiography – soon surfaced. That so much was made of Carlos Santana's participation, displayed the American rock elite's total misapprehension of what Europe had undergone during the intervening years.

A most significant guest at Dylan's Irish show was U2's Bono. Hungry to learn more about what had gone before, an Irish punk rocker with strong spiritual foundations, he edgily paid court to Dylan, and later, gleefully recounted to Steve Turner: "The link between rock 'n' roll and gospel is not at all tenuous. In my walking into walls spiritually I'm not as alone as I once thought I was. When I look back there's Patti Smith and Bob Dylan and Van Morrison and Elvis Presley – right the way down the line." U2 would include 'Maggie's Farm' regularly in their 1987/88 concerts and were swift to cite Dylan as a major influence in interviews, Bono graciously telling him "Your songs will last forever" only to receive the reply from Dylan "Well, I think your songs will too, but who's gonna be able to play them?"

With the release of *The Joshua Tree* in 1987, U2 had become the biggest rock band of the decade, a position cemented by the film/book /double album *Rattle & Hum* in 1988. The latter featuring a free-form adaptation of 'All Along The Watchtower', as well as a haunting, spiritual Dylan/Bono collaboration 'Love Rescue Me'.

The 1984 shows restored at least some lustre to Dylan's crown. With a reconciliation between his secular and his spiritual nature obviously being attempted, there was at last some room for hope; and as the year dwindled into history, for the first time in the decade fans began to look forward to Dylan's future with something approaching relish.

Copenhagen, 12 July 1981

CHAPTER
14

Jesus, who's got time to keep up with the times?"
Bob Dylan, 1984.

While Bob Dylan spent a lifetime not looking
back, others occupied their lives doing just that: the
two eventually came together on *Biograph*. While many
fans felt the five album retrospective concentrated
more on the crumbs than the feast - why not a series of
budget albums chronologically documenting the various
facets of Dylan's career - *Biograph* was at least an admission
from Dylan that there was a past.

With rock 'n' roll entering its fourth decade,
people began to appreciate the huge influence certain
seminal figures had had on its growth. It is true to say
that without Bob Dylan, pop music would still be in
swaddling clothes. To imagine rock without Dylan is
like trying to visualise the Sistine Chapel without a
roof, or acting bereft of Brando and the Method. Rock
without Dylan? Just take any rock encyclopedia and
strike out three quarters of the names. That he had
given the fledgling form a voice was now widely
appreciated, but that huge impact now extended into
the 80s; Even more than his songs, his style and attitude
now increasingly found sanctuary.

Tired of the rigid structures imposed by the rock
establishment and the dull manifestations of formularised
pop during the early 80s, lone balladeers were once
again taking to the road. T-Bone Burnett, Andy
White, Tracy Chapman, Suzanne Vega, Michelle
Shocked and Billy Bragg - who chirpily confided
"being spokesman for a generation's the worst job I've
ever had" - were among the acknowledged heirs.
There was also a resurgence of interest in music which
avoided the increasingly technological direction of
groups like Duran Duran and Frankie Goes To
Hollywood. Nicknamed 'roots' music, new acts like
Los Lobos, Marshall Crenshaw, Lone Justice, REM,
the Beat Farmers, Green On Red, the Long Ryders
and dozens more weren't punks, they weren't out to
destroy, just to remind us of what had gone before.

One of the brightest and best dressed of the bunch
were Jason & The Scorchers, who came steaming out
of Nashville in 1984. They included a killer version of
'Absolutely Sweet Marie' on their debut album, *Fervor*.

Jason Ringenberg remembered Dylan's impact when
I interviewed him at the time: "It was thanks to my
older sister. She went off to college an innocent little
farm girl and she came back in a miniskirt and beads
with a copy of *Blonde On Blonde* under her arm. When
I heard that, I couldn't believe anything could be that
good".

Allied to the return to roots was a campaign to
acquaint audiences with 'New Country' acts like Steve
Earle, Dwight Yoakam, Lyle Lovett, Nanci Griffith
who were once again threatening the Nashville
establishment as Gram Parsons, Waylon Jennings and
Willie Nelson had done a decade before. Interest in the
music of the Third World also blossomed, folk music
from Bulgaria, Hungary and Africa found a wider
audience, and with hip-hop and rap, black music again
found a strident voice. Paul Simon received rock's
Lazarus Achievement Award for his sublime *Graceland*:
the sort of album Dylan badly needed to restore his
critical and commercial esteem, but which he would
never have the patience to make. There was once again
an underground, a rich and rewarding alternative to
the increasingly conservative and sterile Top 40. Rock
was again fragmenting and diversifying, it was too big
to be contained. The only certainties lay in the past.

After a quarter of a century in the public eye, Bob
Dylan was perceived as a symbol of what pop had
achieved. While his contemporary output was
questionable, his presence was unmistakable. But many
felt that he had simply come to represent a rallying
point, an El Cid figure dutifully trotted out in front of
his troops simply as a symbol, with nothing to contribute,
just to be seen was enough. The symbol needed
substance.

For many years there had been rumours of a Dylan
retrospective, taking the form of a collection of those
officially unreleased songs which had by now acquired
the patina of legend. Cynics reasoned that it would
only happen with Dylan's death, when a *Reader's Digest*
boxed set would be released to commemorate his
work. *National Lampoon* in the 70s had an uncannily
accurate Dylan soundalike promoting a Golden Age
Of Protest collection! The trouble with Dylan would
not be what to include, but what to leave out. Such a

With Tom Petty in Jerusalem, 7 September 1987

collection wouldn't need to dwell exclusively on the 60s, there had to be room for the best of recent unreleased works such as 'Blind Willie McTell'.

When *Biograph* finally became available in late 1985, reactions were mixed. At last, such samizdat masterpieces as 'Lay Down Your Weary Tune', 'I'll Keep It With Mine', 'Percy's Song' and 'Abandoned Love' were available in their shining pristine originality. The most frustrating aspect of the set was that it did offer glimpses into the furnace of Dylan's genius but did we really need 'I'll Be Your Baby Tonight' making its third appearance on an official Dylan album? Flaws and imperfections, chaos and impermanence have always been a part of the Dylan myth, but for all its omissions and duplications *Biograph* is nonetheless an essential addition for anyone who has assiduously followed Bob Dylan, and perforce offers a valuable insight into his swingeing effect on the development of rock music. It is to the future that Bob Dylan is condemned now, the past is close behind, with *Biograph* it draws closer. The wayward, haphazard genius that is Bob Dylan is tugging at the reins, it's time to be moving on.

Quite as interesting as the songs were Dylan's comments on them, as elicited by Cameron Crowe. After years of line-by-line critical examination of songs which had embedded themselves in the public consciousness, Dylan punctured plenty of theories while planting the seeds of many more. Conjecture about 'It's All Over Now, Baby Blue', for example, had ranged from the idea that it was written for Paul Clayton - who had blue eyes! - to the possibility of it being Dylan's farewell to Joan Baez; others were equally certain that the composer's inspiration had come from the final verse of W.H. Auden's *The Fall Of Rome:* "Herds of reindeer move across/Miles and miles of golden moss/Silently and very fast". According to Dylan though, the song went back all the way to Hibbing and The Golden Chords, a teenage memory of 'Baby Blue' by Gene Vincent - that "skinny white sailor" with "ashtray eyes and perforated pride" in Ian Dury's incarnation. The comments also revealed that 'Just Like A Woman' was the result of a Kansas City incarceration one Thanksgiving, that 'Like A Rolling Stone' tipped its sombrero to 'La Bamba' and that 'Abandoned Love' had incredibly been ditched in favour of 'Joey'.

Biograph was eulogised in print. *Time* magazine waxed lyrical in a manner which recalled the "We've Got Dylan Back Again" pieces of the early 70s, although strangely enough, *Time* had never honoured Dylan with a cover story. In *Playboy*, Dave Marsh encapsulated the feelings of many when he ended his review: "Sooner or later, anybody this talented has got to experience a revival".

To celebrate the release of the 5 LP set, CBS held a party to honour Dylan at New York's Whitney Museum. In attendance were Pete Townshend, Martin Scorsese, David Bowie, Robbie Robertson, Roy Orbison, Lou Reed, David Byrne, Billy Joel and Robert De Niro. It displayed the enormous esteem in which Dylan was held and also marked the distance of the past and the nearness of the future, which Bruce Springsteen had in mind when he said later "I always wanted to live solidly in the present, always remember the past and always be planning for the future."

The wealth of nostalgic goodwill which accompanied *Biograph* was helped by the coincidence of a strong, new Dylan album. One of the strengths of *Empire Burlesque* was the spacious production from top New York mixmaster Arthur Baker who had previously weaved his magic with New Order, Hall & Oates, Cyndi Lauper and Bruce Springsteen. The album was Dylan's strongest of the decade, with songs encompassing every facet of his career contained on one album: The articulate anger of 'Clean Cut Kid', the stately solo 'Dark Eyes', the sweeping speculation of 'When The Night Comes Falling From The Sky', the slow burning 'I'll Remember You', the relaxed gospel of 'Tight Connection To My Heart'. It wasn't so much a comeback, as a positive reaffirmation. While his role as leader was long past, with this album Dylan proved he could still compete in the marketplace. His 1985 releases provided proof of a glittering past and hope for a brighter future. But as expected with Dylan, the Gemini twin - "that enemy within" - fought for control.

Empire Burlesque was also the album which saw Dylan enter the video age - although the 'Subterranean Homesick Blues' segment at the beginning of *Don't Look Back* has been cited as an early example of the genre. Given Dylan's fascination with the visual, his reluctance to commit himself to promo videos was baffling, but this may have been due in part to the sour reviews his own *Renaldo & Clara* attracted. The few examples which did gain a showing were bizarre and short-lived and Dylan soon stopped dabbling with innovative visual documents to accompany his songs and restricted himself instead to simple performance clips and dreary surrealism. 1990's 'Most Of The Time' promo, for example, was a rudimentary performance, statically shot in an abandoned theatre.

July 1985 saw the greatest gathering of rock stars ever assembled in one show - albeit on two continents. Live Aid was a coming-of-age party for the post-punk tribes. It saw stagnant careers reborn - the record sales

The filming of the video for 'When The Night Comes Falling From The Sky' with Dave Stewart

Brisbane, 1 March 1986

of all the artists who appeared increased dramatically the week after the show - and it saw U2 confirmed as the major band of the decade; it saw reunions which had hitherto seemed impossible, and duets which would never be repeated. It marked the acceptance of responsibility by a music scene which had grown increasingly narcissistic, it alerted a global conscience about the Third World and made the Me Generation look away from the mirror for a moment.

Jack Nicholson's eulogy at the climax of the American leg left few in any doubt about who would close the show, although one still wonders what would have happened if Bruce Springsteen had thrown a guitar into the back of his pink Cadillac and made it down to Philadelphia. Bob Dylan's pivotal position as the act who closed Live Aid confirmed his pre-eminence in the strata of American music; he hadn't had a sizable hit in 20 years and was old enough to have fathered many of the stars performing that day, but Dylan still got top billing at the greatest show of all time.

Predictably, he blew it. There was no quibble about his choice of material, merely its execution. 'When The Ship Comes In' was ideal, particularly as he reached the line about "the whole wide world is watching". But like three demented marionettes in front of a giant curtain, Dylan, Ron Wood and Keith Richard managed to trivialise the whole affair, three middle-aged drunks who'd somehow managed to crash the party. Dylan even managed to make Keith look healthy, and throughout his performance exuded an understandable desire to be 17 other different places.

"One of America's great voices of freedom" looked like shit and sounded like a garbage truck. Then he rambled off on a tangent about the plight of American farmers: a cringingly inappropriate time and place for such a comment. If Dylan felt that strongly he could have organised his own event for them, but instead he tried to hijack Live Aid and in so doing, sounded the only mean spirited note in a day of inspiring unity, generosity and internationalism. Bob Geldof admitted that Dylan's performance was the day's biggest disappointment for him. Live Aid's official biographer Peter Hillmore wrote that Dylan played his greatest songs while diplomatically noting that the 'Stones' played "some laconic background sounds'".

That Dylan should choose the biggest event of the television age to make such a pratfall was par for the course. No quiet defeats for him, no silent humiliations.

Auckland, 7 February 1986

Salvaged from the morass of Dylan at Live Aid though, was the inspiration for September 1985's Farm Aid, a far more low key affair, but one which did focus attention - as Dylan had wished - on the American farmers, ignored by successive governments and suffering in a way unthought of since the 30s' depression. Musically, Farm Aid meant a marrying of minds and Dylan's blazing set with Tom Petty & The Heartbreakers saw him unite with an outfit in a way that hadn't happened since The Band, the collaboration was to colour his music for the next two years. Later in 1985 Dylan was one of innumerable rock stars who contributed to Steve Van Zandt's Sun City project, while Live Aid was avowedly non-political, P.W. Botha's neanderthal style of government was unashamedly the target of Sun City.

Barely a fortnight after Live Aid, came an extraordinarily low key appearance at a poetry festival in Moscow. Alongside fellow poets like Yevgeny Yevtushenko, Dylan sang a solo 'Hard Rain' and 'Blowin' In The Wind'. Strangely, at a time when rock stars like Elton John and Billy Joel were extracting the maximum possible publicity from glasnost and rock stars spoke blithely of breaking down cultural divides, Dylan just went ahead and did it!

Despite the Live Aid débâcle, there was enough happening in the mid 80s to make Dylan fans think this could be the time when it all came back together. The release of *Biograph* at least had Dylan admitting that there were still songs from his past which people wanted to get their hands on, while *Empire Burlesque* sounded a confident note for the future. Dylan received more formal recognition from his peers when the American Society Of Composers, Authors & Publishers (ASCAP) honoured him as a composer and the publication of *Lyrics 1962 - 1985* was another star-studded affair. A further surprise came when Dylan performed at 1987's Gershwin Gala, crooning his way through 'Soon' from the 1930 show *Strike Up The Band* . . . curiouser and curiouser.

Whatever the aberrations, Dylan was still a name to be reckoned with. The British TV première of *Don't Look Back* in 1986 became the subject of intense media accolades and the long awaited publication of Robert Shelton's exhaustive and legendary biography *No Direction Home* recalled attention to his discovery and proved to be, almost, worth its 20-year gestation. Shelton provided illuminating insights into the development of the young Bob Dylan and was particularly revealing on the years between 1962 and 1966.

When ASCAP presented Dylan with their prestigious Founders Award in 1986, it was only the second time the award had been presented. The citation recognised his contributions which "have been a sustaining influence on the music of an entire generation". Elizabeth Taylor smiled and Dylan quoted 1929's 'Without A Song' in his acceptance speech. Elvis had quoted from the same song sixteen years before, when he was honoured as one of the Ten Outstanding Young Men of America alongside Nixon's devious press secretary Ron Ziegler!

Dylan was also getting recognition from the ground up. Andy White couldn't help but be compared with Dylan on the release of his 1986 debut *Rave On Andy White* and when asked about his debt to Dylan he admitted: "It's 20 years ago, it's music from a different country in, hopefully, the same kind of tradition . . . If I wrote plays in 1610 and refused to acknowledge the existence of Shakespeare, it would be unreasonable. You must move on from that form, but the form has been set . . . I've listened to him, absolutely loads. He was a very, very amazingly talented young man".

Nick Christian Sayer, the songwriting muscle behind Transvision Vamp, and one of the few new breeders with an innate understanding of pure pop, told *Melody Maker:* "'It's Alright Ma, I'm Only Bleeding', those are the best lyrics ever written . . . He probably taught everyone a lot about mystique and arrogance; I guess I just haven't learned it!"

Anarcho-buzzsaw minstrels The Jesus & Mary Chain also confessed an unexpected affection for Dylan: "Anything by Bob Dylan before his motorcycle crash was brilliant, anything between '64 and '66 is total genius . . . *Don't Look Back*, Bob Dylan at the Albert Hall with an acoustic guitar - that was genius. There's been nothing like that in folk, rock, pop, whatever you want to call it, before or since. When I saw that I felt as if everything we'd done was worthless. I thought 'God almighty, if we ever did anything as brilliant as that, that would be it, we should retire'. After I saw that, I wanted to do something as good. That's what's good about Bob Dylan, he inspires."

Even now, young pretenders still queue up for Dylan's seal of approval: Eurythmics' Dave Stewart, U2, The Cruzados, Lone Justice, Feargal Sharkey, all have been blessed by the shaman. In 1986, young rocker Charlie Sexton crystalised the fascination and the dilemma of working with Dylan: "He'd just pick up his guitar and start singing and playing without any introduction or explanation - no keys, no chords, nothing! And my job was to figure out all the charts and produce it on the spot. We must have cut about nine or 10 songs. I'd keep asking him 'Is this one of yours?' and he'd just mumble in this gravelly voice 'Nah, it's from the Civil War'! With Dylan you never quite know for sure. They'll all probably surface on one of his albums in about 20 years from now!" Dave Stewart estimated that something around 23 songs were written and demoed with Dylan at Eurythmics' North London studio in three days, only one of which has, so far, surfaced officially!

By and large, from Bob Dylan in the 80s, there was too much of nothing. Too many uninspired blues band riffs, too many insipid performances, too little inspiration. His shows drew the sort of ghoulish crowd whose hobbies include visiting the aftermath of aeroplane crashes. In interview he was growing increasingly crabby and noncommittal, as David Hepworth wrote, everything he did was always someone else's idea, which proved a convenient let-out for a series of dismal career moves. As Peter Kemp wrote of Kenneth Tynan in words which sum up the Bob Dylan of much of the 80s: "For a decade or so (he was) genuinely distinguished, then settled for being merely conspicuous".

The Dylan pacemaker flickered on though. There were sporadic rays of hope: his swaggering performance on a 1984 *David Letterman Show* with The Plugz had Dylan rockin' out with abandon and he was one of Taj Mahal's special guests in early 1987, along with George Harrison and John Fogerty. Politically too, Dylan remained in touch and he was one of an impressive troupe of rock stars on Amnesty International's 1986 Caravan of Hope.

Farm Aid's initial collaboration with Tom Petty & The Heartbreakers was an association which produced some of his most exciting live work for years. Petty was a died-in- the-wool rocker, directly inspired by The Byrds, he had penned 'American Girl' as a soundalike tribute and had enough notches on his pistol to have credibility with rock critics. The 1986 Dylan/Petty shows drew on a rich back catalogue, premiering live versions of 'Positively 4th Street' and 'Watching The River Flow', always allowing plenty of room for improvisation. The resultant concert video, directed by Gillian Armstrong (best known for *My Brilliant Career* and *Mrs Soffel* which starred Diane Keaton) was agreeable, with a restrained use of steadicam capturing the feeling of the event.

Things were looking up and excitement was further fuelled by an exultant piece from *Rolling Stone's* Mikal Gilmore on the sessions for the new Dylan/Petty studio album "so far, well over 20 songs recorded, including gritty R&B, Chicago-steeped blues, rambunctious gospel and raw-toned hillbilly". What we got was *Knocked Out Loaded!*

The album wasn't so much a disappointment as a travesty. Even in collaboration with Carole Bayer Sager - a direct descendant of the tunesmiths who filled the Brill Building - Dylan failed to come up with a single decent tune. As so often in the past the real

Filming Hearts of Fire, in Canada, October 1986

bitterness with the finished album came with the knowledge of what had been excluded. Where was the work with Dave Stewart who had been responsible for some of the brightest moments in 80s' pop or the collaborations with Tom Petty? What was a children's choir doing on 'They Killed Him'? Where was the deftness of touch Dylan could display? Who exactly was going to buy an album like this? Sadly the new generations of Dylan fans were being forced to go back to the past rather than risk their luck with the present. The album was as slipshod and ramshackle a piece of work as any sanctioned by a major artist.

The 11-minute 'Brownsville Girl' was lauded, but as David Hepworth wryly noted "any Bob Dylan song over five minutes long is hailed as a masterpiece". In this instance though, the praise was justified; the song's co-writer Sam Shepard recalled its creation: "It has to do with a guy standing in line and waiting to see an old Gregory Peck movie that he can't quite remember - only pieces of it, and then this whole memory thing happens, unfolding before his very eyes. He starts speaking internally to a woman he'd been hanging out with, recalling their meetings and reliving the whole journey they'd gone on - and then it returns to the guy, who's still standing on line in the rain. The film the song was about was a Gregory Peck western that Bob had once seen, but he couldn't remember the title". The film in question was undoubtedly 1950's *The Gunfighter*, which had Gregory Peck as a legendary gunfighter, tired of lugging his legend around with him. His death at the hands of a snotty young contender sees Peck contemptuously hand down his legend and see how the new kid likes it!

With other things in mind, Dylan sang on 'Brownsville Girl': "Something about that movie though, I just can't get it out of my head. I can't remember why I was in it, or what part I was supposed to play . . ." Time to say hello to Billy Parker and be among the first to hear about something called *Hearts Of Fire*, one sunny Sunday morning in London . . .

I used to go to the National Film Theatre a lot in the 70s. There seemed to be a lot more to be learnt from old movies than what was happening in rock. It always reminded me of a church, the penitents assembled before the Host as that creaky curtain would open and scratchy old black and white prints came to life before your eyes. And afterwards relaxing by the Thames, that dirty old river rolling beneath Waterloo Bridge, where Vivien Leigh had prowled waiting for Robert Taylor and where Terry and Julie went every Friday night.

The NFT was the very last place I expected to see Bob Dylan close as I am to you now, one Sunday morning in August 1986. The hacks had assembled for the press conference of *Hearts Of Fire* ("Hearts On Fire?"

"No, of!"). What do you call a plethora of journalists? A hack? A libel of journalists? Eyes glazed, flicking over your head working the room, looking for someone more important to talk to, exuding control, but belied by the albums clutched like briefcases, held hopefully for possible autographing. All were reduced to slavering groupies, dutifully intoning their "first time", the loss of innocence which accompanied their first hearing Dylan. As the sun filtered in, I reckoned that none of us would be here without that first exposure to those scratchy mono LPs, a distant lifetime ago; and just for one moment, subs from The Caernarvon Bugle, national Sunday columnists, staid magazine editors, were briefly united. Instead of viewing the frizzle haired singer through binoculars here was the chance to get up close. Behind the facade of cool, we had all regressed to teenage fans.

Then the word . . . He was here. Heads twitched like pigeons, the cool melted like ice in a capuccino. Brushing past, shades of course, smaller than you could ever imagine, protected by the sort of people your mother warned you against. Onstage, sulky Rupert Everett, bubbly Fiona, exuberant Richard Marquand, gargoyle Dylan, hectored by reporters asking if he was gonna write any protest songs. Maybe we'd get some of that razor sharp '65 press conference wit. We got monosyllables. The only time Dylan evinced any interest in anything (apart from the customary desire to be someplace else) was when John Bauldie asked about the influence of *The Maltese Falcon* on the lyrics of *Empire Burlesque*! "Oh really?" said Dylan, interest flickering behind the shades, but it soon passed. Then like the drifter, he escaped; except drifters don't have that many minders or limousines.

Sitting outside looking through the synopsis of the film - "It can't be as bad as it sounds can it?" "Whatever happened to his quality control?" - the *Nashville Skyline* sleeve left unautographed, realising that you weren't a 17- year-old star-struck groupie anymore, coming back down to earth, and all the while the river flowed on by. Strange sort of day, the day that Bob Dylan met his Waterloo.

Well of course the film came and went, and yes, it was as bad as it sounded, and although Dylan kept his end up with a performance that at least had charisma on its side, they all ended up with egg on the face. To his credit, Dylan more than held his own against the acting professionals. The *Evening Standard*'s Neil Norman wrote of the film: "It is, ironically, Bob Dylan who emerges with any vestige of dignity from the farrago, which he does simply by keeping his head down and not making more demands of himself than he knows he can deliver." Another paper wrote from the set that Dylan and Fiona's love scenes "sizzle like white-hot

Oakland, California, 24 July 1987

Stills from Hearts of Fire 1986

Stills from Hearts of Fire 1986

1977

charcoal briquettes at a South Fork barbecue" - sorry I missed that bit! The real puzzle was not so much the lacklustre songs Dylan contributed or the risible script - which tediously rewrote that Hollywood chestnut *A Star Is Born* - it was what on earth Dylan of all people was doing in a dump like this?

Then there was the title song that Dylan contributed to the Miami Vice rip-off film *Band Of The Hand*. Then there was Dylan's non-interview for *Whistle Test*. Then there was the evasive interview for *Omnibus*. Then there was . . . just a feeling that it was all a waste of time.

For much of the decade, Bob Dylan had drifted like a rudderless ship, land rarely in sight. In the 80s came the final, sad realisation that Dylan had lost his ability to separate the quality of his work from the quantity. There were too many 12-bar blues with an uninterested Dylan shouting unmemorable lyrics over endlessly repeated, sloppily played riffs. His advisors heaved the plastic of unsold albums at his feet, his quality control had gone down the toilet, the fact that a major artist, any major artist, could sanction albums like *Loaded* and *Down In The Groove* was reprehensible. Dylan's 'punk' attitude to recording was admirable at a time when sampling had become an obsession and many groups worshipped at the altar of the Fairlight, but what was the point in a reckless approach to recording when the songs themselves were so obviously sub-standard?

How on God's earth could Dylan even consider releasing 'My God, They Killed Him' (which simply restated the trite if ideologically right-on sentiments of 'Abraham, Martin & John'), when 'Blind Willie McTell' still lay lost in a vault? Why was 'Groom's Still Waiting At The Altar', with its imaginative rhyming and contemporaneous verses consigned to a B-side when 'Night After Night' took up space on an official album? Why did the lacklustre 'Had A Dream About You, Baby' take up space on two official albums? What was the reasoning behind it all? Surely Dylan knew that 'Caribbean Wind' was a better song than 'Trouble', and if he didn't, he had no business here.

For Britain, the Dylan/Petty shows of October 1987 seemed like they could be the last chance to see the master before the rot set in terminally. Seeing Bob Dylan perform in the 80s was a bit like National Service, you couldn't help but be there, though there were plenty of other places you'd rather be! "Who feels sorry for the centre of attention?" asked Steve Forbert. You had to feel sorry for Bob Dylan when he came onstage at Wembley with what looked like a racoon living in his hair! The Dylan apologists pointed to the wealth of new material he premièred live, but the problem was - they all sounded the same.

All the 60s' favourites were performed with sluggish abandon, 'Watching The River Flow' could just as easily have been 'Rainy Day Women'. He was changing vocal lines, arrangements and lyrics arbitrarily, but it was change for change's sake with no real motivation. There was a steamrollering, big hall sound which rendered the songs virtually indistinguishable from each other, which is why the acoustic break was so welcome, not just because it was nostalgic, but because it signalled a break in the monotony. Tragic to discover of the great communicator, that Dylan's delivery was now sloppy to the point of incoherence.

I felt no sense of moral outrage on hearing 'Chimes Of Freedom' transformed into a singalong finale, I was just resentful at hearing a great song bludgeoned into the ground by an insensitive singer accompanied by a band who couldn't quite keep up with him. Dylan's bludgeoning of that particular song was made all the more a travesty when compared with Bruce Springsteen's sensitive and alert interpretation of 'Chimes Of Freedom' in 1988. Springsteen's pertinent reading of the timeless lyrics, the drama he attached to its performance, the triumph he injected into it made one realise just how curmudgeonly the composer had become.

The 1987 shows with Petty illuminated the dichotomy of being a Dylan watcher in the 80s: feeling the immense frustration, aggravated by the suspicion that when he could be bothered it still came quite easily, but bound to wonder whether it was worth struggling through the frequently mediocre and indifferent performances in the hope of a rare glimpse of the old magic. The frustration was only heightened by the rest of the show, just like the old package tours of the 60s, when every act had 12 minutes before The Beatles' 20.

Roger McGuinn, rescued from beer joints and out in front of thousands who weren't averse to a quick canter through the Byrds catalogue, was a perfect hors d'oeuvre to what was to follow. McGuinn's good-natured performance even made me happily sit through 'Chestnut Mare' though I've always had my doubts about anyone who'd write a love song to a horse!

Tom Petty & The Heartbreakers were not one of the major American bands of the 70s, but a 40-minute condensation of their greatest hits was no bad thing, it was all priming you in an amiable enough manner for the main event. Petty's band and Dylan had, after all, been playing together for over a year, and should have been fully integrated, any sloppiness left behind long ago in a rehearsal studio. But *The Times* called Dylan's performance "perfunctory" and marvelled: "Incredibly, after 25 years as a professional musician, his harmonica playing remained unimproved"! But the fans were willing to mistake ragged indifference for spontaneity, were happy to settle for witnessing Dylan made mortal while overlooking the manifold, obvious flaws in his performance . . . and hell, I went two nights anyway,

With The Grateful Dead, 1987

got to keep the old bugger in work.

To their credit the Heartbreakers worked well under the circumstances and Benmont Tench managed to rescue 'Tomorrow Is A Long Time' with a stately, minuet piano. Most frustrating of all was that on certain songs, when he tried, Dylan still seemed able to weave his old spells: the subtle C&W tinged 'Simple Twist Of Fate', the spectral gris-gris of 'I Dreamed I Saw St Augustine', the taut reading of 'When The Night Comes Falling'. But only rarely were his vocals soulful or imbued with any fervour or identification; all too often the songs fell victim to Dylan's cut-up style of singing, like a battle with an unwilling victim, who refused to lie down and had instead to be pummelled into submission.

There was little or no sense of occasion, even his Israeli debut was risible judging by press accounts of the time. Surely as a Jew, Dylan must have viewed his first appearances in the promised land, the Jewish homeland as something special? Nope, just another ramshackle gig for the man with the dodgy haircut.

Bruce Springsteen struck a poignant chord in an otherwise downward spiral when he inducted Dylan into The Rock & Roll Hall Of Fame in January 1988, he spoke of 'Like A Rolling Stone' "kicking open the door to your mind . . . Bob freed your mind and showed us that just because the music was innately physical did not mean that it was anti-intellect. He had the vision and the talent to make a pop song so that it contained the whole world. He invented a new way a pop singer could sound, broke through the limitations of what a recording artist could achieve, and he changed the face of rock 'n' roll for ever and ever".

The high regard and affection in which Dylan is held by his devoted audience is touching, but "oh what kind of love is this that goes from bad to worse?" Like its predecessor, *Down In The Groove* was pieced together from innumerable sessions over the years which led to its rather obvious lack of cohesion, a fault which was exacerbated by Dylan's declining to pen any original material for the album. The supporting cast was assembled by Central Casting: guitar heroes Eric Clapton and Mark Knopfler, ageing punks Steve Jones and Paul Simonon, Ry Cooder's backing vocalists Bobby King and Willie Green, House outfit Full Force and geriatric acid rockers Grateful Dead.

The finished album wasn't the mess anticipated, it was just another Bob Dylan album of the 80s, with all its concomitant flaws. CBS impishly tried to inject some mystery into its release: "*Down In The Groove* isn't just a contract-filler. It's just gloriously perverse, maybe the last thing you'd expect from Dylan . . . Pretty heavy shit this by anyone's standards." They announced it with glee, like they'd just unearthed another stash of Basement Tapes! This was patently nonsense. While Dylan's vocal on 'Death Is Not The End' was dignified, and 'Ninety Miles An Hour' had an idiosyncratic charm, it was not enough. This was Dylan in neutral, it was much ado about nothing, it showed him hurling away his crown of thorns, but left with the pricks.

In East Berlin, 17 September 1987

If Dylan really wanted to record, and would insist on releasing 'Shenandoah', why not take a leaf out of Springsteen or Costello's book and maximise the potential of 12" singles by filling the B-sides with rarities? Why not release a budget album of cover versions as he's long threatened to do? Compared to the slick sounding albums his contemporaries were releasing, Dylan still sounded like he barely knew one end of a microphone from the other when he went into the studio. For too long during this decade have we had to put up with sub-standard, sloppy albums, wet with perspiration, but bereft of true inspiration.

Contrariwise, Dylan's 1988 shows which pitched him into smaller auditoriums with a stripped down three-piece band had him sounding like he was bothering. This time around, when he blitzed through his back catalogue, he made an effort to emphasise the importance of the songs. Working his way through the list of songs which he'd never performed live, listed in the back of John Bauldie & Michael Gray's *All Across The Telegraph* (Sidgwick & Jackson, 1987), Dylan opened every show with 'Subterranean Homesick Blues' and included such surprising revisits as 'Absolutely Sweet Marie', 'Mama, You Been On My Mind' and 'Man Of Constant Sorrow', as well as reprising 'Masters Of War', 'It's All Over Now, Baby Blue' and 'Boots Of Spanish Leather'.

Rarely playing for more than an action-packed 90 minutes, Dylan managed to infuse life into that which had been pronounced dead on arrival. At the time of

writing, it looks like this is the long-overdue renaissance for Dylan. What Dylan has called his "never ending" tour could also be christened "The Dead Can Walk Tour". While he should be "weary and worn out", Dylan's alive and well, and in his off-stage moments can confidently sit and sift through all his obituaries (1969/70, 1980, 1986/89).

The shows which began in mid-88 begged many questions though, like just why was he doing them? At the tour's commencement, and with a new album to promote, Dylan barely acknowledged its existence, with only 'Silvio' getting an airing from *Down In The Groove*, while *Knocked Out Loaded* was only represented by 'Drifting Too Far From Shore'. As the tour rolled on, and on and on and on, those shows didn't dip back into the 60s, they swam in them!

The 60s' immersion had perhaps started when Dylan toured with the Grateful Dead during 1987. For many, they were the band that still represented the blossoming idealism of the Summer of Love; to others, little more than an embarrassing throwback to a time when 'rock' meant self-indulgent guitar solos. The travesty was compounded when 1989 saw the release of the live album *Dylan & The Dead*, which I regard as the nadir of Dylan's recorded career.

Now I've duly gone out and got 'em all, I've got all Dylan's skeletons on record rattling in my cupboard, and they're occasionally brought out blinking into daylight to see if, yup, they still sounded that bad. But the rarest and most unwelcome visitor is Bob and the

Grateful Dead, these songs of love and Haight are nailed to the mast of a long, gone past. Sure, it included a rare live version of 'Queen Jane Approximately', but served up in such a fashion as to be all but unrecognisable. The only plus for the live 'Joey' is that it's shorter than the studio version, while any lightness of touch on 'I Want You' has been surgically removed. "Bob Dylan and the Grateful Dead?" said Shane MacGowan of The Pogues when they supported Dylan in America during 1989, "they should see us together: Bob Dylan and the Nearly Dead".

"We're a garage band, we come from Garageland" The Clash roared in 1977. The Traveling Wilburys were another garage band, but they came to Malibu via Liverpool; Birmingham; Duluth, Minnesota; Gainesville, Florida and Vernon, Texas. Long thought to be an extinct breed, the last 80s' "supergroup" got together in Bob Dylan's garage in April 1988.

The story goes that George Harrison and producer Jeff Lynne needed an extra track for a Harrison 12" single, and contacted Roy Orbison for moral support. The trio were soon in touch with Tom Petty, who made the journey down to Dylan's garage in a move reminiscent of the superstar jamming which was such a symptom of the late 60s. With the five assembled, a title was plucked out of the air - 'Handle With Care', the Wilburys first single, reputedly came from a label on Dylan's guitar case. It was written and recorded in a refreshingly swift session, and deemed too good for a throwaway bonus track.

Hiding under thinly disguised pseudonyms - 'Lucky', 'Otis', 'Nelson' etc - the Wilburys rattled through their 10-track debut album, *Traveling Wilburys, Volume One* in a matter of days. The spontaneity helped make it one of the most enchanting comeback albums of the decade. Because the Wilburys never really existed, because the superstars could hide behind their fictional faces, it took the pressure off, and helped make the album a one-off wonder. 'Not Alone Any More' gave Roy Orbison a final crack at a big ballad, while the remaining tracks combined old fashioned rockabilly and skiffle with down the line C&W.

Dylan's contributions included the dour 'Congratulations', the Prince-like 'Dirty World', a nod from one Minnesota man to another, and the extraordinary Springsteen by numbers 'Tweeter And The Monkey Man', with its three New Jersey references, as well as namechecking other Boss titles such as 'Stolen Car', 'Mansion On The Hill', 'State Trooper', 'Thunder Road' and 'Jersey Girl'.

Roy Orbison's sad death put the Wilburys on hold, but the album gave the principals an opportunity to sink themselves in being somebody else, and following the dismal *Down In The Groove*, his work with the

Wilburys gave Dylan fans added hope for his future. 'Lucky Wilbury' added another pseudonym to a list which already included 'Elston Gunn', 'Robert Milkwood Thomas', 'Blind Boy Grunt' and 'Bob Dylan'.

Immediately after the Wilburys got into gear, Dylan was off on the road again with his tight, three-piece bar band, tearing round the territories apparently in a bid to try and salvage his reputation before the 80s wrapped. With former Hall & Oates guitarist G.E. Smith, Dylan finally found an accompanist whose talent matched his own mercurial moods onstage.

June 1988 had marked the beginning of what Dylan called his "never-ending tour" and he was rarely off the road for most of the remainder of the decade. One night that brought it all back home was January 12th, 1990, at Toad's Place in New Haven. Dylan selected the 700 capacity venue as a warm-up for his first ever shows in South America and a brief European tour in February. He played 50 songs during a four-hour set. Even for audiences used to Dylan premières during the preceding 18 months, the Toad Show included a baffling and beguiling number of 'firsts' including covers of Joe South's 'Walk A Mile In My Shoes', Springsteen's 'Dancing In The Dark', the Wilburys' 'Congratulations' and Kris Kristofferson's 'Help Me Make It Through The Night'.

The early 90s recalled the Dylan of 20 years before, appearing out of the blue at events like TVs *L'Chaim* telethon, alongside his son-in-law and a tired and emotional Harry Dean Stanton, with Dylan electing to play the recorder on the great Semitic singalong, 'Hava Nagila'. He was there at a tribute to Roy Orbison, and joined The Byrds onstage for their 25th anniversary version of 'Mr Tambourine Man' - I thought Dylan looked rough at Live Aid, here he seemed spritely, especially standing next to David Crosby, who now bears an uncanny resemblance to Jimmy Edwards in *Whacko!*

Otherwise, live, Dylan was roaring, in all his "raging glory". With vim and vigour every night he was digging up his past from the boneyard. He was dispatching his rock 'n' roll songs like bullets from the barrel of a gun, then caressing the acoustic songs as softly as the wind on the sail of a becalmed dhow.

Encouraging as the live work was, Dylan's reputation cried out for an album to bolster his reputation. Neil Young, Lou Reed, Paul Simon, Van Morrison, Paul McCartney, Eric Clapton, Robbie Robertson and Leonard Cohen were all delivering albums which would reach out to whole new audiences as the 80s ended. I always reckoned Dylan had the ability to make one classic album a decade, but he was running out of time. Just in the nick of time, emboldened by his studio

166

work with U2 and the Traveling Wilburys, *Oh Mercy* slipped under the door in September 1989.

Much of the credit for the reinvigorated Dylan must lie with producer Daniel Lanois. As well as giving us one of 1989's most haunting releases with his own New Age, cajun-style *Acadie*, Lanois was acclaimed as one of the decade's most distinctive producers. His co-production work with Brian Eno on U2's *The Unforgettable Fire* and *The Joshua Tree* first brought his name to prominence, before going on to work with Robbie Robertson on his eponymous solo debut, Peter Gabriel on *So* and the Neville Brothers on *Yellow Moon*, which led him to Dylan.

Dylan was particularly impressed with Aaron Neville's handling of his own 'With God On Our Side' (which included an extra verse on Vietnam that Dylan was to later include in his own concert versions of the song) and 'The Ballad Of Hollis Brown'. After years in the wilderness, the Nevilles were suddenly hot again. Their treatment of 'With God On Our Side' particularly aroused enormous interest in Britain, although like Cowboy Junkies' rendering of the Velvet Underground's 'Sweet Jane' the same year, there was a vogue for hailing any version of a classic song, stripped and slowed down, as a classic.

Dylan drifted on down to New Orleans in March 1989 to begin work on his 25th studio album, and was by his standards, effusive in his praise of Lanois. He told Edna Gundersen of *USA Today*: "It's very hard to find a producer that can play. A lot of them can't even engineer. They've just got a big title and know how to spend a lot of money. It was thrilling to run into Daniel because he's a competent musician and he knows how to record with modern facilities. For me, that was lacking in the past".

As *Isis* editor Derek Barker wrote in issue No.28 "Daniel's presence . . . is easily identifiable by that dark, mysterious feel which runs through much of his work; Gabriel's 'Red Rain', Robertson's 'Somewhere Down The Crazy River' and latterly Dylan's own 'Man In A Long Black Coat' all carry that unmistakable Lanois trademark". That "trademark" is an ethereal, wraparound sound; ambient music which draws on Lanois' avowed fondness for music that has gone, but which he is capable of rekindling with state of the art technology. Certainly, Lanois creates a distinctive sound, whether it will - like Trevor Horn's thunderous production work for Frankie Goes To Hollywood - simply be a passing symptom only time can tell. What is certain though is that Bob Dylan found Daniel Lanois at a time when his recorded reputation was at rock bottom, and in tandem they brought it back from the abyss.

While lacking the sustained revitalisation of Lou Reed's *New York* or Paul Simon's *Graceland*, *Oh Mercy* is undeniably the album Bob Dylan needed to make before he bid the 80s adieu. This was the album that marked the welcome return of Dylan as storyteller, not as preacher. You knew he was breaking out when, amidst the chartbound sounds, Radio 1 DJ Simon Mayo began enthusiastically playing 'Man In A Long Black Coat' on his breakfast show. That phantom moment was the single that could have sent Dylan back into the Top 40, predictably it was not lifted, and subsequently the album failed to achieve the breakthrough which could have come on the back of a hit single.

Oh Mercy featured fond memories nestling next to visions of the apocalypse. It embraced the lonesome lap steel Country of 'Where Teardrops Fall' along with the muscular Gospel of 'Ring Them Bells'. The "crickets talkin' back and forth in rhyme" which usher in 'Man In A Long Black Coat' return Dylan to his place in the market as mesmerising weaver of yarns. If anyone had the right to be a victim of the "disease of conceit" it was Bob Dylan: with a body of work as substantial as his, he had every right to have succumbed, but he never fell folly to delusions of grandeur. With *Oh Mercy* Dylan returned like the Angel of Death in a Bergman film, stalking the territory he could now reclaim as his own.

The album had the critics united in its triumph; Gavin Martin in the *NME* summed up the mood, as he welcomed Dylan back with open arms, but not with any unnecessary harking back, rather as a contemporary buddy: "So, Prince can do his party inferno thing on the ruins, Van can ramble round his churchyard cloisters, U2 and the Pogues can be wandering pilgrims, De La Soul can send hieroglyphics from the underground but Dylan's the survivor on the scorched landscape, the wizened and withering prophet on the mount".

Pop has become too diverse, too fragmented to be unified by a Bob Dylan renaissance. Solace can be found though in his renewed vigour, in his determination to keep on going in an industry that is constantly changing, an industry that has changed because of him. As the decade drew to a close, the media love of all things Dylan, gained further momentum with the systematic release of his back catalogue on Compact Disc. Given the primitive studio equipment and Dylan's well known intransigence with recording technique, Bob Dylan On CD provided an opportunity to look back afresh, and proved a fitting curtain on the 80s.

When Robert Hilburn reviewed *No Direction Home*, he asked: "This is the 19th book on Dylan to have appeared. Why do people do it? Are they looking for Dylan or are they looking for themselves?" It cuts both ways: by searching for Dylan we who have followed him assiduously all these years - this happy breed! - can't help but look for ourselves, because his music has been so much a part of our lives. Like diary entries, the songs of Bob Dylan percolate and punctuate our lives; which is why we stick with him stubbornly, through thick and thin, through rough and smooth.

The perennial fascination is, of course, with the work - we can justify that intellectually - but that inevitably simmers alongside the memories. Instead of a lifetime spent studying the *oeuvre* of, say, "an Italian poet of the 16th Century", studying Bob Dylan is a lot more fun. You could stick with the chicaneries of the Schleswig-Holstein affair and end up like Lord Palmertson: "Only three people ever fully understood it - one is dead, one is mad . . . and I can't remember!" Could almost be Bob Dylan talking about 'Sad Eyed Lady Of The Lowlands'.

What we won't admit - as we nuzzle the pampas of middle age - is our fascination with pop stars. Beginning with sketching Hank Marvin's red Fender Stratocaster on a school exercise book, right up to today's irrational behaviour in public, we still remain envious and quietly obsessed. The great thing about Dylan is that he legitimises that adolescent fervour. As 40 stares me in the face, I still find myself poring over Dylan set lists, his whereabouts, his reading matter, his erratic choice of footwear.

Occasionally though, I'll pull myself back. At a reception for Dwight Yoakam at Break For The Border, a little corner of Mexico in the heart of London, a rumour went round the room. Dylan was in London filming *Hearts Of Fire*, and - no it wasn't Him - but one of His kids was said to be there. Putting on my investigative journalist's hat, I scoured the room, then thought: No, this is crazy, what am I doing looking for one of Bob Dylan's children? This isn't what I enlisted for.

On the whole though, being a Dylan watcher is a whole heap more fun than being a weight watcher. It's a damned sight more interesting than being a train spotter. It's fun, it means travelling and meeting people. It stops you becoming a pudding. It's a strange way to make a living. But after all the paths travelled in his company, I guess we ain't complaining none.

In 1972, Andy Warhol's *Interview* magazine looked at the legend of James Dean, their words on that dead actor echo my feelings about Bob Dylan now, pushing 50 and keeping on keeping on, to the irritation of many and the continued delight of others: "James Dean was the perfect embodiment of an eternal struggle. It might be innocence struggling with experience, youth with age, or man with his image. But in every aspect his struggle was a mirror to a generation of rebels without a cause. His anguish was exquisitely genuine on and off

screen; his moments of joy were rare and precious. He is not our hero because he was perfect, but because he perfectly represented the damaged but beautiful soul of our time . . . "

THE END

ANOTHER END: He blew it. Forget perfection, 1990's *Under The Red Sky* didn't even get past first base. There are those who insist that the album tells profound truths in nursery rhyme fashion, that there really is something to sink your teeth into . . . But really, "wiggle, wiggle, wiggle like a bowl of soup". So the critics dusted down their Dylan obituaries again, but then found them mysteriously returned to sender with the release of *Traveling Wilburys Vol.3*. Sadder than Volume 1 (I assume I didn't miss Volume 2) because of the loss of Lefty Wilbury, but if anything, a stronger album than its predecessor.

So the Dylan see-saw dips on and into a new decade, up with *Oh Mercy*, then down with *Red Sky*.

It's unbelievable . . .

THE OTHER END: Like other major artists, Dylan has a reluctance to finish, tenaciously hanging on, pursuing a wayward muse, a distant calling. It has destroyed others before him, the Right butchered Federico Garcia Lorca and Victor Jara. Herman Melville, bitterly resentful of the response to *Moby Dick* on its publication in 1851, spent the last years of his life working as a Deputy Inspector in the New York Custom House, trudging every day from his home at 104 E. 26th Street uptown; it was discovered after his death, that pinned to the desk where he wrote *Billy Budd* - which was only published posthumously - was a cutting "Keep true to the dreams of thy youth". Bob Dylan has; from a teenage ambition to "join Little Richard" he has transcended that.

As Dylan nudges uncomfortably and uncompromisingly towards 50, his restless, hungry feeling is still manifest. That it speaks to successive generations is a testament to his genius. It's not a word to be used lightly in rock, but if anyone merits its appellation, it is Bob Dylan. Dylan has kept true to his dreams, he has poured a lot into the vacuum that is music, he's still doggedly pouring, still keeping true.

While his political tracts remain contemporary, Dylan also acted as a father confessor to a generation; he guided us through the haunted landscapes of the subconscious, turning over stones, unafraid of what he'd find beneath. His love songs contain an urgency which rarely fails to thrill and move, not simply out of cosy nostalgia, but rather their direct emotional confrontation which simply doesn't date. As with any great artist, Dylan's work is a symptom of his times, able to chart those times, yet remain timeless in their quality.

There is still racism rampant, whether in redneck Alabama or the brutal fascist stronghold of South Africa. In rock it runs from the notorious outburst from Public Enemy's Professor Griff that Jews are responsible for "the majority of wickedness that goes on around the globe", or Guns N' Roses Axl Rose sounding off: "I used the word nigger because it's a word to describe somebody that is basically a pain in your life, a problem". It runs through the homophobic and sexist outrages of comedian Andrew Dice Clay and Niggers With Attitude. When asked about South Africa, NWA's Eazy-E responded: "Fuck that black power shit, we don't give a shit. Free South Africa, we don't give a fuck . . . They don't give a damn about us, so why should we give a damn about them?"

That NWA patently don't give a fuck about Nelson Mandela is their problem, but that they can write 'Fuck The Police' is in no small way thanks to Bob Dylan. Nelson Mandela didn't walk free out of prison in 1990 because Jerry Dammers' wrote 'Nelson Mandela' six years before; William Zanzinger was not imprisoned because Bob Dylan wrote 'The Lonesome Death Of Hattie Carroll' in 1963. But Dylan created the climate for such songs to be written.

The victims who Dylan identified are still hounded, whether innocent scapegoats of bombs in Northern Ireland, prisoners of conscience rotting in South American jails or Pakistani families firebombed by racist thugs in the East End of London. There are still farmers evicted from their farms, still victims of religious persecution.

What Bob Dylan has accomplished is a question embracing the value of art itself. Does art change society, or is it merely a reflection of society? At least, thanks to the work of Bob Dylan, we have a vocabulary to register our indignation about the iniquities of racial injustice, religious bigotry, intolerance. That is perhaps Dylan's major achievement, to a generation unable or unwilling to question, he gave "a voice without restraint". A voice to register our protest and indignation, a voice which deserves still to be heard.

THE END

BOB DYLAN — Gallup, N. M. When you tour with the carnival at age fourteen playing piano and guitar, you're bound to learn a lot of life, land and of music. In the course of this learning process, Bob heard Woody Guthrie's "Dust Bowl Ballads" and headed east to meet the great Woody. Arriving in New York, he found that the city people referred to much of the music he had been playing and writing as folk music. To Bob this didn't matter. He's continued to write, sing and dress in a highly individual fashion. This has landed him an enviable record contract with Columbia and the publication by Leeds Music of a collection of his works. The songs he writes (often topical paradies or talkin' blues) and sings relate to what he's heard and seen in America. The closest he comes to international material is the parody of an Israeli song, ("H'ava Ngilla." Plays jazzy blues piano, guitar and harmonica (often both at once). Columbia. 161 West 4th St., N.Y.C.

NOTES

Chronology: Again this is selected rather than comprehensive. It should be assumed that all quotations are by Bob Dylan himself. Where this is *not* the case, the speaker has been identified.

Concerts: For the earliest concerts of which tapes exist in collectors' hands, full track listings have been given. Pre. 1974 concerts for which tapes exist have been marked (★) with the number of songs on the tape indicated. From 1974 onwards, with a very few exceptions, it is to be assumed that tape recordings are in circulation amongst collectors. The "no tape" exceptions are marked (NT).

Bibliography: It should be noted that these are selected listings. All major books are included. Many early interesting magazine articles are listed but a comprehensive bibliography is well beyond the size of the present volume.

Songs written: Unless otherwise indicated, all comments are by Bob Dylan. In some cases the dating of the compositions has been approximated.

Discography: Bracketed details after the catalogue numbers indicate chart position and number of weeks on chart. Eg. (USA No.22, 32 weeks) indicates that the record – in this case the Freewheelin' Bob Dylan – reached Number 22 in the USA and stayed in the top 100 for 32 weeks.

1961

1961 CHRONOLOGY

January

24. Having left Minneapolis in mid–December, Dylan travels via Chicago and Wisconsin, before getting a ride into New York City. He arrives in the middle of a snowstorm. "I knew I had to get to New York. I'd been dreaming about that for a long time." On the night he arrives in New York he plays Woody Guthrie songs at the Cafe Wha? "They flipped. I played there and they flipped. They really did."

25. "I was pretty fanatical about what I wanted to do, so after learning about 200 of Woody's songs, I went to see him. I took a bus from New York, sat with him and sang his songs. Visits Woody Guthrie at Greystone Park Hospital, New Jersey. "I never really talked too much to him. He didn't talk anyway he always liked the songs and he'd ask for certain ones. I knew them all. Hahaha. I was like a Woody Guthrie jukebox."

February

12. Dylan sends a postcard to David Whitaker in Minneapolis. He tells him he visits Woody Guthrie four times a week – he also sees Woody at weekends at the home of Sid and Bob Gleason – and that has been playing at a coffeehouse called The Commons, "where people clap for me".

13. Dylan plays wherever he's allowed to in the coffeehouses in Greenwich Village. For the first time he plays at the Monday night Hootenanny at Gerde's Folk City: "In came this funny looking kid, dressed as if he had just spent a year riding freight trains, and playing songs in a style that you could tap your feet to. Dylan's early style was a combination of blues, rock and country which caught on the very minute that he stepped on to the stage at Gerde's."

14. Bob Dylan writes 'Song To Woody': "I just thought about Woody; I wondered about him, thought harder and wondered harder. I wrote this song in about five minutes." He gives a dated, handwritten copy of the song to the Gleasons, with whom he stays for much of the time. A tape dating from this time, recorded by the Gleasons as Dylan sang to their daughter Kathy, shows Dylan's emergence as a major talent.

April

3. Engaged for his first professional residency at Folk City Dylan joins the Musicians' Union. Club owner Mike Porco acts as his guardian: "When Bob filled in his age as nineteen the union secretary said 'I can't OK this because you're under 21. Come in tomorrow with your father.' Bob says 'I got no father.' The union man says 'Come in with your mother,' and Bob says 'I got no mother either.' The union man leans back behind him and forms the words in his mouth, asking me 'Is he a bastard?' And I said 'I don't know.'"

Bob Dylan's manager Albert Grossman 1965

5. First paid performance in New York at the Loeb Student Center, Washington Square. Seen there by Suze Rotolo.

11. Major professional debut at Folk City, playing support to John Lee Hooker. Dylan's set includes 'Song To Woody' and 'House Of The Rising Sun', in an arrangement which he has learned from Dave Van Ronk.

May

Returns to Minneapolis and plays at a University hootenanny astonishing former friends: "The change in Bob was, to say the least, incredible." (John Pankake). He has written a song, a Woody Guthrie-style talking blues, which summarises his first three months in New York. His friends tape two sessions of the new Dylan, 25 songs which are known as The Minneapolis Party Tape.

June

First professional work in recording studio. Dylan plays harmonica on Harry Belafonte's album *Midnight Special*. Annoyed at repeated takes of the same song - the LP's title track - Dylan walks out. The recording is subsequently released and is thus the earliest commercially available Bob Dylan recording: Harry Belafonte - *Midnight Special* (RCA LMP 2449).

He travels to Boston, the "other" folk music centre, where he meets Eric Von Schmidt, who teaches him 'He Was A Friend Of Mine' and 'Baby Let Me Follow You Down'.

July

At The Gaslight Cafe, Dylan is introduced to Albert Grossman by Robert Shelton, the folk music critic of the New York Times who

NEW SONG WRITERS:

Bob Dylan: Columbia Records CL 1779

Young Bob Dylan is the most gifted poet to appear on the American scene since Woody Guthrie. His output is prodigious, his language direct, personal and of high literary quality. He is not the Woody of his generation, as some believe, but a poet who combines folk vernacular with contemporary poetics. He speaks for the younger generation on issues that vitally concern them, revealing a deep humility and a warm humanity. This disk offers a smattering of his own songs and others picked up in his travels around the country. Unfortunately, it does not present him at his best. The singing is erratic, the words not clear and the manner too undisciplined - but be patient, there will be another along soon.

One of the earliest Album reviews

saw Dylan at Gerde's the previous month. Shelton particularly liked a Dylan song called 'Talkin' Bear Mountain Picnic Massacre Blues'.

29. After performing on the Riverside Church radio show, Dylan spends the evening with Suze Rotolo and her sister Carla.

September

6. A performance at The Gaslight Cafe is taped for posterity.

25. Plays two weeks' residency at Folk City. Is interviewed by Robert Shelton.

29. Shelton writes a review of Dylan's performance for the New York Times. "Shelton, more than anyone, was responsible for Bob Dylan. He pushed and pushed and pushed. He thought Bobby Dylan was a tremendous poet." (Liam Clancy).

Dylan reads part of Shelton's review at Gerde's Folk City, before performing Ain't No More Cane. A tape is made of the evening's performance by Cynthia Gooding.

30. Is hired as harmonica player behind Carolyn Hester. The recording session is produced by John Hammond who is so captured by Dylan's talent that he arranges to sign him up to Columbia Records on a five-year contract. "I couldn't believe it. I remember walking out of the studio. I was like on a cloud. It was one of the most thrilling moments in my life."

October

26. Bob Dylan signs his recording contract with Columbia.

November

4. Dylan's first major concert is promoted by Izzy Young, who runs the Folklore Center. Held in the Carnegie Chapter Hall, it attracts only 53 patrons.

20-22. Recording sessions for Bob Dylan's debut LP. Dylan records two of his own songs: 'Song To Woody' and 'Talkin' New York'. Recording costs are $402. "There was a violent, angry emotion running through me then. I just played the guitar and harmonica and sang those songs and that was it. Mr Hammond asked me if I wanted to sing any of them over again and I said, no. I can't see myself singing the same song twice in a row."

23. Dylan takes Suze Rotolo to dinner with the MacKenzies, who later tape-record a set of songs, including a new composition, 'Hard Times In New York Town'.

December

Dylan returns to Minneapolis to visit friends: "The first thing Bob did was show us the New York Times clipping. He talked with great velocity. 'Listen to what I have done. Listen to what's happened to me.'" (Gretel Whitaker). He allows his friend Tony Glover to record a 26-song tape, large portions of which become famous following the 1969 release of the Great White Wonder bootleg. The tape summarises just how far Dylan has progressed in 1961.

1961 CONCERTS

Various appearances at Coffeehouse Hootenannies.

April

5. NYU Folk Club, Loeb Music Center, New York City.

11-24. Gerde's Folk City, New York City.

May

6. Motowesi Hotel, Branford, Connecticut (★'Talkin' Columbia', 'Slipknot', 'Talkin' Fisherman').

University Hootenanny, Minneapolis, Minnesota.

June

Gerde's Folk City, New York City (Monday night hootenannies).

Cafe Lena, Saratoga Springs (2 nights).

July

Gaslight Cafe, New York City (1 week engagement).

Kiwanis Club, New York City, New York.

September

6. Gaslight Cafe, New York City (★'Man On The Street', 'He

Was A Friend Of Mine', 'Talkin' Bear Mountain Picnic Massacre Disaster Blues', 'Song To Woody', 'Pretty Polly', 'Car Car' (with Dave Van Ronk)).
25-30. Gerde's Folk City, New York City (29th★'Ranger's Command', 'San Francisco Bay Blues', 'The Great Divide','See That My Grave Is Kept Clean', 'Ain't No More Cane', 'Dink's Song', 'He Was A Friend Of Mine', 'Pretty Boy Floyd', 'In The Pines', 'Sally Gal').

October
1-8. Gerde's Folk City, New York City.

November
4. Carnegie Chapter Hall, New York City (★'Pretty Peggy-O', 'In The Pines', 'Gospel Plow', '1913 Massacre', 'Backwater Blues', 'Long Time A-Growin'', 'Fixin' To Die').

December
University Of Minneapolis.
Rutgers University, New Jersey.

1961 BIBLIOGRAPHY
Shelton, Robert, 'A Distinctive Folk Song Stylist', *New York Times*, September 29.

1961 IMPORTANT UNRELEASED MATERIAL
February
The Gleasons' Tape: Recorded in East Orange. (★'San Francisco Bay Blues', 'Jesus Met The Woman At The Well', 'Gypsy Davy', 'Pastures Of Plenty', 'On The Trail Of The Buffalo', 'Jesse James', 'Sweetheart Remember Me').

May
The Minnesota Party Tape: Recorded in Minneapolis. (★'Ramblin' Blues', 'Death Don't Have No Mercy', 'It's Hard To Be Blind', 'This Train', 'Harp Blues', 'Talkin' Fisherman', 'Pastures Of Plenty', 'This Land Is Your Land', 'Two Trains Runnin', 'Wild Mountain Thyme', 'Howja Do', 'Car Car', 'Don't You Push Me Down', 'Come See', 'I Want My Milk', 'San Francisco Bay Blues', 'Long Time A-Growin'', 'Devilish Mary', 'Railroad Bill', 'Will The Circle Be Unbroken', 'Man Of Constant Sorrow', 'Pretty Polly', 'Railroad Boy', 'Times Ain't What They Used To Be', 'Bonnie Why'd You Cut My Hair?').

November 23. and *December* 4.
The MacKenzies' Tapes: Recorded in New York City. (★'Hard Times In New York', 'Wayfaring Stranger', 'It Makes A Long Time Man Feel Bad', 'Lonesome Whistle', 'Worried Blues', 'Baby Of Mine', 'Baby Let Me Follow You Down', 'Fixin' To Die', 'San Francisco Bay Blues', 'You're No Good', 'House Of The Rising Sun', 'This Land Is Your Land', 'Roll In My Sweet Baby's Arms', 'Bells Of Rhymney', 'Come All You Fair And Tender Ladies', 'Roll In My Sweet Baby's Arms', 'Bells Of Rhymney', 'Highway 51', 'This Land Is Your Land').

December
22. Minnesota Hotel Tape: Recorded in Minneapolis. (★'Candy Man', 'Baby Please Don't Go', 'Hard Times In New York Town', 'Stealin'', 'Poor Lazarus', 'I Ain't Got No Home', 'It's Hard To Be Blind', 'Dink's Song', 'Man Of Constant Sorrow', 'East Orange, New Jersey', 'Naomi Wise', 'Wade In The Water', 'I Was Young When I Left Home', 'In The Evening', 'Baby Let Me Follow You Down', 'Sally Gal', 'Gospel Plow', 'Long John', 'Cocaine', 'VD Blues', 'VD Waltz', 'VD City', 'VD Gunner's Blues', 'See That My Grave Is Kept Clean', 'Ramblin' Round', 'Black Cross').

1961 RADIO AND TV APPEARANCES
July
29. WRVR-FM Radio, New York: *Saturday Of Folk Music*. Live from the Riverside Church. (★'Handsome Molly', 'Omie Wise', 'Poor Lazarus', 'Mean Old Southern Railroad' (vocals by Danny Kalb), 'Acne' (with Jack Elliott)).

October
29. WNYC Radio, New York. *Folksong Festival* (with Oscar Brand). Non-extant.

1961 INTERVIEWS
Autumn
Billy James interview (for Columbia Records - for use as liner notes for Dylan's debut LP. Extracts published in *New Musical Express*, April 24, 1976 and July 2, 1977): "I guess I've memorised a lot of what I've heard - things I can remember back - I write a lot of songs and I forget them."
Izzy Young interviews for his Journals. (Published December 1968 in the US underground magazine *Other Scenes*.)

1961 SONGS WRITTEN
Pre-1961 'Blackjack Blues' (Unreleased). No recording extant. Partial lyric extant.
'Bob Dylan's Blues' (Unreleased). No recording extant. No lyric extant.
'Every Time I Hear The Spirit' (Unreleased). No recording

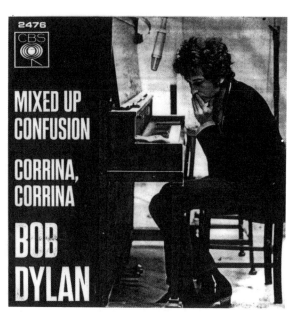

Picture sleeve of the rare Rock 'n' Roll single 'Mixed Up Confusion'

extant. No lyric extant.

'Greyhound Blues' (Unreleased). No recording extant. No lyric extant.

'One-Eyed Jacks' (Unreleased). Recorded on Karen Wallace's tape in May 1960.

'Talkin' Hugh Brown' (Unreleased). Recorded on the September 1960 Minneapolis tape. The song is about Dylan's Dinkytown flatmate.

February

'Song To Woody' (*Bob Dylan*).

May

'Talkin' New York' (*Bob Dylan*).

June

'East Colorado Blues' (Unreleased). No recording extant. Manuscript version owned by MacKenzies.

August

'Talkin' Bear Mountain Picnic Massacre Blues' (*The Bootleg Series*). Recorded for, but not used on, *Freewheelin'*.

September

'He Was A Friend Of Mine'. Recorded on Leeds Demos.

'Man On The Street'. Recorded on Leeds Demos.

'Talkin' Hava Nagila Blues'. Recorded for, but not released on, *Freewheelin'*.

c. October

'California Brown-Eyed Baby' (Unreleased). No recording extant. No lyric extant.

November

'Hard Times In New York Town'. Recorded on Leeds Demos.

December

'Ballad Of The Ox Bow Incident' (Unreleased). No recording extant. No lyric extant.

'I Was Young When I Left Home' (Unreleased). Recorded on Minnesota Hotel Tape, December 22, 1961.

'Strange Rain' (Unreleased). No recording extant. No lyric extant.

1962

1962 CHRONOLOGY

January

Records demo tape for Leeds Music which preserves performances of some of his earliest compositions. He seems to be leaving Woody Guthrie's influence behind: "The influence wore off when he ceased to be an idol to me. I got to know him and I couldn't feel honest any more, things all started looking phoney to me. Singing Woody's songs for money, singing folk songs for money, all of a sudden this seemed very phoney."

February

Broadside magazine is published for the first time. Dylan will be a regular contributor. For the first issue, he gives them his newest talking blues, 'Talkin' John Birch Society'.

March

19. First LP released. "I wasn't even me. I was still learning language then. I was writing then, but what I was writing I was still scared to sing."

April

16. In The Commons coffeehouse, Dylan puts the finishing touches to a new song, 'Blowin' In The Wind'. That evening, Gil Turner performs the song at Gerdes Folk City, and announces Bob Dylan as composer.

May

'Blowin' In The Wind' printed in *Broadside* magazine: "I started writing because things were changing all the time and a certain song needed to be written. I started writing them because I wanted to sing them."

June

8. Suze Rotolo, with whom Dylan has been living for several months, leaves for Italy: "There is something there I see in him that I just don't like negative, pessimistic. But on another level he is so alive, so very much alive, it's frightening. And then there is something in him that is so very funny. That's what made me run away." Suze is away for nine months, during which a distraught Dylan writes some of his greatest early love songs.

Dylan is now managed by Albert Grossman and signs to Witmark publishing. "Albert was one of the few people who saw Dylan's worth early on he refused to let him go on any rinky-dink TV shows, refused to let Columbia do bullshit things with him and Dylan required that kind of handling." (D.A. Pennebaker)

July

9. Records 'Blowin' In The Wind' for his second LP. "I felt real good about doing an album with my own material, and I picked a little on it. Picked the guitar, and it was a big Gibson. I felt real accomplished on that."

August

3. Dylan is mentioned for the first time in the British press when the *New Musical Express* describes him as "the most exciting new folk talent in years".

9. Bob Dylan legally becomes Bob Dylan: "It's a common thing to change your name. Sometimes you are held back by your name I just chose that name and it stuck. That name changed me. I didn't sit around and think about it too much."

November

14. Records 'Talking John Birch Paranoid Blues' - a song which will subsequently not be included on the LP - and 'Mixed Up Confusion' - a rockabilly track. "I played all the folk songs with a rock 'n' roll attitude. This is what made me different and allowed me to cut through all the mess and be heard."

December

14. 'Mixed Up Confusion' released as "folksinger" Bob Dylan's first single.

22. In England for the BBC TV play *Madhouse On Castle Street*, Dylan checks out the London folk clubs - The Troubadour and then The Singers Club at the Pindar Of Wakefield pub in Gray's Inn Road where he performs for an enthusiastic crowd. Club organisers Ewan MacColl and Peggy Seeger do not seem so impressed, however, sitting through Dylan's songs "in stony silence". Meeting MacColl's daughter Kirsty some 23 years later, Dylan tells her "Your daddy didn't like me at all."

1962 BIBLIOGRAPHY

Goddard, J.R., 'Records: Bobby Dylan', *Village Voice*, April 26.
'Bob Dylan Sings In Washington Square', *Seventeen*, September.
Turner, Gil, 'A New Voice Singing New Songs', *Sing Out!*, Oct/Nov.
Pankake, Jon & Nelson, Paul, 'Bob Dylan', *Little Sandy Review*, No.22.

1962 SONGS WRITTEN

January

'Ballad For A Friend' (Unreleased). Recorded on Leeds Demos.

'Poor Boy Blues' (Unreleased). Recorded on Leeds Demos.

'Ramblin' Gamblin' Willie' (The Bootleg Series). "This was about a real person and this is the way it was." Recorded for, but left off, *Freewheelin'*.

'Standing On The Highway' (Unreleased). Recorded for Leeds Demos.

February

'Ballad Of Donald White' (Broadside Reunion). Written after

New York City 1962

watching a television documentary.

'Death Of Emmett Till' (Broadside Reunion). "I used to write songs like I'd say, Yeah, what's bad? Pick out something bad, like segregation. OK, here we go! And I'd pick one of the thousand million little points I can pick and explode it. I wrote a song about Emmett Till which in all honesty was a bullshit song. I realise now that my reasons and motives behind it were phony."

'Death Of Robert Johnson' (Unreleased). No recording extant. No lyrics extant.

'Let Me Die In My Footsteps'. "I was going through some town and they were making this bomb shelter, one of these Coliseum-type things. I was there for about an hour, just looking at them build, and I guess I just wrote the song in my head. It's one song I'm really glad I made a record of." Recorded for, but not released on, *Freewheelin'*.

'Talkin' John Birch Society Blues'. Recorded for, but not released on, *Freewheelin'*.

March

'Talkin' Folklore Center' (Unreleased). No recording extant. Lyrics published as broadsheet by Izzy Young's Folklore Center.

April

'Blowin' In The Wind' (*The Freewheelin' Bob Dylan*). "'Blowin' In The Wind' has always been a spiritual, always. I've always seen it and heard it that way."

'Corrina Corrina' (*The Freewheelin' Bob Dylan*).

'Honey Just Allow Me One More Chance' (*The Freewheelin' Bob Dylan*).

'Rocks And Gravel' (Unreleased). "I learned one verse from Big Joe Williams, and the rest I put together out of lines that seemed to go with this story." Recorded for, but not released on, *Freewheelin'*.

'Suze' (*The Bootleg Series*).

c. June

'Gates Of Hate' (Unreleased). Written about John Henry Faulk, after meeting him at a party hosted by Theodore Bikel. No recording extant. No lyrics extant.

July

'Babe I'm In The Mood For You' (*Biograph*).

'Down The Highway' (*The Freewheelin' Bob Dylan*).

"I really miss my baby" Suze Rotolo sailed to Perugia, Italy on June 8.

'Quit Your Lowdown Ways'. Recorded for, but not released on, *Freewheelin'*.

August

'Ain't Gonna Grieve' (Unreleased). Recorded as demo for Witmark.

'Talkin' Hypocrite' (Unreleased). Recorded on private tape in Minneapolis by Tony Glover.

'Tomorrow Is A Long Time' (*More Bob Dylan Greatest Hits*). For Suze Rotolo.

September

'A Hard Rain's A-Gonna Fall' (*The Freewheelin' Bob Dylan*). "I wrote that in the basement of the Village Gate, at Chip Monck's – he used to have a place down there in the boiler room, an apartment that he slept in. It's a desperate kind of song."

'Ballad Of Hollis Brown' (*The Times They Are A-Changin'*).

October

'Don't Think Twice, It's Alright' (*The Freewheelin' Bob Dylan*). "It isn't a love song. It's a statement that maybe you can say to make yourself feel better. It's as if you were talking to yourself."

'John Brown' (Unreleased). Recorded as demo for Witmark.

November

'I'd Hate To Be You On That Dreadful Day' (Broadside Reunion).

'Long Ago, Far Away'. Recorded as demo for Witmark.

'Mixed Up Confusion' (*Biograph*). Dylan recorded three versions of this song, his first single, before walking out of the sessions in disgust.

'Oxford Town' (*The Freewheelin' Bob Dylan*). "An old banjo tune" about James Meredith.

'Paths Of Victory'. Recorded as demo for Witmark.

'Playboys And Playgirls' (Evening Concerts At Newport Vol 1).

'Walkin' Down The Line'. Recorded as demo for Witmark.

December

'Ballad Of The Gliding Swan' (Unreleased). Written and recorded for BBC TV play, *Madhouse On Castle Street*. Incomplete recording extant. Lyrics extant.

'Bob Dylan's Blues' (*The Freewheelin' Bob Dylan*).

'Hero Blues' (Unreleased). Recorded as demo for Witmark.

'I Shall Be Free' (*The Freewheelin' Bob Dylan*).

'Kingsport Town'. Recorded for, but not used on, *Freewheelin'*.

'Whatcha Gonna Do' (Unreleased). Recorded as demo for Witmark.

1962 CONCERTS

January

San Remo Coffeehouse, Schenectady, New York.

February

Cafe Lena, Saratoga Springs, Mass. Gerde's Folk City, New York City (3 week engagement).

23. CORE Benefit, City College, Manhattan.

April

20-22. Goddard College, Ann Arbor, Michigan.

24-30. Gerde's Folk City, New York City.

May

1-6. Gerde's Folk City, New York City (★'Honey Just Allow Me One More Chance', 'Talkin' New York', 'Corrina, Corrina', 'Deep Ellem Blues', 'Blowin' In The Wind'.)

June

28-30. Potpourri, Montreal, Quebec, Canada.

July

2. Finjan Club, Montreal, Quebec, Canada (★'Death Of Emmett Till', 'Stealin'', 'Hiram Hubbard', 'Blowin' In The Wind', 'Rocks And Gravel', 'Quit Your Lowdown Ways', 'He Was A Friend Of Mine', 'Let Me Die In My Footsteps', 'Two Trains Runnin'',

'Ramblin' On My Mind', 'Muleskinner Blues'.)
September
22. Hootenanny, Carnegie Hall, New York City (*'Sally Gal', 'Highway 51', 'Talking John Birch Paranoid Blues', 'Ballad Of Hollis Brown', 'A Hard Rain's A-Gonna Fall'.)
October
5. Hootenanny, Town Hall, New York City.
November
Gaslight Cafe, New York City (*'Barbara Allen', 'A Hard Rain's A-Gonna Fall', 'Don't Think Twice It's Alright', 'Black Cross', 'No More Auction Block', 'Rocks And Gravel', 'Moonshine Blues', 'John Brown', 'Ballad Of Hollis Brown', 'See That My Grave Is Kept Clean', 'Cocaine', 'The Cuckoo Is A Pretty Bird', 'Ain't No More Cane', 'Motherless Children', 'Handsome Molly', 'Kind Hearted Woman Blues', 'West Texas'.)
December
The Troubadour, London.
22. Singers' Club, Pindar Of Wakefield, London.
23. King & Queen pub, London.

Folk Poet Dylan Weaves a Spell

By BARRY KITTLESON

Folk poet Bob Dylan, who made his New York Town Hall debut last week (12), is the stuff of which legends are made. At 21 singing his own compositions, Dylan turns out to be not just an individual; he is an absolute original.

Dylan is literate, but he affects a hillbilly intonation and diction to subtle purpose, making his story seem all the more profound. And it is profound. Dylan's poetry is born of a painful awareness of the tragedy that underlies the contemporary human condition. But none of it is cliche. Whether he is sermonizing on loneliness, fear, fallout, war or personal tragedy, he has the unbiased perception of a reporter and the compassion of a free spirit.

Dylan, the performer, is unassuming though always in control, and his musicianship is more than competent. But it is his primary purpose to speak, not to entertain. The influence he has already had was evidenced by the many prominent folk singers who turned out for his concert debut.

He has recorded two albums for Columbia. The first, "Bob Dylan," is a document to his rapid growth in the past year. "The Free Wheeling Bob Dylan," which Columbia has readied for May release, is something to look forward to.

Among the young "comers" in the folk scene, Dylan is perhaps the most important. He'll not be lost in the explosion of any overnight ride of popular success. The prediction here is that his talent will be around for a long, long time and his capacity for growth will continue to make each performance a fresh and unique experience.

Review of the New York Town Hall concert of 12 April 1963

Various brief sets at The Troubadour, The King & Queen, Bunjies Coffeehouse, Les Cousins and The Roundhouse in London.

1962 DISCOGRAPHY
March
Bob Dylan (US LP) (Columbia CL 1779/CS 8579) ('You're No Good', 'Talking New York', 'In My Time Of Dyin'', 'Man Of Constant Sorrow', 'Fixin' To Die', 'Pretty Peggy-O', 'Highway 51', 'Gospel Plow', 'Baby Let Me Follow You Down', 'House Of The Risin' Sun', 'Freight Train Blues', 'Song To Woody', 'See That My Grave Is Kept Clean'.)
May
Session on Harry Belafonte's *Midnight Special* (RCA LSP 2449) ('Midnight Special').
Session on Carolyn Hester's *Carolyn Hester* (Columbia CL1796) ('I'll Fly Away', 'Swing And Turn Jubilee', 'Come Back Baby'.)
June
Bob Dylan (UK LP) (CBS BGP 62022).
December
'Mixed Up Confusion'/'Corrina Corrina' (US 45) (Columbia 3-42656)

1962 IMPORTANT UNRELEASED MATERIAL
January-March
Demo recordings for Leeds Music. ('He Was A Friend Of Mine', 'Man On The Street', 'Hard Times In New York', 'Poor Boy Blues', 'Ballad For A Friend', 'Rambling, Gambling Willie', 'Man On The Street' (2), 'Talking Bear Mountain Picnic Massacre Blues', 'Standing On The Highway'.)
February-March
Private recordings at the apartment of Cynthia Gooding.('Ballad Of Donald White', 'Witchita', 'Acne', 'Rocks And Gravel', 'It Makes A Long Time Man Feel Bad'.)
August
11. Private recordings in Minnesota by Tony Glover. ('Tomorrow Is A Long Time', 'This Is Your Land', 'Talking Hypocrite', 'Motherless Children', 'Worried Blues', 'Long Time Gone', 'Deep Clear Blues'.)
April-November
Various recordings at the sessions for *The Freewheelin' Bob Dylan*. 'Baby Please Don't Go', 'Milk Cow Calf's Blues' (x2), 'Witchita' (x2), 'Rocks And Gravel', 'Baby I'm In The Mood For You' (x2), 'Corrina Corrina', 'The Death Of Emmett Till', 'Watcha Gonna Do', 'Sally Gal', 'Going To New Orleans', 'That's All Right Mama', 'Ballad Of Hollis Brown'.
October-November
Recordings in offices of Broadside magazine, New York.('I Shall Be Free', 'Cuban Missile Crisis', 'Playboys And Playgirls', 'Oxford Town', 'Paths Of Victory', 'Walkin' Down The Line').

1962 RADIO AND TV
March
WBAI-FM Radio, New York: *The Broadside Show* ('Ballad Of Donald White', 'Death Of Emmett Till', 'Blowin' In The Wind').
April
WYNC Radio, New York: *Adventures In Folk Music* Interview with Henrietta Yurchenco. Non-extant.
October
WBAI-FM Radio, New York: *The Cynthia Gooding Show* Non-extant.
WBAI-FM Radio, New York: *The Billy Faier Show* ('Baby Let Me Follow You Down', 'Talking John Birch Paranoid Blues',

'Death Of Emmett Till', 'Make Me A Pallet On Your Floor').

1962 INTERVIEWS
September
Edwin Miller for *Seventeen* magazine: "I don't work regularly. I don't want to make a lot of money, really."
October
Rachel Price for *FM-Stereo Guide*: "Some people consider me a poet, but I can't think about it. Right now I'm waiting for my girl to come home."
Gil Turner for *Sing Out!*

1963

1963 CHRONOLOGY
January
In London to play Bobby the hobo in BBC TV play *Madhouse On Castle Street*. "We found he had trouble delivering the lines. Bob wanted to write his own lines." (Philip Saville, director). Dylan is reading *The White Goddess* and is taken, just after New Year, to meet Robert Graves. Unfortunately, he seems not to have made a good impression on the poet, who complained about his manners.
5. Dylan flies to Rome to look for Suze Rotolo. Unfortunately, she has left Italy to return to New York. At this time he composes 'Girl From The North Country', having heard Martin Carthy sing 'Scarborough Fair' in London.
14-15. Dylan records with Richard Farina and Eric Von Schmidt in Dobell's Jazz Record Shop.
February

HOW MANY ROADS
MUST A MAN WALK DOWN...

Bob Dylan has walked down many roads. For most of his 22 years he "rode freight trains for kicks and got beat up for laughs, cut grass for quarters and sang for dimes." And his songs today are the sounds he sopped up all those years on the road — "the coyote's call and the train whistle's moan, the ol' time pals an' first run gals, the faces you can't find again."

Bob does what a true folk singer is supposed to do — sing about the important ideas and events of the times. And he does it better than anybody else. One Dylan fan, Joan Baez, said, "I feel it, but Dylan can say it. He's phenomenal."

His new best-selling album (the first was Bob Dylan) is The Freewheelin' Bob Dylan. It features ten of Bob's own compositions, including the sensational hit, "Blowin' in the Wind." Also, songs on subjects ranging from love ("Girl From The North Country") to atomic fall-out ("A Hard Rain's A-Gonna Fall"). Hear it and you'll know why Bob Dylan is the voice of the times.

BOB DYLAN ON COLUMBIA RECORDS

DON HUNSTEIN

Reunited with Suze, Dylan is photographed in the snow of West 4th Street with her for the cover of his second LP, *The Freewheelin' Bob Dylan*.
April
12. First major solo concert at New York Town Hall. Dylan recites a long poem, 'Last Thoughts On Woody Guthrie' and performs several new songs, including 'With God On Our Side' for an audience of 900.
May
Walks out on Ed Sullivan Show having been forbidden to sing 'Talking John Birch Paranoid Blues'. "I could have done something else, but we'd rehearsed the song so many times, and everybody had heard it. Even Ed Sullivan seemed to really like it! But just before I was going out to sing it - I was just getting ready to play - someone stepped up and said I couldn't sing that song. They wanted me to sing a Clancy Brothers song so, I just left."
18. Gets to know Joan Baez at the Monterey Folk Festival.
27. *The Freewheelin' Bob Dylan* released.
June
Visits Woodstock for the first time with Suze, staying with Peter Yarrow, of Peter, Paul And Mary. "It's the greatest, man, the greatest place. We stop the clouds, turn time back and inside out."
July
6. Sings at Civil Rights Rally in Greenwood, Mississippi. Film of his performance of 'Only A Pawn In Their Game' is included in the later documentary, *Don't Look Back*. 'Blowin' In The Wind' released as a single. Dylan sings the song with Peter, Paul & Mary, Joan Baez and The Freedom Singers at the Newport Folk Festival (26th) and on the *Songs Of Freedom* TV show (30th). The song and its composer become a focal point for the Civil Rights movement.
26-28. Appears at the Newport Folk Festival: "Newport '63 was a turning point for folk song as a new popular music, and for Dylan. Dylan became the festival's emblem. He left Newport a star." (Shelton) Joan Baez and Dylan sing 'With God On Our Side' together.
August
Appears as guest at several Joan Baez concerts. Their relationship develops into a love affair, though Suze doesn't quite realise it.
28. Sings 'Only A Pawn In Their Game' in front of 400,000 people at the March On Washington.
29. In the Washington papers the morning after, Dylan reads of rich wealthy William Zanzinger receiving a six-month sentence for the no reason killing of poor Hattie Carroll.
September
Moves in with Joan Baez in Carmel Valley, California. "I tried to get Bobby to look after his health, cut down on his smoking, clean his teeth."
October
23. Begins the recording of '*The Times They Are A Changin*''
"Those songs were written in the New York atmosphere. I'd never have written any of them - or sung them the way I did - if I hadn't been sitting around listening to performers in New York cafes and the talk in all the dingy parlours. I tried to make the songs genuine." At this time, Dylan is interviewed by Andrea Svedburg for *Newsweek*, but she digs up the subject of Hibbing and his background. A terribly sour piece appears in the magazine, accusing him of phoniness and suggesting that he didn't even write 'Blowin' in The Wind'. An infuriated Dylan never trusts journalists after this experience.
December
Receives the Tom Paine Award from the Emergency Civil Liberties Committee, but creates a furore when, in his acceptance speech he says that he can recognise in himself some of the things that caused Oswald to shoot Kennedy. He subsequently writes a

letter of apology, but knows he has been misunderstood: "They actually thought I was saying it was a good thing Kennedy had been killed."

1963 BIBLIOGRAPHY

Shelton, Robert, 'Bob Dylan Sings His Compositions', *New York Times*, April 13.

Kittleson, Barry, 'A Legend Under Construction: Folk Poet Dylan Weaves A Spell', *Billboard*, April 27.

Dunson, Josh, 'Yevtushenko, Lorca and Bob Dylan', *Broadside*, No.27 June.

Hentoff, Nat, 'Folk, Folkum and the New Citybilly', *Playboy*, June.

Smith, Jack A., 'A World Of His Own', *National Guardian*, August 22.

'Bob Dylan, 22, A Folknik Hero', *Variety*, September.

Levinson, L.L., 'Bob Dylan's "Protest" Songs Fill Carnegie With Teenster Fans', *Variety*, October 30.

'"I Am My Words"', *Newsweek*, November 4.

1963 SONGS WRITTEN

January
'Farewell'. Recorded as demo for Witmark.
'Girl From The North Country' (*The Freewheelin' Bob Dylan*).
'Masters Of War' (*The Freewheelin' Bob Dylan*) "I've never really written anything like that before. I don't sing songs which hope people will die, but I couldn't help it with this one. The song is a sort of striking out, a reaction to the last straw, a feeling of what can you do?"
'Talkin' Devil' (*Broadside Ballads*).

February
'All Over You'. Recorded as demo for Witmark.
'Bob Dylan's Dream' (*The Freewheelin' Bob Dylan*).
'Going Back To Rome' (Unreleased). Recorded in New York City on the private "Banjo Party Tape".
'Only A Hobo' (*Broadside Ballads*).

Bob Dylan, 22, a Folknik Hero

Composer-Performer In Click Groove With His Civil Rights Themes

Bob Dylan is emerging as the big wheel in the current folknik spin. He's scoring in the recording, songwriting and concert field and is considered by many guitar-hooters as the single most important creative force on the folk scene.

In addition to clicking in the pop field with the authorship of "Blowin' In The Wind," the 22-year old singer from the midwest is also in the vanguard of the Negro protest movement with his composition "Only A Pawn In Their Game," a song saga of Medgar Evers. As a disker, he's now clicking with his Columbia Records LP, "The Freewheelin' Bob Dylan," which Col sales execs report to be selling at the rate of about 10,000 copies a week.

Dylan also appears to be shaping as the folksingers' folkster. He's being championed by such folkniks as Peter, Paul & Mary, Pete Seeger, Joan Baez, Odetta, among others. At the recent Newport folk Festival, Peter Yarrow, who was to sing "Blowin' In The Wind" with Peter, Paul & Mary, said, "This song as written by the most important folk artist in America today," Miss Baez called him on stage to share her concert and at the conclusion of Dylan's own performance, every major star at the Festival joined him on stage for a "We Shall Overcome" finale.

Since Newport, Dylan has been appearing, unannounced, as part of Miss Baez's concerts. At the recent Forest Hills (N.Y.) concert, Miss Baez devoted the first half of her program to several of Dylan's songs, and then she introduced him in the second half in which he performed solo and did duets with her. In October, he starts his own concertizing with one-man shows in New York (Carnegie Hall), Philadelphia, Boston and Chicago. Plans are also being made for a college tour.

Dylan started his professional career a little over a year ago singing in Greenwich Village clubs after coming to New York to see veteran folk writer Woodie Guthrie who is ailing in a local hospital. He was signed to a long-term disk deal by John Hammond of Columbia's artists & repertoire department.

The label has released two albums: "Bob Dylan" and "The Freewheelin' Bob Dylan." In the first album, only two selections were written by him; on the second, only one was not written by him.

His song catalog was recently put into folio form by M. Witmark & Sons under the publication title of "The Bob Dylan Song Book."

New York Times enthusiasm 1963

March
'Cuban Blockade' (Unreleased). Recorded for *Broadside* magazine.
'Long Time Gone' (Unreleased). Recorded as demo for Witmark.
'Train A-Travelin'' (*Broadside Reunion*).
'Bound To Lose' (Unreleased). Recorded as demo for Witmark.

April
'Bob Dylan's New Orleans Rag'. Recorded for, but not used on, *The Times They Are A-Changin'*.
'Boots Of Spanish Leather' (*The Times They Are A-Changin'*).
'Dusty Old Fairgrounds' (Unreleased). Recorded at Town Hall, New York City, April 12.
'Ramblin' Down Thru The World' (Unreleased). Recorded at Town Hall, New York City, April 12.
'Talkin' World War III Blues' (*The Freewheelin' Bob Dylan*).
'Walls Of Redwing'. Recorded for, but not used on, *The Times They Are A-Changin'*.
'Who Killed Davey Moore?'. Recorded at Carnegie Hall, New York City, October 26.
'With God On Our Side' (*The Times They Are A-Changin'*).

June
'Eternal Circle'. Recorded for, but not used on, *The Times They Are A-Changin'*.

July
'Only A Pawn In Their Game' (*The Times They Are A-Changin'*).

August
'California' (Unreleased). Recorded for, but not used on, *Another Side Of Bob Dylan*.
'Gypsy Lou' (Unreleased). Recorded as a demo for Witmark.
'North Country Blues' (*The Times They Are A-Changin'*).
'One Too Many Mornings' (*The Times They Are A-Changin'*).
'Percy's Song' (*Biograph*).
'Seven Curses'. Recorded for, but not used on, *The Times They Are A-Changin'*.
'Troubled And I Don't Know Why' (Unreleased). Recorded live at Forest Hills, New York, August 17.
'When The Ship Comes In' (*The Times They Are A-Changin'*).

September
'Lay Down Your Weary Tune' (*Biograph*).
'The Lonesome Death Of Hattie Carroll' (*The Times They Are A-Changin'*). "I wrote Hattie Carroll in a small notebook in a restaurant on 7th Avenue I felt I had a lot in common with this situation and was able to manifest my feelings."
'The Times They Are A-Changin'' (*The Times They Are A-Changin'*). "I wanted to write a big song, some kind of theme song, with short, concise verses that piled up on each other in a hypnotic way."

October
'Restless Farewell' (*The Times They Are A-Changin'*). "Some songs, like Restless Farewell, I've written just to fill up an album."

1963 CONCERTS

January
Various folk club appearances in London and one in Rome.

April
12. Town Hall, New York City (*'Rambling Down Thru The World', 'Bob Dylan's Dream', 'Tomorrow Is A Long Time', 'Bob Dylan's New Orleans Rag', 'Masters Of War', 'Walls Of Red Wing', 'Hero Blues', 'Who Killed Davey Moore?', 'With God On Our Side', 'Dusty Old Fairgrounds', 'All Over You', 'John Brown', 'Last Thoughts On Woody Guthrie').

19 and 20. Cafe Yana, Boston.

21. Hootenanny at Club 47, Cambridge.

25. The Bear, Chicago (*'Honey Just Allow Me One More Chance', 'Talking John Birch Paranoid Blues', 'Bob Dylan's Dream', 'Ballad Of Hollis Brown', 'Talking World War III Blues',

Flushing, N.Y.

Dear Editor:

For a long time, I have been fed up with a great deal about Bob Dylan, but Irwin Silber's review (SING OUT!, February-March) forces me to shout it out.

To start with, let me say that I hold the same "radical" ideas that your magazine and Bob Dylan supposedly stand for. I feel that Dylan and his like are retarding the progressive movement in America. Mainly, I am disgusted at his slob-like appearance. Having his immense head of hair carefully placed to look like it is naturally sloppy by no means helps to combat the "Masters of War." Wearing old and beaten clothes on purpose can only make people shun the thought that "There's A New World A-Coming."

It might be interesting for Dylan to note that most of the civil rights and peace organizations ask people who wish to join their demonstrations to dress decently (also not to smoke on picket lines) in order to create a favorable atmosphere. How can Dylan expect to bring into effect his hopes for a better world if he insists on purposefully associating these hopes with filth and planned sloppiness?

I am not asking for tuxedo and tie, only a little decency in dress indicating an amount of self-respect. (I have never heard of Pete Seeger not being presentably dressed in public)

I could add a few words about Dylan's rather phony Guthrie-exaggerated voice intonation, but will simply close on the note that Dylan's reverse conformity, paticularly in the way he dresses, seems to hint that maybe he himself is "only a pawn in the game."

I omit my name because it is unpopular among the numerous idolizers to criticize the god of "the new world a-coming", Bob Dylan.

Utterly Disgusted

Cruel attack on 'slob-like' Bob in Sing Out!

'A Hard Rain's A-Gonna Fall', 'With God On Our Side').

May

10. Folk Festival, Brandeis University, Boston, Mass.
18. First Monterey Folk Festival, Monterey, California.

July

6. Civil Rights Rally, Greenwood, Mississippi (★'Only A Pawn In Their Game').
26-28. Newport Folk Festival, Newport, Rhode Island (★'Blowin' In The Wind', 'We Shall Overcome', 'Playboys And Playgirls', 'With God On Our Side').

August

3. Camden Music Fair, New Jersey (Guest appearance at Joan Baez concert. Several others in this month too.)
17. Forest Hills Stadium, New York (★'Troubled And I Don't Know Why', 'Blowin' In The Wind').
28. March On Washington, Washington, DC (★'Only A Pawn In Their Game', 'Keep Your Eyes On The Prize').

September

Columbia Records Sales Convention: Puerto Rico.

October

19. Hill Auditorium, Ann Arbor, Michigan.
25. Town Hall, Philadelphia, PA.
26. Carnegie Hall, New York City (★'Lay Down Your Weary Tune', 'When The Ship Comes In', 'Who Killed Davey Moore?', 'Percy's Song', 'Seven Curses').

November

2. Jordan Hall, Boston, Mass.
3. Regent Theater, Syracuse.

30. Mosque Theater, Newark, New Jersey.

December

14. Lisner Auditorium, Washington DC.
27. Orchestra Hall, Chicago, Illinois.

1963 DISCOGRAPHY

May

The Freewheelin' Bob Dylan (US LP) (Columbia CL 1986/CS 8786) (USA No.22, 32 weeks) ('Blowin' In The Wind', 'Girl Of The North Country', 'Masters Of War', 'Down The Highway', 'Bob Dylan's Blues', 'A Hard Rain's A-Gonna Fall', 'Don't Think Twice, It's Alright', 'Bob Dylan's Dream', 'Oxford Town', 'Talkin' World War III Blues', 'Corrina Corrina', 'Honey Just Allow Me One More Chance', 'I Shall Be Free'.)

July

'Blowin' In The Wind'/'Don't Think Twice It's Alright' (US 45) (Columbia 4-42856)

September

Dylan as "Blind Boy Grunt" on Broadside Ballads, Vol.1 (Broadside/Folkways BR 5301) ('John Brown', 'Only A Hobo/Talkin' Devil'.)

November

The Freewheelin' Bob Dylan (UK LP) (CBS BGP 62193) (UK No.1, 49 weeks).

1963 IMPORTANT UNRELEASED RECORDINGS

January

Recordings at offices of Broadside magazine, New York City.(★'Masters Of War', 'Farewell').

February

Recording at Gil Turner's home, New York City.(★'Lonesome River Edge', 'Back Door Blues', 'Bob Dylan's Dream', 'You Can Get Her', 'Farewell', 'All Over You', 'Masters Of War', 'Keep Your Hands Off Her', 'Honey Babe', 'Going Back To Rome', 'Stealin''.)

Spring

Demo recordings for Witmark & Sons, music publishers. (Some probably recorded 1962) (★'Long Ago, Far Away', 'Long Time Gone', 'Ain't Gonna Grieve', 'Blowin' In The Wind', 'Farewell', 'Bob Dylan's Blues', 'Seven Curses', 'Paths Of Victory', 'All Over You', 'When The Ship Comes In', 'The Times They Are A-Changin', 'John Brown', 'Talkin' John Birch Paranoid Blues', 'I Shall Be Free', 'Hero Blues', 'Tomorrow's A Long Time', 'Only A Hobo', 'Watcha Gonna Do', 'Gypsy Lou', 'Baby Let Me Follow You Down', 'A Hard Rain's A-Gonna Fall', 'Don't Think Twice It's Alright', 'Oxford Town', 'Masters Of War', 'Walkin' Down The Line', 'The Death Of Emmett Till', 'Bob Dylan's Dream', 'Quit Your Lowdown Ways', 'Baby I'm In The Mood For You', 'Ballad Of Hollis Brown', 'Girl Of The North Country', 'Boots Of Spanish Leather', 'Let Me Die In My Footsteps', 'Bound To Lose', 'I'd Hate To Be You On That Dreadful Day', 'Percy's Song', 'Moonshine Blues', 'Guess I'm Doin' Fine', 'Eternal Circle', 'Mama You Been On My Mind' (x2), 'Mr Tambourine Man'.)

April

Recordings at the home of Eve & Mac MacKenzie, New York City.(★'See That My Grave Is Kept Clean', 'Ballad Of Donald White', 'A Hard Rain's A-Gonna Fall', 'James Alley Blues', 'I Rode Out One Morning', 'Don't Think Twice It's Alright', 'Long Time Gone', 'Only A Hobo', 'House Of The Risin' Sun', 'Cocaine').

May/June

Recordings at the home of Tony Glover, Minneapolis. (★'Ballad Of Hollis Brown', 'Girl Of The North Country', 'Boots Of Spanish Leather', 'Eternal Circle', 'Hero Blues').

August/October

Anticipating the release of 'The Times They are A-Changin'

Various tracks recorded at the sessions for *The Times They Are A-Changin'* LP. (★'East Laredo Blues', 'Bob Dylan's New Orleans Rag' (x2), 'That's Alright Mama', 'Hero Blues', 'Who Killed Davey Moore?', 'Only A Pawn In Their Game', 'With God On Our Side', 'Tomorrow Is A Long Time'.)

1963 TV AND RADIO APPEARANCES

February
Radio: *The Skip Weshner Show*. (★'Tomorrow Is A Long Time', 'Masters Of War', 'Bob Dylan's Blues').
March
Radio WQXR. New York City. *The World Of Folk Music* Oscar Brand Show (★'Girl From The North Country', 'Only A Hobo').
WBC-TV: *Folk Music Special* compered by John Henry Faulk. No recording extant, but it is known that Dylan played 'Blowin' In The Wind', 'Ballad Of Hollis Brown' and 'Paths Of Victory'.
April
WFMT-FM Radio: Chicago: *Studs Terkel's Wax Museum* (★'Farewell', 'A Hard Rain's A-Gonna Fall', 'Bob Dylan's Dream', 'Boots Of Spanish Leather', 'John Brown', 'Who Killed Davey Moore?', 'Blowin' In The Wind'.)
July
30. WNEW-TV: New York City *Songs Of Freedom* (★'Blowin' In The Wind', 'Only A Pawn In Their Game')
TV: Johnny Carson: 'Tonight'. No recording extant.

1963 INTERVIEWS

January
English Arts magazine *Scene*. Interview conducted in London.
May
Time magazine: "Who can believe him? Hard-lick guitar, whooping harmonica, skinny little voice. Beardless chin porcelain pussy cat eyes."
June
Nat Hentoff for *Playboy* magazine.
August
22. Jack Smith for *The National Guardian*: "Ain't nobody can say anything honest in the United States. Every place you look is cluttered with phoneys and lies."
September
12. Sydney Fields for the *New York Daily Mirror:* "Because Dickens and Dostoyevsky and Woody Guthrie were telling their stories much better than I ever could, I decided to stick to my own mind."
October
20. Michael Iachetta for the *Daily News:* "There's mystery, magic, truth and The Bible in great folk music. I can't hope to touch that. But I'm goin' to try."
November
4. Andrea Svedburg for *Newsweek*.

1964

1964 CHRONOLOGY

February
3. Dylan sets out on a cross-country trip with Victor Maimudes, his road manager, Pete Karman, a writer, and Paul Clayton, a folk singer. They visit striking miners in Hazard, Kentucky, and poet Carl Sandburg in Hendersonville, North Carolina. They go to New Orleans for Mardi Gras – an experience which "made many lasting impressions on Dylan" argues Shelton. During the trip, Dylan composes 'Chimes Of Freedom'.
March
The affair with Suze Rotolo finally ends. "As Dylan got more and more famous, things got more and more oppressive. It was a whole bad time and I really crumbled. I didn't see myself as Bob Dylan's wife. All I wanted to do was to get away from it all." Dylan commemorates the affair's passing by writing 'Ballad In Plain D'. "I understood what he was doing. It was the end of something and we both were hurt and bitter. His art was his outlet, his exorcism. It was healthy. That was the way he wrote out his life." (Suze Rotolo). "That one I look back at and say, 'I must have been a real shmuck to write that'. Of all the songs I've written, maybe I could have left that alone." (Bob Dylan).
May
Visits London for one concert at the Festival Hall, then has a brief holiday in Paris and in Greece. In the village of Vermilya, outside Athens, he writes some of the material which he will record for his next LP, *Another Side Of Bob Dylan*. "Tom Wilson, the producer, titled it that. I begged and pleaded with him not to do it. It seemed like a negation of the past, which in no way was true."
June
9. In one evening in Columbia Studios, New York City, Dylan records 14 songs for his fourth LP, playing piano for the first time on record and moving markedly away from the earlier political "finger-pointing" work. "From now on I want to write from inside me, and to do that I'm going to have to get back to writing like I used to when I was 10 – having everything come out naturally."
July
At the Newport Folk Festival, Dylan disappoints the folkies who are expecting a repeat celebration of Civil Rights protest. Dylan's new material – 'Mr Tambourine Man', 'Chimes Of Freedom' –

and his new hipness take many by surprise. He leaves the confusion and arguments behind him by going up to Woodstock for the summer with Joan Baez, her sister Mimi and Mimi's husband Richard Farina.

August

28. Al Aronowitz takes Dylan from Woodstock to New York to meet The Beatles. At a famous night in the Delmonico Hotel, the Americans introduce the Fabs to cannabis.

October

31. A major solo concert at the Philharmonic Hall, New York City on Hallowe'en has Dylan introducing Joan Baez as guest, after appearing as guest artiste in her concerts in previous months.

December

25. According to a US teen mag, several Bob-given surprises are to be found under Joan Baez's Christmas tree: "a strangely shaped green rock he had found while hitching through Colorado, a brightly coloured African scarf, an old Duncan yo-yo, an autoharp he had swapped from a woman in Maine, a sea-shell he had picked up on the beach at Coney Island, a pogo stick, three *Batman* comics, a copy of Lorca's *Gypsy Ballads*, a record of Blind Lemon Jefferson singing 'Bedbug Blues', an old chewing tobacco tin to keep buttons in, a coon skin cap and two boxes of dried sunflower seed."

1964 BIBLIOGRAPHY

Cash, Johnny, 'A Letter From Johnny Cash', *Broadside*, No.41.
Gleason, Ralph J., 'A Folk Singing Social Critic', *San Francisco Chronicle*, February 24.
'Dylan', *New Statesman*, April.
Wells, Chris, 'The Angry Young Folk Singer', *Life*, April 10.

First UK press advertisement 20 March 1965

THE SOUND OF **DYLAN**

CBS RECORDS

BoB DYLaN NEW SiNGLe RELEASED ToDaY

'THE TiMES THEY aRE a CHaNGiN'' c/w 'Honey, just allow me one more chance' 201751

CBS RECORDS · 104 NEW BOND ST · LONDON W1

Jones, Max, 'Three Folk Missionaries', *Melody Maker*, April 11.
'Bob Dylan (23) Writes Songs Stars Like', *NME*, May 8.
Jones, Max, 'Bob Dylan - Most Important Folk Singer Around Today', *Melody Maker*, May 16.
'A Minnesota Minstrel', *The Times*, May 18.
Ochs, Phil, 'The Art Of Bob Dylan's Hattie Carroll', *Broadside*, No.48, July 20.
Farina, Richard, 'Baez & Dylan: A Generation Singing Out', *Mademoiselle*, August.
Hentoff, Nat, 'The Crackin' Shakin' Breakin' Sounds', *The New Yorker*, October 24.
Silber, Irwin, 'An Open Letter To Bob Dylan', *Sing Out!*, No.5.
Wolfe, Paul, 'The New Dylan', *Broadside*, No.53, December.

1964 SONGS WRITTEN

January

'Guess I'm Doin' Fine' (Unreleased). Recorded as demo for Witmark.

February

'Chimes Of Freedom' (*Another Side Of Bob Dylan*).

May

'It Ain't Me Babe' (*Another Side Of Bob Dylan*).

'Mr Tambourine Man' (*Bringing It All Back Home*). "'Mr Tambourine Man' really isn't a fantasy. There's substance to the dream because you've seen it, you know?"

June

'All I Really Wanna Do' (*Another Side Of Bob Dylan*).

'Ballad In Plain D' (*Another Side Of Bob Dylan*). "That one I look back at and say, 'I must have been a real shmuck to write that.' Of all the songs I've written, maybe I could have left that alone."

'Black Crow Blues' (*Another Side Of Bob Dylan*).

'Denise Denise' (Unreleased). Recorded for, but not used on, *Another Side Of Bob Dylan*.

'East Laredo Blues' (Unreleased). Recorded for, but not used on, *Another Side Of Bob Dylan*.

'I Don't Believe You' (*Another Side Of Bob Dylan*).

'I Shall Be Free No. 10' (*Another Side Of Bob Dylan*).

'I'll Keep It With Mine' (*Biograph*).

'Mama You Bin On My Mind'. Recorded as a demo for Witmark.

'Motorpsycho Nitemare' (*Another Side Of Bob Dylan*).

'My Back Pages' (*Another Side Of Bob Dylan*).

'Spanish Harlem Incident' (*Another Side Of Bob Dylan*).

'To Ramona' (*Another Side Of Bob Dylan*).

September

'It's Alright Ma (I'm Only Bleeding)' (*Bringing It All Back Home*).

October

'Gates Of Eden' (*Bringing It All Back Home*).

'If You Gotta Go, Go Now'.

1964 CONCERTS

January

Zanesville, Ohio.

February

7. Emory University, Atlanta.

12. Tougaloo, Jackson, Mississippi.

15. Denver Civic Auditorium, Denver, Colorado. (This concert marks the first performance of the just-written 'Chimes Of Freedom').

22. Berkeley Community Theater, Berkeley, California. (Dylan performs many unreleased songs - 'Who Killed Davey Moore', 'Walls Of Redwing', 'Eternal Circle' as well as 'One Too Many Mornings', 'Restless Farewell' and others.) Riverside, Los Angeles.

Dear Editor:
It is rather amusing to note that Dylan's most-requested song at Newport was one of those "inner probing and self-concious" ones entitled "Hey, Mister Tambourine Man."

Sincerely yours,
Neil Alan Marks
Forest Hills, N.Y.

Dear Editor:
...Dylan was never the run-of-the mill folk-singer the hippies seem to want...Even his "committed" songs had a deeper irony and a more profound intelligence to them than any other of the worker-war-bomb polemics everyone sings... Anyone with a simple awareness, an elementary grasp of what's going on in this world, can talk about the obvious evil around him, (but this is just) superficial. Dylan has begun to go beneath the surface...

John Sinclair
Detroit, Mich.

Dear Editor:
Your last issue disturbed me somewhat. It seems to me that Mr. Silber's criticisms may prove premature: all artists go through phases of development. It is ridiculous to pounce upon an artist of twenty-three and denounce him for a new trend, in particular, for introspection, which is only natural in a person's early years and these times. It also seems quite evident that he has enough character to know what he's doing and to survive the American Success Machinery. As to Newport, I did not see him "lose contact with people."
...It seems inevitable that a real artist will produce both very bad and very good, and as long as he is unique, he will be very controversial...We get the idea: SING OUT! will re-endorse Bob Dylan when and if he returns to his old song topics.

Very sincerely,
Carol Sheffield
Cambridge, Mass.

Dear Editor:
It took much courage for Mr. Silber to "stick his neck out" in writing the truth about Bob Dylan now. The "open letter" is a respected and highly effective form of journalism, and there is no reason why he shouldn't have used it, but I would hate to see the letters I imagine he will get because of it. Bob Dylan is a public figure; it is good to see such concerned criticism about him. Praise or criticism -- it doesn't matter as long as it is honest.

Yours,
Roger De Lino
Pittsburgh, Pa.

Sing Out! responding to Irwin Silber's famous attack on Dylan in 1964

29. Santa Monica Civic Auditorium.
March
Various concerts as guest artist for Joan Baez, Southern California, Providence, Rhode Island.
April
Boston Symphony Hall.
Club 47, Cambridge.
University of Massachusetts, Amherst.

Brandeis University Folk Festival, Waltham, Massachusetts.
May
Monterey Folk Festival, California.
17. Royal Festival Hall, London (At his first major concert appearance in Great Britain, Dylan performs 'Chimes Of Freedom' and, for the first time, 'It Ain't Me Babe'. Also reported, the only known live version of 'Down The Highway' - an unlikely choice. He plays the songs he had been inspired to write after stealing many of Martin Carthy's tunes on his earlier trip - 'Bob Dylan's Dream' (from 'Lord Franklin'), 'Masters Of War' (from 'Nottamun Town'), 'Girl From The North Country' (from 'Scarborough Fair') - thus returning what's owed, but he does not play 'Blowin' In The Wind'. Dylan holds his audience enthralled for two hours - "like Segovia" claims the reviewer for *The Times*.)
July
Ann Arbor High School Auditorium.
Detroit Masonic Temple Auditorium.
24-26. Newport Folk Festival, Newport, Rhode Island (*'Mr Tambourine Man').
August
8. Forest Hills, New York, guest at Joan Baez concert (*'Mama You Been On My Mind', 'It Ain't Me Babe', 'With God On Our Side').
September
Philadelphia Town Hall 18 songs: Including the last known live version of 'Only A Pawn In Their Game' and new songs 'I Don't Believe You' and 'It's Alright Ma, (It's Life And Life Only)'.
October
Detroit.
Kenyon, Minnesota (First reported version of 'Gates Of Eden').
31. Philharmonic Hall, New York City (*19 songs: First airing of 'If You Gotta Go, Go Now' and the only known live version of 'Spanish Harlem Incident'. The show is recorded for a possible live album. "Don't let that scare ya," Dylan announces after 'Gates Of

Dylan in 1963

Eden', having introduced the song as "a sacriligious lullaby", "it's just Hallowe'en. I have my Bob Dylan mask on."

November

3. Yale University, New Haven, Connecticut.
13. Massey Hall, Toronto, Ontario, Canada.
25. Civic Auditorium, San Jose, California (*10 songs).
27. Masonic Memorial Auditorium, San Francisco, California (*6 songs).
29. Sacramento Auditorium, Sacramento, California.

December

1. College Gymnasium, San Mateo, California.
4. Peterson Gymnasium, San Diego, California.
University of Santa Barbara, California.

1964 DISCOGRAPHY

January

The Times They Are A-Changin' (US LP) (Columbia CL-2105/CS-8905) (USA No.20, 17 weeks) ('The Times They Are A-Changin'', 'Ballad Of Hollis Brown', 'With God On Our Side', 'One Too Many Mornings', 'North Country Blues', 'Only A Pawn In Their Game', 'Boots Of Spanish Leather', 'When The Ship Comes In', 'The Lonesome Death Of Hattie Carroll', 'Restless Farewell').

May

The Times They Are A-Changin' (UK LP) (CBS BGP 62251) (UK No.4, 20 weeks).
'Only A Pawn In Their Game' included on *We Shall Overcome* (US LP) (Folkways FH 5592).
'Playboys And Playgirls' and 'With God On Our Side' included on *Newport Broadside* (US LP) (Vanguard VRS 9144, VSD 79144).
'Blowin' In The Wind' included on *Evening Concerts At Newport Vol 1* (US LP) (Vanguard VRS 9148).

June

As "Bob Landy" on session piano on 'Downtown Blues' on *Blues Project* (US LP) (Elektra EKL 264, EKS 7264).

August

Another Side Of Bob Dylan (US LP) (Columbia CL-2193/CS-8993) (USA No.43, 17 weeks) ('All I Really Want To Do', 'Black Crow Blues', 'Spanish Harlem Incident', 'Chimes Of Freedom', 'I Shall Be Free No.10', 'To Ramona', 'Motorpsycho Nitemare', 'My Back Pages', 'I Don't Believe You', 'Ballad In Plain D', 'It Ain't Me Babe').

November

Another Side Of Bob Dylan (UK LP) (CBS BGP 62429) (UK No.8, 19 weeks).

1964 TV AND RADIO APPEARANCES

February

1. CBC-TV: *Quest* – "Bob Dylan Sings Bob Dylan" (*'The Times They Are A-Changin'', 'Talking World War III Blues', 'The Lonesome Death Of Hattie Carroll', 'Girl From The North Country', 'A Hard Rain's A-Gonna Fall', 'Restless Farewell'.)
25. TV: *The Steve Allen Show*. (*'The Lonesome Death Of Hattie Carroll') "He sang so very softly and his attitude was so off-hand and unprofessional that he seemed rather more a mystery to our studio audience than as a blazing new talent" (Steve Allen).

May

8. BBC-TV: *Tonight* (*'With God On Our Side') ATV: *Halleluiah* (No recording extant, but Dylan is known to have performed 'The Times They Are A-Changin'', 'Blowin' In The Wind' and 'Chimes Of Freedom').

December

KCSB-Radio: Santa Barbara, California. *Interview with Bob Blackmar.

1964 IMPORTANT UNRELEASED MATERIAL

June

Various recordings from sessions for *Another Side Of Bob Dylan* (*'California', 'Denise')

Folk fans mob Bob Dylan

By DON SHORT

AMERICAN folk-singer Bob Dylan was mobbed by fans when he arrived in London last night for his sell-out British tour.

"It's never been like this before," he said after six policemen—and a police girl—managed to escort him through 150 fans at London Airport.

Dylan, 23, was clutching an outsize lamp-bulb. "I got it from an affectionate friend and brought it with me," said the singer, who likes to do odd things.

Inspired

The way-out Dylan, whose first hit was "Blowin' in the Wind," is now selling well in Britain with "Subterranean Homesick Blues."

It was his version of "House of the Rising Sun" that inspired the Animals to make their disc of the number.

Some say Dylan will be as big as the Beatles.

Meanwhile the American gets by on about £85,000 a year.

With him this trip is folk-singer Joan Baez, 24.

A policeman comes between Dylan and an admirer at London Airport

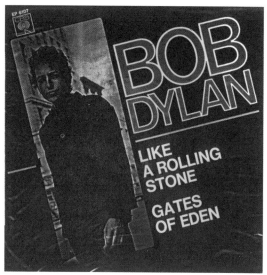

French picture sleeve single

1964 INTERVIEWS

February

3. Helen McNamara for the *Toronto Telegram*.
Canadian magazine *Gargoyle*.

April

10. Chris Wells for *Life* magazine.

May

16. Maureen Cleave for the *London Evening News*.
Julian Holland for the *London Evening Post*.

23. Max Jones for *Melody Maker:* "I'm good, kind, gentle, I think – I mean no harm to anybody – but people pick me apart. Either they like me or they slam me. I get put down a lot."

October

24. Nat Hentoff for the *New Yorker:* "Sometimes I can make myself feel better with music, but other times it's still hard to go to sleep at night."
Stuart Crump for the *Brown University Daily Herald*.

1965

1965 CHRONOLOGY

January

15. Recording sessions for *Bringing It All Back Home* begin. For this LP, Dylan records with electric backing musicians whom he needs to give texture to increasingly complex and obscure lyrical imagery. "Most of the songs went down easily and needed only three or four takes often the first take sounded entirely different from the final one because the material was played at a different tempo or a different chord was chosen." (Daniel Kramer)

April

30. Dylan opens his tour of England in Sheffield: "The audience acted as if they were going into a church. In their minds Dylan was a legend, and you could see the awe on their faces." (Fred Perry, tour manager.) The series of concerts marks the conclusion of a particular phase of his career, with Dylan playing wholly acoustic shows for the last time. "It was too easy. There was nothing happening for me. Every concert was the same it didn't mean anything."

The entire tour is filmed by D.A. Pennebaker, who later edits his footage into the celebrated documentary, *Don't Look Back*. The tour also marks the end of Dylan's affair with Joan Baez: "I thought he would do what I had done with him – would introduce me. I

was very, very hurt. I was miserable." Sara Lowndes, introduced to Dylan by Sally Grossman, comes to London towards the end of the tour to be with him. After Dylan is taken ill and briefly hospitalised, he and Sara go to Portugal for a holiday.

June

15. 'Like A Rolling Stone', arguably Dylan's greatest and certainly one of his most important songs, is recorded in Columbia Studio A, New York City. "No-one knew what they wanted to play, no-one knew what the music was supposed to sound like, other than Bob. Nobody had any idea what to do." (Mike Bloomfield). "The best I could manage was to play kind of hesitantly by sight – I can't even hear the organ – feeling my way through the changes Dylan motions towards Tom Wilson. "Turn the organ up," he orders. Tom says, "That cat's not an organ player." But Dylan isn't buying it. "Hey, now don't tell me who's an organ player and who's not! Just turn the organ up!" (Al Kooper)

July

25. Uproar is caused at the Newport Folk Festival when Dylan is

With Joan Baez, Newport, July 1965

D A Pennebaker filming 1966

backed by the Paul Butterfield Blues Band. "Out comes Dylan, and I'm out there on stage setting up all the amps to exactly the right levels, and when that first note of 'Maggie's Farm' hit, by the standards of the day, it was the loudest thing that anybody had ever heard. The volume. That was the thing, the volume." (Joe Boyd). For the folkies it's the end of an era of Dylan-as-figurehead, but most of the unrest seems not to be in protest at Dylan's playing rock music but at the shortness of his set. His return to the stage to sing 'It's All Over Now, Baby Blue' is one of the most poignant moments of his career. "There are a lot of occasions when you can look back and you can say, 'Well, after that night things were never the same', but it's very rare that you're in a moment where you know it at the time. This was such an event. You knew, as it was happening, that paths were parting." (Joe Boyd)

August
Mary Martin, a secretary in Al Grossman's office, takes Dylan out to a club in New Jersey to see a bar band called The Hawks. They are subsequently hired. "Bob came up to Canada and heard us play a set. We had blown our voices and were playing mostly instrumentals, like 30 minutes of honky-tonk, and Bob loved the group. So we rehearsed that night, went through his songs once, he sent a plane up and we flew down to his gig in Texas. Had one more rehearsal at the sound check, and just started playing." (Rick Danko)

September
3. Concert at Hollywood Bowl, Los Angeles marks the beginning of a world tour with The Hawks - first half acoustic, second half electric. Bob Dylan becomes a pop star poet. "'You wanna play Hollywood Bowl?' Dylan asked Levon Helm. Helm said they had never heard of Dylan, and proceeded to enquire who else was going to be on the show. 'Just us' said Dylan." (Shelton). "Bob Dylan offered them a lot of money they couldn't refuse." (John Hammond)

November
25. Bob marries Sara Shirley Lowndes, much to the dismay of Warhol film starlet Edie Sedgwick, who had her own sights set on him. "Sara was always a very private person, a beautiful woman, fantastic looking, and she had a very strange personality - the kind that went for health food and mysterious life." (D.A. Pennebaker)

1965 BIBLIOGRAPHY

Coleman, Ray, 'Beatles Say: Dylan Shows The Way', *Melody Maker*, January 9.
Gleason, Ralph J., 'The Times They Are A-Changin'', *Ramparts*, April.
Denisoff, R. Serge, 'Dylan: Hero Or Villain?', *Broadside*, No.58, May 15.
Green, Richard, 'Donovan Reviews New Dylan Album', *Record Mirror*, May 15.
Shelton, Bob, 'Bob Dylan: The Charisma', *Cavalier*, July.
Kretchmer, Arthur, 'It's All Right Ma, I'm Only Playing R&R', *Village Voice*, August 5.
Shelton, Bob, 'Pop Singer And Song Writers Racing Down Bob Dylan's Road', *New York Times*, August 27.
MacColl, Ewan, 'Interview', *Melody Maker*, September 18.
'The Great Dylan Row', *Melody Maker*, October 2.
Rose, Stephen C., 'Bob Dylan As Theologian', *Renewal (Chicago)*, Oct/Nov.
Nelson, Paul, 'Newport Folk Festival 1965', *Sing Out!*, November.
Kramer, Daniel, etc., 'A Night With Bob Dylan', *New York Herald Tribune*, December 12.

1965 SONGS WRITTEN

January
'Subterranean Homesick Blues' (*Bringing It All Back Home*). "It's just a little story, really. It's not about anything."
'Bob Dylan's 115th Dream' (*Bringing It All Back Home*).
'It's All Over Now Baby Blue' (*Bringing It All Back Home*).
'I'll Keep It With Mine' (*Biograph*).
'Love Minus Zero/No Limit' (*Bringing It All Back Home*).
'Maggies Farm' (*Bringing It All Back Home*).
'On The Road Again' (*Bringing It All Back Home*).
'Outlaw Blues' (*Bringing It All Back Home*).
'She Belongs To Me' (*Bringing It All Back Home*).

March
'Farewell Angelina'. Joan Baez seems to have adopted the song soon after its composition and her version is well known, until the release on *The Bootleg Series*, it was assumed Bob Dylan had not recorded this song.
'Love Is Just A Four-Letter Word' (Unreleased). No recording extant. Another song covered by Joan Baez, who is pleading with Dylan to finish it several months later.

June
'Like A Rolling Stone' (*Highway 61 Revisited*). "It was ten pages long a rhythm thing on paper telling someone something they didn't know, telling them they were lucky."
'Can You Please Crawl Out Your Window?' (*Biograph*).
'From A Buick 6' (*Highway 61 Revisited*).
'Jet Pilot' (*Biograph*).
'Phantom Engineer' (Unreleased). Early version of 'It Takes A Lot To Laugh, It Takes A Train To Cry', recorded for, but not used on, *Highway 61 Revisited*.
'Sitting On A Barbed Wire Fence'. Recorded for, but not used on, *Highway 61 Revisited*.

July
'Ballad Of A Thin Man' (*Highway 61 Revisited*).
'Desolation Row' (*Highway 61 Revisited*).
'Highway 61 Revisited' (*Highway 61 Revisited*).
'It Takes A Lot To Laugh, It Takes A Train To Cry' (*Highway 61 Revisited*).
'Just Like Tom Thumb's Blues' (*Highway 61 Revisited*).
'Queen Jane Approximately' (*Highway 61 Revisited*).
'Positively 4th Street' (*Biograph*). "Positively 4th Street is extremely one-dimensional, which I like."

From Don't Look Back 1965

'Tombstone Blues' (*Highway 61 Revisited*). "I felt like I'd broken through with this song, that nothing like it had been done before. Just a flash really."

November
'I Wanna Be Your Lover' (*Biograph*).
'Long Distance Operator' (Unreleased). No recording extant. Lyrics published in *Writings & Drawings*.
'Medicine Sunday'. Early version of 'Temporary Like Achilles', recorded at a Columbia session early in 1966.

1965 CONCERTS
February
Bridgewater State University (The first of a series of joint concerts with Joan Baez).
March
5. Philadelphia Convention Hall
6. New Haven Arena, New Haven, Connecticut
24. Pittsburg (2 shows – the last of the joint Dylan/Baez tour)
Santa Monica, California (*13 songs)
April
3. Berkeley Community Theater
7. Berkeley Folk Festival, Berkeley Community Theater (The last time Dylan will appear with Joan Baez for over 10 years).
9. Queen Elizabeth Theater, Vancouver
30. City Hall, Sheffield, England (*6 songs)
May
1. Odeon Theatre, Liverpool, England
2. De Montfort Hall, Leicester, England
5. Town Hall, Birmingham, England
6. City Hall, Newcastle, England
7. Free Trade Hall, Manchester, England (*15 songs)
9. Royal Albert Hall, London, England (*15 songs)
10. Royal Albert Hall, London, England
July
24. Newport Folk Festival, Newport, Rhode Island (*2 songs)

25. Newport Folk Festival, Newport, Rhode Island (*5 songs) (The first electric performance, with the Butterfield Blues Band.)
August
28. Forest Hills Tennis Stadium, New York (*15 songs). "At intermission, Dylan cleared the backstage area and called us into a huddle. 'I don't know what it will be like out there. It's going to be some kind of carnival, and I want you all to know that up front. So just go out there and keep playing no matter how weird it gets.'"(Al Kooper)
September
3. Hollywood Bowl, Los Angeles, California
24. Austin Municipal Auditorium, Austin, Texas. (Dylan's first concert with Levon & The Hawks is well received by the Texan crowd. For the next seven months, Dylan will enthuse about the audience and claim that they're the only ones who really understand him.)
25. Southern Methodist University Coliseum, Dallas, Texas
October
1. Carnegie Hall, New York City
2. Symphony Hall, Newark, New Jersey
10. City Auditorium, Atlanta, Georgia
16. Memorial Auditorium, Worcester, Mass
22. Rhode Island Auditorium, Providence, Rhode Island
23. UVM Patrick Gymnasium, Burlington, Vermont
24. Cobo Hall, Detroit, Michigan
29. Back Bay Theater, Boston, Mass
30. Bushnell Memorial Auditorium, Hartford, Connecticut
31. Back Bay Theater, Boston, Mass
November
5. Auditorium, Minneapolis, Minnesota
6. Kleinham's Music Hall, Buffalo, New York
12. Music Hall, Cleveland, Ohio
14,15. Massey Hall, Toronto, Ontario, Canada
19. Columbus, Ohio
20. Rochester, Vermont
21. Onodago County War Memorial, Syracuse, New York

Promotional picture 1965

With Cathy McGowan, London, 1 May 1965

26,27. Arie Crown Theater, Chicago, Illinois
28. Washington Coliseum, Washington, DC
December
1. Seattle, Washington
3,4. Community Theater, Berkeley, California
5. Masonic Memorial, San Francisco, California
7. Civic Auditorium, Long Beach, California
8. Civic Auditorium, Santa Monica, California
9,18. Civic Auditorium, Pasadena, California
10. Community Concourse Theater, San Diego, California
11. Masonic Memorial, San Francisco, California
12. Civic Auditorium, San Jose, California
19. Civic Auditorium, Santa Monica, California

1965 DISCOGRAPHY
March
Bringing It All Back Home (US LP) (Columbia CL-2328/CS-9128) (USA No.6, 41 weeks) ('Subterranean Homesick Blues', 'She Belongs To Me', 'Maggie's Farm', 'Love Minus Zero/No Limit', 'Outlaw Blues', 'On The Road Again', 'Bob Dylan's 115th Dream', 'Mr Tambourine Man', 'Gates Of Eden', 'It's Alright Ma (I'm Only Bleeding)', 'It's All Over Now, Baby Blue').
'The Times They Are A-Changin''/'Honey Just Allow Me One More Chance' (UK 45) (CBS 201751) (UK No.9, 11 weeks).
April
'Subterranean Homesick Blues'/'She Belongs To Me' (US 45) (Columbia 4-43242) (USA No.39, 8 weeks) (UK 45) (CBS 201753) (UK No.9, 9 weeks).
May
Bringing It All Back Home (UK LP) (CBS BGP 62515) (UK No.1, 29 weeks).

Two tracks on *Newport Folk Festival Evening Concert, Vol 1* (UK LP) (Fontana TFL 6041).
Duet with Joan Baez on *With God On Our Side* (UK EP) (Fontana TFE 18009).
Duet with Pete Seeger on *Ye Playboys And Playgirls* (UK EP) (Fontana 18011).
June
'Maggies Farm'/'On The Road Again' (UK 45) (CBS 201781) (UK No.22, 8 weeks).
July
'Like A Rolling Stone'/'Gates Of Eden' (US 45) (Columbia 4-43346) (USA No.2, 11 weeks).
August
Highway 61 Revisited (US LP) (Columbia CL-2389/CS-9189) (USA No.3, 34 weeks) ('Like A Rolling Stone', 'Tombstone Blues', 'It Takes A Lot To Laugh, It Takes A Train To Cry', 'From A Buick Six', 'Ballad Of A Thin Man', 'Queen Jane Approximately', 'Highway 61 Revisited', 'Just Like Tom Thumb's Blues', 'Desolation Row').
'Like A Rolling Stone'/'Gates Of Eden' (UK 45) (CBS 201811) (UK No.4, 12 weeks).
September
Highway 61 Revisited (UK LP) (CBS BGP62572) (UK No.4, 15 weeks).
'Positively 4th Street'/'From A Buick 6' (US 45) (Columbia 4-43389) (USA No.7, 9 weeks).
October
'Positively 4th Street'/'From A Buick 6' (UK 45) (CBS 201824) (UK No.8, 12 weeks).
December
'Can You Please Crawl Out Your Window?'/'Highway 61 Revisited' (US 45) (Columbia 4-43477) (USA No.58, 6 weeks).

1965 IMPORTANT UNRELEASED RECORDINGS
January
Various recordings from sessions for Bringing It All Back Home. (★'If You Gotta Go, Go Now', 'Keep It With Mine' (instr), 'She Belongs To Me', 'Love Minus Zero/No Limit').
May
Recording in the Savoy Hotel, London (★'I Forgot More Than You'll Ever Know', 'Remember Me', 'More And More', 'Blues Stay Away From Me', 'Weary Blues', 'Lost Highway', 'I'm So Lonesome I Could Cry').
12. Levy's Recording Studios. Session with John Mayall; Eric Clapton on guitar, Tom Wilson producing: "It was just a jam session. We did a lot of his blues songs. He was making it up. We played for about two hours." (Eric Clapton)
June
Various recordings from sessions for Highway 61 Revisited (★'Can You Please Crawl Out Your Window' (x2), 'Sitting On A Barbed Wire Fence' (x2), 'It Takes A Lot To Laugh, It Takes A Train To Cry').
October-December
Columbia recording sessions (★'I Wanna Be Your Lover', 'Can You Please Crawl Out Your Window', 'Number One' (instr), 'Visions Of Johanna').

1965 TV AND RADIO APPEARANCES
February
17 .WABC-TV: New York City: *The Les Crane Show* ('It's All Over Now, Baby Blue', 'It's Alright Ma, I'm Only Bleeding').
April
BBC Radio: London: *Teen Scene*: Interview with Mike Hurst: "I used to play rock 'n'roll, you know, a long time ago."

From left, Bobby Neuwirth, Dylan, D A Pennebaker and Howard Alk in Glasgow, May 1966

28. BBC Radio: *Today*: Interview with Jack de Manio: "What difference does it make if I wear a tie or not? Strapping around my neck just doesn't appeal to me."
June
BBC-TV: London, England: *Bob Dylan* ('Ballad Of Hollis Brown', 'Mr Tambourine Man', 'Gates Of Eden', 'If You Gotta Go, Go Now', 'The Lonesome Death Of Hattie Carroll', 'It Ain't Me Babe', 'Love Minus Zero, No Limit', 'One Too Many Mornings', 'Boots Of Spanish Leather', 'It's Alright Ma, (I'm Only Bleeding)', 'She Belongs To Me', 'It's All Over Now, Baby Blue'.)
October
WDTM-Radio: Detroit, Michigan: Interview with Allen Stone.
December
KQED-TV: San Francisco: Bob Dylan Press Conference.

1965 INTERVIEWS
January
12. *The New York Post.*
February
17. Robert Shelton for *Cavalier:* "All I do is write songs and sing them. I can't dig a ditch, I can't splice an electric wire. I'm no carpenter."
March
25. Jack Goddard for *The Village Voice:* "The world could get along fine without me. Don'tcha know, everybody dies. It don't matter how important you think you are. Look at Shakespeare, Napoleon, Edgar Allen Poe - they're all dead, right?"
27. *Melody Maker.* Phone interview with Max Jones.
April
16. Paul J. Robbins for *LA Free Press.*
26. London Airport Press Conference: "My real message? Keep a good head and always carry a lightbulb."
27. Savoy Hotel Press Conference: "I have no message for anyone. I don't want to influence people in any way."

28. Michael Hellicar for the *Daily Sketch.*
30. Jenny de Yong and Peter Roche for *Darts* magazine.
May
7. *Newcastle Evening Chronicle*: "Why should you want to know about me? I don't want to know about you."
8. Dylan reviews new singles in *Melody Maker*'s 'Blind Date' column.
22. Laurie Henshaw for *Disc:* "Q: Why be so hostile? A: Because you're hostile to me. You're using me. I'm an object to you."
Ray Coleman for *Melody Maker:* "My songs are just me talking to myself just pictures of what I'm seeing."
Dylan fills in "Lifelines" questionnaire for *New Musical Express.*
July
7. KRLA *Beat* magazine: "I guess catastrophe and confusion are the basis of my songs. But basically my songs are really about love. Love of life."
August
27. Robert Shelton for the *New York Times.*
Nora Ephron and Susan Edmiston: "I've never written anything hard to understand, not in my head anyway."
September
4. Beverly Hills Hotel Press Conference.
10. First of three instalments of interview with Paul Robbins in *LA Free Press.*
18. Robert Fulford for the *Toronto Star.*
24. Austin, Texas Press Conference: "I'm not just singing to be singing. There's a much deeper reason for it than that."
September *Newsweek:* "I've never written a political song. Songs can't save the world."
October
17. Frances Taylor for *Long Island Press.*
November
21. Mary Merryfield for the *Chicago Tribune.*
27. Joseph Haas for the *Chicago Daily News:* "It's not folk-rock, it's just instruments. I call it the mathematical sound."

Nat Hentoff for *Playboy* (unpublished).
December
3. San Francisco Press Conference: "I think of myself as a song-and-dance man."
7. Los Angeles Press Conference: "It's been my life-long ambition to be a movie-usher, and I have failed, as far as I am concerned."

1966

1966 CHRONOLOGY
February
4. The world tour with The Hawks recommences.
14-17. Bob Dylan goes to Nashville, Tennessee to begin recording tracks for *Blonde On Blonde*. "In *Blonde On Blonde* I wrote out all the songs in the studio. The musicians played cards, I wrote out a song, we'd do it, they'd go back to their game and I'd write out another song."
April
Concerts and press conferences in Australia establish the controversial and tempestuous nature of the tour. The furore is to continue throughout Europe, but despite the boos and slow-handclaps, Dylan seems to be enjoying playing. "He was having a so much better time with the band than he was by himself. He really liked playing with Robbie and having that electric music all around him." (D.A. Pennebaker)
May
27. The final concert of the tour at London's Royal Albert Hall is as stormy as others which have gone before it. Robbie Robertson reflected on the bewildering experience: "We'd go from town to town, from country to country. We set up, we played, they booed, and threw things at us. Then we went to the next town, played, they booed, threw things, and we left again." Some impression of the tour can be gained from *Eat The Document*, a film again shot by Pennebaker, but edited by Howard Alk and Dylan.
July
25. Dylan falls off his motorcycle in Woodstock. "I was blinded by

Stockholm, 29 April 1966

Stockholm, 29 April 1966

the sun for a second and I kind of panicked or something. I stomped down on the brake and the rear wheel locked up on me and I went flyin'."
He damages his neck, and takes some time to recuperate: "Spent a week in the hospital, then they moved me to this doctor's house in town. In his attic. Had a bed up there with a window looking out. I'd lay there listening to birds chirping, kids playing in the neighbours' yard or rain falling by the window. Then I'd just go back to sleep."
He is able to make use of his enforced convalescence to evade pressing deadlines for film and book and record contracts, all negotiated by Albert Grossman: "I just remembered how bad I wanted to see my kids. I started thinkin' about the short life of trouble. How short life is. I realised how much I'd missed."
During his recuperation Dylan thinks carefully about his relationship with his manager and decides that he's reached a "turning point": "The turning point was back in Woodstock. A little after the accident. Sitting around one night under a full moon, I looked out into the bleak woods and I said, 'Something's gotta change.' There was some business that had to be taken care of."

1966 BIBLIOGRAPHY
Ribakove, Sy and Barbara, *Folk Rock: The Bob Dylan Story*, Dell Publishing, New York.
Paxton, Tom, 'Folk Rot', *Sing Out!*, No.6.
Capel, Maurice, 'The Man In The Middle', *Jazz Monthly*, January.
Gzowski. Peter, 'Dylan: An Explosion Of Poetry', *Macleans*, January 22.
Gleason, Ralph J., 'The Children's Crusade', *Ramparts*, March.
Castin, S., 'Folk Rock's Tambourine Man', *Look*, March 8.

Watt, Douglas, 'Something Is Happening Here', *New Yorker*, March 19.

Silber, Irwin, 'Topical Song: Polarisation Sets In', *Sing Out!*, Feb/March.

Nelson, Paul, 'Bob Dylan: Another View', *Sing Out!*, Feb/March.

Jones, Max, 'Will The Real Bob Dylan Please Stand Up?', *Melody Maker*, May 14.

'With The Uncompromising Bob Dylan', *Salut Les Copains*, July.

Siegel, Jules, 'Well, What Have We Here?', *Saturday Evening Post*, July 30.

Eustis, Helen, 'A Middle-Aged Mother Visits The Teen Scene', *McCall's*, August.

Williams, Paul, 'Understanding Dylan', *Crawdaddy*, August.

'Dylan Hurt In Cycle Mishap', *New York Times*, August 1.

1966 SONGS WRITTEN

January

'One Of Us Must Know(Sooner Or Later)'(*Blonde On Blonde*). "That's one of my favourite songs."

'She's Your Lover Now'. Recorded at the abortive sessions in New York.

February

'Leopardskin Pillbox Hat' (*Blonde On Blonde*). "Mighta seen a picture of one in a department store window. There's really no more to it than that."

'Sad-Eyed Lady Of The Lowlands' (*Blonde On Blonde*). "It started out as just a little thing, but I got carried away. At the session itself I just started writing and I couldn't stop."

'Fourth Time Around' (*Blonde On Blonde*).

'Stuck Inside Of Mobile' (*Blonde On Blonde*).

'Tell Me Momma' (Unreleased). Live recordings from 1966 shows

Bristol 10 May 1966

– this was the opening song of the second half of the shows.

'Visions Of Johanna' (*Blonde On Blonde*).

March

'Absolutely Sweet Marie' (*Blonde On Blonde*).

'I Want You' (*Blonde On Blonde*).

'Just Like A Woman' (*Blonde On Blonde*).

'Most Likely You Go Your Way' (*Blonde On Blonde*).

'Obviously Five Believers' (*Blonde On Blonde*).

'Pledging My Time' (*Blonde On Blonde*).

'Rainy Day Women Nos 12 & 35' (*Blonde On Blonde*). "Rainy Day Women happens to deal with a minority of cripples and orientals and the world in which they live."

'Temporary Like Achilles' (*Blonde On Blonde*).

'What Can I Do For Your Wigwam Right' (Unreleased). A long, slow blues recorded at the sessions for *Blonde On Blonde*. No extant recording.

May

'I Can't Leave Her Behind' (Unreleased). Acoustic unfinished song, featured in the film *Eat The Document*.

'On A Rainy Afternoon' (Unreleased). Acoustic unfinished song, featured in the film *Eat The Document*.

1966 CONCERTS

February

4. Louisville, Kentucky

5. Westchester County Center, White Plains, New York (*9 songs)

6. Syria Mosque, Pittsburgh, Pennsylvania (*8 songs)

10. Ellis Auditorium Amphitheater, Memphis, Tennessee

11. Shrine Mosque, Richmond, Virginia

13. Arena, Norfolk, Virginia

18. New Haven, Connecticut

19. Auditorium, Ottawa, Ontario, Canada

20. Place Des Arts, Montreal, Quebec, Canada

24,25. Academy Of Music, Philadelphia, Pennsylvania

26. Island Gardens, Hempstead, New York (*13 songs)

March

3. Convention Hall, Miami, Florida

In Woodstock, July 1966, just before the motorcycle accident

Stockholm, 29 April 1966

11. Kiel Opera House, St. Louis, Missouri
12. Pershing Memorial Auditorium, Lincoln, Nebraska
13. Municipal Auditorium, Denver, Colorado
 Los Angeles, California
 Santa Monica, California
24. Tacoma, Washington
25. Center Arena, Seattle, Washington
26. PNE Agrodome, Vancouver, BC, Canada
April
9. Honolulu International Center Arena, Honolulu, Hawaii
13. Stadium, Sydney, Australia
15. Festival Hall, Brisbane, Australia
16. Stadium, Sydney, Australia
19. Festival Hall, Melbourne, Australia (★10 songs)
20. Festival Hall, Melbourne, Australia
22. Palais Royal, Adelaide, Australia
23. Capitol Theatre, Perth, Australia
29. Konsert-huset, Stockholm, Sweden (★11 songs)
May
1. KB-Hallen, Copenhagen, Denmark
5. Adelphi Theatre, Dublin, Ireland (★6 songs)
6. ABC, Belfast, N.Ireland
10. Colston Hall, Bristol, England (★15 songs)
11. Capitol Theatre, Cardiff, Wales
12. Odeon, Birmingham, England
14. Odeon, Liverpool, England (★2 songs)
15. De Montfort Hall, Leicester, England
16. Gaumont Theatre, Sheffield, England
17. Free Trade Hall, Manchester, England (★11 songs)
19. Odeon, Glasgow, Scotland
20. ABC Theatre, Edinburgh, Scotland (★15 songs)
21. Odeon, Newcastle, England
24. L'Olympia, Paris, France
26. Royal Albert Hall, London, England (★6 songs)
27. Royal Albert Hall, London, England (★9 songs)

1966 DISCOGRAPHY

January
'Can You Please Crawl Out Your Window?'/'Highway 61 Revisited' (UK 45) (CBS 201900) (UK No.17, 5 weeks).
February

Bob Dylan Destroys His Legend In Melbourne; Concert Strictly Dullsville

Melbourne, April 20.

Over the last two years every overseas folksinger coming Down Under has included a Bob Dylan song in his repertoire, talked of him in tones of awe, and always the response from the Aussie audience has been overwhelming.

Therefore there's been great anticipation over the first Aussie tour of Dylan himself. And it was expected his concerts would be a quick sellout as, has always happened with Peter, Paul & Mary.

But from the very start Dylan blotted his image in Australia. His fans were shocked to read press reports of his arrival in Sydney that he "wouldn't write for Negroes if you paid me $1,000" and to the implicit belief that he was shocked at the "horror of young boys being killed in wars," his glib reply was "this doesn't disturb me

Bob Dylan
Aztec Services Pty. Ltd. and Stadiums Pty. Ltd. presentation in association with Ashes & Sand Inc. of New York. At Festival Hall, Melbourne, April 19, '66; $4 top. VARIETY APRIL 27, 66

at all," adding "in fact I'm quite happy about the state of the world. I don't want to change it."

Undoubtedly these news reports kept some of his fans away from his concerts, as here in Melbourne the Festival Hall has been about 60% full. And of those fans who did brave his concerts, quite a few were disappointed. Some walked out in disgust before the end.

Alone on stage for an hour duration of the first half—which incidentally was over a quarter of an hour late in commencing—Dylan monotonously and untunefully slowly belted out his numbers, accompanying himself on a guitar and harmonica. The harmonica playing was the best part of his act.

His manner towards his audience bordered on insolence. More than once he had a fit of spluttering and coughing, which he seemed to delight in doing right into the mike.

In the second half Dylan was accompanied by an unprogrammed quintet—a pianist, drummer, two guitar players and a fifth member who played an electric organ. The sound of the organ lent a sweet-

ness to the music, that made pleasurable listening. And Dylan's voice, half drowned by the backing, didn't seem so bad. And one could also hear the words.

But he annoyed the audience by taking time to tune up on the guitars so that on two occasions he received a slow handclap. Unlike any other artist who has appeared at the Festival Hall, Dylan made no attempt to introduce his musicians to the audience.

Throughout his performance, considering the number of people present, the applause was lukewarm, and there were no requests for encores at the end. In fact, Dylan left the stage without taking a bow—and no one seemed bothered about this. The performance caught was on the second night. It's understood that at the opening performance there was considerable booing from the audience.

On the basis of this concert Dylan would be advised to remain in the background and let other more seasoned performers with more personality and stage appeal interpret his work. —*Stan.*

Press conference in Stockholm, April 1966

'One Of Us Must Know (Sooner Or Later)'/'Queen Jane Approximately' (US 45) (Columbia 4-43541).
April
'Rainy Day Women Nos 12 & 35'/'Pledging My Time' (US 45) (Columbia 4-43592) (USA No.2, 10 weeks).
'One Of Us Must Know (Sooner Or Later)'/'Queen Jane Approximately' (UK 45) (CBS 202053) (UK No.33, 5 weeks).
Dylan (UK EP) (CBS 6064).
May
Blonde On Blonde (US LP) (Columbia C2L-41/C2S-841) (USA No.9, 21 weeks) ('Rainy Day Women Nos 12 & 35', 'Pledging My Time', 'Visions Of Johanna', 'One Of Us Must Know (Sooner Or Later)', 'I Want You', 'Stuck Inside Of Mobile', 'Leopard-skin Pill-Box Hat', 'Just Like A Woman', 'Most Likely You Go Your Way', 'Temporary Like Achilles', 'Absolutely Sweet Marie', 'Fourth Time Around', 'Obviously Five Believers', 'Sad-Eyed Lady Of The Lowlands').
'Rainy Day Women Nos 12 & 35'/'Pledging My Time' (UK 45) (CBS 202307) (UK No.7, 8 weeks).
June
'I Want You'/'Just Like Tom Thumb's Blues' (US 45) (Columbia 4-43683) (USA No.20, 7 weeks).
One Too Many Mornings (UK EP) (CBS 6070).
July
'I Want You'/'Just Like Tom Thumb's Blues' (UK 45) (CBS 202258) (UK No.16, 9 weeks).
August
Blonde On Blonde (UK LP) (CBS DDP 66012) (UK No.3, 15 weeks).
'Just Like A Woman'/'Obviously Five Believers' (US 45) (Columbia

Bob Dylan Injured In Cycle Mishap

NEW YORK—Bob Dylan, Columbia's 25-year-old folk-rock chanter, is recuperating from fractures of neck vertebrae and a concussion suffered during a motorcycle accident July 29 near Woodstock, N.Y. The artist is said to have been taking his bike to be repaired when the back wheel locked and the vehicle spun out of control. According to his manager, Albert Grossman, Dylan will be out of action for at least 2-months. Grossman also said that the singer is in good condition, but refused to say where he is recuperating.

Oh calamity

4-43792) (USA No.33, 6 weeks).
October
Mr Tambourine Man (UK EP) (CBS 6078).
December
Bob Dylan's Greatest Hits (UK LP) (CBS BGP 62847).

1966 TV AND RADIO APPEARANCES
January
WBAI-FM Radio: New York City: *The Bob Fass Show* Radio phone-in.
February
CBC-Radio: Montreal, Canada Interview with Martin Bronstein: "I don't like to refer to myself as a poet because that puts you into a category with a lot of funny people."
April
Radio 3VZ: Melbourne: Interviews with Stan Profe and Alan

From the concert programme of the first Australian tour April 1966

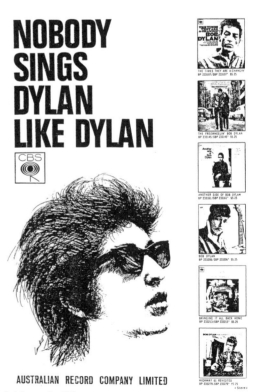

Unappealing Australian promotion 1966

Trengrove.

TV, Adelaide: extracts from Press Conference with questions from Roger Cardwell and Bob Francis.

Swedish Radio-3: Stockholm: Radiohuset Interview with Klas Burling.

1966 INTERVIEWS

January

29. Margaret Steen for the *Toronto Star Weekly:* "Just with the experiences I've experienced already, I could never step outside this room again and still write songs until the end of time."

February

Maura Davies for *Cavalier.*

March

Ralph Gleason for *Ramparts:* "Rolling Stone is the best song I wrote. I had to quit after England. I had to stop, and when I was writing it I knew I had to sing it with a band."

Nat Hentoff for *Playboy:* "It strikes me funny that people actually have the gall to think that I have some kind of fantastic imagination. It gets very lonesome."

8. S. Castan for *Look.*

April

12. Sydney Airport and King's Cross Hotel Press Conferences: "Q: Why did you change your name? A: Wouldn't you change yours if you had a name like William W. Kasonavarich? I couldn't get any girlfriends."

13. Two interviews: Uli Schmetzer and Ron Saw for *Sydney Daily Mirror.* "Terror is my constant emotion. I deal in terror. I buy it, sell it, and make a profit."

15. Brisbane Press Conference.

17. Melbourne Press Conference: "I live a sceptical life among sceptics."

Robert Westfield for *Go-Set* magazine.

21. Adelaide Press Conference: "Most people underestimate my voice, but left alone in an empty room I can sing better than anybody else."

23. Perth Press Conference: "I must have saved up about 75 billion dollars by now. I have it sewed up in my jacket and I never spend it. I'm saving it all up to buy Australia."

28. Stockholm Press Conference.

30. Copenhagen Press Conference: "I don't know myself. I don't know who I am. There's a mirror on the inside of my dark glasses."

May

3. London Press Conference: "You name something, I'll protest about it."

23. Paris Press Conference: "No revolution ever came about because of songs."

June

Australian magazine *Music Maker.*

July

30. Jules Siegel for *Saturday Evening Post.*

September

Louise Sokol for *Datebook.*

1966 IMPORTANT UNRELEASED RECORDINGS

January-March

Various recordings from sessions for *Blonde On Blonde* ('Visions Of Johanna').

1967

1967 CHRONOLOGY

January

Dylan tries to prevent the publication of Daniel Kramer's book of photographs, titled *Bob Dylan*, but Mr Justice Postel finds in favour of Kramer: "The publication does not in any way place the plaintiff in an unfavourable light indeed it would appear that the plaintiff's professional standing and career will be enhanced by the publication."

April

During the months of seclusion in Woodstock, in upper New York state, Dylan spends time with Sara and his children, but continues to make music with the members of The Band who have moved up to Big Pink in West Saugerties to be near him. Al Aronowitz writes: "Dylan was writing ten new songs a week, rehearsing them in his living room with The Hawks." Many recordings are made of afternoons spent making music. Some recordings of new songs are subsequently sent out to music publishers as demo recordings and become known as *"The Basement Tapes"*. Some of the tracks are later bootlegged, and their popularity eventually persuades Dylan to release some of them officially eight years later.

August

Dylan signs new five-year contract with Columbia Records.

October

17. Recording begins in Nashville for *John Wesley Harding*. *"John Wesley Harding* was a fearful album - just dealing with fear, but dealing with the devil in a fearful way, almost. All I wanted to do was to get the words right."

1967 BIBLIOGRAPHY

DeTurk, David A. & Poulin, A. Jr., *The American Folk Scene*, Dell, New York.

Before the Isle Of Wight press conference August 1969

192

Willis, Ellen, 'Dylan', *Cheetah*, March.

Iachetta, Michael, 'Scarred Bob Dylan Is Comin' Back', *New York Daily News*, May 8.

Mood, John J., 'On Behalf Of The Later Dylan: A Study Of Bob Dylan's Lyrics', *Encounter*, Autumn.

Goldstein, Richard, 'Don't Look Back', *New York Times*, October 22.

Willis, Ellen, 'The Sound Of Bob Dylan', *Commentary*, November.

Nelson, Paul, 'Don't Look Back', *Sing Out!*, Dec/Jan.

Ball, Carolyn, *Bob Dylan: Contemporary Minstrel* ??

1967 SONGS WRITTEN

Between April and October

'All American Boy' (Unreleased). Lyrics extant but no recording.

'All You Have To Do Is Dream' (Unreleased). Recorded in Woodstock.

'Apple Suckling Tree' (*The Basement Tapes*).

'Baby, Won't You Be My Baby' (Unreleased). Recorded in Woodstock.

'Bourbon Street' (Unreleased). Lyrics extant but no recording.

'Clothes Line Saga' (*The Basement Tapes*).

'Crash On The Levee' (*The Basement Tapes*).

'Don't Ya Tell Henry' (Unreleased). Recorded in Woodstock.

'Get Your Rocks Off' (Unreleased). Recorded in Woodstock.

'Going To Acapulco' (*The Basement Tapes*).

'Gonna Get You Now' (Unreleased). Recorded in Woodstock.

'I Shall Be Released' (*More Bob Dylan Greatest Hits*).

'I'm Not There (1956)' (Unreleased). Recorded in Woodstock.

'Lo And Behold' (*The Basement Tapes*).

The famous advertising campaign 1966, portrait by Milton Glaser

'Lock Your Door' (Unreleased). Recorded in Woodstock.

'Million Dollar Bash' (*The Basement Tapes*).

'Nothing Was Delivered' (*The Basement Tapes*).

'Odds And Ends' (*The Basement Tapes*).

'One For The Road' (Unreleased). Recorded in Woodstock.

'Open The Door Homer' (*The Basement Tapes*).

'Please Mrs Henry' (*The Basement Tapes*).

'Quinn The Eskimo' (*Biograph*).

'Santa Fe'.

'Sign On The Cross' (Unreleased). Recorded in Woodstock.

'Silent Weekend'.

'Standing Around Shoeing A Horse' (Unreleased). No recording, no lyrics extant.

'Tears Of Rage' (*The Basement Tapes*).

'This Wheel's On Fire' (*The Basement Tapes*).

'Tiny Montgomery' (*The Basement Tapes*).

'Too Much Of Nothing' (*The Basement Tapes*).

'Wild Wolf' (Unreleased). Lyrics extant but no recording.

'Yea Heavy And A Bottle Of Bread' (*The Basement Tapes*).

'You Ain't Goin' Nowhere' (*The Basement Tapes*).

'You Can Change Your Name' (Unreleased). No recording, no lyrics extant.

October

'Ballad Of Frankie Lee And Judas Priest' (*John Wesley Harding*).

'Drifter's Escape' (*John Wesley Harding*).

'I Dreamed I Saw St Augustine' (*John Wesley Harding*).

November

'Wicked Messenger' (*John Wesley Harding*). "The third verse opens it up, and then the time schedule takes a jump, and soon the song becomes wider."

'All Along The Watchtower' (*John Wesley Harding*). "Here we have the cycle of events working in a rather reverse order."

'John Wesley Harding' (*John Wesley Harding*). "It started out to be a real long ballad, but in the middle of the second verse I got tired. So I just wrote a quick third verse. It was a silly little song."

'I'll Be Your Baby Tonight' (*John Wesley Harding*). "It's just a simple song, simple sentiment. Actually, it could have been written from a baby's point of view – that's occurred to me."

'As I Went Out One Morning' (*John Wesley Harding*).

'Dear Landlord' (*John Wesley Harding*).

'Down Along The Cove' (*John Wesley Harding*).

'I Am A Lonesome Hobo' (*John Wesley Harding*).

September 11, 1967

COLUMBIA'S BOB DYLAN IS SUBJECT OF DOCUMENTARY FILM

Label Gives Film Strong Promotional Support

Columbia Records artist Bob Dylan is the subject of the remarkable new documentary feature "Don't Look Back," which opened last week in New York at the 34th Street East Theatre. The film was produced by Albert Grossman, John Court, and Leacock-Pennebaker, Inc., and filmed by D. A. Pennebaker, a specialist in documentary portraits. Pennebaker traveled with Dylan during his 1965 concert tour of England, filming Dylan's performances, his interviews, the parties he attended and the scenes backstage. In "Don't Look Back," he achieves a candid view of Dylan, who has been one of the most private and inaccessible of all performers. The film explores the relationship between the artist and his art, the performer and his legend.

Press and Public Information / 51 West 52 Street, New York, New York 10019 / Telephone (212) 7654321

CBS Press release for announcing Don't Look Back

We found Bob Dylan's hideaway!
In a rambling Cape Cod cottage, miles away from any highway, in a small town in upstate New York, Dylan recuperated from his motorcycle crack-up and the weariness and exhaustion which everybody in the business knew he was suffering.

According to friends, Dylan had some visitors—including poet Allen Ginsberg—and has even received phone calls (from George Harrison, when the Beatles were in New York.)

We'd thought you'd like to see a picture of the house. Behind the house, by the way, is a large swimming pool. Ten cats and two dogs roam the grounds.

We won't tell you the exact location because Bobby might still be there when this is published and we would not want to disturb him.

Dylan discovered after the accident September 1966

'I Pity The Poor Immigrant' (*John Wesley Harding*).

1967 DISCOGRAPHY
March
'Leopard-skin Pill-box Hat'/'Most Likely You Go Your Way (And I'll Go Mine)' (US 45) (Columbia 4-44069).
Bob Dylan's Greatest Hits (US LP) (Columbia KCL-2663/ KCS-

NEWS
FROM COLUMBIA RECORDS

COLUMBIA
CBS Records Division

January 8, 1967

COLUMBIA RECORDS RELEASES "JOHN WESLEY HARDING,"
BOB DYLAN'S FIRST NEW ALBUM SINCE HIS ACCIDENT

Columbia Records has released as an immediate special "John Wesley Harding," Bob Dylan's first new album since his motorcycle accident sixteen months ago. Last April, Columbia Records released a collection of Dylan's best-selling singles, "Bob Dylan's Greatest Hits," which reached the top of the LP charts.

During his absence from the active world of music, Dylan has been composing songs in his Woodstock, New York, home. He traveled to Nashville to record his new compositions for the current album, handpicking the three Nashville musicians who accompany him. The album was produced by Bob Johnston, Executive Producer, Columbia Records.

Press and Public Information / 51 West 52 Street, New York, New York 10019 / Telephone (212) 7654321

Bob's back!

9463) (USA No.10, 86 weeks) ('Rainy Day Women Nos 12 & 35', 'Blowin' In The Wind', 'Subterranean Homesick Blues', 'Like A Rolling Stone' 'Positively 4th Street', 'The Times They Are A-Changin'', 'It Ain't Me Babe', 'Mr Tambourine Man', 'I Want You', 'Just Like A Woman').
May
'Leopard-skin Pill-box Hat'/'Most Likely You Go Your Way (And I'll Go Mine)' (UK 45) (CBS 2700).
June
'If You Gotta Go, Go Now'/'To Ramona' (45-released in Benelux countries only) (CBS 2921).
December
John Wesley Harding (US LP) (Columbia CL-2804/CS-9604) (USA No.2, 49 weeks) ('John Wesley Harding', 'As I Went Out One Morning', 'I Dreamed I Saw St Augustine', 'All Along The Watchtower', 'The Ballad Of Frankie Lee And Judas Priest', 'Drifter's Escape', 'Dear Landlord', 'I Am A Lonesome Hobo', 'I Pity The Poor Immigrant', 'The Wicked Messenger', 'Down Along The Cove', 'I'll Be Your Baby Tonight').

1967 INTERVIEWS
May
8. Michael Iachetta for the *New York Daily News:* "Mainly what I've been doin' is workin' on gettin' better an' makin' better music, which is what my life is all about."

1967 IMPORTANT UNRELEASED RECORDINGS
June-October
Songs recorded in the Basement of Big Pink and in Dylan's house in Upper Byrdcliffe Road, Woodstock (★'Lock Up Your Door', 'Won't You Be My Baby', 'Try Me Little Girl', 'I Can't Make It Alone', 'Don't You Try Me Now', 'A Long Time A-Growin'', 'Bonnie Ship The Diamond', 'Trail Of the Buffalo', 'Down On Me', 'One For My Baby', 'I'm Alright', 'One Single River', 'People Get Ready', ' I Don't Hurt Anymore', 'Be Careful Of Stones That You Throw', 'One Man's Loss', 'All I Have To Do Is Dream' (x3), 'Baby Ain't That Fine', 'Rock Salt And Nails', 'A Fool Such As I', 'Gonna Get You Now', 'Apple Suckling Tree', 'I'm Not There (1956)', 'Get Your Rocks Off', 'I Shall Be Released', 'Too Much Of Nothing', 'Tears Of Rage' (x2), 'Quinn The Eskimo', 'Open The Door Homer' (x2), 'Nothing Was Delivered', 'Don't ya Tell Henry', 'Sign On The Cross'.)

1968

1968 CHRONOLOGY
January
20. Carnegie Chapter Hall, New York City. Dylan performs three Woody Guthrie songs with The Band at the Woody Guthrie Memorial Concert - his first concert appearance since his accident. There are afternoon and evening shows and fans are astonished to see that his hair has been cut very short.
Dylan splits with his manager Albert Grossman, though litigation between them about the terms of the settlement will continue unresolved until the present day. (Grossman's widow, Sally, continued to press Albert's case after his death in February 1986.)
June
5. Dylan's father, Abraham Zimmerman, dies of a heart attack.

1968 BIBLIOGRAPHY
Pennebaker, D.A., *Don't Look Back*, Ballantine, New York.

Gray, Michael, 'What's So Good About Dylan', *OZ*, No.7.
Landau, Jon, 'John Wesley Harding', *Crawdaddy!*
Kramer, Daniel, *Bob Dylan*, Citadel, New York.
Wood, Michael, 'oob Dylan: Wicked Messenger', *New Society*, February 29.
Bloomfield, Mike, 'Impressions Of Bob Dylan', *Hit Parader*, June.
Wenner, Jann, 'Dylan's Basement Tapes Should Be Released', *Rolling Stone*, June 22.
Weberman, A.J., 'John Wesley Harding Is Bob Dylan', *Broadside*, No.93, July.
Strouse, Jean, 'Bob Dylan's Gentle Anarchy', *Commonweal*

1968 CONCERTS

January
20. Appearance at Woody Guthrie Memorial Concert, Carnegie Hall, New York City (★'I Ain't Got No Home', 'Dear Mrs Roosevelt', 'The Grand Coulee Dam', 'This Train Is Bound For Glory').

1968 SONGS WRITTEN

October
'Lay Lady Lay' (*Nashville Skyline*). "I wrote that song for the movie *Midnight Cowboy*. By the time I came up with it though, it was too late. Clive Davis really wanted to release it as a single. Actually, I was slightly embarrassed by it, wasn't even sure I even liked the song. He said it was a smash hit. I was really astonished, you know, when he turned out to be right."

November
'I Threw It All Away' (*Nashville Skyline*).
'I'd Have You Anytime' (Unreleased). Written with George Harrison, who recorded it.
'Every Time Somebody Comes To Town' (Unreleased). Written with George Harrison. Tape extant.

1968 INTERVIEWS

February
26. Hubert Saal for *Newsweek*. "A song is moral just by being a song. I used to think that myself and my songs were the same thing, but I don't believe that anymore."

October/November
John Cohen & Happy Traum for *Sing Out!*: "I expect to be playing music endlessly."

1968 DISCOGRAPHY

February
John Wesley Harding (UK LP) (CBS BGP 63252) (UK No.1, 29 weeks).

1969

1969 CHRONOLOGY

February
13. Recording begins for *Nashville Skyline*. "These are the type of songs that I always felt like writing when I've been alone to do so. The songs reflect more of the inner me than the songs of the past."
17. Dylan is joined in the studio by Johnny Cash. Together they record 16 tracks, one of which – 'Girl From The North Country' – is later included on the LP. Dylan even begins to sound like Johnny Cash. "I don't know what made me sound that way. Today, I don't think I could sound that way if I wanted to."

March
Great White Wonder, the first bootleg record, appears in California. It consists mostly of tracks from the 1967 Basement Tapes and the

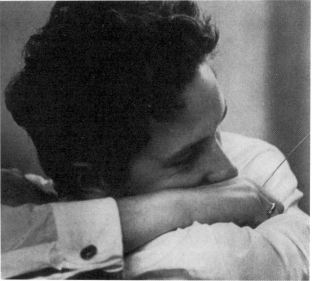

Listening to playback of Self Portrait May 1969

1961 Minneapolis Hotel Tape.

May
3. Recording begins for *Self Portrait*. "I've never been a person that wanted attention so we recorded that album to get people off my back, so they wouldn't like me any more. That's exactly the reason that album was put out – so people would just at that time stop buying my records. And they did. Haha!"

August
Dylan plays three songs at Edwardsville, as a rehearsal for his appearance at the Isle Of Wight festival.
31. Persuaded to the Isle Of Wight by the enterprising Foulke brothers, a short-haired, white-suited, somewhat chubby Dylan plays an hour long set with The Band in front of an estimated 200,000. "If things were like we hoped they would be, we were prepared to play... Bob had an extra list of songs with eight or ten different titles, that we would've went ahead and done, had it seemed like the thing to do. But it seemed like everybody was a little bit tired." (Levon Helm)

1969 BIBLIOGRAPHY

Goldstein, Richard, *The Poetry Of Rock*, Bantam, New York.

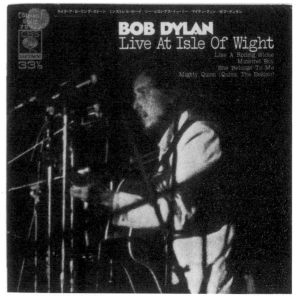

Rare and rather tasteful Japanese EP

Rosenstone, Robert A., 'The Times They Are A-Changin': The Music Of Protest', *AAAPSS*, March.

Sander, Ellen, 'Bob Dylan Revisited', *Saturday Review*, April 26.

Bleasdale, Alan, 'Will The Real Bob Dylan Stand Up And Concentrate', *Melody Maker*, May 17.

Goldman, Albert, 'That Angry Kid Has Gone All Over Romantic', *Life*, May 23.

Botwin, Carol, 'Tracking Dylan In Cash Country', *This Week*, June 15.

Cannon, Geoffrey, 'The Gospel According To Dylan', *Guardian*, September 2.

Logue, Christopher, 'A Fair Feld Ful Of Folk', *The Times*, September 13.

Hopkins, Jerry, '"New" Dylan Album Bootlegged In LA', *Rolling Stone*, September 20.

Smucker, Tom, 'Bob Dylan Meets The Revolution', *Fusion*, October 31.

Marcus, Greil, 'Records', *Rolling Stone*, November 29.

Fowler, Peter, 'Bob Dylan: The Ring Of Confidence', *IT*, 62.

1969 CONCERTS
August
31. Isle Of Wight Festival, Woodside Bay, Isle Of Wight, England (★17 songs).

1969 DISCOGRAPHY
April
Nashville Skyline (US LP) (Columbia KCS-9825/CO-32872) (USA No.3, 46 weeks) ('Girl Of The North Country', 'Nashville Skyline Rag', 'To Be Alone With You', 'I Threw It All Away', 'Peggy Day', 'Lay Lady Lay', 'One More Night', 'Tell Me That It Isn't True', 'Country Pie', 'Tonight I'll Be Staying Here With You').

Recording sessions Nashville, May 1969

Photograph culled by A J Weberman from Dylan's trash, from left, unknown cat litter saleswoman, Bob and Sara

'I Threw It All Away'/'Drifter's Escape' (US 45) (Columbia 4-44826) (USA No.82, 5 weeks).
May
'I Threw It All Away'/'Drifter's Escape' (UK 45) (CBS 4219) (UK No.30, 6 weeks).
Nashville Skyline (UK LP) (CBS 63601) (UK No.1, 42 weeks).
July
'Lay Lady Lay'/'Peggy Day' (US 45) (Columbia 4-44926) (USA No.7, 14 weeks).
September
'Lay Lady Lay'/'Peggy Day' (UK 45) (CBS 4434) (UK No.5, 12 weeks).
October
'Tonight I'll Be Staying Here With You'/'Country Pie' (US 45) (Columbia 4-45004) (USA No.50, 7 weeks).
December
'Tonight I'll Be Staying Here With You'/'Country Pie' (UK 45) (CBS 4611).

1969 TV AND RADIO APPEARANCES
June
ABC-TV: Nashville, Tennessee: *The Johnny Cash Show* (★'I Threw It All Away', 'Living The Blues', 'Girl From The North Country').

1969 INTERVIEWS
March
15. Jann Wenner for *Rolling Stone* (Brief telephone interview).
April
4. Hubert Saal for *Newsweek:* "The smallest line in (*Nashville Skyline*) means more to me than some of the songs on any of the previous albums I've made."
June
Red O'Donnell for the *Nashville Banner:* "I love children. I love animals. I am loyal to my friends. I have a sense of humour. I have a generally happy outlook. I try to be on time for appointments. I have a good relationship with my wife. I take criticism well. I strive to do good work."
August
9. Don Short for the *Daily Mirror.*

16. Ray Connolly for the *London Evening Standard:* "I'm just living a normal happy life like any other guy. I'm very anxious to get back on the stage."
27. Isle Of Wight Press Conference: "My job is to play music. Take it easy and you'll do your job well."
Chris White for the *Daily Sketch.*
September
Ian Brady for *Top Pops* magazine.
November
29. Jann Wenner for *Rolling Stone*: "My songs always sound a lot better in person than they do on the record."

1969 SONGS WRITTEN
Exact date unknown: 'I Don't Want To Do It' (Unreleased). Possibly co-written with George Harrison, who recorded it many years later.
February
'*Champaign, Illinois*' (Unreleased). Recorded by Carl Perkins.
'Country Pie' (*Nashville Skyline*).
'Nashville Skyline Rag' (*Nashville Skyline*).
'One More Night' (*Nashville Skyline*).
'Wanted Man' (Unreleased). Recorded by Johnny Cash.
'Tonight I'll Be Staying Here With You' (*Nashville Skyline*). "Q. On *Nashville Skyline*, do you have a song that you particularly dig? A. 'Tonight I'll Be Staying Here With You'."
'Tell Me That It Isn't True' (*Nashville Skyline*). "It came out completely different than I'd written it. I had it written as sort of a jerky kind of polka-type thing."
'To Be Alone With You' (*Nashville Skyline*). "I wrote it for Jerry Lee Lewis."
'Peggy Day' (*Nashville Skyline*). "I kinda had the Mills Brothers in mind when I did that one."
April
'Living The Blues' (*Self Portrait*).
August
'Minstrel Boy' (*Self Portrait*).

1969 IMPORTANT UNRELEASED MATERIAL
February
Recording session with Johnny Cash, Nashville (★'One Too Many Mornings' (x2), 'Mountain Dew', 'I Still Miss Someone', 'Careless Love', 'Matchbox', 'That's All Right Mama', 'Big River', 'I Walk The Line', 'You Are My Sunshine', 'Guess Things Happen That Way', 'Just A Closer Walk With Thee', 'Blues Yodel No 1', 'Blues Yodel No 5', 'Girl Of The North Country', 'Ring Of Fire'.)
May
Recordings for *Self Portrait* (★'Folsom Prison Blues', 'Ring Of Fire').

1970

1970 CHRONOLOGY
January
In an undated interview with Michele Enghien, Dylan is asked about his lack of activity in recent months: "I believe that at certain periods in a person's existence it's necessary, if not vital, to bring about a change in your life so as not to go under. I have children and I want to watch them grow up - to get to know them and for them to get to know me and know that I'm their father."
June
Dylan is given an honorary Doctorate Of Music by Princeton University. "Although he is now approaching the perilous age of

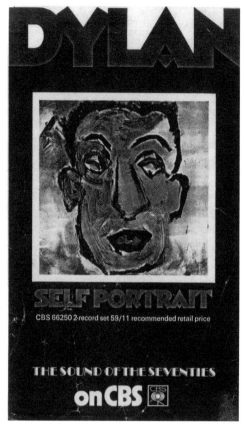

Self portrait flyer, a snip at 59/11d

30, his music remains the authentic expression of the disturbed and concerned conscience of young America." He subsequently writes about the experience in 'Day Of The Locusts'.
August
Recording begins for *New Morning.*
September
Dylan leaves Woodstock to return to New York City. He moves into a townhouse, 94 MacDougal Street, in the heart of Greenwich Village. "Woodstock was a daily excursion to nothingness."

1970 BIBLIOGRAPHY
Thompson, Toby, *Positively Main Street: An Unorthodox View Of Bob Dylan*, Coward-McCann Inc., New York.
Williams, Paul, *Outlaw Blues*, New York.
Marcus, Greil, 'Self Portrait No 25', *Rolling Stone*, July 23.
Williams, Richard, 'Bob Dylan's Confident New Music', *The Times*, Oct 29.
Gleason, Ralph J., 'We've Got Dylan Back Again', *Rolling Stone*, November 26.

1970 DISCOGRAPHY
June
Self Portrait (US LP) (Columbia C2X-30050) (USA No.4, 22 weeks) ('All The Tired Horses', 'Alberta No 1', 'I Forgot More Than You'll Ever Know', 'Days Of '49', 'Early Morning Rain', 'In Search Of Little Sadie', 'Let It Be Me', 'Little Sadie', 'Woogie Boogie', 'Belle Isle', 'Living The Blues', 'Like A Rolling Stone', 'Copper Kettle', 'Gotta Travel On', 'Blue Moon', 'The Boxer', 'Quinn The Eskimo', 'Take Me As I Am', 'Take A Message To Mary', 'It Hurts Me Too', 'Minstrel Boy', 'She Belongs To Me', 'Wigwam', 'Alberta No 2'.)
July
'Wigwam'/'Copper Kettle' (US 45) (Columbia 4-45199) (UK 45) (CBS 5122).

Self Portrait (UK LP) (CBS 66250) (UK No.1, 15 weeks).
October
New Morning (US LP) (Columbia KC-30290) (USA No.7, 23 weeks) ('If Not For You', 'Day Of The Locust', 'Time Passes Slowly', 'Went To See The Gypsy', 'Winterlude', 'If Dogs Run Free', 'New Morning', 'Sign On The Window', 'One More Weekend', 'The Man In Me', 'Three Angels', 'Father Of Night'.)
November
New Morning (UK LP) (CBS 69001) (UK No.1, 18 weeks).

1970 SONGS WRITTEN
Spring
'All The Tired Horses' (*Self Portrait*).
'Wigwam' (*Self Portrait*).
March
'Went To See The Gypsy' (*New Morning*).
'Woogie Boogie' (*Self Portrait*).
May
'If Not For You' (*New Morning*). "I wrote the song thinking about my wife it seemed simple enough."
'Air To Breathe' (Unreleased). No recording, no lyrics extant.
'Time Passes Slowly' (*New Morning*).
'Working On The Guru' (Unreleased). Recording from May session extant.
August
'Day Of The Locusts' (*New Morning*).
'Father Of Night' (*New Morning*).
'If Dogs Run Free' (*New Morning*).
'The Man In Me' (*New Morning*).
'New Morning' (*New Morning*).
'One More Weekend' (*New Morning*).
'Sign On The Window' (*New Morning*).
'Three Angels' (*New Morning*).
'Winterlude' (*New Morning*).

1970 IMPORTANT UNRELEASED RECORDINGS
May
1. New York City recording session with George Harrison (*'Song To Woody', 'Mama You Been On My Mind', 'Yesterday', 'Just Like Tom Thumb's Blues', 'Da Doo Ron Ron', 'One Too Many Mornings' (x2), 'Working On A Guru'.)

1971

1971 CHRONOLOGY
January
Dylan records two tracks, 'East Virginia Blues' and 'Nashville Skyline Rag', with Earl Scruggs. The event is filmed and a documentary programme, *Earl Scruggs, His Family And Friends*, is broadcast on National Educational TV.
19. A.J. Weberman, collector of Bob Dylan's garbage and analyser of his poetry phones him up to discuss an article he's writing for the underground press and records the conversation. It is later scheduled for release by Folkways Records but Dylan files an injunction to prevent its release.
March
16–18. Dylan records six songs, including 'Watching The River Flow' and 'When I Paint My Masterpiece', with Leon Russell. The former song begins: "What's the matter with me? I don't have much to say."
May
Tarantula is published five years after it was written, in response to A.J. Weberman's widespread circulation of bootleg printings of

the text.
Dylan visits Israel and is photographed at the Western Wall wearing his yarmulke. "I'm a Jew. It touches my poetry, my life, in ways I can't describe." Dylan and Sara visit the Kibbutz Givat Haim to discuss the possibility of moving there with the family. The kibbutz apparently think it's not a good idea.
24. Dylan's 30th birthday is spent in Tel Aviv: "We went to see a Gregory Peck movie – I'm quite a fan of his."
August
1. Dylan appears at the Concert For Bangla Desh, organised by George Harrison, at Madison Square Garden. He plays at both the afternoon and evening concerts. "It was very difficult to try and get him to come out. In fact, right up to the moment he stepped on stage I wasn't sure if he was going to come on." (George Harrison)
September
A.J. Weberman is attacked on Elizabeth Street by Dylan, who is furious that the garbologist has renewed his raids on the Dylan trashcans.
October
Dylan records four tracks with Happy Traum. Three of them are subsequently included on *Bob Dylan's Greatest Hits Vol.2* released in November.
Dylan records a TV session with Allen Ginsberg for Channel 13 PBS.
November
4. Dylan records two versions of a new protest song, 'George Jackson', and releases it within a week.
17 & 20. Dylan again records with Allen Ginsberg, this time in a studio. "George Harrison was there, and Gregory Corso and Peter Orlovsky and David Amram – a very great musician – then this

Advertising block for the film of the concert for Bangla Desh

The Greatest Concert
Of The Decade
NOW YOU CAN SEE IT
AND HEAR IT...
AS IF YOU WERE THERE!

THE CONCERT FOR BANGLADESH

apple presents   U
THE CONCERT FOR BANGLADESH
ERIC CLAPTON · BOB DYLAN · GEORGE HARRISON · BILLY PRESTON
LEON RUSSELL · RAVI SHANKAR · RINGO STARR · KLAUS VOORMANN
BADFINGER · PETE HAM · TOM EVANS · JOEY MOLLAND
MIKE GIBBONS · ALLAN BEUTLER · JESSE ED DAVIS · CHUCK FINDLEY
MARLIN GREENE · JEANIE GREENE · JO GREEN · DOLORES HALL
JIM HORN · KAMALA CHAKRAVARTY · JACKIE KELSO · JIM KELTNER
USTED ALIAKBAR KHAN · CLAUDIA LENNEAR · LOU McCREARY
OLLIE MITCHELL · DON NIX · DON PRESTON · CARL RADLE · ALLA RAKAH
Directed by Saul Swimmer · Produced by George Harrison and Allen Klein   Technicolor
Music Recording Produced by George Harrison and Phil Spector   apple / 20th century-fox release

woman who was the high priestess of the Tibetan Buddhists came in." (Happy Traum)

December
Dylan buys a "modest house" from LA sports writer Jim Murray, at Point Dume, past Malibu. He will subsequently add "several adjoining parcels of land" and begin building Xanadu, his huge, copper domed palace, which has - among other attractions - a lounge with doors "big enough to ride a horse through", a cinema, complete with its own Cadillac convertible, and a huge fireplace "with whale motif".

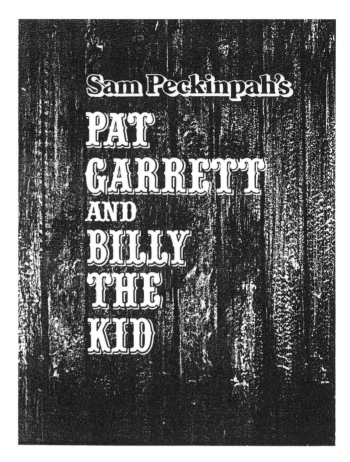

1971 BIBLIOGRAPHY
Remond, Alain, *Les Chemins De Bob Dylan*, Paris, 1971.
Scaduto, Anthony, *Bob Dylan: An Intimate Biography*, Grosset & Dunlap, New York.
Weberman, A.J., 'Something Is Happening To Your Garbage', *IT*, 91, January.
Weberman A.J., 'Dylan Meets Weberman', *East Village Other*, January 19.
Williams, Stacey, 'Defence Of Dylan', *NME*, March 4.
Cott, Jonathan, 'Dylan Film: Opening Night: Fast On The Eye', *Rolling Stone*, March 4.
Pickering, Stephen, *Dylan: A Commemoration*, July.
Cott, Jonathan, 'I Dreamed I Saw Bob Dylan', *Rolling Stone*, September 2.
Ginsberg, Allen, 'On The New Dylan', *IT*, October 21.
Scaduto, Anthony, 'Won't You Listen To The Lambs, Bob Dylan?', *NY Times Magazine*, November 28.
Weberman, Alan J., 'Bob Dylan', (Unpublished).

1971 DISCOGRAPHY
January
Three songs on *A Tribute To Woody Guthrie, Part One* (Columbia KC-31171) (★'Ain't Got No Home', 'Dear Mrs Roosevelt', 'The Grand Coulee Dam').
March
'If Not For You'/'New Morning' (UK 45) (CBS 7092).
June
'Watching The River Flow'/'Spanish Is The Loving Tongue' (US 45) (Columbia 4-45409) (USA No.41, 8 weeks) (UK 45) (CBS 7329) (UK No.24, 9 weeks).
'Nashville Skyline Rag' on *Earl Scruggs, His Family & Friends* (US LP) (Columbia C-30584).
August
Harmonica on 'Sammy's Song', on *David Bromberg* (US LP) (Columbia C-31104).
November
'George Jackson (Big Band Version)'/'George Jackson' (Acoustic Version) (US 45) (Columbia 4-45516) (USA No.33, 8 weeks) (UK 45) (CBS 7688).
Bob Dylan's Greatest Hits, Vol 2 (US LP) (Columbia KG-31120) (USA No.14, 31 weeks) ('Watching The River Flow', 'Don't Think Twice It's Alright', 'Lay Lady Lay', 'Stuck Inside Of Mobile', 'I'll Be Your Baby Tonight', 'All I Really Want To Do', 'My Back Pages', 'Maggies Farm', 'Tonight I'll Be Staying Here With You', 'She Belongs To Me', 'All Along The Watchtower', 'Quinn The Eskimo', 'Just Like Tom Thumb's Blues', 'A Hard Rain's A-Gonna Fall', 'If Not For You', 'It's All Over Now, Baby Blue', 'Tomorrow Is A Long Time', 'When I Paint My Masterpiece', 'I Shall Be Released', 'You Ain't Goin' Nowhere', 'Down In The Flood').
December
Five songs on *The Concert For Bangla Desh* (LP) (Apple STCX-3385) ('A Hard Rain's A-Gonna Fall', 'It Takes A Lot To Laugh, It Takes A Train To Cry', 'Blowin' In The Wind', 'Mr Tambourine Man', 'Just Like A Woman').
More Greatest Hits (UK LP) (CBS 67239) (UK No.12, 15 weeks).

1971 TV AND RADIO APPEARANCES
January
NE-TV: New York City: *Earl Scruggs, His Family And Friends* ('East Virginia Blues', 'Nashville Skyline Rag').
October
Channel 13 PBS-TV: New York City: *Freetime Allen Ginsberg & Friends*.

1971 INTERVIEWS
January
19. A.J. Weberman's account of his meeting with Dylan for the East Village Other.
Anthony Scaduto for his biography.
March
4. A.J. Weberman telephone call. *Rolling Stone* publishes an edited transcript.
May
Yediot Achronot.
June
4. Catherine Rosenheimer for the *Jerusalem Post* "Q: Have you written any songs about Israel? A: No, but I've written one about Yugoslavia."

1971 SONGS WRITTEN
March
'Watching The River Flow' (*More Bob Dylan Greatest Hits*).
'When I Paint My Masterpiece' (*More Bob Dylan Greatest Hits*).
November
'George Jackson' (45 Release).
'Wallflower'. Also recorded on *Doug Sahm & Band* with prominent Dylan vocal.

1971 IMPORTANT UNRELEASED RECORDINGS
January
Recording of telephone conversation with A.J. Weberman.
March
16-18. Blue Lock Studios, New York City. ('Spanish Harlem', 'That Lucky Old Sun', 'Alabama Band', 'Blood Red River').

1972

1972 CHRONOLOGY
September
9. Dylan joins David Bromberg and John Prine onstage at the Bitter End in Greenwich Village. He plays harmonica on three songs and sings along with Prine's 'Donald & Lydia'.
Dylan records two tracks with Steve Goodman.
October
Dylan records five tracks with Doug Sahm and one track with Roger McGuinn.
November
Dylan begins filming in Durango, Mexico, with Sam Peckinpah for *Pat Garrett & Billy The Kid*. He plays Alias, a printer's boy who decides to follow the Kid. "I don't know who I played. I tried to play whoever it was in the story, but I guess it's a known fact that there was nobody in that story that was the character I played." Dylan also writes the music for the film.

1972 BIBLIOGRAPHY
Pichaske, David R., *Beowulf To Beatles: Approaches To Poetry*, The Free Press, New York.
McGregor, Craig, *Bob Dylan: A Retrospective*, William Morrow & Co. Inc., New York.
Gray, Michael, *Song & Dance Man: The Art Of Bob Dylan*, Hart-Davis, MacGibbon, London.
Gonzales, Laurence, 'Persona Bob: Seer And Fool', *Costerus*.
Cohen, Robert H., 'Bob Dylan: His Generation And His Protest', *Les Langues Modernes*, Vol 66 No1.
James, Clive, 'Troubadour Of Protest', *The Observer*, April 23.
Spender, Stephen & Kermode, Frank, 'The Metaphor At The End Of The Funnel', *Esquire*, May.
Pickering, Stephen, *Bob Dylan: Praxis Two*.

1972 DISCOGRAPHY
February
Three songs on *A Tribute To Woody Guthrie, Part One* (UK LP) (CBS 64861).
Five songs on *The Concert For Bangla Desh* (UK LP) (Apple STCX 3385).
December
Five songs on *Doug Sahm And Band* (US LP) (Atlantic SD-7254).
Four songs on *Broadside Reunion* (US LP) (Folkways FR5315).
Bob Dylan vs A.J. Weberman (US LP-withdrawn) (Folkways FR5322).
Session harmonica on one track on *Roger McGuinn* (US LP) (Columbia KC-31946).

1972 SONGS WRITTEN
November
'Billy' (*Pat Garrett & Billy The Kid*).
'Goodbye Holly' (Unreleased). No recording extant. No lyric extant.

1973

1973 CHRONOLOGY
January
Filming continues in Mexico, but all is not well. "I was very uncomfortable in this non-role, but then time started to slip away and there I was trapped deep in the heart of Mexico with some madman, ordering people around like a little king. My wife got fed up almost immediately. She'd say to me, What the hell are we doing here? It was not an easy question to answer."
February
In Burbank Studios, Los Angeles, Dylan records the music for *Pat Garrett & Billy The Kid*, but when the film is eventually released. "The music seemed to be scattered and used in every other place but the scenes in which we did it for. Except for 'Heaven's Door', I can't say I recognised anything I'd done for being in the place that I'd done it for."
August
Dylan records a session with Barry Goldberg and co-produces the LP at Muscle Shoals with Jerry Wexler.
September
Plays harmonica behind John Prine at the Bitter End in New York City.
November
Having refused to renew his recording contract with Columbia Records, Dylan is signed to Asylum by David Geffen. He begins to record tracks with The Band for a new record, which he is planning to call *Ceremonies Of The Horsemen*, though it will be re-titled *Planet Waves*. "The album was fun to do, although it was over before we realised we'd started. We did it in just a couple of days." (Robbie Robertson)
Out of spite, CBS release *Dylan*, a collection of outtakes and warm-up tracks. "They were not to be used. I thought it was well understood. I didn't think it was that bad really!"
Writings And Drawings, a collection of Dylan's work since 1961, is published by Knopf.

1973 BIBLIOGRAPHY
Sarlin, Bob, *Turn It Up! I Can't Hear The Words*, Simon & Schuster, New York.
Karpel, Craig, *The Tarantula In Me: Behind Bob Dylan's Novel*, Klohn, San Francisco.
Hedgepath, William Bowling, 'What Dylan Did', *Intellectual Digest*, Feb.
Monaghan, David, 'Taking Bob Dylan Seriously: The Wasteland Tradition', *English Quarterly*, Summer.
Knobler, Peter, 'Bob Dylan: A Gut Reaction', *Crawdaddy!*, September.
Bruchal, Joseph, *The Poetry Of Pop*, Dustbooks.
Wall, Alan, 'The Passage Of Bob Dylan', *New Blackfriars*.

1973 DISCOGRAPHY
March
'Just Like A Woman'/'I Want You' (UK 45) (CBS 1158).
May
Session harmonica on 'The Crippled Crow' on *Chronicles* by Booker T And Priscilla Jones (US LP) (A&M ST-4413).
July
Pat Garrett & Billy The Kid (US LP) (Columbia KC-32460) (USA No.16, 31 weeks) ('Main Theme', 'Cantina Theme', 'Billy 1', 'Bunkhouse Theme', 'River Theme', 'Turkey Chase', 'Knockin' On Heaven's Door', 'Final Theme', 'Billy 4', 'Billy 7'.)
August
'Knockin' On Heaven's Door'/'Turkey Chase' (US 45) (Columbia

4-45913) (USA No.12, 16 weeks) (UK 45) (CBS 1762) (UK No.14, 7 weeks).

October
Pat Garrett & Billy The Kid (UK LP) (CBS 69042) (UK No.29, 11 weeks).

November
Dylan (US LP) (Columbia PC-32747) (USA No.17, 15 weeks) (UK LP) (CBS 69049) ('Lily Of The West', 'Can't Help Falling In Love', 'Sarah Jane', 'The Ballad Of Ira Hayes', 'Mr Bojangles', 'Mary Ann', 'Big Yellow Taxi', 'A Fool Such As I', 'Spanish Is The Loving Tongue').

December
Session vocals, percussion and co-production on six tracks on *Barry Goldberg* (US LP) (Atco SD 7040).
'A Fool Such As I'/'Lily Of The West' (US 45) (Columbia 4-33259) (USA No.55, 7 weeks).

1973 INTERVIEWS
February
Michael Watts. Brief conversation printed in *Melody Maker*.

1973 SONGS WRITTEN
January
'Billy 4' (*Pat Garrett & Billy The Kid*).
'Billy Surrenders' (Unreleased). Recording on Mexico City session tape.
'Peco's Blues' (Unreleased). Recording on Mexico City session tape.

February
Film score for *Pat Garrett & Billy The Kid*.
'Knockin' On Heaven's Door' (*Pat Garrett & Billy The Kid*).
'Turkey Chase' (*Pat Garrett & Billy The Kid*).

July
'Forever Young' (*Planet Waves*). "I wrote it thinking about one of my boys and not wanting to be too sentimental. The lines came to me, they were done in a minute. The song wrote itself."
'Never Say Goodbye' (*Planet Waves*).
'Nobody 'Cept You'.

November
'Crosswind Jamboree' (Unreleased). No recording, but lyrics extant.
'Dirge' (*Planet Waves*).
'Going Going Gone' (*Planet Waves*).
'Hazel' (*Planet Waves*).
'On A Night Like This' (*Planet Waves*).

From Renaldo and Clara 1975

'Something There Is About You' (*Planet Waves*).
'Tough Mama' (*Planet Waves*).
'Wedding Song' (*Planet Waves*).
'You Angel You' (*Planet Waves*).

1973 IMPORTANT UNRELEASED MATERIAL
January
20. Session for *Pat Garrett* at CBS Studios Mexico City ('Billy', 'Billy 1', 'Billy 2', 'Turkey 1', 'Turkey 2', 'Billy Surrenders', 'And He Killed Me Too 1', 'And He Killed Me Too 2', 'Goodbye Holly', 'Peco's Blues').

1974

1974 CHRONOLOGY
January
3. Dylan's first tour since 1966 begins in Chicago. He opens with a rewritten 'Hero Blues', a song from 1963. He plays 40 concerts in six weeks. The tour earns five million dollars, gross. "There were 5 million envelopes each had an average of three tickets. That's what? 17 million applications?" (David Geffen)
"I was just playing a role on that tour. I was playing Bob Dylan. It was all sort of mindless. The people that came out to see us came mostly to see what they missed the first time around. We were cleaning up, but it was an emotionless trip."

March
Dylan begins two months of painting and philosophy lessons in New York with an old Jewish teacher, Norman Raeben: "It changed me. I went home after that and my wife never did understand me ever since that day. That's when our marriage started breaking up. She never knew what I was talking about, what I was thinking about, and I couldn't possibly explain it."

May
9. Dylan is persuaded by Phil Ochs to play at the Friends Of Chile Benefit Concert in the Felt Forum, Madison Square Garden. Ochs, fearing that Dylan may change his mind about appearing, keeps him locked in the dressing rooms drinking Gallo wine. Dylan performs a hopelessly out-of-control drunken set.

September

12. Dylan, having re-signed with CBS, begins recording *Blood On The Tracks* in New York. "Everybody agrees that was pretty different, and what's different about it is that there's a code in the lyrics and also there's no sense of time. There's no respect for it: you've got yesterday, today and tomorrow all in the same room." Dylan buys a large farm outside of St Paul in Minnesota.

December

27 & 30. Listening to *Blood On The Tracks* over the Christmas holidays in Minneapolis, Dylan is dissatisfied with some of the recordings and goes into a local studio to produce alternate versions of five songs, backed by local musicians. "I didn't perform it well. I was fighting sentimentality all the way down the line."

1974 BIBLIOGRAPHY

Beal, Katherine, *Bob Dylan*, Creative Education, USA.
Yenne, Bill, *One Foot On The Highway: Bob Dylan On Tour 1974*, Klohne Books, San Francisco.
Pickering, Stephen, 'Tour '74', (Booklet).
Eds. Rolling Stone, *Knocking On Dylan's Door: On The Road In '74*, Pocket Books, New York.
Davis, Clive, (with James Willworth), *Clive: Inside The Record Business*, Ballantine Books.
Goldstein, Richard, 'Growing Up With Bob Dylan', *New York*, January 28.
McClure, Michael, 'The Poet's Poet', *Rolling Stone*, March 14.
Smith, Patti, 'Depletion Behind A Positive Mask', *Creem*, April.
Poague, Leland A., 'Dylan As Auteur', *Journal Of Popular Culture*, Summer.
Monteiro, George, 'Dylan In The '60s', *South Atlantic Quarterly*.
Sloman, Larry, 'Blood On The Tracks: Dylan Looks Back', *Rolling Stone*, November 21.

1974 CONCERTS

January

3,4. Stadium, Chicago, Illinois
6.(aft) Spectrum, Philadelphia, Pennsylvania
6.(evg) Spectrum, Philadelphia, Pennsylvania
7. Spectrum, Philadelphia, Pennsylvania
9. Maple Leaf Gardens, Toronto, Ontario, Canada
10. Maple Leaf Gardens, Toronto, Ontario, Canada
11,12. Forum, Montreal, Quebec, Canada
14.(aft) Gardens, Boston, Mass.
14.(evg) Gardens, Boston, Mass.
15,16. Capitol Center, Washington, DC.
17. Coliseum, Charlotte, North Carolina
19.(aft) Hollywood Sportatorium, Miami, Florida
19.(evg) Hollywood Sportatorium, Miami, Florida
21,22. Omni, Atlanta, Georgia
23. Mid-South Coliseum, Memphis, Tennessee
25. Tarrant County Convention Center, Fort Worth, Texas
26.(aft) Hofheinz Pavilion, Houston, Texas
26.(evg) Hofheinz Pavilion, Houston, Texas
28,29. Nassau County Coliseum, Nassau, New York
31.(aft) Madison Square Garden, New York City
31.(evg) Madison Square Garden, New York City

February

2. University Of Michigan, Ann Arbor, Michigan
3. University Of Indiana, Bloomington, Indiana
4.(aft) Missouri Arena, St Louis, Missouri
4.(evg) Missouri Arena, St Louis, Missouri
6.(aft) Coliseum, Denver, Colorado
6.(evg) Coliseum, Denver, Colorado
9.(aft) Coliseum, Seattle, Washington
9.(evg) Coliseum, Seattle, Washington
11.(aft) Coliseum, Oakland, California
11.(evg) Coliseum, Oakland, California
13. Forum, Los Angeles, California
14.(aft) Forum, Los Angeles, California
14.(evg) Forum, Los Angeles, California

1974 DISCOGRAPHY

January

Planet Waves (US LP) (Asylum S-7E-1003) (USA No.1, 21 weeks) (UK LP) (Island ILPS 9261) (UK No.7, 8 weeks) ('On A Night Like This', 'Going Going Gone', 'Tough Mama', 'Hazel', 'Something There Is About You', 'Forever Young', 'Forever Young', 'Dirge', 'You Angel You', 'Never Say Goodbye', 'Wedding Song').
'A Fool Such As I'/'Lily Of The West' (UK 45) (CBS 2006)

February

'On A Night Like This'/'You Angel You' (US 45) (Asylum 11033) (USA No.44, 6 weeks).
'On A Night Like This'/'Forever Young' (UK 45) (Island WIP 6168).
'Something There Is About You'/'Going Going Gone' (US 45) (Asylum 11035).

June

Before The Flood (US LP) (Asylum S-201) (USA No.3, 19 weeks) (UK LP) (Island IDBD 1) (UK No.8, 7 weeks) ('Most Likely You Go Your Way', 'Lay Lady Lay', 'Rainy Day Women Nos 12 & 35', 'Knocking On Heaven's Door', 'It Ain't Me Babe', 'Ballad Of A Thin Man', 'Don't Think Twice It's Alright', 'Just Like A Woman', 'It's Alright Ma, (I'm Only Bleeding)', 'All Along The Watchtower', 'Highway 61 Revisited', 'Like A Rolling Stone', 'Blowin' In The Wind').

July

'Most Likely You Go Your Way (And I'll Go Mine)' (US 45)

Advertisement for Planet Waves 1974

(Asylum 11043) (USA No.66, 5 weeks).
August
'All Along The Watchtower'/'It Ain't Me Babe' (US 45) (Asylum 45212).

1974 INTERVIEWS
January
8. John Rockwell for the *New York Times:* "Being on tour is like being in limbo. It's like going from nowhere to nowhere."
14. Maureen Orth for *Newsweek:* "I'd be doing what I'm doing if I was a millionaire or not, whether I was getting paid for it or not."
16. Tom Zito for the *Washington Post.*
21. David Devoss for *Time:* "All this publicity. Sometimes I think they're talking about somebody else."
February
14. Ben Fong-Torres for *Rolling Stone:* Transcript in *Knocking On Dylan's Door* book.

1974 SONGS WRITTEN
September
'You're A Big Girl Now' (*Blood On The Tracks*). "I read that this was supposed to be about my wife. I wish somebody would ask me first before they go ahead and print stuff like that."
'Tangled Up In Blue' (*Blood On The Tracks*). "I was trying to do something that I didn't think had ever been done before. In terms of trying to tell a story and be a present character in it without it being some kind of fake, sappy attempted tear-jerker. I was trying to be somebody in the present time while conjuring up a lot of past images. I wanted to defy time, so that the story took place in the present and the past at the same time. When you look at a painting, you can see any part of it or see all of it together. I wanted that song to be like a painting."
'Buckets Of Rain' (*Blood On The Tracks*).
'Call Letter Blues' (*The Bootleg Series*).
'Idiot Wind' (*Blood On The Tracks*). "I thought I might have gone a little too far with 'Idiot Wind'. I might have changed some of it. I didn't really think I was giving away too much; I thought that it seemed so personal that people would think it was about so-and-so who was close to me. It wasn't. It didn't pertain to me. It was just a concept of putting in images."
'If You See Her, Say Hello' (*Blood On The Tracks*).
'Lily, Rosemary And The Jack Of Hearts' (*Blood On The Tracks*).
'Meet Me In The Morning' (*Blood On The Tracks*).
'Shelter From The Storm' (*Blood On The Tracks*). "This is the story of my life."
'Simple Twist Of Fate' (*Blood On The Tracks*).
'Up To Me' (*Biograph*).
'You're Gonna Make Me Lonesome When You Go' (*Blood On The Tracks*).

1974 IMPORTANT UNRELEASED RECORDINGS
September
Versions of songs recorded for *Blood On The Tracks* (★'Tangled Up In Blue', 'Idiot Wind', 'Lily, Rosemary And The Jack Of Hearts', 'If You See Her, Say Hello').

1975

1975 CHRONOLOGY
March
23. Dylan plays with three members of The Band and Neil Young at the SNACK benefit in Golden Gate Park, San Francisco. He sings an extraordinary version of 'Knocking On Heaven's Door',

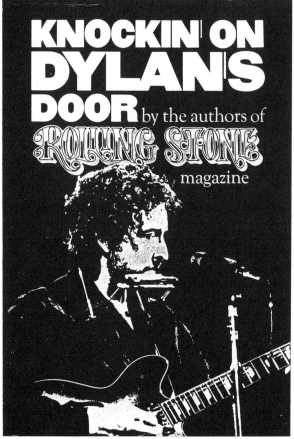

Stone's hardback tour report 1974

called 'Knocking On The Dragon's Door'.
May
Dylan takes a holiday in Corsica and the South of France with painter David Oppenheim, who painted the rear sleeve of the re-issued *Blood On The Tracks*. On his birthday he attends a gypsy festival and meets the King Of The Gypsies. It inspires him to write 'One More Cup Of Coffee'. The gypsies are gathered to worship an unusual black madonna, St Sara.
June
On his return, Dylan visits Hurricane Carter, whose book he has been reading. He takes liberal notes during the conversation and ponders the idea of writing a song about the boxer's case.
July
3. Dylan turns up at The Other End club in Greenwich Village and asks Rambling Jack Elliott if he can play a new song. He performs a marvellous version of 'Abandoned Love'. He pops into various other clubs during the month, playing with Muddy Waters, Bobby Neuwirth, Patti Smith and Roger McGuinn. He begins to think of the idea for the Rolling Thunder Revue.
Dylan meets Jacques Levy on the street in New York. The two get together that evening and write 'Isis'. The following day they write two more songs. Feeling excited about the possibilities of their collaboration, they go out to Dylan's house in East Hampton, Long Island for two weeks where they complete a further 14 songs.
28. Recording begins for *Desire*. "The songs on the *Desire* album, that's kind of a fog to me."
October
23. At Folk City the newly assembled Rolling Thunder troupe turn up to celebrate Mike Porco's 61st birthday.
24. The first version of the song 'Hurricane' turns out to have some potentially libellous factual inaccuracy in its lyrics, so Dylan has to

hurriedly re-record the song for it to be released as a single. "Bob Dylan wrote 'The Hurricane' and sent it to me and said This is what I can do for you I can get people to listen to me, to this song. That was fantastic for me." (Hurricane Carter)

Dylan records 'Buckets Of Rain' with Bette Midler, who tries – and fails – to seduce him. "He absolutely charmed the pants off me – well, not literally but close. Actually, I tried to charm the pants off him but everyone will be disappointed to learn I was unsuccessful. But I got close. A couple of first bases in the front seat of his Cadillac. He drives an hysterically long red Cadillac convertible and he can't drive worth a pea. He's not a big guy and he always drives with the seat well back."

The Rolling Thunder troupe set off in a Greyhound bus named Phydeaux for Plymouth, Massachusetts.

December

Rolling Thunder Revue plays at New Jersey State Penitentiary at Clinton for Hurricane Carter and the following night at Madison Square Garden – The Night Of The Hurricane. "I enjoyed that tour, I suppose, but I was drunk the entire time. I didn't even realise I was on that tour until afterwards when they charged me $2,000 for my liquor bills." (Jack Elliott)

1975 BIBLIOGRAPHY

Ducray, Francois, et al., *Dylan*, Albin Michel, Paris.

Ed. Stibal, Brian, 'Talkin' Bob Zimmerman Blues', (*Fan magazine*) Issue 1, February.

King, Bill, 'The Artist In The Marketplace', (Unpublished thesis).

Scalet, Elizabeth Butler, 'The Song Was There Before Me: The Influence Of Traditional Music On The Songs Of Bob Dylan', *Heritage Of Kansas*, Vol 8 No 2.

Pickering, Stephen, *Bob Dylan Approximately: A Portrait Of The Jewish Poet In Search Of God – A Midrash*, McKay, New York.

Friesen, Gordon, (with Bookbinder, David), 'The Radicalisation Of Bob Dylan', *Broadside*.

Campbell, Gregg M., 'Bob Dylan And The Pastoral Apocalypse', *Journal Of Popular Culture*, Spring.

Gray, Michael, 'Signs Of Life', *Let It Rock*, April.

Lhamon, W.T., 'A Cut Above: Blood On The Tracks', *The New Republic*, April 5.

Bond, Alan, 'Blood On The Tracks', *Texas Guardian*.

Hinton, Nigel, 'Narrative And Dramatic Elements In Bob Dylan's Poetry', (University Of Kent thesis).

McDonough, Jack, *It Takes A Train To Cry*, (Unpublished).

1975 SONGS WRITTEN

May

'One More Cup Of Coffee' (*Desire*).

June

'Abandoned Love' (*Biograph*).

July

'Isis' (*Desire*). "It's kind of like a journey sort of a journey-like trip. I don't really know too much in depth what it would mean."

'Black Diamond Bay' (*Desire*).

'Catfish'.

'Golden Loom'.

'Hurricane' (*Desire*).

'Joey' (*Desire*).

'Money Blues' (Unreleased). No recording extant. Co-writer Jacques Levy sang the song on radio WBAI some years later.

'Mozambique' (*Desire*).

'Oh Sister' (*Desire*).

'Rita Mae' (45 Release).

'Romance In Durango' (*Desire*).

'Sara' (*Desire*).

'Sign Language' (Unreleased). Dylan vocal version featured on Eric Clapton's *No Reason To Cry*.

'Wiretappin'' (Unreleased). No recording extant, no lyric extant.

1975 CONCERTS

October

30. War Memorial Auditorium, Plymouth, Mass.
31. War Memorial Auditorium, Plymouth, Mass.

November

1. South Eastern Massachusetts University, North Dartmouth, Mass. (NT)
2. Technical University, Lowell, Mass. (NT)
4.(aft) Civic Center, Providence, Rhode Island
4.(evg) Civic Center, Providence, Rhode Island
6.(aft) Civic Center, Springfield, Mass.
6.(evg) Civic Center, Springfield, Mass.
8. UVM Patrick Gymnasium, Burlington, Vermont
9. University Of New Hampshire, Durham, New Hampshire
11. Palace Theater, Waterbury, Connecticut
13.(aft) Veterans' Memorial Coliseum, New Haven, Connecticut
13.(evg) Veterans' Memorial Coliseum, New Haven, Connecticut
15.(aft) Convention Center, Niagara Falls, New York (NT)
15.(evg) Convention Center, Niagara Falls, New York
17.(aft) War Memorial Coliseum, Rochester, New York
17.(evg) War Memorial Coliseum, Rochester, New York
19. Memorial Auditorium, Worcester, Mass.
20. Harvard Square Theater, Cambridge, Mass.
21.(aft) Music Hall, Boston, Mass.
21.(evg) Music Hall, Boston, Mass.
22. Brandeis University, Waltham, Mass.
24. Civic Center Arena, Hartford, Connecticut
26. Civic Center, Augusta, Maine (NT)
27. Municipal Auditorium, Bangor, Maine
29. Coliseum, Quebec, Canada

December

1. Maple Leaf Gardens, Toronto, Ontario, Canada
2. Maple Leaf Gardens, Toronto, Ontario, Canada
4. Forum, Montreal, Canada
7. Correctional Institution For Women, Clinton, New Jersey
8. Madison Square Garden, New York City

1975 DISCOGRAPHY

January

Blood On The Tracks (US LP) (Columbia PC 33235) (USA No.1, 24 weeks) (UK LP) (CBS 69097) (UK No.4, 16 weeks) ('Tangled Up In Blue', 'Simple Twist Of Fate', 'You're A Big Girl Now', 'Idiot Wind', 'You're Gonna Make Me Lonesome When You Go', 'Meet Me In The Morning', 'Lily, Rosemary And The Jack Of Hearts', 'If You See Her, Say Hello', 'Shelter From The Storm', 'Buckets Of Rain').

February

'Tangled Up In Blue'/'If You See Her, Say Hello' (US 45) (Columbia 3-10106) (USA No.31, 7 weeks).

June

The Basement Tapes (US LP) (Columbia C2-33682) (USA No.7, 14 weeks) ('Odds And Ends', 'Million Dollar Bash', 'Goin' To Acapulco', 'Lo And Behold!', 'Clothes Line Saga', 'Apple Suckling Tree', 'Please Mrs Henry', 'Tears Of Rage', 'Too Much Of Nothing', 'Yea Heavy And A Bottle Of Bread', 'Crash On The Levee', 'Tiny Montgomery', 'You Ain't Goin' Nowhere', 'Nothing Was Delivered', 'Open The Door Homer', 'This Wheel's On Fire').

July

'Million Dollar Bash'/'Tears Of Rage' (US 45) (Columbia 3-

Film poster, The Last Waltz

10217).
August
The Basement Tapes (UK LP) (CBS 88147) (UK No.8, 10 weeks).
Session harmonica for David Blue on *Comin' Back For More* (US LP) (Asylum 7E-1043).
October
'Million Dollar Bash'/'Tears Of Rage' (UK 45) (CBS 3665).
November
'Hurricane Pt.1'/'Hurricane Pt.2' (US 45) (Columbia 3-10245) (USA No.33, 11 weeks).

1975 TV AND RADIO APPEARANCES
April
KNX-FM Radio: Los Angeles: *Mary Travers & Friend* Interview with Mary Travers.
December
WTTW-TV: Chicago, Illinois: *The World Of John Hammond* (★'Hurricane', 'Oh Sister', 'Simple Twist Of Fate').

1975 INTERVIEWS
October
Larry Sloman for *Rolling Stone*.
Sam Shepard for *Rolling Thunder Logbook*.
November
10. Jim Jerome for *People:* "Writing a song, it can drive you crazy. My head is so crammed full of things I tend to lose a lot of what I think are my best songs, and I don't carry around a tape-recorder."

1976

1976 CHRONOLOGY
January
25. The Night Of The Hurricane - 2 at Houston Astrodome. The concert is badly organised in a venue whose acoustics are far from satisfactory. Because of a lack of publicity the Astrodome is barely a quarter full. The show makes a loss of over $50,000. *Rolling Stone* later runs an investigative feature which suspects the show's promoters of shady dealings. Bob Dylan is personally $15,000 out of pocket, having kitted out his musicians in country glitter outfits from Nudie The Tailor. Hurricane Carter is not disappointed by the exercise, seeing it as valuable furthering of his cause. He is granted a retrial within seven weeks of the show.
April
18. The Rolling Thunder tour reconvenes in Florida, without Ronee Blakley and Luther Rix.
22. Two concerts at the Belleview Biltmore Hotel in Clearwater Florida are videotaped for a *Midnight Special* TV show. Dylan is unhappy with the results - he says it looks too much like a *Midnight Special* TV show - and scraps it.
May
23. TVTV crew are called in at 36 hours' notice to video the concert at Fort Collins, Colorado. Incessant rain helps give the film its title - *Hard Rain*.
July
Dylan records his own song, 'Sign Language', with Eric Clapton in Shangri-la Studios, Malibu. It is subsequently included on Clapton's *No Reason To Cry* LP. "I put the chords in and he wrote the words to the song. He was just hanging out at Shangri-la. He was actually living in a tent in the bottom of the garden. He would keep sneaking into the studio to find out what was going on - trying to catch me there." (Eric Clapton)
Contributes to the recording of Leonard Cohen's Phil Spector-produced LP, *Death Of A Ladies Man*, as does Allen Ginsberg.
August
In an interview with Neil Hickey for *TV Guide*, Dylan is asked how he imagines God. "How come nobody ever asks Kris Kristofferson questions like that?" he replies.
November
25. Dylan performs at *The Last Waltz*, the farewell concert by The Band at Winterland in San Francisco. As he leaves the stage Neil Diamond comments to Dylan: "You'll have to be pretty good to follow me." Dylan replies: "What do I have to do, go onstage and fall asleep?"

1976 BIBLIOGRAPHY
Bliss, Carolyn Jane, 'Younger Now', (Unpublished thesis).
Rodnitzky, Jerome L., *Minstrels Of The Dawn: The Folk Protest Singer As Cultural Hero*, Nelson Hall, Chicago.
Lhamon, W.T., 'Bicentennial Dylan: Desire', *The New Republic*, February 14.
Bangs, Lester, 'Bob Dylan's Dalliance With Mafia Chic', *Creem*, April.
Gant, Sandy, 'A Discography Of Bob Dylan', *New York*, July.
Farren, Mick, 'Journey To The Centre Of The Psyche', *NME*, December 25.
Lindstrom, Naomi, 'Dylan: Song Returns To Poetry', *Texas Quarterly*, Winter.
Hinton, Nigel, 'Visions Of Bob Dylan', (Unpublished).

1976 CONCERTS
January
23. Troubador, Los Angeles, California

25. Astrodome, Houston, Texas
April
18. Civic Center, Lakeland, Florida
20. Bayfront Civic Center Auditorium, St Petersburg, Florida
21. Curtis Hixon Convention Center, Tampa, Florida
22.(aft) Belleview Biltmore Hotel, Clearwater, Florida
22.(evg) Belleview Biltmore Hotel, Clearwater, Florida
23. Sports Stadium, Orlando, Florida
25. University Of Florida, Gainesville, Florida
27. Florida State University, Tallahassee, Florida
28. University Of West Florida, Pensacola, Florida
29.(aft) Expo Hall, Municipal Auditorium, Mobile, Alabama
29.(evg) Expo Hall, Municipal Auditorium, Mobile, Alabama
May
1. Reid Green Coliseum, Hattiesburg, Mississippi
3.(aft) The Warehouse, New Orleans, Louisiana
4. L.S.U. Assembly Center, Baton Rouge, Louisiana
6. The Warehouse, New Orleans, Louisiana
8. Hofheinz Pavilion, Houston, Texas
10. Memorial Coliseum, Corpus Christi, Texas (NT)
11. Municipal Auditorium, San Antonio, Texas
12. Municipal Auditorium, Austin, Texas (NT)
15. State School For Boys, Gatesville, Texas (NT)
16. Tarrant County Convention Center, Fort Worth, Texas
18. State Fair Arena, Oklahoma City, Oklahoma
19. Henry Levitt Arena, Witchita, Kansas
23. Colorado State University, Hughes Stadium, Fort Collins, Colorado
25. Salt Palace, Salt Lake City, Utah (NT)

1976 DISCOGRAPHY
January
Session vocals on 'Buckets Of Rain' for Bette Midler on *Songs For The New Depression* (US LP) (Atlantic SD-18155).
Desire (US LP) (Columbia PC-33893) (USA No.1, 35 weeks) (UK LP) (CBS 86003) (UK No.3, 35 weeks) ('Hurricane', 'Isis', 'Mozambique', 'One More Cup Of Coffee', 'Oh Sister', 'Joey', 'Romance In Durango', 'Black Diamond Bay', 'Sara'.)
'Hurricane Pt.1'/'Hurricane' (Full version) (UK 45) (CBS 3878) (UK No.43, 4 weeks).
February
'Mozambique'/'Oh Sister' (US 45) (Columbia 3-10298) (USA No.54, 5 weeks) 'Lay Lady Lay'/'I Threw It All Away' (UK 45) (CBS 3945).
March
'Hurricane'/'Mozambique' (US 45) (Columbia 13-33324).
April
'Mozambique'/'Oh Sister' (UK 45) (CBS 4113).
September
Shared vocal and guitar for Eric Clapton on 'Sign Language' on *No Reason To Cry* (Polydor RSO RS1-3004).
Hard Rain (US LP) (Columbia PC-34349) (USA No.17, 12 weeks) (UK LP) (CBS 86016) (UK No.3, 7 weeks) ('Maggies Farm', 'One Too Many Mornings', 'Stuck Inside Of Mobile', 'Oh Sister', 'Lay Lady Lay', 'Shelter From The Storm', 'You're A Big Girl Now', 'I Threw It All Away', 'Idiot Wind').
November
'Rita Mae'/'Stuck Inside Of Mobile With The Memphis Blues Again' (US 45) (Columbia 3-10454).

1976 TV AND RADIO APPEARANCES
September
NBC-TV Network: *Hard Rain* TV Movie (*'A Hard Rain's A-Gonna Fall', 'Blowin' In The Wind', 'Deportees', 'I Pity The Poor Immigrant', 'Shelter From The Storm', 'Maggie's Farm', 'One Too Many Mornings', 'Mozambique', 'Idiot Wind', 'Knockin' On Heaven's Door'.)

1976 INTERVIEWS
September
11. Neil Hickey for *TV Guide:* "I can see God in a daisy in the wind and rain. The highest form of song is prayer."

1976 SONGS WRITTEN
April
'Seven Days'.

1976 IMPORTANT UNRELEASED RECORDINGS
April
15. Rehearsal for Rolling Thunder tour, Clearwater, Florida (*'Just Like Tom Thumb's Blues' (x4), 'The Sun Is Shining', 'Lay Lady Lay', 'One More Cup Of Coffee', 'It Takes A Lot To Laugh, It Takes A Train To Cry', 'Ballad Of Hollis Brown', 'Hold Me In Your Arms', 'Mozambique', 'Idiot Wind', 'One More Cup Of Coffee', 'Shelter From The Storm', 'Isis', 'Rita May', 'I Threw It All Away').

1977

1977 CHRONOLOGY
February
Bob Dylan's marriage seems set to break up when Sara comes down to breakfast to find "a woman named Malka" at the table with Dylan and the kids. Sara claims that she was then "struck on the face" by Dylan and "ordered to leave".

In Paris, July 1978

Brisbane, March 1978

March

Sara Dylan's divorce petition is heard at the Santa Monica Superior Court. "I can't go home without fear for my safety," Sara claimed in the papers she filed. "I was in such fear of him that I locked my doors to protect myself from his violent outbursts and temper tantrums. He has struck me in the face, injuring my jaw." "Marriage was a failure. Husband and wife was a failure, but father and mother wasn't a failure, I wasn't a very good husband." (Bob Dylan). Sara is represented by the famous divorce lawyer, Marvin Mitchelson, who said: "It was horrendous. He had bodyguards and armed guards and there was a tremendous fight. We battled it out and it was a very emotional thing, involving psychiatrists and psychologists."

May

Dylan signs a management deal with Jerry Weintraub, who thus becomes his first manager in 10 years.

September

Divorce hearings continue in Santa Monica Superior Court.

October

Dylan and Allen Ginsberg call in on a Leonard Cohen recording session being produced by Phil Spector: "Spector was taking a lot of cocaine and was in a kind of hysterical frenzy - totally Hitlerian and dictatorial and sort of crazed. He started pushing us around, ordered Dylan around. Cohen was in despair. Spector went in, twiddled the dials, mixed it, and it sounded perfect." (Allen Ginsberg). During this time, Ginsberg resolves to write a critical discourse about *Renaldo & Clara*. He interviews Dylan but the singer confiscates the tapes because he feels he's said too much. Further interviews take place in which Dylan explains the characters of the movie in great detail.

November

The divorce proceedings draw to a conclusion, (Sara is reported to have been awarded $13.5 million and to have 50 per cent rights to every song written during the 12 years of marriage), though there

are protracted battles for custody of the children. Sara accuses Dylan and a nanny of "attempting to brainwash the minor children", but is herself accused of battery when she bursts into a school classroom and "punches and chokes" a teacher who asks to see her court order of custody. With three private detectives, she chases the kids - who reportedly "resisted going with Mrs Dylan" - through the school.

December

Calling in on an Etta James session, Dylan plays some new tunes on piano for producer Jerry Wexler. It is reported to be religious material. Tour rehearsals begin for a huge worldwide tour with a big band. They will continue for some six weeks, until the final line-up is determined.

1977 BIBLIOGRAPHY

Kooper, Al, *Backstage Passes*, Stein & Day, New York.
Shepard, Sam, *Rolling Thunder Logbook*, Viking, New York.
Denisoff, R. Serge and Fandray, David, 'The Political Side Of Bob Dylan', *Popular Music And Society*, Vol 5 No 5.
Miles, 'Renaldo Zimmerman And The Cubist Movie', *NME*, December 10.

1977 DISCOGRAPHY

February

'Rita Mae'/'Stuck Inside Of Mobile With The Memphis Blues Again' (UK 45) (CBS 4859).
Backing vocals on one track for Leonard Cohen on *Death Of A Ladies' Man* (US LP) (Warner Bros BS-3125).

1977 SONGS WRITTEN

'Patty's Gone To Laredo' (Unreleased) Used as part of the soundtrack for *Renaldo & Clara*.
'What Will You Do When Jesus Comes?' (Unreleased). Used as part of the soundtrack for *Renaldo & Clara*.

1977 INTERVIEWS

October

28-31. Allen Ginsberg and Pierre Cotrell. Printed in *The Telegraph* March 1989.

1977 IMPORTANT UNRELEASED MATERIAL

December

30. Tour rehearsals at Rundown Studios, Santa Monica (★'It's All Over Now Baby Blue' (x3), 'Blowin' In The Wind' (x2), 'Maggies Farm', 'Like A Rolling Stone', 'The Man In Me', 'To Ramona', 'Most Likely You Go Your Way', 'Simple Twist Of Fate', 'Leopard-skin Pill-box Hat', 'If Not For You', 'I Threw It All Away', 'I'll Be Your Baby Tonight').

1978

1978 CHRONOLOGY

January

Renaldo & Clara is released to a generally mixed reception: "It is difficult to understand why a man of his sensibilities has allowed such a hotch potch of unfinished, rambling jumble to appear under his name." (*The Times*) "It's about the essence of man being alienated from himself and how, in order to free himself, to be reborn, he has to go outside himself it's a story that means a great deal to me."

March

In the preamble to his *Playboy* interview, there's a mention of Dylan's "psychic adviser" Tamara Rand. She helps Dylan delve into his past and into previous existences through hypnosis. She is

Auckland 9 March 1978

convinced that Dylan has had several lives before, the first being in Roman times. According to Rand, Dylan even sends his girlfriends to her for approval, but she adds "I would not betray Bob. I know many of his secrets but they will remain secret."

Sneaking out of his Auckland hotel in disguise for a midnight jog, Dylan spots a beautiful Maori princess called Ra Aranga. The silver-tongued devil lost no time in making a move, as Ra recalled: "He looked at me, walked over and said, Hello lady, how about coming with me for a run? I said something like, Push off you scruffy little man." But it seems Ra fell under Dylan's charismatic spell and Dylan subsequently arranged a romantic rendezvous in Christchurch, where the couple spent "three beautiful days" together.

May

Between the Far East concerts and the brief USA warm-up for Europe, Dylan records the songs for *Street-Legal*, which is released in June. "We made *Street-Legal* in a rehearsal hall all I had was two weeks. If I hadn't done it in two weeks I wouldn't have a record out, and you know how it is – after after a certain amount of time, you won't do these songs any more, so you lose them. *Street-Legal* comes closest to where my music is going for the rest of the time. It has to do with an illusion of time."

July

15. The European tour concludes at Blackbushe in front of some 250,000 people.

1978 BIBLIOGRAPHY

Cable, Paul, *Bob Dylan: His Unreleased Recordings*, Scorpion/Dark Star, London.

Hoggard, Stuart And Shields, Jim, *Bob Dylan: An Illustrated Discography*, Transmedia Express, Scotland.

Sloman, Larry, *On The Road With Bob Dylan: Rolling With The Thunder*, Bantam Books, New York.

Rinzler, Alan, *Bob Dylan: The Illustrated Record*, Harmony Books, New York.

Miles, *Bob Dylan: In His Own Words*, Omnibus, London.

Miles, *Bob Dylan*, Big O, London.

Bangs, Lester, 'Oh Mama, Can This Really Be The End?', *NME*, February 4.

Weberman, A.J., 'Bob Dylan's Renaldo & Clara', *High Times*, May.

Gray, Michael, 'Why did I spend 11 hours in a queue to get four tickets to see this man?', *Melody Maker*, June 17.

Jones, D.A.N., 'By The Waters Of Bob Dylan', *The Listener*, June 22.

Shelton, Robert, 'How Does It Feel To Be On Your Own?', *Melody Maker*, July 29.

Lhamon, W.T., 'Poplore & Bob Dylan', *Bennington Review*, December.

Medcalf, Laurence, 'The Rhetoric Of Bob Dylan', (Unpublished).

1978 SONGS WRITTEN

February

'Is Your Love In Vain?' (*Street-Legal*). "When a man's looking for a woman he's looking for a woman to help him out and support him, to hold up one end while he holds up another."

March

'Changing Of The Guard' (*Street-Legal*). "It means something different every time I sing it. 'Changing Of The Guard' is a thousand years old."

'Brown Skin Girl' (Unreleased). Co-written with Helena Springs. No Dylan version extant.

'Coming From The Heart' (Unreleased). Performed at various shows in 1978 and covered by The Searchers.

'If I Don't Be There By Morning' (Unreleased). Co-written with Helena Springs. No Dylan version extant. Covered by Eric Clapton.

'Walk Out In The Rain' (Unreleased). Co-written with Helena Springs. No Dylan version extant. Covered by Eric Clapton.

Arriving at Brisbane Airport 11 March 1978

In Paris, July 1978

April
'Senor (Tales Of Yankee Power)' (*Street-Legal*). "Senor was one of them border type things – Nuevo Laredo, Rio Bravo, Brownsville, Juarez, ya know – sort of like lost yankee on gloomy Sunday-carnival-embassy-type of thing having to pay for sins that you didn't commit when all the while you were getting away with murder."
'New Pony' (*Street-Legal*). "The Miss X in that song is Miss X, not ex-."
'Baby Stop Crying' (*Street-Legal*). "The man in that song has his hand out and is not afraid of getting it bit."
'No Time To Think' (*Street-Legal*). "I wonder if people are comfortable with those broad terminologies like pacifism, rightism, leftism, militarianism, republicanism humanism and secularism. Everything's got an –ism. Not that I'm so stupid that I can't understand what they mean, but I don't think anybody else knows what they mean."
'True Love Tends To Forget' (*Street-Legal*).
'We'd Better Talk This Over' (*Street-Legal*).
'Where Are You Tonight (Journey Through Dark Heat)' (*Street-Legal*).
May
'Stop Now' (Unreleased). No recording extant. No lyrics extant.
September
'Stepchild' (Unreleased). Performed at various 1978 concerts.
'I Love You Too Much' (Unreleased). Performed at various 1978 concerts.
'This Way That Way' (Unreleased). Performed at a soundcheck in New Haven, Connecticut, September 17.
'You'd Like Me To Go' (Unreleased). Performed at a soundcheck in New Haven, Connecticut, September 17.
October
'Legionnaires' Disease' (Unreleased). Performed at a soundcheck

in Detriot, October 13. Covered by The Delta Cross Band.
'One More Time' (Unreleased). Performed at a soundcheck in Carbondale, Illinois, October 28.
'Take It Or Leave It' (Unreleased). Performed at a soundcheck in Carbondale, Illinois, October 28.
November
'Your Rockin' Chair' (Unreleased). Performed at a soundcheck in Carbondale, Illinois, October 28.
December
'Do Right To Me Baby' (*Slow Train Coming*).

1978 CONCERTS
February
20,21,23. Nippon Budokan Hall, Tokyo, Japan
24,25,26. Matsishita Denki Taiikukan, Hirakata City, Osaka Fu, Japan
28. Nippon Budokan Hall, Tokyo, Japan
March
1,2,3,4. Nippon Budokan Hall, Tokyo, Japan
9. Western Springs, Auckland, New Zealand
12,13,14. Festival Hall, Brisbane, Australia
18. Westlake Stadium, Adelaide, Australia
20,21,22. Myer Music Bowl, Melbourne, Australia
25,27,28. Entertainment Centre, Perth, Australia
April
1. Sportsground, Sydney, Australia
June
1,2,3,4,5,6,7. Universal Amphitheater, Los Angeles, California
15,16,17,18,19,20. Earl's Court, London, England
23. Feyenoord Stadium, Rotterdam, Netherlands
26,27. Westfalenhalle, Dortmund, West Germany
29. Deutschlandhalle, West Berlin, West Germany
July
1. Zeppelindfeld, Nurnberg, West Germany

Blackbushe special newspaper 1978

BRITAIN'S BIGGEST EVENING SALE **Evening News** LONDON, SATURDAY, JULY 15, 1978 10p

Thousands pay tribute to the rock genius

A GREAT DAY WITH DYLAN

Top stars at Blackbushe for the festival

By JOHN BLAKE

SUPER-STAR, , Dylan, the little man with a giant talent.

3,4,5,6,8. Pavilion De Paris, Paris, France
11,12. Scandinavium, Goteborg, Sweden
15. Blackbushe Aerodrome, Camberley, England
September
15. Civic Center, Augusta, Maine
16. Cumberland Civic Center, Portland, Maine
17. Veterans Coliseum, New Haven, Connecticut
19. The Forum, Montreal, Canada
20. Boston Garden, Boston, Mass.
22. War Memorial Auditorium, Syracuse, New York
23. War Memorial Auditorium, Rochester, New York
24. Broome County Veterans Memorial Arena, Binghampton, NY
26. Civic Center, Springfield, Mass.
27. Nassau County Coliseum, Uniondale, New York
29,30. Madison Square Garden, New York City
October
3. Scope Arena, Norfolk, Virginia
4. Civic Center, Baltimore, Maryland
5. Capitol Center, Washington, DC
6. The Spectrum, Philadelphia, Pennsylvania
7. Civic Center, Providence, Rhode Island
9. Memorial Auditorium, Buffalo, New York
12. Maple Leaf Gardens, Toronto, Canada
13. The Olympia, Detroit, Michigan
14. Hulman Center, Terre Haute, Indiana
15. Riverfront Stadium, Cincinatti, Ohio
17,18. Stadium, Chicago, Illinois

Rehearsing in San Francisco, November, 1979

20. Richfield Coliseum, Cleveland, Ohio
21. Centennial Arena, Toledo, Ohio
22. University Arena, Dayton, Ohio
24. Freedom Hall, Louisville, Kentucky (NT)
25. Market Square Arena, Indianapolis
27. Wings Stadium, Kalamazoo, Michigan
28. SIU Arena, Carbondale, Illinois
29. The Checkerdome, St Louis, Missouri
31. Civic Center, St Paul, Minnesota
November
1. Dane County Coliseum, Madison, Wisconsin
3. Kemper Arena, Kansas City, Missouri
4. Civic Auditorium, Omaha, Nebraska
6. McNichols Arena, Denver, Colorado (NT)
9. Memorial Coliseum, Portland, Oregon
10. Hec Edmondson Pavilion, Seattle, Washington
11. Pacific Coliseum, Vancouver, Canada
13,14. Oakland Coliseum, Oakland, California
15. The Forum, Los Angeles, California
17. Sports Arena, San Diego, California
18. ASU Activities Center, Tempe, Arizona
19. McKale Memorial Center, Tucson, Arizona
21. Special Events Arena, El Paso, Texas
23. Lloyd Noble Center, Norman, Oklahoma
24. Tarrant County Convention Center, Fort Worth, Texas
25. Special Events Arena, Austin, Texas
26. The Summit, Houston, Texas
28. The Coliseum, Jackson, Mississippi
29. LSU Arena, Baton Rouge, Louisiana
December
1. Mid–South Coliseum, Memphis, Tennessee
2. Municipal Auditorium, Nashville, Tennessee
3. Jefferson Civic Center, Birmingham, Alabama
5. Municipal Auditorium, Mobile, Alabama
7. Coliseum, Greensboro, North Carolina
8. Civic Center, Savannah, Georgia
9. Carolina Coliseum, Columbia, South Carolina

21 November 1980 San Francisco

10. Coliseum, Charlotte, North Carolina
12. The Omni, Atlanta, Georgia
13. The Coliseum, Jacksonville, Florida
15. Civic Center, Lakeland, Florida
16. Hollywood Sportatorium, Miami, Florida

1978 DISCOGRAPHY

April

Five songs on *The Last Waltz* (US LP) (Warner Bros 3 WS 3146) (UK LP) (Warner Bros WBK 66076) ('Baby Let Me Follow You Down', 'I Don't Believe You', 'Forever Young', 'Baby Let Me Follow You Down', 'I Shall Be Released').

June

Street-Legal (US LP) (Columbia JC 35453) (USA No.11, 23 weeks) (UK LP) (CBS 86067) (UK No.2, 20 weeks) ('Changing Of The Guards', 'New Pony', 'No Time To Think', 'Baby Stop Crying', 'Is Your Love In Vain?', 'Senor', 'True Love Tends To Forget', 'We Better Talk This Over', 'Where Are You Tonight?').
'Baby Stop Crying'/'New Pony' (US 45) (Columbia 3-10805).

July

Bob Dylan At Budokan (Japan-only, later US & UK) (CBS/Sony 40 AP 1100-1) ('Mr Tambourine Man', 'Shelter From The Storm', 'Love Minus Zero/No Limit', 'Ballad Of A Thin Man', 'Don't Think Twice It's Alright', 'Maggies Farm', 'One More Cup Of Coffee', 'Like A Rolling Stone', 'I Shall Be Released', 'Is Your Love In Vain?', 'Going Going Gone', 'Blowin' In The Wind', 'Just Like A Woman', 'Oh Sister', 'Simple Twist Of Fate', 'All Along The Watchtower', 'I Want You', 'All I Really Want To Do', 'Knockin' On Heaven's Door', 'It's Alright Ma (I'm Only Bleeding)', 'Forever Young', 'The Times They Are A-Changin''.)
'Baby Stop Crying'/'New Pony' (UK 45) (UK No.13, 11 weeks) (CBS 6499-also 12-inch).

September

'Changing Of The Guard'/'Senor (Tales Of Yankee Power)' (US 45) (Columbia 3-10851).

With Roger McGuinn San Francisco 21 November 1980

With Regina Havis San Francisco 21 November 1980

1978 World tour

Bob Dylan At Budokan (US LP) (Columbia PC2-36067) (USA No.13, 25 weeks).
October
'Is Your Love In Vain?'/'We Better Talk This Over' (UK 45) (CBS 6718-also 12-inch) (UK No.56, 3 weeks).
December
'Changing Of The Guard'/'Senor' (UK 45) (CBS 6935).

1978 RADIO & TV APPEARANCES
March
Radio 2GB, Australia. Julia Orange Interview: "I think we need examples to follow and we need people to show us the way. I used to worship Woody Guthrie, Robert Johnson. I know what hero worship is. I also know that it's an enlightening thing - it's nothing that holds you back."
July
Mette Fugl for Danish TV report, *TV-Aktuelt*.
Swedish TV reporter.
September
Marc Rowland for radio: "My songs are intense. There's a wide range of emotions in there. To me, it's like a Shakespeare play."
Matt Damsker for radio (printed in *Circus*): "I've tried to be very moral in all my dealings. I've tried to remain very moral, even in my sinful ways."

1978 INTERVIEWS
January
Ron Rosenbaum for *Playboy*.
8. John Rockwell for *New York Times*.
20. Joel Kotkin for the *Washington Post*.
22. Gregg Kilday for the *LA Times*.
24. Press Conferences at Rundown Studios, Santa Monica.
26. Jonathan Cott for *Rolling Stone*: "Art is the perpetual motion of illusion. The highest purpose of Art is to inspire. I live in my dreams, I don't live in the actual world."
February
Randy Anderson for the *Minnesota Daily*: "I feel the same exact way as those old tribesmen about having your picture taken. I don't believe it's really proper to do that to somebody else."

3. Jon Bream for the *Minneapolis Star*.
12. Mary Campbell for the *Houston Post*.
17. Tokyo Press Conference.
March
15. Helen Thomas for *The Age*.
20. Philip Fleishman for *Macleans* magazine: "There's no way I should or could explain (*Renaldo & Clara*)."
26. Barbara Kerr for *Chicago Daily News*.
April
11. Karen Hughes for *The Australian:* "I seldom like to talk to anybody because it's false. Because when you talk and you speak, that's all you're doing."
May
28. Robert Hilburn for the *LA Times*.
June
29. Robert Shelton for *Melody Maker:* "All I have in this world are those songs. Nobody else gives those songs life. It's up to me to do it. I live like a poet and I'll die like a poet."
July
3. Philippe Adler for *L'Expresse*.
October
7. Peter Goddard for the *Toronto Sun*.
18. Pam Coyle for *Hibbing High Times* (brief telephone interview).
November
12. Robert Hilburn for *LA Times*.
12. John Mankiewicz for West Coast music paper *Sound*.
16. Jonathan Cott for *Rolling Stone:* "I didn't create Bob Dylan. Bob Dylan has always been here always was. When I was a child there was Bob Dylan. And before I was born, there was Bob Dylan."
18. First of a six-part interview by Peter Oppel for *Dallas Morning News*.

1978 IMPORTANT UNRELEASED RECORDINGS
Various rehearsal tapes from Rundown Studios, Santa Monica.
January (★'You're Gonna Make Me Lonesome When You Go', 'Simple Twist Of Fate', 'Going Going Gone')
27. (★'All I Really Want To Do' (x2), 'Absolutely Sweet Marie' (x2), 'Tomorrow's A Long Time' (x11), 'Oh Sister', 'The Times They Are A-Changin'', 'My Gal', 'Shelter From The Storm').
30. (★'I'll Be Your Baby Tonight', 'The Times They Are A-Changin', 'If You See Her Say Hello', 'The Man In Me', 'I Don't Believe You', 'Tomorrow's A Long Time', 'You're A Big Girl Now', 'Knockin' On Heaven's Door', 'It's Alright Ma (I'm Only Bleeding)', 'Forever Young').
February
1. (★'Repossession Blues', 'One Of Us Must Know', 'Girl Of The North Country').
April
(★'We Better Talk This Over', 'Coming From The Heart', 'I Threw It All Away', 'Maggies Farm', 'Ballad Of A Thin Man', 'Simple Twist Of Fate', 'To Ramona', 'If You See Her Say Hello', 'I Don't Believe You', 'Love Minus Zero/No Limit').

1979

1979 CHRONOLOGY
Spring
Towards the end of 1978, Dylan - prompted by his girlfriend, Mary Alice Artes - takes a serious interest in Christianity, and is converted: "Jesus put his hand on me. It was a physical thing. I felt my whole body tremble. The glory of the Lord knocked me down and picked me up." He attends Bible study classes for the first three

months of 1979.

May

1-11. *Slow Train Coming* is recorded at Muscle Shoals Sound Studio, Alabama. Produced by Jerry Wexler and Barry Beckett, the LP featured Mark Knopfler and Pick Withers from Dire Straits. "Those songs - I didn't plan to write them, didn't like writing them, didn't want to write them, but I found myself writing these songs, and after I had a certain amount of them, I thought I didn't want to sing them, but I wanted the songs out. So I had a girl sing them for me - Carolyn Dennis. I gave them all to her and had her record them."

October

20. Dylan appears on *Saturday Night Live*, performing three of his new Christian songs. After the show he is photographed with autograph collector Mark Chapman, who will later assassinate John Lennon.

November

1. Dylan begins a 14-night residency at the Fox-Warfield Theatre in San Francisco. "I played no song that I had ever played before live. It was a whole different show, and I thought that was a pretty amazing thing to do. I don't know any other artist who has done that." "If you are an artist like Bob Dylan, you got to make the crowd follow you. I can tell you that it doesn't mean anything to him that people might not like what he is doing. Him still do it. And that is the most important thing. Him still do it." (Bob Marley)

1979 BIBLIOGRAPHY

Williams, Paul, *Dylan: What Happened?*, Entwhistle Books, CA.
Parsons, Tony and Burchill, Julie, 'Take This God And Stuff It', *NME*, January 6.
Wenner, Jann S., 'The Slow Train Is Coming', *Rolling Stone*, September 20.
Phillips, David, 'Bob Dylan: A Pony Ride Past The Gate', *Hot Wacks*, 20.

1979 CONCERTS

November

1,2,3,4,6,7,8,9,10,11,13,14,15,16. Fox-Warfield Theater, San Francisco, California
18,19,20,21. Civic Auditorium, Santa Monica, California
25,26. Gammage Center, Tempe, Arizona
27,28. Golden Hall, San Diego, California

December

4,5. Convention Center, Albuquerque, New Mexico
8,9. Community Center, Tucson, Arizona

1979 DISCOGRAPHY

May

Bob Dylan At Budokan (UK LP) (CBS 96004) (UK No.4, 19 weeks).

June

'Forever Young'/'All Along The Watchtower' (UK 45) (CBS 7473).

August

'Gotta Serve Somebody'/'Trouble In Mind' (US 45) (Columbia 1-11072) (USA No.24).

Slow Train Coming (US LP) (Columbia FC-36120) (USA No.3, 26 weeks) (UK LP) (CBS 86095) (UK No.2, 13 weeks) (★'Gotta Serve Somebody', 'Precious Angel', 'I Believe In You', 'Slow Train', 'Gonna Change My Way Of Thinking', 'Do Right To Me Baby', 'When You Gonna Wake Up?', 'Man Gave Names To All The Animals', 'When He Returns').

'Precious Angel'/'Trouble In Mind' (UK 45) (CBS 7828).

October

'Man Gave Names To All The Animals'/'When He Returns' (UK 45) (CBS 7970).

November

'When You Gonna Wake Up'/'Man Gave Names To All The Animals' (US 45) (Columbia 1-11168).

1979 TV AND RADIO APPEARANCES

October

NBC-TV Network: *Saturday Night Live* (★'Gotta Serve Somebody', 'I Believe In You', 'When You Gonna Wake Up').

December

7. KMEX Radio, Tucson, Arizona: Interview with Bruce Heiman: "I follow God, so if my followers are following me, indirectly they're gonna be following God too, because I don't sing any song which hasn't been given to me by the Lord to sing."

1979 SONGS WRITTEN

April

'Baby Give It Up' (Unreleased). Co-written with Helena Springs. No extant recording. Lyrics extant.
'Gonna Change My Way Of Thinking' (*Slow Train Coming*).
'Gotta Serve Somebody' (*Slow Train Coming*).
'I Believe In You' (*Slow Train Coming*).
'Man Gave Names To All The Animals' (*Slow Train Coming*).
'No Man Righteous' (Unreleased). Performed live in 1979. Cover version by Jah Malla.
'Precious Angel' (*Slow Train Coming*).
'Slow Train' (*Slow Train Coming*).
'Trouble In Mind' (45 Release).
'When He Returns' (*Slow Train Coming*).
'When You Gonna Wake Up' (*Slow Train Coming*).
'Ye Shall Be Changed' (Unreleased). No recording extant. Lyrics extant.

Autographed photograph 1980

San Francisco 21 November

Wearing his cross in 1980

September

'More Than Flesh And Blood' (Unreleased). Co-written with Helena Springs. No extant recording. Lyrics extant.

'Responsibility' (Unreleased). Co-written with Helena Springs. No extant recording. Lyrics extant.

'Saving Grace' (*Saved*).

'Someone Else's Arms' (Unreleased). Co-written with Helena Springs. No extant recording. Lyrics extant.

'Tell Me The Truth One Time' (Unreleased). Co-written with Helena Springs. No extant recording. Lyrics extant.

'The Wandering Kind' (Unreleased). Co-written with Helena Springs. No extant recording. Lyrics extant.

'What's The Matter' (Unreleased). Co-written with Helena Springs. No extant recording. Lyrics extant.

'Without You' (Unreleased). Co-written with Helena Springs. No extant recording. Lyrics extant.

October

'Covenant Woman' (*Saved*).

'In The Garden' (*Saved*). "'In The Garden' is actually a classical piece. I don't know how in the world I wrote it but I was playing at the piano, closed my eyes, and the chords just came to me."

'Pressing On' (*Saved*).

'Saved (By The Blood Of The Lamb)' (*Saved*).

'Solid Rock' (*Saved*). "Well, you just don't hear things like that, full gospel, half gospel or otherwise white gospel, black gospel, forget it."

'Stand By Faith' (Unreleased). No recording extant. Lyrics extant.

'What Can I Do For You' (*Saved*).

1979 INTERVIEWS

June

Lynne Allen for *Trouser Press*.

1980

1980 CHRONOLOGY

January

25. In his concerts, Dylan continues to deliver little sermons from the stage. In Omaha, Nebraska for instance: "Years ago they used

Drammen, Norway, 9 July 1981

Dylan playing saxophone on stage with former schoolfriend Larry Kegan 1981

to say I was a prophet. I'd say, No I'm not a prophet. They'd say, Yes, you are a prophet. Now I come out and say, Jesus is the answer. They say, Bob Dylan? He's no prophet."

February

27. Dylan wins Grammy Award for Best Male Rock Vocal Performance on 'Gotta Serve Somebody'. He performs a remarkably powerful version of the song, wearing a tuxedo and bow-tie.

April

"Dylan had this black chick following him everywhere, carrying a Bible and praising the Lord every two seconds. Dylan told me

Toulouse 21 June 1981

that he had sold 12 million records since he became a Christian. I told him to become a Moslem and he might sell 60 million." (Ronnie Hawkins)

Summer

Records backing harmonica for Christian singer Keith Green on 'Pledge My Head To Heaven', from the LP *So You Wanna Go Back To Egypt*. Green will later be killed in a plane crash.

November

9. Begins a series of "retrospective" concerts in San Francisco, in which old songs are mingled with new. In 12 nights at the Fox-Warfield Theater, Dylan introduces occasional guests, including Roger McGuinn, Jerry Garcia, Maria Muldaur and Michael Bloomfield. Bloomfield will die of a drugs overdose two months later.

1980 BIBLIOGRAPHY

Gross, Michael, *Bob Dylan: An Illustrated History*, Grossett & Dunlap, New York.

Krogsgaard, Michael, *Twenty Years Of Recording: The Bob Dylan Reference Book*, Scandinavian Institute For Rock Research.

Roques, Dominique, *The Great White Answers-The Bob Dylan Bootleg Records*, Southern Live Oak, Paris.

Williams, Paul, *Dylan-One Year Later,* (Private pamphlet).

Ed. Thomson, Elizabeth M., *Conclusions On The Wall: New Essays On Bob Dylan*, Thin Man, Manchester.

Weberman, A.J., *My Life In Garbology*, Stonehill, New York.

Ed. Woodward, Ian, *Bob Dylan Occasionally*, (Fan magazine) Issue 1.

McAuliffe, Jon, 'Bob One', *Music World*, May.

Gillespie, Dana, 'I Was Dylan's Cuddly Teddy Bear', *News Of The World*, August 31.

Wooding, Dan, 'Dylan-By His Pastor', *Buzz*, November.

Bauldie, John, *The Camelion Poet: Bob Dylan & The Search For Self*, (Unpublished).

1980 CONCERTS

January
11,12. Paramount Theater, Portland, Oregon (NT)
13,14. Paramount Northwest Theater, Seattle, Washington
15. Paramount Northwest Theater, Seattle, Washington (NT)
17,18. Opera House, Spokane, Washington (NT)
21,22,23. Rainbow Music Hall, Denver, Colorado
25,26. Orpheum Theater, Omaha, Nebraska
27,28,29. Uptown Theater, Kansas City, Missouri
31. Orpheum Theater, Memphis, Tennessee
February
1. Orpheum Theater, Memphis, Tennessee
2,3. Jefferson Civic Center, Birmingham, Alabama
5,6. Civic Auditorium, Knoxville, Tennessee
8,9. Municipal Auditorium, Charleston, West Virginia
April
17,18,19,20. Massey Hall, Toronto, Canada
22,23,24,25. Theatre St Denis, Montreal, Canada
27,28. Palace Theater, Albany, New York
30. Kleinhan's Music Hall, Buffalo, New York
May
1. Kleinhan's Music Hall, Buffalo, New York
2,3. Memorial Theater, Worcester, Mass.
4,5. Area Landmark Theater, Syracuse, New York
7,8. Bushnell Memorial Auditorium, Hartford, Connecticut
9,10. City Hall, Portland, Maine
11,12. Ocean State Performing Arts Center, Providence, Rhode Island
14,15,16. Stanley Theater, Pittsburgh, Pennsylvania
17,18. Civic Theater, Akron, Ohio
20. Franklin County Veterans Memorial Auditorium, Columbus, Ohio
21. Memorial Hall, Dayton, Ohio
November
9,10,11,12,13,15,16,17,18,19,21,22. Fox-Warfield Theater, San Francisco, California
24. Community Center, Tucson, Arizona
26. Golden Hall, San Diego, California
29,30. Paramount Northwest Theater, Seattle, Washington
December
2. The Armory, Salem, Oregon
3,4. Paramount Theater, Portland, Oregon

1980 DISCOGRAPHY

January
'Gotta Serve Somebody'/'Gonna Change My Way Of Thinking'

Communication breakdown in the long-running Dylan v's Grossman Court battle

This is Dylan . . . give me rewrite

HOW *many times can a man turn his head / And pretend that he just doesn't see?* That is the musical question posed in court papers by Albert Grossman, who's suing the author of those words, one Bob Dylan. Grossman was Dylan's manager from 1962 through 1969, and now Grossman has filed a multi-million-dollar suit against his former charge, alleging breach of contract and claiming that Bob owes him royalties and other sums. When we last left this case, Dylan had filed with the court a response to Grossman's charges. But, in October, 1983, a Manhattan Supreme Court Justice decided that what Bob had turned in was "jumbled and disorderly," and told him to redraft it into something a little more lucid. Dylan did just that, but now Grossman and his attorney, Roy Grutman, say that his second response is every bit as incomprehensible as the first. "Dylan," Grutman complains in papers filed in court, "has claimed a lack of understanding of the effect of certain agreements. But the words which he does not understand are simple English words like 'partnership,' 'purchase' and simple numerical concepts like '10 years' and '25 percent.' This man is a master of the English language whose lyrics, along with his music, have made him into a superstar . . ." Grutman and Grossman are asking for the court to request a *third* redraft from Dylan.

Roy Lichtenstein inspiration for Shot Of Love sleeve

(UK 45) (CBS 8134).
June
Saved (US LP) (Columbia FC 36553) (USA No.24, 11 weeks) (UK LP) (CBS 86113) (UK No.3, 8 weeks) ('A Satisfied Mind', 'Saved', 'Covenant Woman', 'What Can I Do For You?', 'Solid Rock', 'Pressing On', 'In The Garden', 'Saving Grace', 'Are You Ready?') It was mixed wrong or something, it didn't sound right to me anyway."
'Saved'/'Are You Ready?' (UK 45) (CBS 8743).
August
'Saved'/'Are You Ready?' (US 45) (Columbia 1-11370).
Summer
Session harmonica on 'Pledge My Head To Heaven', from *So You Wanna Go Back To Egypt* by Keith Green (Pretty Good Records PGR-1).

1980 TV AND RADIO APPEARANCES

February
TV: *Grammy Awards Ceremony* ('Gotta Serve Somebody').
May
15. Pat Crosby for KDKA-TV.
November
19. Paul Vincent for KMEL-Radio: "Right now I'm just content to play these shows - it's a stage show we're doing, not a salvation ceremony."
21. Ernesto Bladden for KPRI-Radio.

1980 INTERVIEWS

May
7. Karen Hughes for the *Village Voice*.
August
2. Karen Hughes for *The Dominion*: "Jesus put his hand on me. It

Dylan finally makes the News Of The World 1980

was a physical thing. I felt it. I felt it all over me. I felt my whole body tremble. The glory of the Lord knocked me down and picked me up."

November
23. Robert Hilburn for the *LA Times*.

1980 SONGS WRITTEN
February
'Are You Ready?' (*Saved*).
April
'Ain't Gonna Go To Hell' (Unreleased). Performed live at various 1980 concerts.
'Coverdown Breakthrough' (Unreleased). Performed live at various 1980 concerts.
'I Will Love Him' (Unreleased). Performed live in Toronto.
'Why'd They Talk About Me' (Unreleased). No recording extant. No lyric extant.
September
'Her Memory' (Unreleased). No recording extant. No lyric extant.
October
'Every Grain Of Sand' (*Shot Of Love*). "Sometimes you're in an area where there isn't anybody there and never was. So you just have to be real sensitive to where you're walking at the time. You must keep it balanced. And there's no footnotes around. It's the kind of an area where there's no precedent for it. 'Every Grain Of Sand' is a song like that."
'Groom's Still Waiting At The Altar' (45 Release, on later version of *Shot Of Love*).
'Let's Keep It Between Us' (Unreleased). Performed live at various 1980 concerts.
'Yonder Comes Sin' (Unreleased). Performed on rehearsal tape, October 1980.

November
'City Of Gold' (Unreleased). Performed live at various 1980 concerts.

1980 IMPORTANT UNRELEASED MATERIAL
October
Rehearsals at Rundown Studios, Santa Monica (★'Yonder Comes Sin', and incomplete fragments of 'Blowin' In The Wind', 'Gotta Serve Somebody', 'Mr Tambourine Man', 'Slow Train').

1981

1981 CHRONOLOGY
April
Recording begins for *Shot Of Love*. "'Shot Of Love' was one of the last songs Bumps Blackwell produced, and even though he only produced one song, I gotta say that of all the producers I ever used, he had the best instincts but 'Shot Of Love' didn't fit into the current formula. It probably never will. Anyway, people were always looking for some excuse to write me off, and this was as good as any."
July
Albert Grossman sues Dylan for more than $1 million, claiming that Dylan "overpaid songwriter's royalties to himself" and withheld other payments.
August
Shot Of Love released with pop art illustration on cover – apparently Dylan's idea, based on Lichtenstein but executed by Pearl Beach. However, a drawing on the back was replaced at the last minute

Ralph Steadman illustration for the programme of the first Bob Dylan fan convention

by a photo of Dylan sniffing a rose. "He wanted the back of a Cadillac, with exhaust coming out of it. So I did a collage of photographs and hand-painted them with the car in the sky and the exhaust blending into the clouds. There's a quote from the Bible on the album sleeve, from Matthew 11-25, so I put M1125 on the license plate, but he changed it to 666." (Pearl Beach). The "Cadillac cover" was actually released in Brazil.

1981 BIBLIOGRAPHY

Heylin, C.M., 'The Bob Dylan Interviews - A List', (Pamphlet).
Ledbury, John, 'Mysteriously Saved', (Pamphlet) Quest, London.
Gray, Michael, *The Art Of Bob Dylan*, Hamlyn, London.
Anderson, Dennis, *The Hollow Horn*, Hobo Press, Munich.
Hattenhauer, Darryl, 'Bob Dylan As Hero', *Southern Folklore Quarterly*.
Norman, Philip, 'Dylan And The Angels', *Sunday Times*, June 28.
Franks, Alan, 'With Bob On His Side', *The Times*, July 3.
Spencer, Neil, 'The Diamond Voice Within', *NME*, August 15.
Ed. Bauldie, John, *The Telegraph* (Fan magazine) Issue 1, November.
Sumner, Carolyn, 'The Ballad Of Dylan & Bob', *Southwest Review*, Winter.

1981 CONCERTS

June
10. Poplar Creek Music Theater, Chicago, Illinois
11,12. Pine Knob Music Theater, Clarkston, Michigan
14. Merriweather Post Pavilion, Columbia, Maryland
21. Stade Municipal Des Minimes, Toulouse, France
23. Stade de Colombes, Colombes, France
26,27.28,29,30. Earl's Court, London, England
July
1. Earl's Court, London, England
4,5. NEC Arena, Birmingham, England
8. Johanneshovs Isstadion, Stockholm, Sweden
9,10. Drammenshallen, Drammen, Norway
12. Brondby-Hallen, Copenhagen, Denmark
14,15. Freilichttheatre, Bad Segeberg, West Germany
17. Freilichtbuhne, Loreley, St Goarshausen, West Germany
18. Eisstadion, Mannheim, West Germany
19,20. Olympiahalle, Munchen, West Germany
21. Stadthalle, Wien, Austria

On stage in Madrid 26 June 1984

Verona press conference 27th May 1984

23. Sporthalle St Jakob, Basel, Switzerland
25. Palace des Sports, Avignon, France
October
16,17. The Auditorium, University of Wisconsin, Milwaukee, Wisconsin
18. Dane County Coliseum, Madison, Wisconsin
19. Holiday Star Music Theater, Merrilville, Indiana
21. The Orpheum, Boston, Mass.
23. The Spectrum, Philadelphia, Pennsylvania
24. Recreation Building, Pennsylvania State University, State College, Pennsylvania
25. University Of Bethlehem, Bethlehem, Pennsylvania
27. Meadowlands BTB Sports Arena, East Rutherford, New Jersey
29. Maple Leaf Gardens, Toronto, Canada
30. The Forum, Montreal, Quebec, Canada
31. Kitchener Arena, Kitchener, Ontario, Canada
November
2. Civic Center, Ottawa, Canada
4,5. Cincinnati Music Hall, Cincinnati, Ohio
6. Perdue University, Lafayette, Indiana
7,8. Hill Auditorium, Ann Arbor, Michigan
10, 11. Saenger Performing Arts Center, New Orleans, Louisiana
12. Houston, Texas
14. Nashville, Tennessee
15, 16. The Fox Theater, Atlanta, Georgia
18, 19. Sunrise Musical Theater, Miami, Florida

1981 RADIO & TV APPEARANCES

June
20. Paul Gambaccini for *Rock On*, Radio One.
21. Tim Blackmore for Capitol Radio, London.
22. Radio Europe No.1. Interview with Yves Bigot.
July
2. Radio WNEW-FM, New York. Interview with Dave Herman.
22. Brief street interview in Vienna with Andreas Forst for Austrian TV. ORF Channel 02, *Ohne Maulkorb*.

1981 INTERVIEWS

July
13. Travemunde Press Conference: "Being re-born changes everything. I mean, it's like re-awaking one day and, can you imagine being re-born? Can you imagine turning into another person? It's pretty scary if you think about it."
August
15. Neil Spencer for *NME*.
October
Divina Infusino for the *Milwaukee Journal* (brief interview).

1981 DISCOGRAPHY

July

3. 'Heart Of Mine'/'Let It Be Me' (UK 45) (CBS A 1406)

August

Shot Of Love (US LP) (Columbia TC 37496) (USA No.33, 9 weeks) 20. (UK LP) (CBS 85178) (UK No.6, 8 weeks) ('Shot Of Love', 'Heart Of Mine', 'Property Of Jesus', 'Lenny Bruce', 'Watered Down Love', 'Dead Man, Dead Man', 'In The Summertime', 'Trouble', 'Every Grain Of Sand').

September

12. 'Lenny Bruce'/'Dead Man, Dead Man' (UK 45) (CBS A 1604).

'Heart Of Mine'/'Groom Still Waiting At The Altar' (US 45) (Columbia 18-02510).

1981 SONGS WRITTEN

May

'Caribbean Wind' (*Biograph*). "I started it in St Vincent when I woke up from a strange dream in the hot sun. I was thinking about living with somebody for all the wrong reasons."

'Heart Of Mine' (*Shot Of Love*). "I had somebody specific in mind when I wrote this, somebody who liked having me around."

'Dead Man, Dead Man' (*Shot Of Love*). "I wrote this song while looking into the mirror."

'Angelina'. Recorded for, but not used on, *Shot Of Love*.

'Need A Woman'.

'Trouble' (*Shot Of Love*).

'Watered Down Love' (*Shot Of Love*).

'Shot Of Love' (*Shot Of Love*). "The purpose of music is to elevate and inspire the spirit. To those who care where Bob Dylan is at, they should listen to 'Shot Of Love'. It's my most perfect song. It defines where I am spiritually, musically, romantically and whatever else. It shows where my sympathies lie. It's all there in that one song."

'Property Of Jesus' (*Shot Of Love*).

'Lenny Bruce' (*Shot Of Love*).

'In The Summertime' (*Shot Of Love*).

July

'Jesus Is The One' (Unreleased). Performed at various 1981 concerts.

November

'Thief On The Cross' (Unreleased). Performed in New Orleans, November 10.

'You Changed My Life' (*The Bootleg Series*).

1981 IMPORTANT UNRELEASED RECORDINGS

April-May

Recordings from sessions for *Shot Of Love* (★'Angelina', 'Need A Woman', 'Mystery Train').

1982

1982 CHRONOLOGY

January

Howard Alk, a former partner of Albert Grossman and friend of Dylan's since the early '60s as well as collaborator on *Eat The Document* and *Renaldo & Clara* is found dead in Rundown Studios.

February

Records in Rundown Studios, Santa Monica, with Allen Ginsberg.

March

6. Appears at the "Peace Sunday" concert at the Pasadena Rose Bowl with Joan Baez, and sings three songs, including the song by Jimmy Buffett, 'Pirate Looks At Forty', the lyrics of which Dylan has written on his shirt cuff.

With Chrissie Hynde, Van Morrison and Eric Clapton, Wembley Stadium, 1 July 1984

15. Admitted to the Songwriters' Hall Of Fame, New York City. "It's thrilling. Kinda like the Baseball Hall Of Fame."
UPI carry a story that Dylan has declined to present the Gospel Song Award of the National Music Publishers Association and quote a "source close to Dylan": "The evidence is that his Christian period is over. In a sense, he never left Judaism."
July
22. The first annual Bob Dylan imitators' contest is held at The Speakeasy club on MacDougal Street in Greenwich Village. There are 51 competitors. Frank Christian, the winner, receives a golden harmonica.
December
22. Frank Zappa is surprised when his entry phone beeps: "This is Bob Dylan. I want to play you my new songs." Zappa commented, "I looked at the video screen to see who was at the gate and there, in the freezing cold, was a figure with no coat and an open shirt, it was him." Dylan sat at the piano, played 11 songs, and asked Zappa if he would produce the next album.

1982 BIBLIOGRAPHY

Van Estrik, Robert, 'Concerted Efforts', (Pamphlet), Holland.
Heylin, Clinton, *Rain Unravelled Tales-A Rumourography*, Manchester.
Dowley, Tim & Dunnage, *Barry From A Hard Rain To A Slow Train*, Midas Books, Kent.
Dorman, James E., *Recorded Dylan*, Soma Press, California.
Bowden, Betsy, *Performed Literature*, Indiana UP.
Herdman, John, *Voice Without Restraint*, Harris, Edinburgh.

1982 SONGS WRITTEN

May
'Don't Ever Take Yourself Away' (Unreleased). No recording extant. Lyric extant.
'Fur Slippers' (Unreleased). No recording extant. Lyric extant.??
'All The Way Down' (Unreleased). Recorded on rehearsal tape, possibly dating from summer 1982, but as yet unidentified. Title provisional.
'Hallelujah' (Unreleased). Recorded on rehearsal tape, possibly dating from summer 1982, but as yet unidentified. Title provisional.
'High Away' (Unreleased). Recorded on rehearsal tape, possibly dating from summer 1982, but as yet unidentified. Title provisional.
'Is It Worth It?' (Unreleased). Recorded on rehearsal tape, possibly dating from summer 1982, but as yet unidentified. Title provisional.
'Magic' (Unreleased). Recorded on rehearsal tape, possibly dating from summer 1982, but as yet unidentified. Title provisional.
'On Borrowed Time' (Unreleased). Recorded on rehearsal tape, possibly dating from summer 1982, but as yet unidentified. Title provisional.

Press advertisement for Wembley 1984

'Red Boat' (Unreleased). Recorded on rehearsal tape, possibly dating from summer 1982, but as yet unidentified. Title provisional.
'Rockin Boat' (Unreleased). Recorded on rehearsal tape, possibly dating from summer 1982, but as yet unidentified. Title provisional.
'Say That' (Unreleased). Recorded on rehearsal tape, possibly dating from summer 1982, but as yet unidentified. Title provisional.
'Tryin' To Make It On Your Own' (Unreleased). Recorded on rehearsal tape, possibly dating from summer 1982, but as yet unidentified. Title provisional.

1982 RADIO AND TV APPEARANCES

March
15. NBC-TV, New York. Interview with Jane Hansen, after Songwriters' Hall Of Fame presentation.
June
6. ABC-TV. 'Entertainment Tonight'. Part of Peace Sunday concert, Pasadena, California.

1982 CONCERTS

June
6. Peace Sunday, Rose Bowl, Pasadena, California (★'With God On Our Side', 'Pirate Looks At Forty', 'Blowin' In The Wind'.)

1983

1983 CHRONOLOGY

February
16. Appears as tipsy guest at a show by Levon Helm & Rick Dankoat New York's Lone Star Cafe.
A case brought against Bob Dylan by Hurricane case witness Patty Valentine (claiming that Dylan's song implied that she had conspired to convict Carter unjustly) is thrown out of court. A federal appeals court decides that "a review of the entire song makes it clear this interpretation is not reasonably possible. It is obvious that the lyrics

Enjoying the Verona press conference 27 May 1984

are substantially and materially true."

April

3. Arriving at LA International Airport from New York, Dylan attacks a photographer, Gary Aloian, who is annoying him. The skirmish is snapped by another lensman and Aloian files charges against Dylan, accusing the singer of "battery". Dylan, it is reported, used to study Kung Fu with David Carradine.

11. Recording begins for *Infidels*, again with Mark Knopfler whom Dylan has asked to produce the record, after having been turned down by Elvis Costello and, reputedly, by David Bowie. Many tracks are recorded, some of which will not be released. It remains a mystery to those who have heard the unreleased songs, why Dylan appears to be unconscious of their merit.

May

8. The *Infidels* sessions end. Mark Knopfler, engaged to produce the LP, has to leave to join Dire Straits for their tour. The press report that "Knopfler Walks Out". *Infidels* is mixed and finished without his participation, and he is subsequently quoted as being "disappointed" with the way the album turned out. "I wasn't given the final mix or the choice of songs on the album: Bob decided to do those himself, and I must say that listening to it makes me wish I'd done it. He overdubbed certain things, re-sang certain things. I think I've got some roughs at home which are better than what's on the record. Infidels is not my album. I look at that as a job half done." (Mark Knopfler)

19. LA Deputy City Attorney Susan L. Kaplan concludes there was no criminal conduct in the "battering of Aloian" case and that no charges would be preferred against Bob Dylan.

June

New York magazine reports that Dylan has been spending time in Brooklyn with the Lubavitcher community.

September

19. Dylan is photographed at the Western Wall in Jerusalem at the bar mitzvah of his son, wearing prayer shawl.

October

6. The Grossman vs Dylan case comes to court. Dylan's eight-page submission to the court is handed back by Justice Martin Evans because it makes no sense. He instructs Bob to write it again "in discrete, self-contained paragraphs containing concise factual statements."

November

Dylan's first-ever promo video is released. 'Sweetheart Like You' has the singer and a multi-ethnic band playing to a sweeper-up in a deserted nightclub. The charlady is mistakenly identified as Bob's mother.

1983 BIBLIOGRAPHY

Gans, Terry A., *What's Real And What Is Not: The Myth Of Protest*, Hobo Press, Munich.
Diddle, Gavin, *Images & Assorted Facts*, Manchester.
Hinchey, John, *Bob Dylan's Slow Train*, Wanted Man, Study Series 1.
Bauldie, John, *Bob Dylan & Desire*, Wanted Man, Study Series 2.
Gilmore, Mikal, 'Dylan Returns To The Material World', *LA Herald Examiner*, October 28.
Hilburn, Robert, 'Bob Dylan At 42', *LA Times*, October 30.

1983 SONGS WRITTEN

April

'I & I' (*Infidels*) "The 'I', like in 'I & I', changes. It could be I, or it could be the 'I' who created me. And also, it could be another person who's saying 'I'. It's sorta like Childe Harold in Babylon."

'Blind Willie McTell'. "It had a kinda broad landscape setting. That's how it was envisioned anyway. It never really reached that proportion for me lyrically. It never got developed . . ."

Hamburg, 31 May 1984.

'Clean Cut Kid' (*Empire Burlesque*).

'Death Is Not The End' (*Down In The Groove*).

'Don't Fall Apart On Me Tonight' (*Infidels*). "A lot of times you'll just hear things and you'll know that these are the things that you want to put in your song. Whether you say them or not. They don't have to be your particular thoughts. They just sound good and somebody thinks them. A song like 'Don't Fall Apart On Me Tonight' sort of falls into that category. A guy's getting out of bed saying don't talk to me, it's leaving time."

'Foot Of Pride'.

'Jokerman' (*Infidels*).

'Julius And Ethel' (Unreleased). Recorded for, but not used on, *Infidels*.

'License To Kill' (*Infidels*). "Women are the only hope. I think they're a lot more stable than men. Only trouble with women is they let things go on too long."

'Lord Protect My Child'.

'Man Of Peace' (*Infidels*).

'Neighbourhood Bully' (*Infidels*).

'Someone's Gotta Hold Of My Heart'.

'Sweetheart Like You' (*Infidels*).

'Tell Me'.

'Union Sundown' (*Infidels*).

1983 DISCOGRAPHY

August

Appears on one track on Will Powers LP, *Dancing For Mental Health*.

October

'Union Sundown'/'Angel Flying Too Close To The Ground' (UK 45) (CBS A-3916).

Infidels (US LP) (Columbia QC 38819) (USA No.20, 23 weeks) ('Jokerman', 'Sweetheart Like You', 'Neighbourhood Bully', 'License To Kill', 'Man Of Peace', 'Union Sundown', 'I & I', 'Don't Fall Apart On Me Tonight').

November

Infidels (UK LP) (CBS 25539) (UK No.9, 12 weeks).

December

'Union Sundown'/'Sweetheart Like You' (US 45) (Columbia 38-04301) (USA No.55, 8 weeks).

1983 INTERVIEWS

October

30. Robert Hilburn for *LA Times*: "There was always some kind of resistance. If it wasn't about religion, it was about the style of music. If it wasn't style, it was about the clothes you wore. If it wasn't clothes, it was about the people you knew. There was

always something that people didn't like. I've been used to that since I was born."

1983 IMPORTANT UNRELEASED RECORDINGS
April-May
Various recordings from the sessions for *Infidels*. (★'Clean Cut Kid', 'Union Sundown', 'Jokerman', 'Don't Fall Apart On Me Tonight', 'Blind Willie McTell' (x2), 'Sweetheart Like You' (x9), 'Foot Of Pride', 'Julius And Ethel', 'Someone's Got A Hold Of My Heart', 'Lord Protect My Child', 'Tell Me', 'This Was My Love').

1984

1984 CHRONOLOGY
February
28. Dylan appears with Stevie Wonder at the Grammy Awards to present the song of the year award. Sting, who wins with 'Every Breath You Take', is in Australia, so Dylan walks off with the prize.
March
22. Dylan appears live on the *David Letterman TV Show*, backed by an LA band called The Cruzados. Although he has rehearsed many songs with the group on the previous evening, come showtime they still have no idea what he's going to do. In fact, the opener, Sonny Boy Williamson's 'Don't Start Me To Talking', is one song that the band have never even tried out before, but the show is a triumph.

With Mick Taylor and Carlos Santana, Brussels, 7 June 1984

April
Dylan's second video is 'Jokerman', highly acclaimed – chiefly by those who made it – but Dylan has mixed feelings: "They filmed me from 30 yards away. When I saw the videos, all I saw was a shot of me from my mouth to my forehead on the screen. I figure 'Isn't that somethin'? I'm payin' for that?'"
May
Rehearsals begin for the European tour with Santana, but it takes some time for Dylan and guitarist Mick Taylor to put a band together and the somewhat disorganised opening performance in Verona proves that some further rehearsal would have been preferable.
July
30. A fascinating interview is taped for a Westwood One Radio special, *Dylan On Dylan*. It is notable for its detailed retrospection and Dylan's affirmation that playing live is what matters above all else: "If I went out to play and nobody showed up, that would be the end of me. I only make records because people see me live."
Winter
Some sessions are recorded for a new LP, which will be called *Empire Burlesque*. Dylan's already becoming a little despondent about his lack of commercial appeal: "If the records I do make are only going to sell a certain amount, then why do I have to spend a lot of time putting them together?"

1984 BIBLIOGRAPHY
Mellers, Wilfrid, *A Darker Shade Of Pale*, Faber & Faber, London.
Landy, Elliott, *Woodstock Vision*, Rowohlt, West Germany.
Heylin, Clinton, *More Rain Unravelled Tales*, Manchester.
Day, Aidan, *Escaping On The Run*, Wanted Man, Study Series 3.
Cott, Jonathan, *Dylan*, Doubleday, New York.
Bicker, Stewart P., *The Red Rose & The Briar*, Private.
Rowley, Chris, *Blood On The Tracks*, Proteus.

1984 CONCERTS
May
28,29. Arena di Verona, Verona, Italy
31. St Pauli Stadion, Hamburg, West Germany
June
2. St Jakob Stadion, Basel, Switzerland
3. Olympia Stadion, Munchen, West Germany
4,6. Sportpaleis Ahoy', Rotterdam, Netherlands
7. Stade de Schaerbeek Stadion, Bruxelles, Belgium
9. Ullevi Stadion, Goteborg, Sweden
10. Idraetsparken, Copenhagen, Denmark
11. Stadion Bieberer Berg, Offenbach, West Germany
13. Waldbuhne, West Berlin, West Germany

With Manager Bill Graham, Verona May 1984

With Van Morrison at Slane Castle 8 July 1984

14. Wiener Stadthalle-Kiba, Wien, Austria
16. Mungersdorfer Stadion, Koln, West Germany
17. Stade de l'Ouest, Nice, France
19,20,21. Palaeur, Roma, Italy
24. Stadio San Siro, Milano, Italy
26. Estadio del Rayo Vallecano, Madrid, Spain
28. Ministadio CF Barcelona, Barcelona, Spain
30. Stade Marcel Saupin, Nantes, France
July
1. Parc de Sceaux, Paris, France
3. Alpexpo, Grenoble, France
5. St James Park, Newcastle, England
7. Wembley Stadium, London, England
8. Slane Castle, Slane, Ireland

1984 TV AND RADIO APPEARANCES
February
28. TV: Guest co-presenter on the Grammy Awards. "I wasn't doing anything that night. For me, it was just going down to the place and changing my clothes."
March
TV: *The David Letterman Show* 'Don't Start Me To Talking', 'License To Kill', 'Jokerman').
June
30. TV: *Antenne 2* (France) Antoine De Caunes Interview: "I write because I need something to sing. Sometimes it's painful, you know, you're up days and nights, walking around."
July
7. Interview with Martha Quinn for MTV, backstage at Wembley: "We've been playing for mostly foreign audiences. In Spain, they were Spanish audiences, in France mostly French, and in Germany they were mostly German audiences."
November
Radio: *Westwood One*: Interview with Bert Kleinman: "I don't know if I've ever been happy. I've just never thought of life in terms of happiness and unhappiness. It just never occurred to me."

1984 INTERVIEWS
May
26. Kurt Loder for *Rolling Stone*.
29. Verona (Sirmione) Press Conference: "We like the world ruled by violence. We don't want the world ruled by democracy."
31. Hamburg Press Conference: "I might have been a protest singer, but I've never been into politics."
July
1. Mick Brown for *The Sunday Times*: "I'm a realist. Or maybe a surrealist. But you can't beat your head against the wall forever." With David Hammond and Derek Bailey for Clancy Brothers documentary. (Printed in full in *The Telegraph*)
16. Pamela Andriotakis for *People*: "I think you have to be old to get good."
August
5. Robert Hilburn for *LA Times:* "I don't think I'll be perceived properly 'til a hundred years after I'm gone. I really believe that."
24. Bono for *Hot Press*: "You go into a studio now and they got rugs on the floors, settees and pinball machines and videos and sandwiches coming every ten minutes once you'd make an album in three or four days, and it was over; now it takes four days to get a drum sound."

1984 DISCOGRAPHY
January
'Sweetheart Like You'/'Union Sundown' (US 45) (Columbia 38 04301).

Outtake of Down In The Groove sleeve photograph

In Tel Aviv, 5 September 1987

December
'New Danville Girl' (Unreleased). Early version of 'Brownsville Girl'. Recorded for, but not used on, *Empire Burlesque*.
'Something's Burning' (*Empire Burlesque*).

1984 IMPORTANT UNRELEASED RECORDINGS
March
22. Rehearsal for *David Letterman TV Show* (★'I Once Knew A Man', 'Jokerman', 'License To Kill', 'Treat Her Right').
May
23. Rehearsal for tour. Beverly Theater, Los Angeles (★'Maggies Farm', 'All Along The Watchtower', 'Just Like A Woman' (x2), 'When You Gonna Wake Up?' (x2), 'Shelter From The Storm', 'Watered Down Love', 'Masters Of War', 'Jokerman', 'Simple Twist Of Fate' (x2), 'Man Of Peace' (x2), 'I And I', 'It's All Over Now, Baby Blue', 'Ballad Of A Thin Man', 'Heart Of Mine', 'Highway 61 Revisited', 'I See You Around And Around', 'Leopard-skin Pill-box Hat', 'It's All Over Now Baby Blue', 'Always On My Mind' (x3), 'Every Grain Of Sand' (x2), 'Girl Of The North Country').
27. Rehearsal session from Verona, Italy (★Various instrumentals, 'Almost Done', 'Enough Is Enough', 'Dirty Lies', 'Why Do I Have To Choose', 'To Each His Own').
28. Rehearsal session from Verona, Italy (★'Jokerman', 'All Along The Watchtower', 'Just Like A Woman', 'Highway 61 Revisited', 'I And I', 'Girl From The North Country', 'Shelter From The Storm', 'License To Kill', 'Ballad Of A Thin Man', 'When You Gonna WakeUp', 'To Ramona').
Autumn
Various studio recordings, New York (★'Driftin' Too Far From Shore', 'Firebird' (instr), 'Who Loves You More', 'Straight A's In

May
'Jokerman'/'Isis' (live 1975) (US 45) (Columbia 38-04425).
June
'Jokerman'/'License To Kill' (UK 45) (CBS A4055)
December
Real Live (US LP) (Columbia FC 39546) (UK LP) (CBS 26334) (UK No.54, 2 weeks) ('Highway 61 Revisited', 'Maggies Farm', 'I And I', 'License To Kill', 'It Ain't Me Babe', 'Tangled Up In Blue', 'Masters Of War', 'Ballad Of A Thin Man', 'Girl Of The North Country', 'Tombstone Blues').

1984 SONGS WRITTEN
May
'Angel Of Rain' (Unreleased). No recording extant. No lyric extant.
'Dirty Lies' (Unreleased) (Recording on rehearsal tape of May 27).
'Enough Is Enough' (Unreleased). Various live performances in 1984.
July
'Driftin Too Far From Shore' (*Knocked Out Loaded*). "To hear the way he's let producers just take his stuff and bury it has surprised me. 'Driftin' Too Far From Shore' is a good example of this, a brilliant, fantastic, really vibrant rock'n'roll track - but when you hear it on the record . . . " (Ron Wood)
'Go Way Little Boy' (Unreleased). Recorded at sessions for *Empire Burlesque* and covered by Lone Justice.
'When The Night Comes Falling From The Sky' (*Empire Burlesque*).
'Who Loves You More' (Unreleased). Recorded for, but not used on, *Empire Burlesque*.
'Wolf' (Unreleased). Recorded for, but not used on, *Empire Burlesque*.

Wearing an SAS T-shirt Brisbane, 1 March 1986

Wellington Airport, 4 February 1986

With Dire Straits in Australia, Feb 1986

Love', 'Clean Cut Kid' (x2), 'The Very Thought Of You') (★'Go Way Little Boy').
Studio recordings, Hollywood, California (★'New Danville Girl', 'Something's Burning Baby').

1985

1985 CHRONOLOGY
January
29. Dylan contributes to the recording of 'We Are The World', though he has trouble with the phrasing of his line and has to run through many takes before he's satisfied. "It's a worthwhile idea, but I wasn't so convinced about the message of the song. To tell you the truth, I don't think people can save themselves."
March
Dylan plays harmonica on 'No Name On The Bullet' on Sly & Robbie's *Language Barrier* LP.
April
The Dylan/Grossman case continues in New York. Grossman having sued for $1 million, Dylan counter-sues for $7 million. The thrust of Dylan's defence is that "Grossman induced an unsophisticated 21-year-old to enter into various agreements while acting in a fiduciary capacity and that Grossman owed Dylan a duty of undivided loyalty and honesty and had no right to take advantage of him."
July
5. London's *Daily Mirror* runs a curious story: "Bob Dylan has become a religious fanatic since his return to the Jewish faith friends say Dylan hopes to be ordained as a rabbi."

13. Dylan is the final act on 'Live Aid', the transatlantic concert in aid of famine relief for Ethiopia. Introduced as being "transcendent" by Jack Nicholson, Dylan's performance is ragged. Cohorts Ron Wood and Keith Richards don't help, and the lack of stage monitors and noises off as the rest of the cast assemble behind Dylan's back cause a great deal of uneasiness. Dylan makes controversial comments about the plight of American farmers and later walks offstage during the massed finale. "Some guy halfway round the world is starving so, OK, put 10 bucks in the barrel, then you can feel you don't have to have a guilty conscience about it. Obviously, on some level it does help, but as far as any sweeping movement to destroy hunger and poverty, I don't see that happening." "We came off looking like real idiots. But I'd do it again, for Bob." (Ron Wood)
25. Invited to Moscow by Yevgeny Yevtushenko, Dylan is introduced to a packed Lenin Stadium Luzhniki Sports Hall as "a singing poet." He performs three songs at an event sponsored by the Soviet Writers' Union. "I didn't understand too much of it, the peculiar thing was there wasn't anybody at this particular poetry reading that I figured had even heard of me a little bit."
August
21 & 22. Dylan makes promo videos with Dave Stewart for 'When The Night Comes Falling' and 'Emotionally Yours', directed by Eddie Arno and Markus Innocenti. Dylan says he wants the videos in black and white so they'll look like "an old Japanese movie".
September
22. Performs with Tom Petty & The Heartbreakers at 'Farm Aid'. "The idea came to me when all that money was being raised for the famine in Africa. I'd gotten a lot of letters from people who were having their farms repossessed." "The combination of Dylan's spontaneity and the ability of The Heartbreakers to respond quickly to it is a great success and the alliance is to continue for almost two years. "We rehearsed about a week, playing maybe a million different songs. That was one of the best times I ever had. We were blazing. So we went off to Farm Aid and had a great night." (Tom Petty).
Dylan contributes to Steve Van Zandt's "Artists Against Apartheid"

Empire Burlesque promotion photograph 1985

record, 'Sun City'. Remix engineer Jay Burnett had his work cut out: "Bob Dylan sang the whole song and we had to pick out one line that sounded good. That was a bigger problem than it sounds because we couldn't find a line that a) sounded like Dylan and b) was in time and c) was in tune. Good old Bob!"

November

13. CBS Walter Yetnikoff throws a party to celebrate Bob Dylan's 25-year career. A star-studded event at the Whitney Museum in New York sees Dylan presented with a plaque, a platinum disc (for cumulative sales of 35 million records) and an original Woody Guthrie drawing and 1945 songbook. He is also hugged by lots of people.

Dylan records with Eurythmic Dave Stewart in his recording studio, The Church, Crouch End, London. "I was excited to work with Dave because I've always liked his work a lot."

December

The 5-LP, 53-track retrospective *Biograph* is released and sells unexpectedly well. It features some previously unreleased material, including live recordings from the 1966 concerts. "I've never really known what this thing is supposed to be most of my stuff has already been bootlegged so to anybody in the know, there's nothing on it that they haven't heard before. I didn't put it together and I haven't been very excited about this thing. All it is, really, is repackaging, and it'll just cost a lot of money."

A book, *Lyrics: 1962-1985*, an updating of *Writings And Drawings*, is published.

1985 BIBLIOGRAPHY

Amendt, Gunter, *Reunion Sundown*, Hobo Press, Munich.

Bicker, Stewart P., *Friends & Other Strangers*, Private.

Cartwright, Bert, *The Bible In The Lyrics Of Bob Dylan*, Wanted Man, Study Series 4.

De Somogyi, *Jokermen & Thieves*, Wanted Man, Study Series 5.

Dierks, Barbara and Angela, *It Ain't Me Babe*, Isis, W. Germany.

Williams, Don, *Bob Dylan: The Man, The Music, The Message*, Revell, New Jersey.

Neve, Michael, 'Queen Mary', *London Review Of Books*.

1985 SONGS WRITTEN

January

'Emotionally Yours' (*Empire Burlesque*). "Dylan told us that 'Emotionally Yours' had been written with Liz Taylor in mind." (Markus Innocenti).

'I'll Remember You' (*Empire Burlesque*).

'Trust Yourself' (*Empire Burlesque*).

'Seeing The Real You At Last' (*Empire Burlesque*).

February

'Tight Connection To My Heart' (*Empire Burlesque*). "'Tight Connection To My Heart' is a very visual song. I want to make a movie out of it. Of all the songs I've ever written, that's the one that's got characters that can be identified with I can see people in it."

'Never Gonna Be The Same Again' (*Empire Burlesque*).

'Straight A's In Love' (Unreleased). Recorded for, but not used on, *Empire Burlesque*. Cover version by The Williams Brothers.

'The Very Thought Of You' (Unreleased). Recorded for, but not used on, *Empire Burlesque*.

'Waiting To Get Beat' (Unreleased). Recorded for, but not used on, *Empire Burlesque*.

March

'Dark Eyes' (*Empire Burlesque*). "That particular song just sort of came I won't say easy but all in one piece like that."

November

'Under Your Spell' (*Knocked Out Loaded*).

1985 RADIO & TV APPEARANCES

June

17. Radio: Rockline Phone-In, with Bob Coburn: "Q: What poets have had the most influence on your writing? A: John Keats. I used to read him quite a bit."

September

22. Farm Aid on US TV ('Clean Cut Kid', 'Shake', 'I'll Remember You', 'Trust Yourself', 'Lucky Old Sun', 'Maggies Farm'.)

29. TV: MTV: Interview with Charles M. Young: "I feel healthy. I'm not doing anything differently - maybe the longer you do it, the healthier you get!"

October

10. TV: ABC: *20/20*: Interview with Bob Brown: "I don't know what a Robert Frost or Keats or T.S. Eliot would think of my stuff. It's more a visual type thing for me. I could picture the colour of the song or the shape of it."

November

22. TV: BBC: *Old Grey Whistle Test*: Interview with Andy Kershaw. "Bob had just been out to Russia reading poetry in football stadiums and he thought he'd like to talk about that, but Andy Kershaw said, 'So, Bob, are you gonna have your hair cut like Dave's?' and the papers said, 'Bob Dylan - what a jerk, stoned out of his mind. What's he doing on telly?'" (Dave Stewart)

1985 INTERVIEWS

March

Bill Flanagan for his book *Written In My Soul* (published Autumn 1986): "Songs are just thoughts. For the moment they stop time. Songs are supposed to be heroic enough to give the illusion of stopping time."

October

13. Mikal Gilmore for *LA Herald-Examiner*. "I know I've done a lot of things, but if I'm proud of anything it's maybe that I helped bring somebody like Woody Guthrie to a little more attention."

Brisbane, 1 March 1986

At the Lone Star Cafe New York 25 May 1988

November

17. Robert Hilburn for *LA Times*: "When I see my name anywhere, it's the '60s this or the '60s that. I can't figure out sometimes if people think I'm dead or alive."

25. Denise Worrell for *Time* magazine: "My favourite poets are Shelley and Keats. Rimbaud is so identifiable. Lately, if I read poems, it's like I can always hear the guitar. Even with Shakespeare's Sonnets, I can hear a melody because it's all broken up into timed phrases."

December

5. David Fricke for *Rolling Stone*.

Scott Cohen for *Spin*. "I've never been able to understand the seriousness of it all, the seriousness of pride. People talk, act, live as if they're never gonna die. And what do they leave behind? Nothing. Nothing but a mask."

1985 DISCOGRAPHY

January

'We Are The World' – USA For Africa Single (Columbia 78EN 04839).

22. 'Highway 61 Revisited'/'It Ain't Me Babe' (UK 45) (CBS (G)A5020).

June

Empire Burlesque LP (US Columbia FC 40110) (USA No.33, 17 weeks) (UK CBS 86313) (UK No.11, 6 weeks) ('Tight Connection To My Heart', 'Seeing The Real You At Last', 'I'll Remember You', 'Clean-Cut Kid', 'Never Gonna Be The Same Again', 'Trust Yourself', 'Emotionally Yours', 'When The Night Comes Falling From The Sky', 'Something's Burning Baby', 'Dark Eyes') 'Tight Connection To My Heart'/'We Better Talk This Over' (UK 45) (CBS A6303).

August

'When The Night Comes Falling From The Sky'/'Dark Eyes' (UK 45) (CBS A6469–also 12-inch).

Harmonica on 'No Name On The Bullet', on *Language Barrier*. Sly Dunbar and Robbie Shakespeare (Island 90286).

December

Biograph 5LP Box-set (US Columbia C5X 38830) (USA No.33, 22 weeks) (UK CBS 66509) ('Lay Lady Lay', 'Baby Let Me Follow You Down', 'If Not For You', 'I'll Be Your Baby Tonight', 'I'll Keep It With Mine', 'The Times They Are A-Changin'', 'Blowin' In The Wind', 'Masters Of War', 'Lonesome Death Of Hattie Carroll', 'Percy's Song', 'Mixed-Up Confusion', 'Tombstone Blues', 'Groom's Still Waiting At The Altar', 'Most Likely You Go Your Way', 'Like A Rolling Stone', 'Jet Pilot', 'Lay Down Your Weary Tune', 'Subterranean Homesick Blues', 'I Don't Believe You', 'Visions Of Johanna', 'Every Grain Of Sand', 'Quinn The Eskimo', 'Mr Tambourine Man', 'Dear Landlord', 'It Ain't Me Babe', 'You Angel You', 'Million Dollar Bash', 'To Ramona', 'You're A Big Girl Now', 'Abandoned Love', 'Tangled Up In Blue', 'It's All Over Now Baby Blue', 'Can You Please Crawl Out Your Window?', 'Positively 4th Street', 'Isis', 'Caribbean Wind', 'Up To Me', 'Baby I'm In The Mood For You', 'I Wanna Be Your Lover', 'I Want You', 'Heart Of Mine', 'On A Night Like This', 'Just Like A Woman', 'Romance In Durango', 'Senor', 'Gotta Serve Somebody', 'I Believe In You', 'Time Passes Slowly', 'I Shall Be Released', 'Knockin' On Heaven's Door', 'All Along The Watchtower', 'Solid Rock', 'Forever Young').

'Sun City'/'Not So Far Away' (US 45) (Manhattan ST53019).

1985 IMPORTANT UNRELEASED RECORDINGS

January

Several takes of 'We Are The World' at A&M Studios, Hollywood.

March

Tracks from sessions for *Empire Burlesque*. ('Waiting To Get Beat', 'When The Night Comes Falling From The Sky').

September

19. Universal Studios, Los Angeles. Rehearsals for Farm Aid.

Oakland California, 24 July 1987

('Forever Young', 'Then He Kissed Me', 'Louie Louie', 'What'd I Say', 'Baby What You Want Me To Do', 'Shake', 'I'll Remember You', 'Alabama Band', 'Trust Yourself', 'That Lucky Old Sun').

1986

1986 CHRONOLOGY

January

20. Appears at the Martin Luther King birthday celebration, which is televised. Dylan sings 'I Shall Be Released' with new words - "You're laughing now, you should be praying/Could be the midnight hour of your life" - and is joined by Peter, Paul & Mary for 'Blowin' In The Wind'. Also contributes to 'Let The Bells Of Freedom Ring' (with Stevie Wonder) and the finale, 'Happy Birthday', standing with Elizabeth Taylor - once a dream girl, recently a dinnerdate.

25. Dylan's former manager Albert Grossman dies of a heart attack on a flight to London.

February

5. The Far East True Confessions Tour begins. "You never know what's coming. There'll be different songs, or we'll do the same songs in different keys. It reminds me of a high school dance band. It's more polished, maybe, but it has that looseness, that freshness, that, uh - chaos." (Guitarist Mike Campbell). The first concert, in Wellington, New Zealand, doesn't impress the critics: "The Heartbreakers were obviously out of sorts with Dylan's material and for the most part they floundered around like a B-grade pub group".

9. Records 'Band Of The Hand' in Festival Records Studio, Sydney.

March

4. The Band's pianist, Richard Manuel, hangs himself in his motel bathroom in Winter Park, Florida.

Dylan records tracks which will be included on his next LP, *Knocked Out Loaded*. "It's all sorts of stuff. It doesn't really have a theme or purpose."

31. Dylan receives the Founder's Award of the American Society Of Composers, Authors and Publishers. (ASCAP). Quotes from 'Without A Song' in his acceptance speech.

April

When Liz Taylor is in hospital for dental surgery, Dylan sends her a ten-foot square "get well soon" card - a poster of himself that she had admired at the ASCAP awards ceremony.

June-August

The concerts in the USA with Tom Petty & The Heartbreakers attract audiences of over 1 million people. "Since 1974 I've never stopped working. I'm not getting caught up in all this excitement of a big tour. I mean, what's such a big deal about this one?" At some dates, The Grateful Dead also appear. "Those were the best shows, with The Dead," Dylan comments later.

August

Dylan raps on 'Street Rock' from Kurtis Blow's album *Kingdom Blow*. "He raps, he really raps. The man raps." (Kurtis Blow)

17. Dylan, shortly to begin filming in England and Wales for the Richard Marquand-directed movie *Hearts Of Fire*, holds a Press Conference at the National Film Theatre in London.

September

14. Dylan appears on the Chabad anti-drugs Telethon. He gives a brief message and performs Hank Williams's 'Thank God' with The Heartbreakers.

October

Filming for *Hearts Of Fire* continues in Canada.

November
10. A long-time fan of Gordon Lightfoot, Dylan turns up at the Canadian Academy of Recording Arts to help induct Lightfoot into the Hall Of Fame. He describes Lightfoot as "a rare talent".

1986 BIBLIOGRAPHY

Ashenmacher, Bob, 'Dylan Talks', *Duluth News-Tribune & Herald*, June 29.
Bream, Jon, 'The Many Faces Of Bob Dylan', *Minneapolis Star & Tribune*.
Shelton, Robert, *No Direction Home*, NEL.
Hepworth, David, 'The Invisible Man', *Q*, October.
Wyman, Bill, 'Don't Think Twice', *Oakland Express*, November 28.
Chase, Donald, 'Blood On The Tracks', *City Lights*, November.

1986 CONCERTS
February
5. Athletic Park, Wellington, New Zealand
7. Mt. Smart Stadium, Auckland, New Zealand
10,11,12,13. Entertainment Centre, Sydney, Australia
15. Memorial Drive, Adelaide, Australia
17,18. Entertainment Centre, Perth, Australia (NT)
20,21,22. Kooyong Stadium, Melbourne, Australia
24,25. Entertainment Centre, Sydney, Australia
28. Lang Park, Brisbane, Australia
March
1. Lang Park, Brisbane, Australia (NT)
5. Nippon Budokan Hall, Tokyo, Japan
6. Castle Hall, Osaka Fu, Japan
8. Gymnasium, Nagoya, Japan
10. Nippon Budokan Hall, Tokyo, Japan
June
9. Sports Arena, San Diego, California
11. Lawlor Events Center, Reno, Nevada
12. Cal Expo Amphitheater, Sacramento, California
13,14. Greek Theater, University Of California, Berkeley, California
16,17. Pacific Amphitheater, Costa Mesa, California
18. Veterans Memorial Coliseum, Phoenix, Arizona
20. Southern Star Amphitheater (Astroworld), Houston, Texas
21. Irwin Center, Austin, Texas
22. Reunion Arena, Dallas, Texas
24. Market Square Arena, Indianapolis, Indiana
26. Hubert H. Humphrey Metrodome, Minneapolis, Minnesota
27. Alpine Valley Amphitheater, Milwaukee, Wisconsin
29. Poplar Creek Music Theater, Chicago, Illinois
30. Pine Knob Music Theater, Detroit, Michigan
July
1. Pine Knob Music Theater, Detroit, Michigan
2. Rubber Bowl, Akron, Ohio
4. Rich Stadium, Buffalo, New York
6,7. RFK Stadium, Washington, DC
8,9. Great Woods, Mansfield, Mass.
11. Civic Center Auditorium, Hartford, Connecticut
13. Performing Arts Center, Saratoga Springs, New York
15, 16, 17. Madison Square Garden, New York City
19,20. The Spectrum, Philadelphia, Pennsylvania
21. Meadowlands BTB Arena, East Rutherford, New Jersey
24. Sandstorm, Kansas City, Missouri
26,27. Red Rock, Denver, Colorado
29. Portland, Oregon
31. Tacoma Dome, Tacoma, Washington
August
1. The BC Place, Vancouver, Canada

Japanese advertisement for the ten-LP Biograph bustin' bootleg box Ten Of Swords

3. The Forum, Los Angeles, California
5. Shoreline Amphitheater, Mountain View, California
6. Mid-State Fairground, Paso Robles, California

1986 RADIO & TV APPEARANCES
January
20. NBC-TV. Martin Luther King Day Concert. ('The Bells Of Freedom', 'I Shall Be Released', 'Blowin' In The Wind', 'Happy Birthday'.)
27. US TV. Congratulation speech to Willie Nelson. National Appreciation Awards Ceremony, Los Angeles.
February
9. Channel 9 TV. Australia. 60 Minutes. Interview with George Negus.
19. Channel 7 TV. Australia. Interview with Maurice Parker for State Affair.
March
31. CNN-TV. Extracts from ASCAP Founder's Award Ceremony.
April
10. Extracts from Press Conference, Los Angeles.
May
21. Radio. WBAI. New York. Telephone interview with Bob Fass.
June
HBO cable TV. In Concert Special – Hard To Handle. Concert in Sydney, Australia.
July
4. TV. Broadcast of part of concert in Buffalo, New York for Farm Aid II. FM Simulcast.
September
14. TV. Chabad Telethon. Dylan & Heartbreakers sing 'Thank God', and Dylan delivers anti-drug message.

1986 INTERVIEWS
January
16. Toby Cresswell for Australian *Rolling Stone*: "I wouldn't do half the things I do if I was thinking about having to live up to a Bob Dylan myth."
26. Don McLeese for the *Chicago Sun Times*.

```
RE:   SALE OF BOB DYLAN'S BOYHOOD HOME AND ORIGINAL FURNISHINGS


The following items will be placed on bid effective 1-1-87. Bids will be accepted
no later than 3-1-87. All correspondence and details of items shall be the re-
sponsibility of the proposed purchaser.

We, the seller, reserve the right to reject any placed bids we find unacceptable.


3 Bedroom Home - 2 story approximately 3,000 sq. feet.  Attached single stall
              garage, additional double stall garage - corner lot 100 x 175'
              2 baths, 2 fireplaces, formal dining room, recreation room in
              basement.


Miscellaneous items of original Bob Dylan home -

       Crystal chandelier

       Complete dining room set, table, 5 chairs, breakfront, buffet

       Original bedroom set, bed, dresser, dresser with mirror, box
       spring and mattress

       Nautical light fixture from Bob Dylan's bedroom

       Bedroom lamp - silverplate base

       Lavabo (matches dining room set)

       Sofa

       Living room chair

       Kitchen Set (chrome)

       Recliner Chair

       4 Ceramic Kitchen Plates (decorative plates)

       Original bath tub


Send all correspondence to:  P. O. Box 124
                             Hibbing, Minnesota   55746
```

Bob's Boyhood home for sale, including nautical light fixture

February
10. Press Conference. Sydney: "I'm only Bob Dylan when I have to be Bob Dylan. Most of the time I'm just myself."
21. Stuart Coupe for *The Age*.
April
10. Press Conference, Los Angeles.
Charles Kaiser for the *Boston Review*.
June
22. Jon Bream for *Minneapolis Star And Tribune*.
29. Bob Ashenmacher for the *Duluth News Tribune And Herald*.
July
Mikal Gilmore for *Rolling Stone*: "Obviously I'm not gonna be around forever. That day's gonna come when there aren't gonna be any more records, and then people won't be able to say, Well this one's not as good as the last one."
August
17. Press Conference, National Film Theatre, London: "I'm just taking some time off here."
October
David Hepworth for Q magazine: "I can go most places and nobody will recognise me except people who know who I am."
November
23. Comments to Donald Chase for *San Francisco Chronicle*.

1986 DISCOGRAPHY

July
Knocked Out Loaded (US LP) (Columbia OC 40439) (USA No.55, 13 weeks) (UK LP) (CBS 86326) (UK No.10, 5 weeks) ('You Wanna Ramble', 'They Killed Him', 'Driftin' Too Far From Shore', 'Precious Memories', 'Maybe Someday', 'Brownsville Girl', 'Got My Mind Made Up', 'Under Your Spell').
August
11. 'Band Of The Hand' (US 45) (MCA 52811) (UK 45) (MCA 1076).
September
Rap on 'Street Rock', on *Kingdom Blow* by Kurtis Blow (Mercury

830-215).

1986 SONGS WRITTEN

February
'Band Of The Hand' (45 Release).
April
'Brownsville Girl' (*Knocked Out Loaded*).
May
'Got My Mind Made Up' (*Knocked Out Loaded*).
'Jammin Me' (Unreleased). Cover version by Tom Petty & The Heartbreakers. "Bob came out and said 'I got this idea for a song called Jammin' Me. Like too much information.' So we put a pad down and picked up a newspaper and just started coming up with lines, saying the lines out loud to each other. We wrote eight or nine verses." (Tom Petty)
'Maybe Someday' (*Knocked Out Loaded*).
September
'Had A Dream About You Baby' (*Down In The Groove*).
'Night After Night' (*Hearts Of Fire* Soundtrack LP).

1987

1987 CHRONOLOGY

February
19. Dylan turns up at the Palomino Club in LA with George Harrison and the two join Taj Mahal and John Fogerty on stage for an extended jam session.
28. Dylan duets with Michael Jackson at Elizabeth Taylor's 55th birthday party in Hollywood, held at Burt Bacharach's home.
March
11. Dylan is invited to appear at a tribute to George Gershwin, at the Brooklyn Academy Of Music, on the 50th anniversary of the composer's death. "I said, 'Are you sure? You sure there might not be another Bob Dylan?'" He does, however, express a liking for Gershwin's music and performs the little-known 'Soon' at the concert.
April
20. Dylan appears as guest artist at U2's concert at the LA Sports Arena singing two songs with Bono.
May
4. Paul Butterfield dies aged 44.
August
Dylan is asked to comment on Elvis Presley for US magazine for the anniversary of Presley's death: "When I first heard Elvis's voice I just knew that I wasn't going to work for anybody and nobody was gonna be my boss. Hearing him for the first time was like busting out of jail."
September
5. Richard Marquand, director of *Hearts Of Fire*, dies aged 49. Dylan plays in Israel for the first time in his life. His concert in Tel Aviv's Hayarkon Park is not very well received by either concertgoers or critics.
October
9. Première of *Hearts Of Fire*, Marble Arch Odeon, London. Co-stars Rupert Everett and Fiona attend, Dylan doesn't – even though he is in London. Audience sniggers suggest that the movie is not likely to be a success. It plays for seven days and is never shown in theatres again. A UK video release follows some months later. In the USA the film is not released at all.

1987 BIBLIOGRAPHY

Aaseng, Nathan, *Bob Dylan: Spellbinding Songwriter*, Lerner, Minneapolis.

Karlin, Danny, 'It Ain't Him Babe', *London Review Of Books*, February 5.
Ed. Gray, Michael and Bauldie, John, *All Across The Telegraph*, Sidgwick & Jackson, London.
Dundas, Glen, 'Tangled Up In Tapes', (Pamphlet), Canada.
Shepard, Sam, 'Dylan', *Esquire*, July.
Hampton, Wayne, *Guerrilla Minstrels*, Tennessee UP.

1987 CONCERTS

July
4. Sullivan Stadium, Foxboro, Mass.
10. John F. Kennedy Stadium, Philadelphia, Pennsylvania
12. Giants Stadium, East Rutherford, New Jersey
19. Autzen Stadium, Eugene, Oregon
24. Oakland County Stadium, Oakland, California
26. Anaheim Stadium, Anaheim, California
September
5. Hayarkon Park, Tel Aviv, Israel
7. Sultan's Pool, Jerusalem, Israel
10. St Jacobshalle, Basel, Switzerland
12. Arena Ex Autodromo, Modena, Italy
13. Palasport, Torino, Italy
15. Westfalenhalle 1, Dortmund, West Germany
16. Frankenhalle, Nuremberg, West Germany
17. Trep Tower Festwiese, East Berlin, East Germany
19. Sportpaleis Ahoy', Rotterdam, Netherlands
20. Halle 20, Messeplatz, Hanover, West Germany
21. Valby Hallen, Copenhagen, Denmark
23. Jaahalli, Helsinki, Finland
25. Scandinavium, Goteborg, Sweden
26. Johanneshovs Isstadion, Stockholm, Sweden
28. Festhalle, Frankfurt, West Germany
29. Hanns Martin Scheyerhalle, Stuttgart, West Germany
30. Olympiahalle, Munich, West Germany
October
1. Arena di Verona, Verona, Italy
3. Palaeur, Roma, Italy
4. Arena Civica, Milano, Italy
5. Piazza Grande, Locarno, Switzerland
7. POPB, Bercy, Paris, France
8. Forest National, Bruxelles, Belgium
10,11,12. NEC Arena, Birmingham, England
14,15,16,17. Wembley Arena, London, England

1987 INTERVIEWS

July
Sam Shepard for *Esquire*: "You always know who you are. I just don't know who I'm gonna become."
September
Brief comments to Robert Hilburn for *LA Times* Kurt Loder for *Rolling Stone*.

1987 APPEARANCES

September
19. BBC TV *Omnibus* TV special. Interview with Christopher Sykes and footage from *Hearts Of Fire* shooting.
October
BBC Radio 2. Dylan interview sections in *The Woody Guthrie Story*.

1987 DISCOGRAPHY

April
'Got My Mind Made Up'/'They Killed Him' (UK 45) (CBS BA 3471).
May

Harmonica on 'Factory' on Warren Zevon's LP *Sentimental Hygiene* (Virgin 90603).
September
Hearts Of Fire Soundtrack (UK LP) (CBS)
October
Hearts Of Fire Soundtrack (US LP) (Columbia SC 40870)
'The Usual'/'Got My Mind Made Up' (UK 45) (CBS 6511487)
'The Usual'/'Got My Mind Made Up'/'They Killed Him' (UK 45 12-inch) (CBS 6511486)

1987 SONGS WRITTEN

April
'Silvio' (with Robert Hunter) (*Down In The Groove*).
'The Ugliest Girl In The World' (with Robert Hunter) (*Down In The Groove*).

1987 IMPORTANT UNRELEASED MATERIAL

Summer
Two outtakes from *Down In The Groove*, 'Got Love If You Want It' and 'Important Words'.
June
Three-hour rehearsal tape with The Grateful Dead. Tracks include: Buddy Holly's 'Oh Boy', Paul Simon's 'Boy In The Bubble', 'Ballad Of Ira Hayes', 'Stealin'', 'Walking Down The Line' and 'Rolling In My Sweet Baby's Arms'.

1988

1988 CHRONOLOGY

January
20. Dylan is inducted to the Rock 'n' Roll Hall Of Fame. He is introduced by Bruce Springsteen, who says: "The way that Elvis freed your body, Bob freed your mind he had the vision and the talent to make a pop song so that it contained the whole world." Dylan and the assembled company attempt 'All Along The Watchtower' and 'Like A Rolling Stone'.
29. Dylan shares a table with Martin Scorsese and Steven Spielberg at a party at LA's Museum Of Contemporary Art to première the latest Giorgio Armani Collection. Most guests wear black tie; Dylan wore an "angora knit hat".
February
26. The case against Hurricane Carter is finally overturned and Hurricane is freed.
April
George Harrison, Tom Petty, Roy Orbison and Jeff Lynne turn up on Dylan's doorstep to use his garage studio to record a song as a C-side for a George Harrison single. The odd bunch enjoy each other's company so much that they resolve to meet up again and make an LP of self-penned songs - thus The Traveling Wilburys. "Bob was just a prince. I still think of him as the greatest poet of our age." (Roy Orbison)
May
29. Dylan turns up at the Lone Star in New York City, where he sits in on a session by Levon Helm, singing 'The Weight' and 'Nadine'.
June
Dylan begins an extensive tour of the US with a three-piece band, though for two of the first three shows the line-up is augmented by Neil Young on lead guitar. Marshall Crenshaw was advertised as playing bass, but he was replaced shortly before the tour began by Kenny Aaronson.
July
1. After his show at Jones Beach, Dylan meets light heavyweight

San Francisco, 21 November 1980

boxing champion Donny 'Golden Boy' Lalonde. Lalonde plays Dylan's music in his dressing room before he fights and gives Bob a pair of boxing gloves. He is made to promise to send tickets for his fight with Sugar Ray Leonard. Dylan, he reveals, shadow boxes to keep himself fit.

15. After a show in Indianapolis, Dylan drives to Fairmount, Indiana, arriving some time after midnight. He goes to look at James Dean's grave, at the house where Dean grew up, and somehow persuades the Fairmount police to open up the Historical Museum for him, to see the room of James Dean relics. Dylan leaves around 3am.

November

7. 'Golden Boy' Lalonde is true to his word and gives Dylan a $1,000 ringside seat for his title fight. Unfortunately he is quickly knocked senseless. "I thought it was sad," says Bob. "I thought Donny was gonna go a little longer, ya know?"

December

4. Appears in Oakland, California as a solo performer at the Bridge School Benefit, a concert organised by Neil Young and his wife Pegi to raise funds for handicapped children.

7. Roy Orbison, aka Lefty Wilbury, suffers a fatal heartattack.

1988 DISCOGRAPHY

June

13. *Down In The Groove* (US LP) (Columbia OC40957) (UK LP) (CBS 460267 No.32, 6 weeks) ('Let's Stick Together', 'When Did You Leave Heaven?', 'Sally Sue Brown', 'Death Is Not The End', 'Had A Dream About You Baby', 'Ugliest Girl In The World', 'Silvio', 'Ninety Miles An Hour (Down A Dead End Street)', 'Shenandoah', 'Rank Strangers To Me').

"There's no rule that claims that anyone must write their own songs. You could take another song somebody else has written and you can make it yours. I'm not saying I made a definitive version of anything with this last record, but I liked the songs. Every so often you've gotta sing songs that're out there. You just have to, just to keep yourself straight."

July

'Silvio'/'When Did You Leave Heaven?' (UK 45 CBS 651406).
'Silvio'/'When Did You Leave Heaven?'/'Driftin' Too Far From Shore' (UK 12-inch 45 CBS 651406).

August

'Pretty Boy Floyd' on Folkways: *A Vision Shared* (US LP Columbia OC44034) (UK LP CBS 460905).

October

Vocal on 'Love Rescue Me' and organ on 'Hawkmoon 269' on U2's *Rattle & Hum* (US/UK LP Island A2 91003).

November

Several tracks on *The Traveling Wilburys: Volume One* (US LP) (UK LP Warners 925796 No.2, 15 weeks).

1988 BIBLIOGRAPHY

Liff, Dennis R., 'Raging Glory', (Booklet) Privately published.
Cooper, Chris and Marsh, Keith, 'The Circus Is In Town', (Booklet) Private.
Milne, Larry, *Hearts Of Fire*, NEL.
Day, Aidan, *Jokerman: Reading The Lyrics Of Bob Dylan*, Blackwell.
Heylin, Clinton, *Stolen Moments: The Ultimate Reference Book*, Wanted Man.
Krogsgaard, Michael, *Master Of The Tracks: The Bob Dylan Reference Book Of Recording* , S.I.R.R., Denmark.
Spitz, Bob, *Dylan: A Biography*, McGraw Hill.
Dylan, Bob, *Lyrics 1961-1985*, Grafton paperback.
Ed Smith, Joe, *Off The Record-An Oral History Of Popular Music*, Warner.

1988 CONCERTS

June

7. Concord Pavilion, California
9. Cal Expo, Sacramento, California
10. Greek Theater, Berkeley, California
11. Shoreline Amphitheater, Mountain View, California
13. Park West, Park City, Utah
15. Fiddler's Green Amphitheater, Denver, Colorado
17. The Muni, St Louis, Missouri
18. Alpine Valley, East Troy, Wisconsin
21. Blossom Music Center, Cuyahoga Falls, Ohio
22. River Bend Music Center, Cincinnati, Ohio
24,25. Garden State Arts Center, Holmdel, New Jersey
26. Performing Arts Center, Saratoga Springs, New York
28. Finger Lakes Performing Arts Center, Canandaigua, New York
30. Jones Beach Music Theater, New York

July

1. Jones Beach Music Theater, New York
2. Great Woods Amphitheater, Mansfield, Massachusetts
3. The Ballpark, Old Orchard Beach, Maine
6. Mann Music Center, Philadelphia, Pennsylvania
8. The Forum, Montreal, Canada
9. Civic Center, Ottawa, Canada
11. Copps Coliseum, Hamilton, Ontario, Canada
13. The Castle, Charlevoix, Michigan
14. Poplar Creek Music Theater, Hoffman Estates, Illinois
15. State Fairgrounds, Indianapolis, Indiana
17,18. Meadowbrook, Detroit, Michigan
20. Merriweather Post Pavilion, Columbia, Maryland
22. Starwood Amphitheater, Nashville, Tennessee
24,25. Chastain Park Amphitheater, Atlanta, Georgia
26. Mud Island, Memphis Tennessee
28. Starplex, Dallas, Texas
30. Compton Terrace, Phoenix, Arizona
31. Pacific Amphitheater, Costa Mesa, California

August

2,3,4. Greek Theater, Los Angeles, California
6. Sammis Pavilion, Batiquitos, Carlsbadd, California
7. County Bowl, Santa Barbara, California
19. Civic Auditorium, Portland, Oregon
20. Champs De Brionne Summer Music Theater, George, Washington
21. P.N.E., Pacific Coliseum, Vancouver, Canada
23. Olympic Saddledome, Calgary, Canada
24. Northlands Coliseum, Edmonton, Canada
26. Arena, Winnipeg, Canada
29. Exhibition Stadium, Toronto, Canada
31. New York State Fairground, Syracuse, New York

September

2. Orange County Fair, Middletown, New York
3. Riverfront Park, Manchester, Connecticut
4. Lake Compounce Festival Park, Bristol, Connecticut
7. Champlain Valley Fairgrounds, Burlington, New Jersey
8. Broome Memorial Arena, Binghampton, New York
10. Waterloo Village, Stanhope, New Jersey
11. George Mason U.C., Fairfax, New York
13. Civic Arena, Pittsburg, Pennsylvania
15. University of N.C., Chapel Hill, North Carolina
16. University of S.C., Columbia, South Carolina
17. New Charlotte Coliseum, Charlotte, North Carolina
18. Univerisity of Tennessee, Knoxville, Tennessee
19. University Hall, Charlottesville, Virginia
22. University Of Southern Florida Sundome, Tampa, Florida
23. Miami Arena, Miami, Florida

Goes to New Orleans to record *Oh Mercy* with Daniel Lanois producing. "It was thrilling to run into Daniel because he's a competent musician and he knows how to record with modern facilities. For me that was lacking in the past."

May

27. European tour begins in Sweden at the Christinehof Slott. Dylan surprises everyone – including the band – by wearing a cap and hood combination throughout the show.

September

24. Dylan makes an unexpected appearance on the Chabad Telethon with his son-in-law Peter Himmelman and Harry Dean Stanton (they claim this band is called Chopped Liver). Looking positively odd, Dylan makes an inglorious attempt to play the flute and the recorder, the band play 'Hava Naghila', and Bob is subsequently blessed by a dancing rabbi.

November

20. A recording of 'People Get Ready' is made in a studio in Bloomington, Indiana, with Barry Goldberg producing, for use in the movie *Flashback*. While there, Dylan also makes a promotional video for 'Political World', with John Cougar Mellencamp directing.

1989 SONGS WRITTEN

March

'Political World' (*Oh Mercy*). "Just because it's called 'Political World' doesn't necessarily mean it's a political song."
'Where Teardrops Fall' (*Oh Mercy*).
'Everything Is Broken' (*Oh Mercy*).
'Ring Them Bells' (*Oh Mercy*).
'Man In A Long Black Coat' (*Oh Mercy*). "There was another line in there. The beginning of the line was 'People don't live or die, people just are'. It was tough trying to come up with a rhyme for that."
'Most Of The Time' (*Oh Mercy*).
'What Good Am I?' (*Oh Mercy*).
'Disease Of Conceit' (*Oh Mercy*).
'What Was It You Wanted?' (*Oh Mercy*).
'Shooting Star' (*Oh Mercy*).
'Series Of Dreams'. Recorded for, but not used on, *Oh Mercy*. "'Series Of Dreams' was a fantastic, turbulent track that I felt should have been on the record but he had the last word." (Daniel Lanois).
'God Knows' (*Under The Red Sky*)
'Born In Time' (*Under The Red Sky*)

1989 DISCOGRAPHY

January

30. 'End Of The Line'/'Congratulations' The Traveling Wilburys (US 45) (Warners 27637).

February

6. *Dylan & The Dead* (US LP) (Columbia OC 45056)(UK LP) (CBS 463381 No.38, 7 weeks) ('Slow Train', 'I Want You', 'Gotta Serve Somebody', 'Queen Jane Approximately', 'Joey', 'All Along The Watchtower', 'Knockin' On Heaven's Door'). "We were trying to back up a singer on songs that no one knew. It was not our finest hour, nor his. I don't know why it was even made into a record." (The Dead's Mickey Hart).

20. 'End Of The Line'/'Congratulations' The Traveling Wilburys (UK 45) (Warners 7673).

October

2. *Oh Mercy* (US LP) (Columbia OC45281) (UK LP) (CBS 465800 No.6 6 weeks) ('Political World', 'Where Teardrops Fall', 'Everything Is Broken', 'Ring Them Bells', 'Man In A Long Black Coat', 'Most Of The Time', 'What Good Am I?', 'Disease Of Conceit', 'What Was It You Wanted?', 'Shooting Star').

Singing 'A Couple More Years' in Hearts Of Fire 1986

24. University Of Florida O'Connell Center, Gainesville, Florida
25. Audubon Zoo, New Orleans, Louisiana

October

13,14. The Tower, Philadelphia, Pennsylvania
16,17,18,19. Radio City Music Hall, New York

1988 IMPORTANT UNRELEASED RECORDINGS

December

A PA tape of the solo set at the Bridge School Benefit, Oakland, California. (★'San Francisco Bay Blues', 'Pretty Boy Floyd', 'With God On Our Side', 'Girl From The North Country', 'Gates Of Eden', 'Forever Young').

1988 INTERVIEWS

August

Syndicated interview with Kathryn Baker of Associated Press: "Writing is such an isolated thing, you're in such an isolated frame of mind. In the old days I could get to it real quick. I can't get to it like that no more. It's not that simple."

1989

1989 CHRONOLOGY

February

By sending back his lobster to have its shell removed, Dylan offends Sergio Pertot, the chef at R. J. Scotty's on New York's Ninth Avenue. Only when Dylan apologises personally is the irate cuisine-meister calmed.

12. Appears as surprise guest at a Grateful Dead show in LA, singing 'Stuck Inside Of Mobile'.

March

"Most of them are stream-of-consciousness songs, the kind that come to you in the middle of the night."
23. 'Everything Is Broken'/'Death Is Not The End' (UK 45) (CBS 655358).
'Everything Is Broken'/'Dead Man, Dead Man' (live '81)/'I Want You' (from *Dylan & The Dead*) (UK 12-inch) (CBS 655358 6).
'Everything Is Broken'/'Where Teardrops Fall'/'Dead Man, Dead Man' (live '81)/'Ugliest Girl In The World' (UK CD5) (CBS 655358 2).

1989 INTERVIEWS

Summer
Interviewed by Dan Neer for WNEW/Media America Radio: "My music is structured. Nobody realises it but it is."
June
Brief interview for Spanish newspaper *El Diaro Vasco*: "Recalling the past is almost masochistic for me. There were some beautiful times I want to keep, but I've been in the darkness for a long time. I'm looking forward to the light again now."
Brief interview for Greek newspaper *Elegtherotoupia*: "I'm trying to get rid of my myth. I'm more alive now than I was in the '60s and I still have a lot to offer for the '90s."
September
With Edna Gundersen for *USA Today*: "My songs aren't written for great singers, they're written for me."
October
With Adrian Deevoy for *Q Magazine*: "No-one has ever said to me, 'Change that lyric, make it more this way or that way.' I mean, that might be an unfortunate thing that no-one has ever done that. Sometimes you wish somebody would."

1989 BIBLIOGRAPHY

Heylin, Clinton, *To Live Outside The Law: A Guide To Bob Dylan Bootlegs*, Labour Of Love Productions.
Dreau, Jean Louis & Schlockoff, Robert, *Hypnotist Collectors: An International Illustrated Discography*, Media Presse, Paris.
Stein, Georg, *Bob Dylan-Temples In Flames*, Palmyra, W. Germany.
Bauldie, John, '*The Ghost Of Electricity: Bob Dylan's 1966 World Tour*' Privately published.

1989 CONCERTS

May
27. Christinehof Slott, Andarum, Sweden
28. Globen Arena, Stockholm, Sweden
29. Jaahalli, Helsinki, Finland
June
3,4. RDS, Simmons Court, Dublin, Ireland
6. Scottish Exhibition Centre, Glasgow, Scotland
7. National Exhibition Centre, Birmingham
8. Wembley Arena, London
10. Statenhal, Den Haag, Netherlands
11. Vorst Nationaal, Brussels, Belgium
13. Les Arenes, Frejus, France
15. Sportpalace, Madrid, Spain
16. Sportpalace, Barcelona, Spain
17. Velodromo de Anoeta, San Sebastian, Spain
19. Paltrussardi, Milan, Italy
20. Gradinate, Rome, Italy
21. Stadio Lamberti, Cava dei Tirreni, Italy
22. Stadio di Ardenza, Livorno, Italy
24. Istanbul, Turkey
26. National Stadium, Patras, Greece
28. Panathenaika Stadium, Athens, Greece
July
1. Civic Center Arena, Peoria, Illinois

2. Poplar Creek Music Theatre, Hoffman Estates, Illinois
3. Marcus Amphitheatre, Milwaukee, Wisconsin
5,6. Baldwin Memorial Pavilion, Rochester, Michigan
8. Deer Creek Pavilion, Noblesville, Indiana
9. Blossom Music Centre, Cuyahoga Falls, Ohio
11. Skyline Sports Complex, Harrisburg, Pennsylvania
12. Fairgrounds, Allentown, Pennsylvania
13. Great Woods Amphitheatre, Mansfield, Massachusetts
15. Seashore Performing Arts Ctr, Old Orchard Beach, Maine
16. Lake Compounce Park, Bristol, Connecticut
17. Waterloo Village, Stanhope, New Jersey
19. Merriweather Post Pavilion, Columbia, Maryland
20. Bally's Grand Hotel, Atlantic City, New Jersey
21. Garden State Arts Centre, Holmdel, New Jersey
23. Jones Beach Music Theatre, New York
25. Finger Lakes PAC, Canandaigua, New York
26. Performing Arts Centre, Saratoga Springs, New York
28. Civic Arena, Pittsburgh, Pennsylvania
29. Kingswood Music Theatre, Maple, Ontario, Canada
30. Ottawa Civic Centre, Ottawa, Ontario, Canada
31. L'Amphitheatre, Jolliet, Quebec, Canada
August
3. Harriet Island Riverfest, St Paul, Minnesota
4. Dane County Coliseum, Madison, Wisconsin
5. Welsh Auditorium, Grand Rapids, Michigan
6. Cooper Stadium, Columbus, Ohio
8. Savage Hall, Toledo, Ohio
9. The Muni, St Louis, Missouri
10. River Bend Music Centre, Cincinnati, Ohio
12. KD Amusement Park, Doswell, Virginia
13. Carowinds Amusement Park, Charlotte, North Carolina
15,16. Chastain Memorial Amphitheatre, Atlanta, Georgia
18. Freedom Hall, Louisville, Kentucky
19. State Fair, Springfield, Missouri
20. Starwood Amphitheatre, Nashville, Tennessee
22. Sandstone Amphitheatre, Bonner Springs, Kansas
23. The Zoo, Oklahoma City, Oklahoma
25. Kiefer UNO Arena, New Orleans, Louisiana
26. The Summitt, Houston, Texas
27. Starplex Amphitheatre, Dallas, Texas
29. Pan American Theatre, Las Cruces, New Mexico
31. Fiddler's Green, Englewood, Colorado
September
1. Park West, Park City, Utah
3. Greek Theatre, Berkeley, California
5. County Bowl, Santa Barbara, California
6. Starlight Bowl, San Diego, California
8. Pacific Amphitheatre, Costa Mesa, California
9,10. Greek Theatre, Los Angeles, California
October
10,11,12,13. Beacon Theatre, New York
15,16. The Tower, Philadelphia, Pennsylvania
17,18. Constitution Hall, Washington, DC
20. Mid-Hudson Arena, Poughkeepsie, New York
22. University Of Rhode Island, Kingston, Rhode Island
23,24,25. Opera House, Boston, Massachusetts
27. Rensseaer Polytechnical, Troy, New York
29. Ithica College, Ithica, New York
31. Arie Crown Theatre, Chicago, Illinois
November
1. Hill Auditorium, Ann Arbor, Michigan
2. State Theatre, Cleveland, Ohio
4. University Of Pennsylvania, Indiana, Pennsylvania
6. Virginia Polytechnic, Blacksburg, Virginia
7. Chrysler Hall, Norfolk, Virginia

8. Duke University, Durham, North Carolina
10. Fox Theatre, Atlanta, Georgia
12,13. Sunrise Musical Theatre, Sunrise, Florida
14,15. Performing Arts Centre, Tampa, Florida

1990

1990 CHRONOLOGY

January

Dylan records four songs in LA with Don Was producing. These will later be included on *Under The Red Sky*. Among those guesting on the sessions is Slash from Guns N' Roses. Slash is surprised to find Dylan in cap, hood and shades – "all I could see was his nose and upper lip". Dylan asks him to play, on 'Wiggle Wiggle', "exactly like Django Reinhardt". Slash notes that looking on from the control booth are George Harrison and Elizabeth Taylor.

Dylan films a live performance (though in a deserted studio) of 'Most Of The Time', for use as a promo video. The song, however, is never scheduled to be released as a single.

12. Dylan appears at Toad's Place, a small club in New Haven, Connecticut, where he plays four separate sets which amount to some five and a half hours of music. He also does requests, laughs, speaks to the audience and offers unusual cover versions of, amongst others, 'Help Me Make It Through The Night' and Bruce Springsteen's 'Dancing In The Dark'.

30. In Paris, at the Ministry Of Culture, Dylan is formally awarded the medal of Commandeur Des Arts Et Des Lettres by French Minister of Culture Jack Lang. It is the highest cultural honour which can be bestowed on a foreigner and Dylan is acclaimed as representing "an ideal of music, life and poetry". "Thank you a thousand times," says Dylan, in perfectly intelligible French.

February

24. Dylan is reunited with The Byrds at a Roy Orbison Tribute concert at the Universal Amphitheatre, Los Angeles. They perform 'Mr Tambourine Man' and 'He Was A Friend Of Mine'.

March

1. Dylan appears as a surprise guest at a Tom Petty concert at the LA Forum, singing 'Rainy Day Women Nos 12 & 35'. Bruce Springsteen, another surprise guest, trips off arm in arm with Bob after a rousing version of The Animals' 'I'm Crying'.

April

The Traveling Wilburys reassemble in a rented house in Beverly Hills to begin work on a possible Volume Two.

June

Dylan makes a promo video for 'It's Unbelievable' with Molly Ringwald and a pig. Dylan plays the part of a chauffeur.

August

26. Stevie Ray Vaughan, who played lead guitar on the January session for *Under The Red Sky* is killed in a helicopter crash in the USA, along with other members of Eric Clapton's touring entourage.

September

17. *Under The Red Sky*, Dylan's strongest LP for several years, is released to a critical trashing, in the UK at least. "Good reviews don't hurt you, but they don't help either. It's better to have a record the critics hate that sells 10 million copies than one the critics love that sells 10."

22. At a Beach Boys' fan convention in England, a videotape sent over by Brian Wilson is played. Wilson talks about a song called The Spirit Of Rock 'n' Roll he's just finished rescording with some friends. He plays a little of the tape, which features Bob Dylan singing along.

29. Life magazine publishes a list of the 20th century's "Most Influential Americans". Bob Dylan is included, sandwiched on the list between Allen Dulles, founding director of the CIA, and Albert Einstein.

October

Bob Dylan's boyhood home, 2425 E. Seventh Street, Hibbing, Minnesota, is sold to local couple Donna and Gregg French for $57,000. Curt Curtis, the estate agent who thought he'd make a fortune, is disgusted that the Hibbing town council insisted that the house should not be exploited as a commercial venture. Bob Dylan advises the young couple to "check the furnace".

December

It is announced that Bob Dylan will be honoured at the 1991 Grammy Awards Ceremony with a Lifetime Achievement award. At the same time, CBS Records reveal that a 4-CD box set of previously unreleased material is in preparation for release in Spring.

1990 INTERVIEWS

September

With Edna Gundersen in *USA Today*.

"People can learn everything about me through my songs – if they know where to look..."

1990 BIBLIOGRAPHY

Ed. Thomson, Elizabeth & Gutman, David, *A Dylan Companion*, Macmillan.

Williams, Paul, *Performing Artist-The Music Of Bob Dylan*, Underwood Miller.

Dundas, Glen, *Tangled Up In Tapes Revisited*, SMA.

Dunn, Tim, 'I Just Write 'Em As They Come', Private.

Ed. Bauldie, John, *Wanted Man-In Search Of Bob Dylan*, Black Spring.

1990 DISCOGRAPHY

January

29. 'Political World'/'Ring Them Bells' (UK 45) (CBS 655643 7)

Brisbane, 1 March 1986

'Political World'/'Ring Them Bells'/'Silvio'/'All Along The Watchtower' (Dead version) (UK CD5) (CBS 655643 2).

'Political World'/'Caribbean Wind'/'You're A Big Girl Now'/'It's All Over Now Baby Blue' (UK Picture CD) (CBS 655643 5).

30. 'People Get Ready' on soundtrack LP, *Flashback* (US LP WTG 46042).

July

'Nobody's Child' The Traveling Wilburys (US 45 Wilbury/Warners 26280) (UK 45 Wilbury/Warners W9773).

September

17. *Under The Red Sky* (US LP Columbia 46794) (UK LP CBS 467188) ('Wiggle Wiggle', 'Under The Red Sky', 'Unbelievable', 'Born In Time', 'TV Talkin' Song', '10,000 Men', 'Two By Two', 'God Knows', 'Handy Dandy', 'Cat's In The Well'.)

"It's just another record. You can only make the records as good as you can and hope they sell."

'Unbelievable'/'10,000 Men' (UK45).

'Unbelievable'/'10,000 Men'/'Jokerman'/'In The Summertime' (UK CD5)

October

1. *Volume 3*

The Traveling Wilburys (US LP Wilbury/Warners 26324) (UK LP Wilbury/Warners 26324)

('She's My Baby', 'Inside Out', 'If You Belonged To Me', 'The Devil's Been Busy', '7 Deadly Sins', 'Poor House', 'Where Were You Last Night?', 'Cool Dry Place', 'New Blue Moon', 'You Took My Breath Away', 'Wilbury Twist').

November

'Mr Tambourine Man' (live with The Byrds from the Roy Orbison Tribute Show) is included on the 4-CD set, *The Byrds* (CBS C4K 46773)

13. 'She's My Baby'/'New Blue Moon' (instrumental)/'Runaway' The Traveling Wilburys (UK CD5 Warners W7523CD)

1990 SONGS WRITTEN

January

'10,000 Men' (*Under The Red Sky*).

'Two By Two' (*Under The Red Sky*).

'Cat's In The Well' (*Under The Red Sky*).

March

'Wiggle Wiggle' (*Under The Red Sky*).

'Under The Red Sky' (*Under The Red Sky*). ("It's intentionally broad and short, so you can draw all kinds of conclusions.")

'It's Unbelievable' (*Under The Red Sky*).

'TV Talkin' Song' (*Under The Red Sky*).

'Handy Dandy' (*Under The Red Sky*).

1990 CONCERTS

January

14. Penn State College, Pennsylvania

15. Princeton University, Princeton, New Jersey

18. Morumbi Stadium, Sao Paulo, Brazil

25. Sambodromo, Rio de Janeiro, Brazil

29,30,31. Grand Rex Theatre, Paris, France

February

1. Grand Rex Theatre, Paris, France

3,4,5,6,7,8. Hammersmith Odeon, London

May

29. University Of Montreal, Montreal, Quebec, Canada

30. Memorial Arena, Kingston, Ontario, Canada

June

1,2. National Arts Centre, Ottawa, Canada

4. University Of Western Ontario, London, Ontario, Canada

5,6,7. O'Keefe Centre, Toronto, Canada

9. Alpine Valley, East Troy, Wisconsin

10. Adler Theatre, Davenport, Iowa

12. Lacrosse Centre, Lacrosse, Wisconsin

13. Civic Arena, Sioux Falls, South Dakota

14. Civic Centre, Fargo, North Dakota

15. Civic Centre, Bismark, North Dakota

17,18. Centennial Hall, Winnipeg, Manitoba, Canada

27. Laugardalsholl, Reykjavik, Iceland

29. Roskilde Festival, Denmark

30. Kalvoya Festival, Norway

July

1. Abo Festival, Turku, Finland

3. Stadtpark, Hamburg, West Germany

5. International Congress Centre, Berlin, West Germany

7. Tourhout Festival, Belgium

8. Werchter Festival, Belgium

9. Casino, Montreux, Switzerland

August

12, 13. Jubilee Auditorium, Edmonton, Alberta, Canada

15,16. Jubilee Auditorium, Calgary, Alberta, Canada

18. Champs De Brionne, George, Washington

19. Memorial Auditorium, Victoria, British Columbia, Canada

20. Pacific Coliseum, Vancouver, British Columbia, Canada

21. Arelen Schnitzer Concert Hall, Portland, Oregon

24. State Fair, Pueblo, Colorado

26. Iowa State Fair, Des Moines, Iowa

27,28. Star Plaza Theatre, Merrillville, Indiana

29. Minnesota State Fair, St Paul, Minnesota

31. Bob Devaney Sports Centre, Lincoln, Nebraska

September

1. Swiss Villa, Lampe, Missouri

2. Riverfront Amphitheatre, Hannibal, Missouri

4. Riverpart Amphitheatre, Tulsa, Oklahoma

5. Civic Centre, Oklahoma City, Oklahoma

6. Fairpark Music Hall, Dallas, Texas

8. Sunken Garden Theatre, San Antonio, Texas

9. Palmer Auditorium, Austin, Texas

11. Pablo Soleri Amphitheatre, Santa Fe, New Mexico

12. Mesa Amphitheatre, Mesa, Arizona

October

11. Tilles Centre, C.W.Post College, Brookville, New York

12. Paramount Theatre, Springfield, Massachusetts

13. Eisenhower Hall Theatre, West Point, New York

15,16,17,18,19. Beacon Theatre, New York City

21. Mosque Theatre, Richmond, Virginia

22. Syria Mosque, Pittsburgh, Pennsylvania

23. Municipal Auditorium, Charlotte, North Carolina

25. Tad Smith Coliseum, Oxford, Mississippi

26. Coleman Coliseum, University Of Alabama, Tuscaloosa, Alabama

27. Vanderbilt University, Nashville, Tennessee

28. University of Georgia Coliseum, Athens, Georgia

30. Varsity Gym, Appalacian St. College, Boone, North Carolina

31. Ovens Auditorium, Charlotte, North Carolina

November

2. University Of Kentucky, Lexington, Kentucky

3. S.I.U. Arena, Carbondale, Illinois

4. The Fox Theater, St Louis, Missouri

6. Chick Evans Fieldhouse, De Kalb, Illinois

8. Carver Hockey Arena, Iowa City, Iowa

9. Chicago Theater, Chicago, Illinois

10. Riverside Theater, Milwaukee, Wisconsin

12. Wharton Centre, Michigan S.U., East Lansing, Michigan

13. University Of Dayton Arena, Dayton, Ohio
14. Normal, Illinois
16. Palace Theatre, Columbus, Ohio
17. Music Hall, Cleveland, Ohio
18. Fox Theater, Detroit, Michigan

1991

1991 CHRONOLOGY
January
Bob Dylan rehearses in New York for a further series of concerts in Europe. Both G.E. Smith and drummer Christopher Parker have now left the band. The new guitar player is the previously unheard of John Jackson and the drummer Bury-born Ian Wallace, veteran of the 1978 tour, and of *Street-Legal*.
February
20. At the 20th Grammy Awards ceremony, Bob Dylan accepts a Lifetime Achievement award. A 5-minute "career summary video" is premièred.
March
1. An extensive summary of Bob Dylan's unreleased recordings from the past 30 years is released in the USA by the newly re-christened Sony Records company. Among the previously unheard gems are 'Blind Willie McTell', 'Farewell Angelina', 'Series Of Dreams'.
May
24. Bob Dylan "celebrates" his 50th birthday. As he observed in 'When I Paint My Masterpiece', "It sure has been one hell of a ride ..."

1991 CONCERTS
January
28. Zurich, Switzerland
30. Brussels, Belgium
31. Musik Centrum, Utrecht, Holland
February
2,3. SECC, Glasgow, Scotland
5. The Point, Dublin, Eire
6. Icebowl, Belfast, N. Ireland
8,9,10,12,13,15,16,17. Hammersmith Odeon, London, England

1991 DISCOGRAPHY
March
The Bootleg Series, Vols 1-3, Rare And Unreleased 1961-1989 (US 3-CD Sony) (UK 3-CD Columbia)
CD1
'Hard Times In New York Town', 'He Was A Friend Of Mine', 'Man On The Street', 'No More Auction Block', 'House Carpenter', 'Talking Bear Mountain Picnic Massacre Blues', 'Let Me Die In My Footsteps', 'Rambling, Gambling Willie', 'Talkin' Hava Nagilah Blues', 'Quit Your Low Down Ways', 'Worried Blues', 'Kingsport Town', 'Walkin' Down The Line', 'Walls Of Red Wing', 'Paths Of Victory', 'Talkin' John Birch Paranoid Blues', 'Who Killed Davey Moore?', 'Only A Hobo', 'Moonshiner', 'When The Ship Comes In', 'Times They Are A-Changin'', ' The Last Thoughts On Woody Guthrie'.
CD2
'Seven Curses', 'Eternal Circle', 'Suze (The Cough Song)', 'Mama, You Been On My Mind', 'Farewell, Angelina', 'Subterranean Homesick Blues', 'If You Gotta Go, Go Now (Or Else You Got To Stay All Night)', 'Sitting On a Barbed Wire Fence', 'Like A Rolling Stone', 'It Takes A Lot To Laugh, It Takes A Train To Cry', 'I'll Keep It With Mine', 'She's Your Lover Now', 'I Shall Be Released', 'Santa-Fe', 'If Not For You', 'Wallflower', 'Nobody 'Cept You', 'Tangled Up In Blue', 'Call Letter Blues', 'Idiot Wind'.
CD3
'If You See Her, Say Hello', 'Golden Loom', 'Catfish', 'Seven Days', 'Ye Shall Be Changed', 'Every Grain Of Sand', 'You Changed My Life', 'Need A Woman', 'Angelina', 'Someone's Got A Hold Of My Heart', 'Tell Me', 'Lord Protect My Child', 'Foot Of Pride', 'Blind Willie McTell', 'When The Night Comes Falling From The Sky', 'Series Of Dreams'.

1991 BIBLIOGRAPHY
May
Behind The Shades, Clinton Heylin, (Summit).
Absolutely Dylan, Patrick Humphries & John Bauldie, (Viking Studio Books).